PRAISE for *Going Public*

This is not a book about ideas alone, but about all the nitty-gritty details, the specificities that make big ideas possible in the mundane daily life of schooling. It's irresistible. I can't wait to get it into the hands of our staff, parents, and allies up here in Boston. I know they'll discover, as I have, that by the time they put one of these marvelous ideas to use it won't look just the way it did at the Manhattan New School. That's what's so much fun about the book. After I write down some practical to-dos for tomorrow I begin thinking about them and come up with a slightly different list that fits our school. I just wish I had put all Shelley's ideas into practice yesterday.

Thank you, thank you, Shelley. How ever did you find the time—to create the school itself and write so wonderfully about it?

—**Deborah Meier**, Principal of the Mission Hill School
Author of *The Power of Their Ideas*

Shelley Harwayne is the most gifted educator I know. In *Going Public* she describes how she and her colleagues transformed the institution of public school into a school*house* and created a culture of trust, respect, character, rigor, common vision, and love. In aiming to discover what really matters in the life of a city elementary school, Shelley demonstrates how imagination, intelligence, and grit can turn the status quo on its head. She invites public school teachers and administrators who argue that schools can't be humanized, because rules and bureaucracy prevent it, to understand, detail by detail, how she did it and how they can, too. *Going Public* is packed with inspiring messages and practical ideas. As I read I took notes nonstop about things I want to do, try, and get *tomorrow*. This is a book for anyone who cares about the future of our schools and everyone who wants to learn how to create a place where teachers, children, and their parents can discover together what it means to be fully human.

—**Nancie Atwell**, Director of the Center for Teaching and Learning
Author of *In the Middle, Second Edition*

Going Public is the most important book on education and schooling that I've read in quite a while—and certainly one of the most enjoyable. Harwayne's work is smart, deep, practical, thought provoking, and instructive—equal parts Dewey's *Education & Democracy* and Kaufman's *Up the Down Staircase*. It can inspire all teachers and should be *required* reading for all principals and superintendents.

—**David B. Sherman**, Vice-President, United Federation of Teachers

Going Public

Priorities & Practice at The Manhattan New School

SHELLEY HARWAYNE

HEINEMANN
Portsmouth, NH

Heinemann

A division of Reed Elsevier Inc.

361 Hanover Street

Portsmouth, NH 03801–3912

http://www.heinemann.com

Offices and agents throughout the world

The author and publisher thank those who have generously given permission to reprint borrowed material:

Excerpt from "In New York City There Are Schools That Work." From *Teaching K–8 Magazine* (May 1994). Reprinted by permission of *Teaching K–8*, Norwalk, CT 06854.

"Qualities of Leadership" by David B. Sherman was originally published in the *New York Teacher City Edition* (May 25, 1998). Reprinted by permission of the Publisher.

"Mary and Sarah", from *A Mouse in my Roof* by Richard Edwards. Copyright © 1988 by Richard Edwards. Used by permission of Delacorte Press, a division of Random House, Inc.; Felicity Bryan; and the author.

Excerpt from "Somewhere Over the Rainbow" by Laura Benson. From *The Colorado Reading Council Journal*. Reprinted by permission of the Author.

Excerpts from "Whole Language: The Debate" by Shelley Harwayne. Reprinted by permission of ERIC/EDINFO Press.

Excerpt from "Together" by Paul Engle. From *Embrace: Selected Love Poems* by Paul Engle. Copyright © 1969 by Paul Engle. Reprinted by permission of Random House, Inc.

Credits continue on p. 339.

Library of Congress Cataloging-in-Publication Data

Harwayne, Shelley.

    Going public : priorities and practice at the Manhattan New

School / Shelley Harwayne.

      p. cm.

    Iincludes bibliographical references and index.

    ISBN 0-325-00175-8

    1. Elementary school administration—New York (State)—New York

Case studies.   2. Manhattan New School (New York, N.Y.) I. Title.

LB2822.5.H37   1999

372.9747'1—dc21

                              99-35451

                              CIP

Editor: Lois Bridges

Production service: Patricia Adams

Production coordination: Abigail M. Heim

Cover design: Catherine Hawkes, Cat and Mouse

Interior photographs: Herb Shapiro, Tammy DiPaolo, and Shelley Harwayne

Cover photographs: Donnelly Marks and Colleen Croft

Cover illustrations: Maxine Getz and Suzy Campbell & students

Manufacturing: Louise Richardson

Printed in the United States of America on acid-free paper

03 02 01 00 99   RRD   1 2 3 4 5 6 7 8 9

To all
the children
who will call
the Manhattan New School
their very first alma mater,
and
to all
the teachers
they will remember
with love and admiration

CONTENTS

8. SING ABOUT IT!   273

APPENDICES   287

ACKNOWLEDGMENTS

I have been working on this book for almost three years, but I have been living the story of this book for eight years. I must admit that during the first few years of our school's existence I never imagined writing a book. I hardly had time to read a book, let alone write one. Those early years were particularly exhausting and at the same time exhilarating. I can't imagine writing a book about our school without acknowledging the role those pioneer teachers played, as well as giving credit to *all* the wonderful people who have since joined our staff. Isabel Beaton, one of the teachers acknowledged below, told me that a "school is a chorus, not a solo performance." You are about to meet the members of the choir.

This grand thank-you note begins with an acknowledgement of the seven teachers who dreamed the impossible dream. Thankfully, five of the original staff members who founded this school still call the Manhattan New School home.

Tara Fishman began as a special education teacher in our school and now serves as my part-time administrative assistant. I thank her for her expertise, dedication, warmth, humor, and her unconditional love for all that the Manhattan New School stands for. It is a privilege to teach her daughter Sydney, and I look forward to working with her son Lucas.

Layne Hudes readily shares her early-childhood expertise with all members of the staff. She also shares her passion for literature, both old and new, with her fortunate first graders. She can also be counted on to recommend great adult books, give travel advice, share Knicks anecdotes, and add humor to her work with children or adults. I also thank her for her devotion to the special education students across the hall.

Eve Mutchnick has the distinction of being the only teacher who has consistently taught kindergarten throughout our eight-year history. She brings to this role a rich professional know-how, a dedication to and compassion for young children, and a heart of pure gold for all members of the community. I also thank her for being so easy with visitors and for hanging out so frequently in other people's classrooms. She understands camaraderie.

Joan Backer has brought many years' experience as a literacy staff developer to our school community. I thank her especially for the patience, trust, and confidence she has in her students, along with her spirit of adventure. She always graciously invites students to take big risks. I also thank her for her fourth-grade leadership, her pioneer math work, and her participation in so many late-night events.

Joanne Hindley Salch's personal and professional life is marked by beauty, integrity, and clarity of purpose. She can teach you as much about reading and writing when she relaxes on your living room sofa as when she delivers a keynote address. I thank her for her brilliant contributions to our school and to our profession and especially for being such a wonderful friend. We have spent many hours sharing the important stories of our lives. Whenever Joanne is dazzled by her students, she can be heard saying, "Hot stuff!" It's easy to say the same about her.

Julie Liebersohn and Elizabeth Servidio, two founding faculty members, have since departed from the New York City schools, but they have clearly left their mark on the way we still live our lives together. I thank Julie for taking on big projects. She created our very first class museum, our schoolwide bookswap, and she even agreed to serve as our first school treasurer. Elizabeth taught us all about the need for clarity in our teaching, made an art of teaching reading to beginning readers, and taught us a great deal about working with families.

Over the following years, new teachers joined our staff, adding additional warmth, vibrancy, and unique areas of expertise.

Lorraine Shapiro has a mesmerizing dedication to the profession, an insatiable curiosity about the teaching of reading, boundless energy, a passion for the study of architecture, weaving, and countless other topics. I thank her for reminding me to take care of my health, sit down when I eat, and avoid stress at all cost. It is a privilege to teach her granddaughter Eliza, and I look forward to teaching her grandson Jake.

Sharon Taberski's teaching is marked by an exquisite sense of order, clarity, rigor, purpose, as well as an elegance of design. I thank her for always pushing our professional envelope and for the sparkle in her eye when she spots a former student walking down the hall. She can always be heard to say, "There's my buddy." Most of all I thank her for her willingness to share her expertise and passion for the teaching of reading.

Pam Mayer has an unconditional love for her early-childhood students and their families. Gentle nurturing, serenity, and joy mark her teaching, and yet she is always ready to welcome visitors, try out new teaching ideas, write book reviews, share her computer expertise, or help a colleague. I especially thank her for inviting me into her classroom so frequently. She has a way of taking small ideas and turning them into magnificent rituals.

Debby Yellin brings her background as an artist, voracious reader, and learning disabilities specialist to bear in her early-childhood special education classroom. I appreciate her total commitment to mainstreaming, decertification, and the inclusion of special youngsters in the full life of a school community. Debby has helped us realize as well that the special education teacher must be fully integrated into the life of the school community.

Paula Rogovin brings new meaning to tapping resources, family involvement, and educating for social responsibility. She has taught us all how to use the classroom interview to open up a wide world of learning for children and adults. I thank her for her commitment to social change, her important contributions to the field of education, and the daily kindness she bestows on all who enter her classroom.

Judy Davis not only greets visiting educators with open arms, but usually with hugs and kisses. Her vibrant personality is a perfect match for her brilliant teaching. I thank her for setting high standards in her professional world and welcoming me into her personal one. I am grateful for our comforting conversations about our families, our health, our writing, and our reading. I especially want to thank her for always believing that this year's class is the most beautiful of her career.

Carmen Colon has taught kindergarten at the Manhattan New School as well as Spanish as a second language to all our students. I thank her for the equity and justice she brings to her work as well as her admiration and appreciation for all the children and their languages, literacies, and family stories. It is a privilege to teach her daughter Maia Montes de Oca, and I look forward to teaching her son Emilio.

Regina Chiou's integrity, humanity, peacefulness, and professionalism all radiate in the second-grade environment she and her students create. As her students learn to read and write, they learn to become caring stewards of the Earth and all its living things. I especially want to thank her for giving her colleagues seemingly endless opportunities to talk, ponder, reflect, and otherwise marvel at their chosen profession.

Lisa Siegman has worn many hats in our school, all of them with style, brilliance, and dedication. In addition to being the mother of two accomplished graduates, Alexei and Gabe Beltrone, Lisa teaches science to all our students, has spearheaded our growth in technology, and has given incredible support to our school's role as book reviewers for *The New Advocate*. I always appreciate her ability to think through problems and offer an array of solutions.

Isabel Beaton's presence graces our school. Her compassion, generosity, spirituality, and kindness is felt in every corner of her classroom. I have learned to count on Isabel for thoughtful advice, memorable stories, brilliant metaphors, and breathtaking teaching. Isabel not only teaches kindergartners, she serves as a powerful mentor to family members, colleagues, student teachers, volunteers, doctoral students, and all those fortunate enough to work alongside her. I thank her as well for her gifts of song, serenity, and all those sweet surprises in our mailboxes.

Roberta Pantel Rhodes plays many roles in our school community. In addition to being our resource room/learning disabilities teacher, she also serves as the chapter leader for the teachers' union, the United Federation of Teachers. As a published author of short stories and children's books, Roberta is also an important literacy model for students and colleagues. I am especially grateful to her for her wise counsel throughout the year, her deep concern for our struggling students, and for lightening my load during the season of standardized testing.

Renay Sadis returned to New York City from her position as a staff developer in Quito, Ecuador. I am grateful for her professional expertise, humor, and straightforwardness. She not only takes care of children's academic growth but she also tends to their emotional well-being. I am especially appreciative of her participation in our technology advances and her willingness to organize our social get-togethers. She and her beloved dog Canela have thrown some great parties.

Diane Lederman is our caring and easygoing music teacher. I'd like to thank her for teaching our children to lift their beautiful voices in song, play their instruments with gusto, and rock and roll down East Eighty-second Street. I never imagined that our little fledgling school would one day have an orchestra and a grand piano taking center stage.

Michael Miller, our physical education instructor, enables all our students to feel comfortable in the sports arena, but more importantly he teaches our children about good health, collegiality, and compassion. I'm grateful to Mike for reminding me every day just how lucky we are to be surrounded by children, and for making Fire Island a summer hangout for the Manhattan New School community.

Pam Saturday, artist extraordinaire, not only provides our children with the inspiration and techniques they need to create their own works of art, she eagerly works with colleagues to weave art into their everyday studies. I want to especially thank Pam for adding so much of her original art to our school environment.

Denise Rickles proves to us that special education youngsters deserve the very same beautiful classroom and effective classroom instruction as all children. I am grateful to her for reminding me to appreciate all the small steps along the way.

Karen Ruzzo is a gift from New England. I'd like to thank her for her exquisite teaching, her even-tempered and gracious presence, her calm and soothing way with children and adults, and her willingness to always let me work with her children. When Karen sings to her students, they stop what they are doing and look up in awe. She teaches with voice in more ways than one.

Amy Mandel began her career as a student teacher in our school. Her dedication to the children and to teaching made her a natural choice for a full-time position. I am grateful to her for her gentle and caring ways, her participation in all aspects of the school's life, and her ability to make children simply fall in love with her.

Kathy Park came to us from middle school and brought a passion for literacy learning, an expertise in working with the second-language learner, and a commitment to treat every student with individual attention and the utmost respect. Kathy inspires us all to lead dignified professional lives.

Jennifer Feinberg, in her first year of teaching, was so poised, confident, and effective, it was hard to believe that she was just beginning her career. I am grateful to Jenn for having the wisdom beyond her years to know what supports she needed, to ask for them graciously, and then to use what she was learning to create an enriched, tranquil, and nurturing classroom for her second graders.

David Besancon is a fourth-grade teacher whose classroom is marked by his calm and caring nature, as well as a determination to make every minute count. I am grateful for his enthusiastic participation in all aspects of professional study and his awe and appreciation for our school setting.

Sharon Hill's expertise in the teaching of reading and writing, combined with her rich experiences as a staff developer, make her an incredible asset to our school community. In addition to her know-how, I am grateful for her honesty, integrity, and gentle ways. I am as honored that she teaches in the penthouse of our school as I am to be entrusted with the education of her daughter Daniella.

Constance Foland brings all that she knows about reading and writing to her work with our English as a second language students. I thank her for her dedication, flexibility, spirituality, and willingness to cut back on her personal writing time in order to add Reading Recovery to her daily schedule.

Pat Werner has believed in the Manhattan New School ever since her daughter Chelsea began here as a student. She brings to her teaching a passion for reading and books, a commitment to professional growth, and a deep respect and admiration for her colleagues. I'm especially grateful to Pat for her heartfelt letters, her willingness to organize our professional library, and the most beautiful bowl of cherries I have ever seen in my life.

Tammy DiPaolo recently joined our staff as a kindergarten teacher. I am particularly grateful to her for handling her complicated move to New York City with such determination, creativity, graciousness, and humor. It is virtually impossible for me to walk out of her classroom if she happens to be reading aloud, singing, or telling stories. She knows what literacy is all about.

Meggan Towell Friedman has worked part time at our school over a number of years. I am grateful to her for her passion for literacy and for her dedication to the children and her colleagues. She can always be counted on for precise assessments, brilliant teaching, as well as boundless nurturing and nourishment for young and old alike. I am additionally grateful to her for her honest and reflective letters. Hers are the kind one keeps forever.

I am also grateful to student teachers Diana Baron, Elissa Eisen, and Mindy Gerstenhaber, for being available whenever they were needed and then accepting teaching positions that they carried off with pride and professionalism.

Kevin Tallat-Kelpsa, Sungho Pak, Dawn Harris Martine, Cindy Michaels, and Julie Taubes have all moved away from the Manhattan New School, but they have left their footprints in the snow. I especially want to thank Dawn for entrusting us with her granddaughter Chelsea, and Kevin for his willingness to substitute teach whenever he was needed.

Other teachers have passed through our copper swinging doors for short periods of time. We still have coffee mugs inscribed with the names of Andrea, Brad, Cindi, Elyse, Henry, Jamie, Jeanne, Jessica, Jill, Kathy, Lamson, Maxine, Peter, and Rachel. Your contributions are remembered with gratitude.

In the last several years, the incredible Jacques d'Amboise and his National Dance Institute have taught us the meaning of having high standards. In particular, I'd like to thank Tracy Straus, our dance instructor, for sharing her vibrancy, expertise, and magical teaching with all of our fourth graders. Tracy's devotion to her field and to her students makes her a marvelous mentor.

There are many family members who have greatly added to the quality of life in our school. I could never mention all their names, but let the following few who spend so much time at the Manhattan New School represent the entire parent body. Barbara Santella and Judi Klein, parents as well as staff members, maintain our main office as a gracious and welcoming reception area. Barbara has added so many beautiful touches to our school, including gourmet meals, flowering plants, and splashes of red everywhere. I thank her for placing her sons, Jeremy and Alex, in our hands and for accepting the role of supervising school aide, director of our after-school program, and past co-president of the PTA. Judi, our dependable secretary, who works in quiet, gracious ways, has also placed her daughter Kimberly in our care. I thank her for being patient with all those long-distance callers, the seemingly endless faxes, and her ability to tend to all the paperwork without complaints.

Ellen Afromsky, mother of Leah and Matthew Blank and a past co-president of the PTA, has been a full participant in the life of our school since our doors first opened. I thank her for all her contributions and especially for sharing her literature and book reviewer expertise. I thank Susan Geller Ettenheim, mother of Rosie and Mattie, for bringing us into the twenty-first century with technological elegance, along with Gem Barut, father of Kate, for sharing his computer brilliance. I'd also like to thank the current co-presidents of the PTA, Gail King, mother of Gregory Schwedock, and Barbara Carren-LeSauter, mother of Isabelle, for all their hard work and support and for all our early morning get-togethers.

My thanks go as well to Herb Shapiro for the beautiful black-and-white photographs that grace most chapters of this book, and for his unwavering commitment to our school. He is not only able to look at our school through the eyes of an accomplished photographer and artist, but also through the lens of a retired principal, a mentor for new principals, as well as a devoted husband to our colleague Lorraine and grandfather to our student Eliza. He wears all these hats with distinction and flare.

In addition, parents Sheila Shapira, graphic designer and mother of graduate Ivan Cortez, and Colleen Croft, photographer and mother of Luca Guaitolini, so graciously accepted the invitation to inspire the cover of this book. I so appreciate their generosity and remain in awe of their artistic talents.

Karen Feuer has been a pioneering parent of two graduates, Alix and Noah Liiv, a past co-president of our PTA, and the current president of our school board. I am ever indebted to her for her unconditional love for and confidence in the Manhattan New School. How many principals can say that their school board president has read all the right books, done incredible graphic designs for their schools, answered telephones when they were short help in the office, served food and cleaned sidewalks at school fairs, and even fried potato pancakes in the holiday season?

Our school would never have become the beautiful setting it is without the total commitment and professionalism of our custodian Neil Donovan and his assistants James Smith and Gonzalo Serrano. In addition to the endless maintenance work they do, it is comforting to know that they care about the colors on our walls, the arrangement of furniture and works of art, and even the plants on our windowsills. They handle all our concerns with humor, patience, and understanding.

A very special thank-you goes to John D'Antonio, our founding custodian. John cared about people and their stories. His humanity and sense of humor sent us off in the right direction. I am ever indebted to him for his willingness to get involved in so many aspects of our school's life and for his willingness to allow me to share so much of his story in this book. He will always be thought of with love by the parents, teachers, and especially the children.

There are also several staff members who take care of the day-to-day nitty-gritty and the annoying loose ends that when cared for properly allow smooth sailing for the entire school community. Hats off to school aides Rachele Lisi and Dora Cruz, security guard Ida Mae Chaplin, and volunteer par excellence Dilta Sanchez.

Community School District 2 provided us with a lovely place to hang our hats and continues to shower us with trust, support, confidence, and expertise. I am grateful to Tony Alvarado and Elaine Fink, superintendents, and our local school board for their willingness to take a chance on a group of teachers with a dream. I am grateful as well to Ilene Friedman, Brenda Goodheart, Beverly Hershkowitz, Bea Johnstone, Fred Kaesar, Andrew Lachman, Ed Levine, Marjorie Robbins, Howard Simms, Lorraine Smith, Maria Utevsky, Lucy West, and Bob Wilson, for all their day-to-day wise counsel.

I am especially indebted to the colleagues in my District 2 reading group. They make me proud of my chosen career. Francine Ballan, longtime friend and colleague, always offers wise counsel that brims with honesty and integrity. Tanya Kaufman, the perfect mentor, helps me make sense of the myriad tasks that come across a principal's desk. Anna Switzer, an important role model, reminds me to stay true to my beliefs and speak out against any hint of mediocrity. Lesley Gordon reminds me to place humanity first in the work we do. Denise Levine's unconditional commitment to the researcher's stance keeps me on my professional toes. I am inspired as well by Sandi Cangiolosi's determination to make a difference in the lives of students and Jill Myers's vision of the principal as teacher. (Hindy List, an essential member of this reading group, is acknowledged below.) All of these women have their own important stories to tell.

I am also grateful to Sandra Feldman, president of the American Federation of Teachers, and to the leadership of the United Federation of Teachers, including Randi Weingarten, president; David Sherman, vice president; and Ivan Tiger, district representative. Through their visits to the school, as well as through their columns, letters, and phone calls, they encourage us with admiration and support. They make us all proud to be part of public education in New York City.

There is also a cluster of familiar faces who frequently drop by to visit old friends, catch up on school news, pitch in to help, and add heartfelt camaraderie to our classrooms and corridors. I thank Mimi Aronson, Doris Levy, Andrea Lowenkopf, Sue Smith, Jim Sullivan, and Arty Voigt for understanding and appreciating what the Manhattan New School is all about.

I'd also like to thank many of the renowned educators whose groundbreaking writing and teaching has inspired and informed us all and whose visits to our school provided us with exhilarating nourishment. They include Bess Altwerger, Nancie Atwell, Laura Benson, Courtney Cazden, Carol Edelsky, Karen Ernst, Bobbi Fisher, Ralph Fletcher, Irene Fountas, Danling Fu, Mary Ellen Giacobbe, Jerry Harste, Steph Harvey, Georgia Heard, Martha Horn, Bonnie Campbell Hill, Ellin Keene, Barbara Kiefer, Peter Johnston, Tom Newkirk, Joann Portaluppi, Linda Rief, Regie Routman, Susan Stires, Connie Weaver, and Bob Wortman.

Over the years we have also been graced with frequent visits by such luminaries as Maureen Barbieri, Bee Cullinan, and Di Snowball. These brilliant educators have left their mark through their words and deeds as well as through their friendship. I'd especially like to thank Donald Graves, whose annual visits always touch the bottom of our hearts and souls through his gracious compliments, incredible insights, and brilliant and far-reaching observations and inquiries.

There are also several additional researchers whose commitment to literacy and to the future of public education gives us proud shoulders to stand on. These include Ken and Yetta Goodman, Karen Smith, Denny Taylor, and Kathy Short. We'd be honored to show them our school.

The publication of this book has a complicated history. I am especially grateful to all the folks at Heinemann for understanding and appreciating this very long story and for their unconditional love, trust, and support. I am particularly indebted to my editor, Lois Bridges, for thinking that my writing was like New York City, dense and full of surprises, to Mike Gibbons, general manager, for his enthusiasm and expertise and for sending all those huge boxes filled with incredible gifts to our school, and to Ray Coutu, marketing director, for his friendship, advice, and the time he spent tutoring our students. I am also grateful for the support of Leigh Peake, the editorial director, Renee Le Verrier, managing editor, Abby Heim, production supervisor, and Patty Adams, production editor. Likewise, I thank Heinemann for sending photographer Donnelly Marks to us on a very first day of school to capture some very special moments.

Hindy List always deserves special recognition. She is the only friend and colleague I regularly call upon for lengthy telephone writing conferences. Her own leadership in literacy and her unconditional love for the children and teachers of New York City always makes her advice astute and compassionate. Her enthusiasm for fiction, family, theater, travel, and world politics also helps me to keep my work in perspective. I can't thank her enough for her interest in my work and the expertise she so willingly shares.

My own children, who took such full advantage of all that the New York City public schools had to offer, inspire me to create similar opportunities for the students we teach. I thank my son Michael for his ever present interest in the work I do. He is always clipping articles, downloading information, and sharing memorable stories that become grist for my writing mill. My daughter J.J. was studying for the bar during the final summer in which I wrote this book. I thank her for all the phone calls that enabled us both to take the breaks we needed. I also thank her for finding the time to visit our school and for being swept off her feet by so many of our remarkable children. Thank you both for adding so much beauty, humor, and tenderness to my life.

Most of all, I am forever in love with my husband, Neil. With the turn of every page, I can recall the close of each long summer writing day. It was so much easier to stay at my desk knowing I could look forward to his dinners on the back porch. Even now I can taste the grilled salmon, the fresh bread, the small red potatoes covered in basil olive oil, and the chilled English cider. He continues to make my life easy.

INTRODUCTION

When you start a school from scratch, you are conscious on that very first day that no such school existed on the day before. We opened the Manhattan New School in a warm New York autumn, and I became obsessed with recording our history and documenting our every move. It was a clean slate, just begging to be filled.

Some of my data collections, although a bit unorthodox, are rather easy to explain. I have a special shelf filled with the works of such writers as Janet Ahlberg, Pam Conrad, Myra Cohn Livingstone, James Marshall, Eve Merriam, David McCord, Peggy Parish, Richard Scarry, Dr. Seuss, Alvin Schwartz, Shel Silverstein, and Valerie Worth. These are all wonderful writers who've left incredible literary legacies for our students and who have all unfortunately passed away since September of 1991, our opening season. I know this because I've been keeping records, archives if you will. I keep this special collection of children's literature because whenever a beloved writer dies, we pay tribute to their life and work. I also have a list of all the novels we've read together as a staff. In fact, on the wall of one school restroom, each tile boasts the title and author of one of these shared readings. You read the wall and reminisce. I also keep a growing list of all the languages our students speak. These are mounted on our language board. You can not only find the names of all our bilingual students, but you can find out the country they come from and which classroom you can find them in. This list comes in very handy when you're looking for a translator, or when newcomers to our school want to meet other families from their home country. I've also painted a mural on my office wall that has come to serve as an archive of sorts. It's a scene of two children reading, sitting atop stacks of books. On each book spine is the name of a carefully chosen children's author. These include Arnold Adoff, Louise Borden, Paula Danziger, Allan A. De Fina, Rebecca Dotlich, Ralph Fletcher, Mem Fox, Monica Gunning, David Harrison, Virginia Hamilton, Ben Mikelson, Ann Morris, Emily Arnold McCully, Sheldon Oberman, Marci Ridlon, Faith Ringgold, Michael Rosen, and Sarah Weeks. They are, in fact, writers who have visited our school; this always-in-progress mural also has blank spines, for the names of those to come. There are all kinds of ways to keep records.

I have drawers filled with common schoolhouse artifacts. I've saved every note from every child, teacher, and family member. I've saved every memo from our district supervisors, central board personnel, superintendent, and chancellor. I have hundreds of slides and snapshots capturing memorable moments. I have several journals filled with observations, reflections, concerns, and questions. I have a copy of every letter I've ever written to our staff and every note a visitor has ever sent us. I have every cartoon or newspaper clipping someone has mounted on our walls. I have eight years of logbook pages from our school. (See Appendix 1.) Each day this prominent open book becomes filled with announcements, reminders, messages, gossip, changes in schedule, and names of visitors.

I've saved all these things, because these artifacts help me tell a very new story. I am now the principal of a New York City public school. Several teachers I met through my work at the Teachers College Writing Project at Columbia University joined me in an attempt to show what's possible when enthusiastic, well-informed educators, who share a common vision for what rich teaching and learning environments can be, come together under one roof and are thoroughly supported by a district leadership that shares their vision.

In the late spring of 1991, we sent a proposal to the school board of Community School District 2, outlining our hopes for a new school. We described our plan to create a school in which students would apprentice themselves to teachers who were readers, writers, and researchers. We described our vision of creating workshop studios across the curriculum in which students would learn by doing, talking, and messing up, and teachers would be close at hand, advising, coaching, demonstrating, encouraging, guiding, teaching, and no doubt occasionally messing up themselves. With the school board's approval, we hung signs in supermarkets and laundromats, announcing our plans to reopen the former P.S. 190. We held a few evening open houses, letting the neighborhood parents in on our vision for the Manhattan New School. When we opened the following fall, we had one hundred and fifty students, in grades kindergarten through three. Each year, we have enrolled at least three new kindergarten classes, and our first group of entering third graders became our first sixth-grade graduating class in 1995.

Today the Manhattan New School has more than 550 children working in twenty-two different classrooms. We are not a charter school, not an alternative school, not an option school, but a regular neighborhood public school. Approximately 45 percent of our students come from minority backgrounds, and 55 percent come from a wide range of nonminority backgrounds. Our students speak upwards of thirty different first languages.

Whenever I speak or write about our school, I feel like Dorothy in the Wizard of Oz, clicking my heels and beginning with the words, "There's no place like home." There really is no place like home when you're talking about New York City. We are part of an enormous city system serving more than one million public school children. When the Yankees won the World Series in 1996, more than twelve thousand children were absent in order to attend the ticker-tape parade in honor of their heroes! Every community, no doubt, offers its own unique challenges, but perhaps our crowded, complicated city offers some rather surprising ones.

It is a challenge not to get swallowed up and depressed by central board of education memoranda that announce, "Violence Prevention Anti-Gun Poster Contests," "Child-Abuse Prevention Month," or "Stop the Violence Week."

It is a challenge not to get caught on your way to work in gridlock traffic and then have to search half an hour for a parking spot, knowing your students are gathering on the rug eagerly awaiting your arrival. It's even worse to have to run out at eleven o'clock to move your car to the alternate side of the street to avoid a parking ticket or having your car towed away.

It is a challenge to work in a schoolhouse built at the turn of the century, with no gymnasium, no formal library, insufficient playground space, insufficient restrooms and water fountains, and an old-fashioned ground-floor cafeteria designed at a time when most children went home for lunch and no breakfasts were served. It's also a challenge to work in a five-story building with no elevator, and to have existed for many years with no working intercom system, without the help of a full-time secretary or nurse or guidance counselor. It's a challenge to work with classroom registers nearing thirty children per class, children who speak so many first languages. And of course, it's a challenge to work with such low budgets that our parents have to donate everything from Band-Aids to postage stamps to photocopy paper to help us through the year.

It's a challenge and at the same time, it's a rare privilege. Where else could we have a school that is five blocks from the Metropolitan Museum of Art, five blocks from Central Park and a subway ride away from Broadway, the World Trade Center, the Empire State Building, the United Nations? Where else could I learn what the story of Snow White sounds like in Maltese, what the Macedonian alphabet looks like, how it feels to leave your grandparents in Kosovo? Where else could we enroll students who live in neighborhood luxury apartment buildings alongside the children of the custodians who take care of those buildings and the children of the domestic workers who care for the families in those buildings? Where else could I have the opportunity to give back to the children of immigrants what the New York City public schools gave to me, a child of immigrants?

It's also a privilege to be surrounded by so many children and parents who are a product of their surroundings. Where else would I receive a request from a student for her class to watch her performance on the soap opera *All My Children*? Or a letter from a mother requesting that I hail a taxicab for her daughters at three o'clock? Or a page from a "fill in the blank" play-date pad, sent by a parent to let us know changes in her son's after-school plans? Where else would I find a student writing safety tips for her teacher, who had recently moved to Manhattan? And others writing photographic essays about street vendors, architecture, and the world of specialty bookstores? Where else would lateness excuses include "A passenger got sick on the subway," or "The president was at the U.N. so they closed First Avenue?" Where else would I find children entertaining themselves in an empty playground by turning a stale bagel into a hockey puck?

Above all, I feel privileged to be at the Manhattan New School, because where else would I have the opportunity to teach and learn alongside so many of my old friends, each an exquisite teacher and learner? I once heard the director of the Mendelsohn Choir say that he imagined going to heaven one day and describing to the gatekeeper the wonderful choir he had been working with. The gatekeeper would turn him away saying, "You better go back, we have nothing that comes close, even in heaven." I completely understand that choir director's sentiment.

It comes as no surprise to me that unknowing first-time visitors to our school ask if it is a private institution. I think it's the antique stained glass windows and copper swinging doors that welcome you as you climb up the front staircase. I think it's the oak benches and small tables with bouquets of flowers and baskets filled with magazines that provide a cozy corner for you to wait until your visit begins. I think it's the calm, beautiful corridors filled with children's artwork and children at work that inspire our guests to ask, "Is this really a public school?" After all, only the public school nightmare stories usually make the evening news. "Yes, it's a public school," I proudly announce, "and I can show you many more in our city that you'd be proud to call your own."

It also comes as no surprise to me that each year we have a long waiting list of families hoping to send their children to our school. "Can't you open a Manhattan New School West?" a parent from the other side of town once asked me. "No," I answered, "You can never re-create the same school in another setting. You can't make the same thing happen again." It's true: the life story of every school is so unique, so dependent on the particular people involved, the history of the world at the time, each community's needs, and even the physical space allotted. Just as teachers can't plan all of the next year's teaching during the summer months, but instead have to weave the year's fabric together with the needs, interests, and passions of their new students, so too, we can't dream up a perfect school and then pour it into an empty vessel. No, every school is uniquely different, and each evolves as the members of the community live, dream, and work alongside one another.

So why this book? I have no clever list of absolutes for starting a school, no "thou shalts, shoulds, or musts." But I do have a few suggestions for educators intent on making change, either by starting a brand-new school or transforming an existing one. I have learned some big lessons in the last few years, ones that have made me rethink my beliefs about students, teachers, parents, administrators, schools, and literacy learning. (Although I never intended to separate my administrative leadership from the literacy work I do because the two inform one another, I pitied the reader of one such lengthy story. Information about literacy appears therefore in two companion volumes, *Lifetime Guarantees: Literacy lessons from the Manhattan New School* and *Writing Through Childhood: Lessons from Young Writers at the Manhattan New School*.

I read several years ago that Frank Smith wrote his classic book *Understanding Reading* in order to help himself understand the reading process. Similarly, writing a book about creating an elementary school where students and teachers are joyfully literate has enabled me to understand what makes our schoolhouse tick. In essence, I have aimed to discover what really matters in our school lives. I have searched for what has been essential in creating a schoolhouse that is simultaneously rigorous, nurturing, and successful by many standards. Above all, I have learned to set priorities and create and support the kind of practices that enable us to turn our dreams into reality.

My colleague Regina Chiou recently suggested that I reread E. B. White's *Stuart Little*, particularly "The Schoolroom" chapter. In it, Stuart serves as a substitute teacher and asks his students to "tell us what is important." Henry responds, "A shaft of sunlight at the end of a dark afternoon, a note in music, and the way a baby's neck smells if its mother keeps it tidy." In writing this book, I have been asking myself the same question, "What is important?" It is my hope that the answers to that question and the lessons I have been learning will serve as conversation starters in the faculty rooms of those of you reading this text.

Countless times, when I speak at seminars, conferences, or summer institutes, teachers come up to me and say, "I wish my principal were here." This book is intended for teachers *and* their principals. Through years of work as a staff developer, I've come to understand the frustration a teacher feels when she attempts to make significant changes in her reading/writing classroom, but realizes that those changes are limited by the culture of the building outside her classroom door. She needs the entire school community to rally round and extend and enrich those changes. I have spent the last eight years thinking through how, as a building principal, I can initiate, demonstrate, and nurture that rallying round.

Each day I'm privileged to see master teachers at work. Each has his or her own story to tell. Several have already published their own books, videos, and articles and others are well on their way. They each know best the story of what happens day to day inside their classrooms. My story is a different one. What I know best is what happens outside the classrooms, what happens in the corridors, in the tiny reading rooms studded throughout our building, what happens at parent meetings, at faculty conferences, and of course, what happens in my own little cluttered office. What has become my turf is how best to support the efforts of students, teachers, and parents who are determined to lead literate lives. Nothing would make me happier than to win an Academy Award for best supporting role.

Choosing a title for this book became a long and arduous task. The book has been in the making for many years and has lived through several working formats and possible designs. I finally selected *Going Public* because of the possible interpretations it contains. I am of course "going public" when I tell this story and let the world know what is happening behind the walls of that red brick building on East Eighty-second Street in New York City. The title also serves to advocate *for* public education. The families in our community are "going public" when they choose a public school over the many private, parochial, and soon-to-be charter schools in our city. I hope readers will understand their choice as I share what I consider the non-negotiable elements in our school lives. Finally, my friends who understand the workings of the financial district have told me that, on Wall Street, "going public" indicates a successful enterprise, one that people will eagerly and confidently invest in. The Manhattan New School fits that description as well.

We're more than ready to go public, in every sense of the term.

CHAPTER 1

SHARING THE SECRETS OF OUR SUCCESS

Priorities

- Educators must meet the challenges of teaching and learning head on.
- Educators must choose their colleagues carefully.
- A new school should start small in order that a core culture can be developed.
- The work of all members of a school community, not only that of the teaching staff, must be valued.
- Adult learning must be taken seriously if schools are to thrive.
- Staff members must be encouraged to trade places with one another on occasion.
- A school's belief system must be focused and strong, to enable good decisions to be made about programs and procedures.
- To make a difference in the lives of children, educators must be willing to challenge the status quo.
- Educators must be willing to become political in order to fight for what they believe in.

Practice

- On tackling problems such as insufficient parent involvement, literacy issues of the struggling child, and uncivilized cafeteria life
- On developing criteria for selecting teachers to work in our school
- On treating all members of the school community with professional courtesy
- On minimizing the obstacles that prevent educators from taking care of their own learning
- On challenging the givens of public school life, including the use of time, space, personnel, and resources
- On getting political, including writing letters to public officials, letters to the editor, and speaking out publicly

Donald Graves paid me a very high compliment when he told me I was running a sanitarium. Our school, he suggested, is a "place that heals any sickness an educator might have. Walk in sick; walk out whole."

I appreciated and understood Don's comments. There is a lot of smiling, laughing, and hugging in our school. Teachers, children, and parents genuinely like one another, pay attention to one another, and take care of one another. Teachers and students are proud to call this place home. Some incoming neighborhood parents act as if they've won the lottery when they find out that their address is in our zoned catchment area. The school is quiet, calm, and beautiful. We take pride in the architecture, in the views out the window, in the carefully designed classrooms, in the students' work, and in the beautiful faces of the children, who come from over forty different countries. Above all, people aren't afraid to roll up their sleeves and get lost in the rigorous and scholarly work that takes place around here.

We are a successful school by many standards. We have a waiting list of prospective students. We qualify for extra funding because of our wonderfully diverse student population. Our organization sheet reads like a Who's Who in New York education circles. Educators from near and far request to visit with us. Graduate students want to conduct research in our classrooms. Student teachers feel privileged to be assigned to us. Even our standardized test scores, if you care about such things, are worth writing home about.

Tackling Problems

Of course, in no way do we think we've arrived. There are many questions tugging at our sleeves. We have yet to figure out how to fully involve our nonEnglish-speaking parents in the life of the school. And although we've made a difference in the life of many children who struggle with learning to read, we continue to puzzle over many literacy questions. We have not yet come to terms with the standards movement and we have big questions about special education. We struggle to find the best ways to make use of volunteers, and we are continually rethinking the place of programs that pull children out of their regular classrooms. We still need to solve the mystery of how to create a civilized cafeteria life, especially on long rainy or snowy afternoons and we continue to think through ways to guarantee that all the children we educate will resolve their conflicts peacefully. Perhaps one of the biggest issues currently on my mind, and one I doubt is talked about often enough in most schools, is prejudice. We pride ourselves on living a respectful, multicultural, harmonious life together, but every once in awhile we overhear a child make a hurtful comment about someone's color of skin, country of origin, or ethnic background. And even one comment is too much.

Yes, there is still much work to be done, but part of the magic of this place is that when we know a problem exists, we tackle it. When I began this book three years ago, I originally included in our list of shortcomings such items as behind-the-times technology (we had rotary telephones when our school first opened), gaps in our study of

American history, the unpolished use of portfolios, and inconsistent assessment tools for communicating with parents.

I am thrilled to look back and realize that we have made progress in all these areas. (We can even boast having over sixty-five computers, as well as half a dozen laptops, e-mail and access to the Internet through a T-1 line, digital cameras, a school Web site, and an after-school video workshop utilizing computer editing.) This realization is a good reminder that school problems can be solved. All it takes is time, priorities, people with expertise (including people who know how to write grants or contact politicians for funding), and a refusal to sweep things under the rug. I suppose that refusing to look the other way is one of the secrets of our success, and writing this book has pushed me to wonder if there aren't others.

Guidelines for Successful School Administration

If I were teaching one of those graduate courses in educational administration, I'd probably devote the first class to the lessons I learned early on in starting this school. The list on the chalkboard would probably look something like this:

- Choose colleagues carefully
- Start small
- Value everyone's work
- Take adult learning seriously
- Walk a mile in one another's shoes
- Believe in something
- Challenge the givens
- Get political

I'd then explain each of these points in the following way:

Choose Colleagues Carefully

I know that I've been incredibly lucky. Through my previous role at the Teachers College Writing Project, I had an enviable little black book filled with the names and telephone numbers of wonderful teachers and staff developers from all parts of the city. In the closing chapters of my book *Lasting Impressions: Weaving Literature into the Writing Workshop*, I suggested that my work in starting the Manhattan New School would begin with gathering the finest of teachers, and that is indeed where my efforts began. And as soon as a few wonderful teachers agreed to join me in this venture, they began talking to their friends. Word of mouth and serious networking enabled us to open this school with a cluster of seven good friends who happened to be great teachers. As years went on, staff members kept urging friends with similar teaching visions to apply. They also recommended their favorite student teachers and contacted former colleagues. In eight years, our staff has grown to twenty-nine full-time teachers.

I know that every city has different hiring procedures and union regulations. In order to do my job well, I became familiar with all the New York City requirements. I learned about such possibilities as hardship transfers, minority transfers, and seniority transfers. Several years ago the teachers' union enabled us to become part of its School-Based Option program, acknowledging that our school had a unique perspective and therefore did not necessarily have to hire the most senior teacher who applies to work in our school. We are very grateful for this status. There is a world of wonderful teachers out there and it is worth all the time and effort it takes to surround ourselves with colleagues with whom we can joyfully teach and learn.

Each year we inevitably have to add new staff to our growing school and we continue to be very discriminating. The teachers' union requires our school-based selection committee to have formal criteria for choosing new teachers, but my colleagues know that I also have my own unwritten list of requirements. There are several things I wonder about even before we formally interview candidates or observe them teaching. First I want to know if the candidate considers it a privilege to be around children. Next I want to know if the candidate reads. Does he/she take care of his/her own literacy? And finally I ask myself, "Would I want to have dinner with this person?" I think children deserve to be surrounded by people who find the world a fascinating place, people who have interests and passions and who aren't hesitant to talk about them. A few of the actual questions we have asked candidates are listed below:

- If colleagues were visiting your classroom, how would you facilitate their learning?
- How would you plan for an inquiry-based social studies course of study?
- How would you launch a writing workshop?
- How would you organize a classroom library?
- Who are your mentors and what have you learned from them?
- How do you assess your own professional growth and the growth of your students?
- What are you currently reading for your own pleasure and for your professional growth, and what are you reading to your students?

(See Appendix 2 for reproducible interview questionnaire.)

The Manhattan New School is filled with exquisite educators, and I make no apologies for demanding such a fine crew. The most important job a principal has is leading the search for just the right teachers.

A word about professional courtesy is in order here. Even though I don't think every teacher is appropriate for teaching in every school setting, I am unconditionally pro-teacher. I root for teachers on quiz shows. I clip pro-teacher stories from the newspaper. I vote for pro-teacher candidates. Despite my pro-teacher stance, I recognize that there are very different ways teachers think about teaching and learning. In other words, even though I am pro-teacher, I must admit that there are teachers I don't want to see working in our school. One year, we were assigned a learning-disabilities teacher who had a diagnostic/prescriptive approach to working with struggling readers. She brought cartons of worksheets to "cure" whatever ailed our students. I disagreed with her methods, but I treated her with dignity. She worked hard. She cared about children. (In *Lifetime Guarantee*, I explain how it came to pass that this hardworking teacher found a new home, better suited to her philosophical beliefs.) At a recent gathering of the National Council of Teachers of English (NCTE), Frankey Jones delivered a speech entitled "Curb your Dogma." Even when we disagree with other educators, we must find ways to treat one another civilly and professionally. I recently spent a frustrating morning with two new substitute teachers in our school. One blew a whistle each time she wanted to get the children's attention. The other held "a quiet contest," pitting the boys against the girls. It was clear that these newcomers to our school did not understand our way of life. Their methods enraged me but I resisted the urge to rant and rave. They were hardworking teachers who were in the wrong place. They still deserved to be treated with respect.

Start Small

Choosing the right teachers was just the beginning. We had to learn to live together. We had to carve out a school culture together. Again, we have been incredibly lucky. Our district allowed us to start small. We opened with only seven classes, kindergarten through third grade. Today we have twenty-two classes, moving up through grade five, but starting out small made an incredible difference. We had ample opportunities to meet, to talk, to listen, to negotiate, to appreciate, and for all of us to get to know one another's students and parents. Together with that first crew of seven teachers, and those 150 students and their parents, all of us became ambassadors. We were able to demonstrate to the next year's students and families and to the newly hired teachers our way of life. It's as if we announced to the incoming folks, "This is what we value. This is how we do it here." As each year passed, we took in more and more students and hired new staff, ever so carefully. Each year the newcomers learned from the students and staff who had lived here the year before. This is how we talk to one another. This is how we share literature. This is how we treat visitors. This is how we create beautiful settings. And then of course we began to take lessons from the newcomers. Each new student, parent, and teacher added their own passions and areas of expertise to our growing community, but having started small allowed us to create the kind of school culture that fosters a willingness to listen to new ideas, that welcomes change, and accepts new challenges.

Selecting the right colleagues and starting small are always my first bits of advice to educators interested in opening new schools. In fact, educators interested in making changes in existing schools also need to think long and hard about hiring new staff, and even if their schools are huge, faculties need to continually search for ways for people to meet in small groups, in order that all voices be listened to, appreciated, and respected.

I used to think that schools shouldn't have more children than the number of days in a school year. I was thinking about 180. Then quite conveniently as our school grew, I revised my thinking to 365, the number of days in a calendar year. As our school grew even larger and we continued to feel intimate and be successful, I revised my thinking once again. I now believe that schools shouldn't have more children than the number of fine teachers we can attract to teach those children successfully. All that being said, it bears repeating that starting small with a group of colleagues who can work well and productively together enables a school to grow bigger and stay successful.

Value Everyone's Work

I learned several other important lessons early on. In the weeks before the school opened, our staff met regularly to think through our opening days. One of the decisions we made was to try and live environmentally conscious lives. To that end we agreed to avoid Styrofoam in the building. We would bring in ceramic mugs instead. One of the mugs I brought from home was a gift from a teacher friend. It read, "Those who can, teach. Those who can't go into some less significant line of work." It was, no doubt, an answer to that old saw, "Those who can, do. Those who can't, teach." One early morning I was drinking out of that mug when John, our custodian, walked in. He took one look at that mug and asked, "How do you think that mug makes me feel?" Needless to say, it was a revelation for me. I felt the blood drain from my face. I was speechless. I never intended to hurt the custodian's feelings, nor the paraprofessionals, school aides, security guards, kitchen workers, nurses, or secretaries. I know the work they do is very significant. The school wouldn't run well without them. But I had never paused to think about the inscription on that mug from anyone else's point of view. No, I had thought of it simply as a compliment to the teaching profession. I remain grateful to John for having the courage and wisdom to teach me not to be elitist or exclusionary in a school building. You don't have to have a teaching license to make a difference in children's lives. Everyone counts in a school building. If you label a room the teachers' lounge, does that mean that custodians and secretaries are unable to enter to get a cup of coffee? We have a staff room that everyone's invited to use. In fact, we have painted the door to our staff room. It looks like a giant sheet of lined loose-leaf paper that is filled top to bottom with job titles, including all the people who work in our building as well as parents and visitors.

That coffee mug is no longer at school. I keep it on my desk at home, filled with assorted pens and pencils. It serves as a constant reminder that everyone counts in a school building. Everyone deserves a sincere "Good morning."

Take Adult Learning Seriously

I also learned quite dramatically, that first year, the importance of taking care of our own adult learning. I had been based at the Teachers College Writing Project for seven years and I had forgotten what it is like to live in an elementary school building five days a week. I had forgotten how hard it is to be a really fine classroom teacher, how many hours of reflection and preparation it takes. And I had forgotten what it is like to try and find time in your life to visit the dentist, renew a driver's license, or get a haircut. I had forgotten what it's like not to be able to get a cup of coffee whenever you want one, or make a phone call (heaven forbid it's a long-distance one!) or use the restroom when you need to.

I sensed that starting a school from scratch, taking over a few floors in an old building with barely a piece of chalk, would be difficult, but I never imagined that it would require twelve-hour days, six or seven days a week. Our bodies ached from moving furniture, carrying cartons of books, and cleaning out closets. For several months we were all-consumed, packing and unpacking, arranging and rearranging, scheduling and rescheduling, planning and then revising our plans.

The remarkable thing about a school is that it has to work on day one. It's not like starting a marriage. You don't start out with a fully furnished home, children, and a big bank account. You live out of boxes, and live on pasta and canned soups. You work up to things. You don't have to be good at cooking and cleaning and parenting and entertaining immediately. You get there in time, sometimes, but starting a school is oh, so different.

From the very first day, the rooms have to be ready, the record keeping in order, and what seems like carton upon carton of regulations need to be followed. The students need to know where to enter and where to exit. They need to know where to sit and stand and wait. They need to be fed and toileted and transported. They need not only to be taught but also loved and comforted. And it all begins on the very first day. It all has to work.

But even later on, when we were settled in a bit, we were still putting in long days. The work never seemed to end. Putting in long hours was not the hard part though. Teachers are used to that. The most difficult part, perhaps the saddest part for all of us, was forgetting to take care of our own learning. We were all so busy. The teachers were working so hard to set up their classrooms and teach their students that they forgot to take care of themselves. I suffered from the same overload. I was consumed with health records, variances, auditors, security measures, bus schedules, purchase orders, lunch coverages, fire drills, forming a PTA, and what seemed like dozens of other getting-started necessities.

Starting this school has been a humbling experience. Many of us on staff were embarrassed to realize that in our former jobs as staff developers, teacher trainers, mentor teachers, and teacher researchers, we were the ones who went about the city encouraging teachers to take care of their own learning. We were the ones who suggested that teachers keep journals on their teaching, write for publication, form adult reading and writing groups, do case studies, collect data, form study groups, attend conferences, tape-record and videotape their teaching, and visit colleagues in their classrooms. It was so easy to encourage others to do these important things, and yet we were forgetting to do them ourselves. We were so caught up in doing for others that we forgot to make time for ourselves. It took us awhile, but we have finally figured out ways to take our own learning as seriously as we take that of our students.

Walk a Mile in One Another's Shoes

There is not enough back-and-forth educational movement in this country. People become staff developers and then rarely return to full-time classroom teaching. People become principals and then rarely return to full-time staff development positions. People accept university positions and then rarely become school principals. Not only do I think educators should change jobs every few years, I think they should return to their former roles every once in awhile. The staff developer who returns to full-time classroom teaching and then becomes a staff developer again will return with new compassion in her heart. Likewise, the university professor who becomes a school principal and then returns to university teaching will have new concerns, priorities, and understandings to share.

Trading places not only has value in the educational community at large, but also within any one educational community. At the end of Donald Graves's first visit to our school several years ago, he asked me if I had read Che Guevera's *Handbook on Guerrilla Warfare* recently. "No, I haven't. What makes you ask?" I responded. Don, the supreme researcher, had noticed how each of us in the building had taken on many roles. "One of the first rules of revolution," Don explained, "is that everyone must know everyone else's job, because in a revolution you never know when you might have to trade places." I suppose there is something revolutionary about walking into a school and seeing the custodian reading to children, the principal teaching, the security guard helping a child solve a math problem, or teachers filling out purchase orders. We are not, however, trying to be revolutionary; we are simply trying to create the kind of setting in which we can live out our dreams of becoming accomplished and effective teachers and learners. It is essential that we know one another's jobs. If we are really going to have well-run, joyous, successful schoolhouses, we all need to walk a mile in one another's shoes. We need to redefine our roles and be willing to trade places.

One day Joanne Hindley Salch noticed an eyelash resting on my cheek. "Don't you feel it?" she asked. I answered no, and began swatting away at the side of my face, completely missing the eyelash. "Can't you see it?" Joanne then asked. "See it?" I answered. "How can I see my own cheek, without a mirror?" "I can see mine when I look down," she responded. I thought she was kidding, but she wasn't. It was as surprising for Joanne to learn that I couldn't see my own cheek as it was for me to grasp that the shape of her cheekbone allows her to look down and see her cheek. Amazon Indians eat termites and grubs, and retch at the thought of drinking cow's milk, secretion from an animal. It takes a lot of work to understand someone else's point of view.

Would I have a new respect for cafeteria life if I spent the morning alongside the kitchen workers serving food? Would the kitchen workers have a new appreciation for preparing bag lunches if they were involved in planning the class trip? It never ceases to amaze me when I roll out my file cabinet drawer, the wide range of subject matter that's within—that a file labeled "lice" is tucked between "letter-writing" and "multiage grouping." Teachers need to understand the full range of *my* job as I do theirs.

I was once interviewed on a radio program. The host began one of her questions with the words, "Pretend you're a teacher." "No need to pretend," I answered, "I am a teacher." Principals must stay close to teaching. How else can I help my colleagues, understand students' needs, or counsel parents? Besides, I'm a really good teacher. How can I not participate in the teaching life of the school? I disagree with those textbooks on administration which suggest that the teacher's main area of concern is the classroom and the principal's is the school at large. No, we both need two lenses in our cameras, the wide angle and the zoom. Schools become better places when all of us can step back and see the big picture and pull in close to do the nitty-gritty work. The reverse is probably also true. It's probably near to impossible to have a truly wonderful and effective school if the principal doesn't care about the teaching and the teachers don't care about what happens outside their classroom doors.

Believe in Something

In *Lasting Impressions: Weaving Literature into the Writing Workshop*, when I wrote about my hopes for this school I described my use of "authenticity" as a filter to decide what is worth sharing with children. I suggested that we wouldn't ask students to do things we don't value in our own lives. We planned to invite the students to read, write, solve problems, and create art in the same ways that you and I read, write, solve problems, and create art outside of school. Just as I don't pretend to be a teacher, students shouldn't pretend to be learners. We need to give them the real stuff, not fill them with pretend activities. In the last eight years, I've deepened my thinking about "authenticity." I've come to realize that we are raising activists in our school. All the classroom methods we appreciate—process reading and writing, inquiry-based studies, reader-response opportunities, real-world problem solving—all these add up to raising activists. All these approaches require students to take in their world, to take responsibility for their world, to see the strengths and weaknesses of their world, and to improve the quality of their world. Authenticity for me is now aligned with things that really matter. We have only six hours a day with our students. The time is precious. From the very first day, we need to eliminate the busywork, the boring work, the things that don't add up. Every community that sets out to start a school or transform an existing one needs to grapple with the issue of what's really important. All schools need an organizing vision, one that helps the members of the community sift through all the possibilities that come their way. When you truly believe in something, you can critically look at some new curriculum item or teaching technique and honestly say, "That's not for us."

After visiting our school, Helena Linna, an educator from Finland, sent me the following quote taken off of an old church wall in Sussex, England. It reads, "A vision without a struggle is only a dream. Works and deeds without a vision are mere labor. A vision and action together bring hope to the world." Those are words for educators to live by.

Challenge the Givens

The final crucial lesson I learned during the early years of our school was the absolute need to be willing to challenge the givens of public school life. Julia Alvarez in *In the Time of the Butterflies*, an account of life in the Dominican Republic under the dictator Trujillo writes, "The givens, all I'd been taught, fell away like so many covers when you sit up in bed." If we really have a vision in mind, we have to be willing to rethink all that we've been taught. We have to be willing to renegotiate and redesign our choices and commitments.We don't have to accept the status quo; we don't have to do things simply because they have always been done.

During the fall of 1992, in the second year of our school, I sent the following note to the new staff members:

> *9-30-92*
>
> *Dear Pam, Debby, Lorraine, and Sharon,*
>
> *Just a few reminders.*
> *As a school we stay away from:*
>
> > *store-bought decorations*
> > *contests and competitions*
> > *religious holiday celebrations*
> > *pink for girls and blue for boys and other sexist stuff*
> > *using edible foods in collage or as math manipulatives*
>
> *We will also be rethinking Columbus Day and Thanksgiving perspectives together.*
>
> *Please bring your thoughts and questions to our Wednesday gathering.*
>
> > *Love,*
> > *Shelley*

The note clearly reveals that we have strong opinions and beliefs. The note hints that we have taken a political stance. The note suggests that we are all gazing in the same direction. Above all, the note clearly states that we are willing to challenge the givens of public school life.

We will not allow our school to become "P.S. Anywhere," a phrase Joanne coined as soon as she thought we were starting to settle, or become satisfied with less than our dreams. We do feel like P.S. Anywhere whenever we let bureaucratic paperwork get in the way of having a good day with children, when we let hallway artwork become ragged or poorly displayed, or when we find ourselves griping and groaning about how tired we are. Jessie, a few weeks after she graduated from our school, reminded us that our school does look and feel very different from most. She sent Judy, her sixth-grade teacher, and I a letter from camp in which she describes a conversation with the other girls in her bunk, who no doubt were surprised at her description of her city school (see Figure 1.1)

When you are determined to create a spectacularly simple school in a complicated city, you must be ever on the lookout for hints of mediocrity. You must be willing to challenge the givens that unfortunately and frequently attach themselves to public school life in a big city.

We have challenged some of the givens in seemingly small ways. We gave ourselves a name instead of using a number. We are known as the Manhattan New School, not the traditional P.S. 290. We call each other by our first names. The students are often surprised to learn our last names. The principal's office is not center stage. I use a small room way off the beaten track that was once part of a medical suite in the days

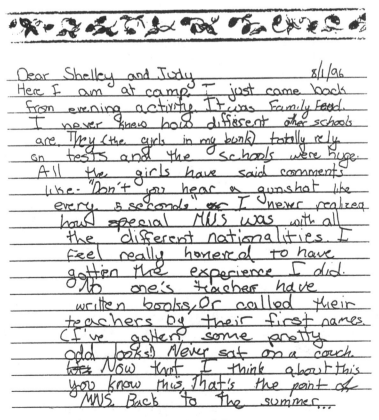

Dear Shelley and Judy   8/1/96
Here I am at camp. I just came back
from evening activity. It was Family Feud.
I never knew how different other schools
are. They (the girls in my bunk) totally rely
on tests and the schools were huge.
All the girls have said comments
like- "Don't you hear a gunshot like
every 5 seconds." I never realized
how special MNS was with all
the different nationalities. I
feel really honored to have
gotten the experience I did.
No one's teacher have
written books, Or called their
teachers by their first names.
(I've gotten some pretty
odd looks!) Never sat on a couch.
Now that I think about this
you know this, That's the point of
MNS. Back to the summer...

Figure 1.1

when public schools had nurses, doctors, and dentists. I don't need to have a room with a view of all the action. I don't need to okay everyone's decisions. I don't want to lead that kind of hierarchical life. We also took lessons from a thoughtful and successful neighboring principal, Tanya Kaufman, and removed the huge metal counter that traditionally separates parents from the staff in the main office and we removed the bolted-down folding seats from the auditorium. We now have a beautiful ballroom just right for music, dance, and social gatherings.

We have challenged the givens of public school life in large ways as well. We devote big blocks of time to our studies. It's not surprising to pass by a classroom and see children reading and pass by that same classroom an hour later and see children still reading. Teachers also know that they have the freedom and flexibility to move away from their usually busy agendas and every once in awhile devote an entire day to a math project, an art mural, or a science investigation. We also minimize interruptions. We don't allow frequent specials and extravaganzas to keep us from our everyday practice of tackling hard work. We don't allow bells, buzzers, and public-address announcements to get in the way of really listening to one another. When that shrill bell does go off, it means someone needs the custodian quickly. I've come to refer to it as the "vomit bell." (Someone had better have vomited and the custodian's mop-up services are immediately needed if all of us have been interrupted.) We've hung white metal mailboxes on classroom doors to avoid unnecessary opening and closing of doors for deliveries. Sharon Taberski, a first- and second-grade teacher, even teaches her students how to turn the doorknob without making a sound, so that they won't disturb others when they need to leave or reenter their classrooms. I've also realized that you can't lead a whole language classroom if you never have your whole class together. We therefore avoid lots of special pullout programs and we continue to fight for push-in specialists if the need arises.

From the very first day, we became conscious that schools built in 1904 were not designed for today's teaching styles. The rooms were too small to allow for workshops filled with small-group, hands-on conversational activities. We needed softer noise levels in our classrooms. And so we invited children to create their own comfortable workspaces in the nooks, crannies, and corridors that dot our building. When fewer students are in any one area, the volume goes down. Of course, this kind of movement requires trusting your students, another important way we challenge the givens of public school life.

In the first year of our school, Joanne created a simple way to increase space and lower the volume in her primary classroom. She removed the lower legs from many of her classroom tables. The tables now stood knee-high and the children no longer needed chairs. Instead, they happily sat on rug squares and the absence of chairs created more space and eliminated the often harsh sounds of moving chairs. Likewise, Judy Davis, a fifth- and sixth-grade teacher, created lots of additional workspace by attaching a deep wooden shelf clear across the top of the low, built-in oak cabinets that line one wall of her classroom. She carted in a half dozen stools, and her students had a wall of prime workspace.

Our school doesn't have a traditional library. Instead, we have turned all the small offices into reading rooms. We have a fiction reading room, a poetry reading room, and a nonfiction reading room. We have clearly rethought the use of space in our building. (Before our school grew to its current size, staff members even toyed with the idea of having a room devoted to block construction alone, and another one used exclusively for map study.) We also have staff members determined to turn one of our restrooms into a photography darkroom. We have learned never to say never, although our increasing enrollments year after year make these dreams seem more and more impossible.

However we decide to use our allotted space, one thing remains constant. It is up to us to make those spaces beautiful. Again we must challenge the given that schools must have an institutional, sterile look. One summer we had a temporary custodian, substituting for our beloved John. The man walked up and down the corridors and in and out of the classrooms, and announced, "This isn't a school. It's a fucking apartment building!" Thankfully his stay was short-lived. But what is here forever is our determination to create a homey setting. Why not? It is our home away from home. We have met with fire marshals and we are living proof that there are safe ways to create inviting settings for teachers and children who have important work to do. (See discussion on the role of the interior decorator in Chapter 2, "Rethinking the Role of Principal.")

We must also rethink how personnel are used in a building. When we opened our school, we deliberately hired specialists who might be able to teach more than one class at a time, so that two regular teachers could meet together during the schoolday to discuss problems and practice. Early on we hired a storyteller, a physical education teacher, and a music teacher, specialists who could thoughtfully work with large groups of children. (New York City public school teachers are contractually entitled to one free period a day for preparation. Hence, all the specialists are needed to provide instruction when regular classroom teachers are freed up from teaching assignments.) Today we have a music, physical education, and art teacher as well as two teachers sharing science and technology responsibilities.

We are also very good at gathering extra hands in our classrooms. Each fall we look to the arrival of new student teachers, new high school interns, and new community volunteers. Each year we become more thoughtful about how to best tap our people resources. We know which grandparents can sew, which parents can type, which family members can build shelves, teach instrumental music, write lyrics, or prepare gourmet meals.

We also need to challenge the givens of how money is spent in public schools. I've been told that during one school year, ours was the only New York City elementary school without a full-time secretary. The reasons were clear. With that year's budget cut, I had to give back twenty-six thousand dollars from my allotment. One way I did that was to cut back on secretarial help. We missed our secretary Judi on Fridays, but parent volunteers were there to keep the office going. I was determined not to cut direct services to children. Thankfully I'm in a district that trusts school communities to make decisions like these. During times of fiscal crisis, we need to be especially careful of how we spend the little money that we do have. The only way I know of to make those decisions wisely is to put the choice into the hands of teachers.

Get Political

When I say that we are raising activists in our school, I am referring to the adults as well as the children. When I suggest that we need to take responsibility for our world, see the strengths and weaknesses in our world, and work to improve the quality of our world, I am referring to the adults as well as the children. Not only do we need to let the powers that be know the good work that *we* are doing, we also need to tell others when we think that *they* are doing good work. Those folks include the members of the school board, those who work on the local newspaper, and the politicians at city hall and in the state capitol. The reverse is also essential. If new schools and schools undergoing change are to survive and prosper, we need to protest policies we disagree with and fight for the supports we need to make a difference in the lives of children.

We need to attend rallies, public hearings, and town hall meetings. We need to invite central board administrators, journalists, union delegates, and city council members to our front door. We need to write letters to the editor and make public speeches. Every day, we need to take a stand for children. Seven-year-old Alexandra Viola should not be the only one corresponding with city officials. In her letter to the mayor of New York (see Figure 1.2), Alexandra asked for all the right things. We live in a five-story building and have been requesting window guards for many years. We must keep fighting for the things that will make a difference in the lives of children.

Several years ago, our schools were in danger of being redistricted. None of us wanted to belong to another community. We were determined not to let the politicians' plan become a reality. Hundreds of people attended the public hearings, waving strong signs of protest. Some of us asked to speak. Below is the text of the short speech I delivered. Thankfully, our district lines have never been changed. The public wouldn't allow it.

> There is a Japanese belief that in heaven, there is a network of pearls so arranged that if you look at any one pearl, you see all the others reflected in it.
>
> As a member of the District 2 community, I'd like to suggest that we too form a network of pearls, and that if you look at any one school, you will see all the others reflected in it.
>
> We share deep-rooted beliefs about teaching and learning. We share deep-rooted beliefs about parents and community. We share deep-rooted beliefs about school priorities, professional development, and social responsibility.
>
> Within our network of pearls, we know our resources. We know who to turn to. We know our ways of working together. We know our ways of entering professional conversations.

Jan. 27

Dear Mayor Giuliani,
My name is Alexandra Rose Vida.
Can you please give Manhattan
New School some more
computers and some window
guards. And can you please
 bring back some more teachers
 and give some more
 afterschool programs like:
 Music, Dance and Games and
 other Opportunities.
 Thanks Alexandra Viola
 age 7 2nd grade Class 201 P.S. 290

Figure 1.2

This speech was delivered several weeks before the publication of the May 1994 issue of the professional magazine *Teaching Pre K–8*. I continued my presentation by referring to the upcoming article.

In the May issue, I am proud to say, our school will be the cover story. The reporters who visited entitled the article, "In New York City—There Are Schools that Work." They wrote, "In the city of New York, on the island of Manhattan, there exists a school filled with teachers who, while perhaps too modest to admit they're on a mission to change the world, are indeed doing exactly that. . . . It was created by a bit of luck, no doubt, but also by the visionary support of the Superintendent in New York's Community District Number 2, and by the complementary vision of teachers who had been nurturing their own dream, which was to launch a new public school in the heart of New York City." They go on to say that "the school is a vivid example of the dedication, skills and commitment to be found on the teaching staffs of urban schools . . . throughout this country." "For the most part," they conclude, "city schools get a bum rap."

We do have a wonderful school, but that school does not stand alone.

We have a wonderful District 2 school.

We have a school that, as it grows, will continue to need the support of our district superintendent, school board, and colleagues. Our school would not be the same if it were uprooted. I learned a long time ago that if the work we do is fed by the world, it will return to feed the world. Our work is fed by the world of District 2. We rely on district resources, priorities, experts, initiatives, and ways of working together.

Family holidays are soon approaching. My sister called and asked me to bring a favorite family dish. "Why don't you come early and prepare it at my house?" she asked.

"No thanks," I said, "I need to cook at home." Have you ever tried to cook in someone else's kitchen? It just doesn't feel right. The ingredients are never the brands you love. The utensils feel different in your hands. The kitchen layout doesn't feel quite as comfortable as the one you are used to. "No thanks, I'll work at home, where I can do my best work." And so I say likewise to all of you. Let us stay home with our families, where we can continue to do our best work.

Educators need to stand up for what they believe in, through public speaking as well as through the printed word. Last December, I became furious when reading a seemingly harmless article about matchmaking in the *New York Times*. The article caught my eye because it referred to a store owned by a parent of a child who attends our school. The store is called The Little Shop of Plaster, and it is a place where people can make and decorate their own plaster figures. The story was about a matchmaking party that took place at this establishment. I became outraged when the reporter described the matchmaker's method of choosing guests to invite to these singles get-togethers. I sent the following letter to the editor.

> *Dear Editor,*
>
> *I read with much displeasure David Gonzalez', "Elevating Matchmaking to a Fine Art." It's not that I have anything against single folks meeting one another or the meeting place described, The Little Shop of Plaster. In fact the owner of the shop is a parent of a student at the Manhattan New School, where I am principal. What saddened me was the matchmaker's comment. She only invites to her parties "investment bankers, stock brokers, female attorneys, and professional people. Not any teachers. People that are more quality."*
>
> *It's clear that the matchmaker is uninformed. Just what qualities is she looking for? Teachers' lives are marked by generosity, compassion, humanity, and involvement. Teachers are one of the most well-educated professional groups in this country. They are well read and well informed. They know drama, art, music, and literature. Clearly the matchmaker chooses her guests based on their pay stubs. The last thing hard-working educators need is to be judged by their unfortunately paltry salaries. (She also admits to choosing guests based on their looks, which is as well a small-minded act). The irony is, several years from now, if any of that matchmaking succeeds, those very same couples will be knocking on our door, asking to put their children's names on our waiting list, because they've heard about all the* high-quality *teachers in our school.*

The New York Times did not publish my letter, but I did include it in a school newsletter. The matchmaker involved happened to see it and wrote me an angry letter saying that she had never said those awful things and that she had asked the newspaper to print a correction. I'm sorry that this person was misquoted. (In fact, because of her response, I have deleted her name and softened my tone for reprinting here.) But I will never apologize for writing that letter. As I explained to the woman, the issue for me was not the embarrassment of one matchmaker, it was the public humiliation of the thousands of teachers who read *The New York Times*.

Our school began as a small alternative or option school in New York's Community School District 2. The Manhattan New School was a bit of an oxymoron back then, as we were described as a "zoned-option" school, meaning we could accept students from all over the city but we could not turn down anyone in our carved-out zone. We grew quite rapidly and left the world of option schools several years ago. We became the neighborhood school. In New York, though, parents have choice. You need not attend your neighborhood school. Many parents "shop around," looking for the best school for their children. Some neighborhood parents opt out of our school, having a different image in mind of the right educational place for their child. This is as it should be. As long as there is a space available, a child can attend any school to which he is accepted. Several years ago our district superintendent, Anthony Alvarado, wrote an op-ed piece for *The New York Times*, in which he suggested, "Promoting choice as the primary method of educational change is like rearranging the deck chairs on the Titanic." The issue is not just for parents to have choice, the issue is to have quality choices. Tony went on to stress the need for schools to always be searching for the best educational methods and strategies, so that we can meet the needs of all children. I agree, and I would add that fine educational strategies only become effective if you choose your colleagues carefully, give serious attention to continued adult learning and professional development, become willing to challenge the givens of public school life, and become political. I know my former superintendent would agree.

RELATED READINGS IN COMPANION VOLUMES

Lifetime Guarantees (Heinemann, forthcoming), will be abbreviated as LG.
Writing Through Childhood (Heinemann, forthcoming), will be abbreviated as WC.

Puzzling over literacy questions	**LG**: Ch. 2, Ch. 7.
Having questions about the standards movement	**LG**: Ch. 8.
Launching a writing workshop	**WC**: Ch. 3, Ch. 6.
Organizing a class library	**LG**: Ch. 1, Ch. 6.
Assessing professional growth	**WC**: Ch. 11, Ch. 7.
Reading for your own pleasure	**LG**: Ch. 7.
Professional courtesy	**WC**: Ch. 11. **LG**: Ch. 7.
Taking adult learning seriously	**WC**: Ch. 11. **LG**: Ch. 7.
Raising activists	**LG**: Ch. 4. **WC**: Ch. 9.
Having big blocks of time	**WC**: Ch. 2. **LG**: Ch. 2.
Making schools beautiful	**LG**: Ch. 1.

CHAPTER 2

RETHINKING THE ROLE OF PRINCIPAL

Priorities

- School principals must be comfortable wearing many hats, including that of troubadour, knower of names, switchboard operator, substitute teacher, devoted grandma, interior decorator, housekeeper, and literacy lover.
- Principals must maintain control in the face of inevitable obstacles, including the plague of standardized testing and the scheduling of pullout programs.
- Principals must stay true to the passions of his/her teaching life.

Practice

- On the importance of sharing one another's stories
- On the importance of knowing and celebrating students' names
- On getting to know students well and being able to hook up like-minded groups and individuals
- On ensuring worthwhile substitute teaching
- On successful and rewarding tutoring of struggling students
- On decorating the school, including suggestions for eliminating eyesores and aligning design with purpose
- On keeping the school tidy using schoolwide house-keeping structures
- On informing children about your own literacy

November 1995. I was walking through our school in the late afternoon, knowing I would be absent for several days to attend the NCTE convention in San Diego. I said goodbye to Isabel Beaton's kindergarten children, explaining that I wouldn't be in for awhile. Canaan, a sparkling redhead with a serious look on her face, looked up at me and made several attempts to ask a question. "Who's gonna be the new . . . ? Who's gonna be the new . . . ? Who's gonna be the new . . . ?" I realized that Canaan couldn't finish her question because she didn't know what to call me. She didn't know my job title. Finally she asked, "Is there school tomorrow?" hoping that a school holiday would eliminate her dilemma. "Of course there is," I answered. Canaan stared at me a moment and then finally found a way to ask her question. "Who's gonna be the new *of you*?" she asked.

Sometimes I am just as much at a loss as Canaan. It's not that I don't know my job title; I get enough mail addressed to the school principal. It's that my job is so very hard to explain. There are days when I have to pinch myself and ask, "Am I really doing this?" Sometimes it all seems so surreal. One opening day, I had to secure the building because there was a sniper a block away and police and FBI agents had cordoned off our street. After taking all the commonsense emergency precautions, I couldn't help but think, "But I know children's literature. I'm sort of a *maven* in writing process. What am I doing here?"

The Changing Face of School Administrators

I recently dug up my old autograph album from elementary school. There was a fading photograph of Mr. Gartenlaub, the principal. I remembered him as a tall, smiling man, although I don't recall ever having spoken to him. In the photo, he's seated at his desk with pen in hand, as if ready to signoff on some memo. His office looks squeaky clean. His desktop is clear except for what looks like a crystal inkwell and one of those rolling calendars in a brass tube. He's wearing a suit and tie and has a white handkerchief positioned tastefully in his breast pocket. The only item in the background is a small American flag standing on a side cabinet. The photograph speaks volumes to me about the life of a principal in 1959, the year I graduated.

But I won't let that photo fool me. Mr. Gartenlaub was a kind man. I wouldn't be surprised to learn that he too had to escort a child into foster care, appear in court in a custody battle, or help a dying parent prepare a bedside will. And no doubt, some of the administrative chores I'm asked to do are exactly the same ones he did in the 1950s. Of course, the computer has changed the way we take attendance, order purchases, and receive standardized test scores. And the fax machine has changed the way we correspond with our school board members, our superintendent, and district office staff. But my old principal would understand if I spoke of leading fire drills, reporting teacher observations, and attending PTA meetings. Some things never change.

There are many things, however, that would make Mr. Gartenlaub's tightly cropped and neatly parted gray hair stand on end. What would he think if he heard that the children call me Shelley? I doubt if the students at P.S. 179 even knew his name was Louis. I even doubt if the teachers would have thought to call him by his first name. And what would he make of monthly suicide attempt forms, AIDS-awareness curriculum guides, and weapon-confiscation surveys? What would he think on learning that most New York schools haven't had a nurse on staff for many years? Would he be good at removing wooden beads stuck on five-year-old fingers, protecting the tongue of an epileptic child, administering inhalers to asthmatic children? And what would he have said to eight-year-old Bailey, who tried to look cool by wearing magnetic nose rings, but failed to read the instructions carefully and sucked up both magnets into her nasal passages?

Filling in for a nurse is not the only role that would surprise my old principal. Lots of the activities that fill my days would probably startle him. And he wouldn't be able to appreciate why I do what I do unless he was able to deeply understand our beliefs about how children learn best. No doubt, he'd be surprised about the kind of teaching and learning that fills our classrooms and spills out into our corridors. He'd wonder why there are no textbooks, no workbooks, no basal readers. He'd wonder why there are no chalkboards, no teachers' desks positioned prominently in the front of every classroom, and no bolted-down student desks in neat rows—even no desks at all. No doubt he'd have real concerns about all those round oak tables brimming with chatting children. I'd probably have to offer Mr. Gartenlaub a primer on whole language, the writing process approach, reader-response theory, alternative assessment, and inquiry-based studies.

The Wearer of Many Hats

Although this is the chapter that focuses on the role of principal, I think that my presence in that role will be felt in all the chapters to come. After all, I'm not a neutral observer. I do take part in curriculum discussions, parent education, professional development, and so on. My intention in this chapter, however, is to share the roles that I delight in that are perhaps more unexpected.

But first a disclaimer is in order. This chapter is the hardest one for me to write, for fear I make myself too central to the life of the school. In a recent article by David Sherman, vice president of the United Federation of Teachers, in the publication *New York Teacher* (May 25, 1998), the union leader described the work I do as a combination of "coach, staff developer, advocate, author, illustrator, cheerleader, intellect, teacher, bulletin board fixer-upper, muse, confidante and friend." I certainly appreciated that the leadership of the teachers' union had such complimentary things to say about an elementary school principal, but I in turn must return the favor. I sense that I have influenced our school and left my mark, but I'm also quite sure that I couldn't do what I do if I weren't surrounded by such hardworking and brilliant colleagues, who inspire me to burst the traditional image of building supervisor. I'm aware as well that my colleagues would be as thoughtful and successful no matter where they chose to teach. They arrived on our doorstep with much energy and enthusiasm and many areas of expertise. I'd like to think, however, that our setting has invited them all to shine just a bit more brightly.

If I kept a principal's portfolio, the following roles would be those I'd share with the most pride.

Troubadour

I share stories. I've become a great gatherer of people's stories, which I tell and retell up and down the halls and throughout the five floors of our school building. Peter Johnston, a literacy professor from Albany, New York, sent me a greeting card that read, "You never engage in idle gossip, only meaningful gossip!" I'm really not gossiping, I'm a troubadour, spreading the wealth. Kitty Kaczmarek from Glendale, Arizona, sent me a silver pin as a gift. She explained that it was a parrot from the Hopi tradition and represented the "teller of tales." I wear it proudly.

The Importance of Story   I started working on this book during the summer of 1996, the summer of the TWA Flight 800 crash, the Atlanta Olympics, political conventions, and the Yankees World Series victory. With each news report, I became keenly aware of people's hunger for story. The following thoughts were included in my back-to-school letter to my colleagues:

> This was a summer to be especially conscious of the power of people's stories. I'm sure many of you wondered, as I did, how we would have responded to the TWA tragedy in the presence of our students. All of us shared in that incredible loss of human life and we were all interested in the life stories of those unfortunate passengers. So too, many of us got caught up in those televised vignettes detailing the life stories of all those Olympic athletes. Even the speeches at the political conventions were filled with people's life stories. And you may have been rooting for the Yankees to win ball games, but it was manager Joe Torre's family story that really captured our hearts. We worried about his ailing brother Frank and cared about his sister's prayers. . . . So now we are back at work, with the challenge of taking care of five hundred young people, each with their own stories to tell. . . .

Stories remind us to appreciate one another and to take care of one another. They help us cope, understand, make sense of the world, and make it a better place.

When our custodian John challenged me about my coffee mug, I told everyone about it. When people in a community know one another's stories, relationships change. Those who heard the story of the mug responded to John in a new, more respectful way. During the first year of the school, I began a writing workshop for parents. When parents and I swapped stories, relationships changed. (See more on parent writing workshops in Chapter 5, "Reaching Out to Families.") My daughter J.J., in law school, called home to tell me about a course she was taking in subordination. The professors asked the students to introduce themselves by telling the story of their maternal grandmothers. When the students heard one another's stories, relationships changed. People were no longer judged in stereotypical fashion, by their names, outward appearances, or regional accents.

Paula Rogovin is an experienced and innovative first-grade teacher. Interviewing family and community members is at the heart of her reading, writing, and social studies curriculum. (This innovative curriculum is the subject of Paula's book *Classroom Interviews: A World of Learning* and her video, *The Classroom Interview in Action*). Paula and her six-year-olds spend most of the school year researching their cultural backgrounds. When they began a study on students of African-American ancestry, Paula invited Ida Mae Chaplin, our security guard, to sit in the rocking chair reserved for special guests and answer the children's questions. I'll never forget Paula's excitement at sharing what they had discovered.

Ida was a key figure in the civil rights movement. There is a classic photo of her in many journals, newspapers, and even hanging on the wall at the Smithsonian in Washington, D.C. Ida was one of the courageous college students who participated in a sit-in at the Woolworth's counter in Greensboro, North Carolina, in 1960. If you remember this classic photograph, you can't miss our Ida. She's the one with pie being thrown on her by angry white students. Ida told Paula and her students her story and then they told the entire school community. All of us continue to tell Ida's story to everyone who enters. (Read the details of the first graders' discovery in Paula's book, cited above).

Today, no one passes Ida's desk without saying good morning. She's a real hero around here. Knowing one another's stories does change relationships. We become the stories we tell. Knowing one another's stories also enables us to tap our resources. I can't imagine any class studying the civil rights movement without asking Ida to be a guest speaker.

Paul Filippini was the most determined child I had ever seen in kindergarten. He seemed obsessed with learning to read. When I met his mother, Elizabeth Hernandez, I thought I understood his interest in becoming literate. Elizabeth, a single parent, is blind. I assumed Paul's determination came from his savvy understanding that he could be a big help to his mom if he could read all those everyday things that aren't available in Braille. I began observing Paul's growing literacy in school and at the same time began interviewing Paul and his mother. Their tale of love and literacy seemed so special, I even began crafting a picture book about the two of them. It begins, "My mom always wanted a boy. I was born on Mother's Day. I was her best present ever." I went on to explain how hard Paul worked at learning to read in school and about all the unique ways he was using his newfound literacy. He was our only six-year-old who knew how to read the expiration dates on dairy products in the supermarket.

I was surprised one afternoon when Paul, now a third grader, told me his mom would be in for a three o'clock interview. I hadn't arranged the meeting. In fact, I thought my research was complete. But I didn't have the heart to tell this to Paul, who loved being the center of attention. I didn't cancel the interview and it was lucky for me, because that day, Elizabeth told me more than I ever imagined. Having no prepared topic in mind, I simply said, "Elizabeth, tell me how you think Paul learned to read so well." And for the next half hour I sat back spellbound as this tiny Latino woman, holding onto her cane, proceeded to tell me all that *she* had done to make Paul the reader he is today.

Her story began in nursery school. Elizabeth used her Braille typewriter to place alphabet letters on the back of picture cards. She did the same with Sesame Street word cards. She then made up different letter- and word-recognition games to play with Paul. She also took him to the library for the blind every week. Elizabeth explained that she read aloud too slowly in Braille to keep Paul's interest, so she began borrowing books on tape for him. The books were all twin-text ones, with both Braille and standard print. Paul listened to these over and over again at home, and each week they took out new ones. In his kindergarten and first-grade class, Elizabeth admits, he learned a lot about reading; but she kept on providing him with lots of books on tape at home. "Finally," she continued, "Paul was reading well enough to begin reading aloud to me at bedtime." She then began to worry that he might be making mistakes. "Like if he said "boat" for "ship," I wouldn't know. It was only when it didn't make sense that I would ask him to spell the words out loud so I could help him." Paul's teacher let her know that what she was doing was just right. Elizabeth came to understand why the reading of "boat" for "ship" was an "okay mistake." Elizabeth continued her story by explaining how she now buys books for Paul. "He went through all those series books, *Frog and Toad, Amelia Bedelia, Nate the Great, The Magic Schoolbus,* and then he got into those *Goosebumps* books. I even took him to Central Park on Halloween when they were giving away small *Goosebumps* books for free." Elizabeth gets help when choosing books to buy Paul. The clerks in the local bookstore are more than willing to read aloud the first few pages from possible choices to help her decide.

Paul and Elizabeth continue to play word games. They own a twin-text Scrabble set, but Paul prefers to play their homemade games. They sometimes play oral spelling games. They take turns spelling entire sentences out loud and they each call out the other's creation. Sometimes Paul opens to any page in what he calls a difficult book, then his mom points to a word, and Paul spells it out loud and then tries to pronounce it. Elizabeth lets him know how he is doing.

Naturally, Paul does a lot of everyday kinds of reading for his mother. He reads the mail aloud, giving her the gist by reading only the first and last paragraphs of letters. He reads greeting cards aloud in the stationery store to help his mother choose. He reads lots of street signs, supermarket fliers, and television listings. And of course, he continues to read the expiration dates on bread, milk, and meats in the supermarket. Elizabeth had quite a story to tell and she graciously allowed me to share it at our next PTA meeting. The topic was at-home reading, and Elizabeth's ways of working at home with her child became wonderful suggestions for our sighted parents. We talked at that meeting about the importance of playing with language, reading aloud and books on tape, acceptable mistakes, choice of reading materials, the value of books in a series, and the reading of environmental print. When you know people's stories, they become a well to draw from.

Knower of Names

We have a yearly tradition at school, inviting grandparents to visit every Monday following the Thanksgiving break. Lots of relatives often come to town for the family get-togethers, so we run a bit of an open house. Aunts, uncles, and cousins often attend as well. Last year, I passed a third grader and her grandparents sitting on a couch in the fifth-floor corridor. "Hi, Audrey!" I called out as I walked by. Her grandparents stopped me, stunned that I knew their granddaughter's name without hesitation. Audrey commented, "Yeah, in my old school my principal used to call me, "Hey, you in the blue shirt." I can't imagine having this job, if I didn't know all our students' names.

I delight in knowing names. In the late spring months of every school year I meet individually with every new student who will be attending our school come the fall, along with members of their family. I have two main purposes for holding these meetings. First, I want to make sure the parents fully understand our ways of teaching before they register their students in our school. If parents really understand our approaches, from even before day one, they are much less likely to ask me where the phonics workbooks, basal readers, and ditto masters are. Secondly, these short family meetings give me a head start in learning the names of our new students. I don't remember all their names on that first day of school in September, but I remember enough to lighten my load. And besides, it delights kindergarten parents to know they're leaving their children with at least one person who already knows their names. I continue in September going out of my way to spend more time with the newcomers, so that I can greet every student by name. I'm not sure that I have an unusually good memory for names, or I simply work harder at it. I do know I stare intently trying to attach a name to every face. With identical twins, I work overtime.

A few helpful ways of remembering children's names includes greeting children by name all the time. I never say "Hi," when I pass children in the halls, I say "Hi, Samantha," thereby reinforcing the name in my mind. I also periodically read the list of names for students registered in each class, thereby keeping all the names fresh in my mind. If I can't place a face with a name, you can be sure I seek that child out immediately. I also pay attention whenever teachers call on children. I am always holding names and faces together in my mind's eye.

Whenever I enter classrooms and draw a blank on a student's name, I madly search for clues. (I hesitate to ask a child outright because students come to expect me to know their names. I worry that a child will feel insulted if I can't remember just one name.) I begin by trying to see the names printed on his/her folder or mounted near their cubby, closet hook, or work tray. If that doesn't work I look over the attendance sheet, knowing that if I spot the name I'll be able to connect it to the face. Sometimes I eavesdrop, hoping someone will address the child by name. Occasionally, when I pass a student in the hall and realize that I've forgotten his or her name and there are no context clues around, I simply say, "I was wondering how you spell your name," as if I remember the name, but am checking the spelling. You can't resort to this ploy too often. Similarly, I've asked children, "Do you know if there are other children in the school with your same name?" With any luck, the child responds, "Yes, there's another David in second grade."

I'm not the only one who should be trying to learn students' names. Each year we update a labeled and framed collection of staff photographs in the main lobby, to ensure that every student knows the name of every teacher. Likewise, we need to guarantee that no adult will ever need to say, "Hey, you in the blue shirt!" A few years ago I drove my family and friends half crazy trying to recall the exact words to the *Cheers* theme song, because the sentiment contained was so important. Don't we all want to be in places where everyone knows our name and everyone delights in our presence? This is true for a bar in Boston; it's also true for a school in the big city. Schools are more effective when all the grown-ups, including teachers, school aides, secretaries, security guards, and paraprofessionals know the names of all the students.

One year I was interviewing a potential art teacher by inviting her to teach a lesson. She quickly set up her materials in a second-grade classroom and began to teach. Jessica, an outspoken seven-year-old interrupted her. "Don't you want to know our names?" she began. I wasn't too concerned that a visiting teacher didn't attempt to learn students' names, but I would worry if teachers only cared to learn the names of the children in their own class. I always find it frustrating to hear a teacher voice concerns or compliments about a student at a staff meeting and realize that many of the people in the room can't visualize the child being discussed. Students are too interesting for us not to make an effort to learn their names.

We must invent ways for all members of the community to get to know a few more names. We have over 550 children in our school, rather small by New York standards, but big enough for people *not* to know one another's names if we don't make that knowledge a top priority. We need to see students' names everywhere.

One year I began a weekly ritual. We collected discarded plastic badges from convention goers and bought additional ones, so that every one in the school had a durable name tag. We pinned them on once a week and did nothing special except to wear them as we went about our usual business. I suppose lots of students whose paths didn't cross too often got to know the names of some new schoolmates. I know that this idea enabled lots of teachers to finally place a child's face with a name they had often heard a colleague use.

We do hang framed class photographs in our main lobby, but there are no captions supplying names. Occasionally I see a teacher pointing out a child to a colleague, but these photographs really don't help us learn each other's names in an ongoing way.

Last year our new school photographer gave me a strip of five small photographs of each student, as a bonus for placing our order with his company. Each photograph peels off a self-sticking back. No doubt we will be devising ways for these pictures to help more people know the names of more students in our school. We can now cluster names and faces on posters labeled, "Meet the Yankee Fans," "Meet the Piano Players," "Meet the Gymnasts," et cetera. We can now cluster name twins and triplets on posters labeled "Meet all our Stephanie's" or "Meet all our Michael's." These handy stick-on photographs will probably encourage us to ask students to regularly bring in more photographs of themselves, so we can always have a steady supply. Each time a student hangs their work in the hallway, why not have a photo next to their name? What an easy way for people to get to know a few more names. So too, we can be sure to attach photos to cumulative record folders and portfolios. We can also hang name and photo directories outside *every* classroom door.

Celebrating Names   Over the years, we have begun collecting and displaying book jackets of works whose title contains the name of one of our students. Of course, Patricia MacLachlan's *Sarah, Plain and Tall* and *Arthur for the Very First Time* are up there, along with E. B. White's *Charlotte's Web,* Kathryn Lasky's *A Baby for Max,* and Marissa Moss's *Amelia's Notebook.* In eight years, we've collected well over one hundred titles, as well as many poems with our students' names in them. Perhaps surprisingly, we were even able to find a picture book with our student Pavel's name in the title and a poem with our student Nefertiti's name in it. Some of our students' names are *so* unusual that we need to encourage our young authors to write original books and poems with their friends' names in the titles. Then we need to tack up student photos on those book jackets and alongside those poems.

Children are always eager to read books or poems in which the main character shares their name. When I posted the following poem by Richard Edwards, two first graders named Mary and Sarah went through it line by line to see if they had the same likes and dislikes as the characters described.

Mary and Sarah

Mary likes smooth things,
Things that glide:
Sleek skis swishing down a mountainside.

Sarah likes rough things,
Things that snatch:
Boats with barnacled bottoms, thatch.

Mary says—polish,
Sarah says—rust,
Mary says—mayonnaise,
Sarah says—crust.

Sarah says—hedgehogs,
Mary says—seals,
Sarah says—sticklebacks,
Mary says—eels.

Give me, says Mary,
The slide of a stream,
The touch of a petal,
A bowl of ice cream.

Give me, says Sarah,
The gales of a coast,
The husk of a chestnut,
A plate of burnt toast.

Mary and Sarah—
They'll never agree
Till peaches and coconuts
Grow on one tree.

Students' names are also displayed on our perpetual birthday calendar that lines the second-floor hallway. We write "alumnus" next to the children who graduate, but we never remove their names. We'd be wise to devise a way to mount photos on those birthday displays so that people could greet one another appropriately on their special days. We could also mount photographs near students' names on our language board, described in the introduction.

Schools need to find ways to celebrate students' names. One year our kindergarten students sorted all the students' first names by their first letter. Later they shared their findings and told us which first letters were the most popular and which the least. They also counted how many name twins we had and triplets as well. They counted so many Sarahs, Samuels, Rachels, Davids, and Jacobs that they proved to us that biblical names are alive and well in the Big Apple. Later older students alphabetized and displayed all the names gathered for each letter.

Pam Mayer pays special tribute each year to her kindergarten students' names, and at the same time provides a tool for these young writers who are still spelling as best they can using invented spelling. Each student selects words that begin with the same initial consonant sound as their names. Pam encourages them to select concrete nouns, ones they can easily illustrate. Underneath his name, for example, Matthew drew a monkey, some money, and math manipulatives. (Only 1990s five-year-olds are familiar with the word *manipulatives*. Sounds like a college-board word to me.) Griselle used grapes, guitar, and gum. Nonconforming Nat had narwhal, Nanotyrannus, and numbat! Pam then covers an entire wall with these large name charts. Classmates' names become important early sight words for young readers and writers and these charts extend their use. Students use these charts as reference to remind them which letter to use when they are searching for a letter to match a desired sound. They come to appreciate that other words begin with the same beginning sound as their friend Matthew's name.

As you walk up the staircases, you can also see our students' names prominently displayed. I invite every student to select and decorate a wall tile, including of course his or her name. These tiles let the students know that they count in this school. They have made their permanent mark. The children, in fact, use permanent markers and we intend to keep their marks forever. (There are so many square white tiles lining our stairwells, we can never imagine running out of space.)

We also need to delight in learning the accurate pronunciation of difficult-sounding names. I worked for days learning to say Tugba Hacialioglu the way a Turkish speaker would say it. I feel bad each time I realize that I've mispronounced Chanetta or Ernad's name. I feel even worse when I hear that a student has Americanized his name because the native name is so often mispronounced. I wanted to pronounce Kwaw's name as "Jaw," the way a Burmese speaker would pronounce it. Instead, Kwaw chose to call himself Joe. Barbara Robinson has written a poem entitled "Foreign Student." In it a young Chinese girl changes her beautiful name Si Lan to Lani. This saddens me every time I read the surprising line. So too, in *The House on Mango Street,* Sandra Cisneros, writing about a girl named Esperanza, sadly comments, "At school they say my name funny as if the syllables were made out of tin and hurt the roof of your mouth." In Jean Craighead George's picture book *Arctic Son,* on the other hand, a child is joyfully given an Inupiat Eskimo name to accompany his English name. At school, when there is more than one child in a class with the same first name, I discourage students from distinguishing between their friends by using initials—a child isn't Alan T., he's Alan Townley. Not Alan R., but Alan Ramirez. Names need to be celebrated, not shortened.

Then too, children must never be allowed to tease one another because of an unusual name. Riri, a young Japanese student, once complained to her teacher Renay that her classmate Zieyik was teasing her about her name. I would like to have been there to hear Renay help the children resolve that ironic conflict! So many of our children have names that are uncommon that it is relatively rare for anyone to be teased because their name sounds different. Historically, children are known to tease other classmates by making up painful rhymes or nicknames. Of course these needn't be unusual names. Being called "Plain Jane" is just as hurtful as being teased because you have an unusual-sounding name. No matter the circumstance, we have zero tolerance for name teasing (or any kind of teasing). Our names are too precious to each and every one.

We also celebrate names by asking students to tell us the story of how they were named. (Reading aloud from Eve Sanders's picture book *What's Your Name?: From Ariel to Zoe* is a great way to get that conversation going). We also invite parents to include that information in their letter of introduction when they first register a child in our school. (See additional information on page 159). Ella's mother begins:

First of all, thank you for giving us the opportunity to write to you about our daughter, Ella Bina Pultinas. It's hard to put a beginning to all this, but here it goes. Ella was born in Queens on February 11, 1990. This was the day that Nelson Mandela was released from prison and Ella has innately acquired much of the leader's determination and joy of freedom. Ella takes her first name from her father's late aunt who was a deeply generous and beautiful woman and role model. Bina is the name of her late grandmother on her mother's side, who lived in Calcutta, India and who loved to sing beautiful and holy songs. Pultinas is a Lithuanian name which means "not to fall," or in other words, to succeed. We are confident that Ella will live up to her name and make both sides of her family proud.

How could I ever forget Ella's name; how could anyone who hears this story?

Several years ago, the first student named Shelly registered in our school. She spelled her name without the final *e* that appears in mine, but I did feel a special bond with my name twin. In fact, realizing that other name twins might share a special bond, I created another very special wall display. We hung photographs of all the name twins alongside their family's explanation of their choice of names. (In addition to the biblical name twins listed above, our community also boasted several Mergims and Arjetas, names which speak to our Eastern European community.) Parents wrote most of the stories, but several children chose to write their own understanding of how their names were chosen. The board literally stopped traffic in our main lobby. Young and old alike were curious to hear the name choice explanations, and teachers began distinguishing all the Alex's, Nicholas's, Chelseas, Ashleys, and Stevens from one another. A few examples follow:

On a recent trip to Hawaii, Mark found his baby book in a closet. In it, a list of possible names for him, scribbled during my pregnancy. Alexander—Nicholas—Sidney–Max–Seymour—he was horrified to secretly discover that he almost became somebody BESIDES Mark!

I considered everything—how his name would sound with "Sage," how it would look on his business cards . . . even how his initials would look on a shirt monogram someday. Would he be called "Dr. Mark?" or "Professor Mark?"

Trendy friends were sure I'd spell it Marc. Or Marque. But "Mark Matthew Sage" was the winner, hands down. Mark means Warrior, strong and brave fighter. Matthew is Hebrew for Gift of God. His first nickname was M&M's (for Mark Matthew). Most special is that while his brother's name is unique because it's been carried through six generations, Mark is an original—one of a kind—Mark Matthew Sage the first! Who knows? Maybe his son will be Mark Matthew Sage, Jr., and he can tell this story all over again.

Years before she was born I was asked what I would name my daughter. I don't know why or how it came to me, but I said, "Isabelle."

Since she was born I have come across some Isabelles that I would be proud to name my daughter after; a mischievous, strong-minded Isabelle whose father was a great king called Babar, an independent woman adventurer named Isabelle who traveled through Algeria in 1900 disguising herself as a boy in order to study Islam, and an Isabelle who would raise "excellent hell" in a song by Bjork.

But I know that when I was asked what I would name my daughter, that Isabelle already existed and it was her that day letting me know she was there and waiting for me, waiting for her, waiting for each other.

Mommy, why is my name Maya?

When mommies are pregnant, many people believe that they can tell whether the child to be born will be a girl or a boy by looking at the mother's face and/or her belly. Many of these "wise" people predicted that I would have a boy. I just wanted a healthy baby, boy or girl didn't matter. So, confident that I was having a boy, I chose the name Michael. I never chose a girl's name.

But a funny thing happened.

About a week before my baby was due to be born, I dreamt that I was at a family picnic. The picnic blanket was pink! The umbrella was pink. The decorations were pink. The beach ball was pink. There were even pink milkshakes! I awoke startled and immediately began to search my heart for girls' names, just in case.

Without much searching, I thought of Maya because I always loved not only the writings and other artistic works of Maya Angelou, but also I admired her spirit! Your spirit or soul was my major concern. I believed giving you that name, exposing you to as many aspects of life as possible and telling you about this wonderful woman as you grew older, would somehow bless you with a life of courage and perseverance. I believe you are on your way. So that, my love, is why your name is Maya.

The wall above was so popular that children who did not have a name twin asked for equal time. I didn't have adequate wall space to display all the explanations that were sent in, but I did collect them and enter them into a three-ring binder that sits in our main lobby. Each year we will be adding new pages to our own "A to Z Name Book." Visitors can now discover how Annaliese, Bari, and Christopher got their names as well as how Xanyani, Yuri, and Zakiya got theirs. (We also added several poems to the inside covers of that binder including James Berry's "Isn't My Name Magical?".)

Switchboard Operator

Of course, learning students' names is just the beginning. You also have to get to know the students well. And there are lots of ways to do that. You hang out with them, pull up alongside them in their classrooms, invite them to lunch, watch them in the playground, read their writing, stop and chat when you pass them in the hall. I also learn a great deal whenever I create a schoolwide ritual that regularly pulls small groups of students together. Our student council meets every other Friday afternoon. I host a baseball club when the season opens in April. (Only Yankee fans need apply!) I also encourage students to teach courses in my office if they have an area of expertise. Zippering, shoe-tying, and origami lessons have been offered on my gray leather couch. I've also learned a great deal about individual students by inviting them to keep a dialogue journal with me. I get to know others by hanging out a help-wanted sign that reads, "Needed: Principal for a Day." When students shadow me for the day they learn as much about me as I do about them. Our teachers ask parents to sign a generic, walking permission slip during the first week of school. Occasionally I ask a student to accompany me as I run an errand at lunchtime. I've learned a great deal about students as they walk me to the photo store to drop off slides for a PTA presentation or to the bakery to pick up snacks for a late-afternoon meeting. Of course, I also get the scoop on our students when I listen carefully to what teachers and family members have to say.

Once I know the students well, my switchboard operator's role can begin. New York City is host to lots of television and movie production. Over the years, I've gotten calls from producers looking for a child who could play Meg Ryan's daughter, or one who looks like Michael J. Fox when he was seven, or one who has an exotic look and could play the role of Mowgli in a new movie version of *The Jungle Book*. These requests are fairly easy for me to honor. After all, it doesn't take much to know physical appearances. It's much more of a challenge to be asked for students with certain inner qualities.

The crew from the television show *Reading Rainbow* frequently calls me in need of children for a particular episode. They usually have a certain type of child in mind. One time they needed children who could improvise, on other occasions they were looking for musical children and humorous ones. Most recently they needed children who could tell stories about legacies they've been left, not tangible riches but attitudes, interests, and ways of looking at the world they had inherited from family members. It gives me great pleasure that I can quickly recommend such students.

Connecting People   My real interest of course is not to launch acting careers but to lead a fine school, and so it is with even greater pleasure that I bring together like-minded individuals. When Grady is writing a picture book about how hard it is to wait in the doctor's office and complains that he is running out of things for his main character to do while he waits, what better way to enrich Grady's draft than to introduce him to other children who have strong opinions about waiting-room life? (See *Writing Through Childhood*.) When I know children well, I can serve as the switchboard operator connecting them to worthwhile people and places. That's part of our job, to create networks and to help students tap resources. Schools should be scholarly communities. When I pay attention, eavesdrop, and gently stick my nose into lots of people's business, I know who knows about losing a grandparent, having a new baby brother, or wanting a dog so badly you could cry.

When Isabel's class got interested in origami, I introduced them to Frances, our resident expert. When Danny was drawing a street mural and worried about sketching animals well, I introduced him to Stephanie, another artist who specialized in sketching animals. When Brittany was looking for another title in the *American Girls* series, I suggested she talk to Carmen, whose backpack was bulging with them.

Of course, when you allow your head to become filled with children and you start keeping inventory of who knows what, you can take advantage of the experts yourself. When the auditors were coming and I needed to get our inventory in order quickly, I called on Tugba, a young Turkish student with a knack for numbers and efficiency. When a French-speaking family arrived for a tour of the school, I knew Vanesa and Sebastian would make the perfect escorts. When lost-and-found items started taking over our living spaces, I knew which young writers to call upon to craft a letter to families detailing all those homeless scarves, sweatshirts, and mittens.

My ability to connect people with one another carries over to the adult community as well. Pam Mayer tells me she is stunned at my ability to place student teachers with just the right cooperating teachers. Fordham University allows me to play matchmaker, and after talking to the student teachers for half an hour, I seem to know just who to place them with. It's not that difficult when you know people's interests, strengths, and styles. I can also connect family members with one another. I can make sure all the Maltese, Burmese, Russian, and Korean families have met. I can introduce all the opera buffs, baseball fans, and flea market enthusiasts to one another. And more importantly for the life of the school, I know who to call upon when we need fabric swatches, rug squares, or planks of wood. I know who to call upon when we need couches mended, paint mixed, furniture moved, or party hors d'oeuvres prepared. I know which parents can arrange a visit to the Metropolitan Museum of Art, the United Nations, or a Broadway show. I know who to invite when we crave information on stocks and bonds, French cooking, the history of Haiti, or how to become a citizen. When I keep tabs on this kind of information, teachers' resources are never limited to the family members of the children in their current class. Instead, 550 family members and all their friends and relations become this huge smorgasbord of possibilities, each person eager to enrich the life of our school.

Teachers and other staff members, apart from their professional areas of expertise, bring their own personal gifts, talents, and areas of interest to the school community. Lorraine knows Hebrew. Layne knows basketball. Pam knows Spanish. Joan teaches skiing. Lisa is a cetacean expert (she knows whales and dolphins). Debby is a printmaker. Renay is a photographer. Eve knows rock music. Paula knows gardening. Regina knows how to raise finches. Judy knows about fitness. Mike knows how to make pizza. Tara knows Broadway shows. David builds stone walls. Tammy is a gourmet cook. Karen is an expert skiier. Roberta can belly dance. Constance performs ballroom dancing. Sharon Hill is well versed in the psalms and hymns from the Bible. Amy knows all there is to know about Paris. And on the list goes. When people come to me for help, advice, or information, I know how to say, "Why don't you talk to _____?"

This role of switchboard operator becomes significant as well when it comes to professional development. When you know who the experts are, you can recommend teachers as well as their students to help a colleague launch writer's notebooks, revise poetry, or reorganize their classroom libraries. (See Chapter 7, "Turning Schools into Centers for Professional Study.")

Substitute Teacher

Occasionally a child will look up at me, and with a bit of disbelief in her voice, decide to check out a rumor. "You're the principal?" she asks. Perhaps someone had shared with her the old-fashioned image of being sent to the principal's office. Perhaps the child envisions a towering authoritarian adult sitting behind a huge desk, laying down the law, scolding the child for her misdeeds, and threatening to call home. (I did over-hear a child on the playground once, attempting to scare off a bully with the words, "I'm telling Shelley." I was startled, to say the least.)

Children are rarely sent to my office for misbehavior. And if they are, I'm probably not there. I like to think of my workplace not as any one office, but as all the rooms and corridors of the school. The children are surprised to discover that I'm the principal, not so much because I'm not a very impressive authority figure, but because they've seen me teach. When Pam Mayer sends her five-year-olds to look for me, they often return un-successful. They tell her, "Shelley's not in her office. They think she's reading with the third graders." Or they return saying, "They think she's working on that music mural with Sharon Hill's kids," or "They think she's writing with Karen's class."

I once heard Marilyn Burns say that when she taught, she felt like the grandma who takes her grandchildren for an hour or two. I do feel a bit like the grandma when I teach. Not for a minute do I think my teaching is as important as the classroom teacher's, but when I am called upon to cover a class I do take this responsibility seri-ously. After all, I'm expected to be the instructional leader in the school. School boards need to hire principals who can teach. Our new superintendent, Elaine Fink, suggests, and rightfully so, that before we hire a teacher we watch her teach. I would add that be-fore school boards, superintendents, and parents select principals, they too go out and watch them teach. If, when the superintendent calls, I'm always in my office, she should be worried. Principals need to stay close to teaching.

There are lots of reasons I might cover a teacher's class. Perhaps the teacher is not feeling well, has a family emergency, or needs one-on-one time with a student or must attend an important meeting with a parent. There are also *many* professional develop-ment reasons for principals to cover classes, co-teach them, or conduct demonstration lessons in a school. These will be addressed in Chapter 7, "Turning Schools into Cen-ters for Professional Study."

Whatever the reason for covering classes, the rewards are wide ranging. When principals carve out time to teach, they begin to deeply and personally understand cur-riculum goals, the availability of appropriate materials, the frustrations attached to un-necessary interruptions, the shortage of time during the school day, and the challenges of working with disruptive children, unusually sophisticated children, or children with a multitude of disabilities. Covering classes also enables principals to fine-tune their teaching abilities and is an excellent way for principals to get to know students well. I've also discovered that covering a class, with an inventive idea in mind, can also result in instant bulletin board displays. (See *Writing Through Childhood*.)

Strategies for Successful Subbing   On many of these occasions, which are frequently very last-minute, I find myself turning to read-alouds. I keep a stack of new, surefire books on my shelves, ones I know can't miss. To the uninformed eye, the books on my office shelves probably appear to be shelved randomly. There is however a method to my cluttered madness. I begin each year with fairly discrete categories of books. (I'm not very good at returning books to their appropriate places and therefore I forever need to straighten up. I'm only half-kidding when I say that most of the folders in my file cabinets are labeled "miscellaneous".)

Whatever book I choose, I try to share it in ways that allow for lots of classroom interactions and follow-up talk, art, or writing. After all, I am usually interested in covering classes for substantial amounts of time, frequently for an hour at a time. I am always delighted when a book can be shared throughout the grades. I like studying different-aged students' reactions to the same text and I think it comforts students to know that they share a schoolwide literary heritage. Children love knowing a book that their brother, sister, or upstairs neighbor knows. I love hearing a child ask another, "Has Shelley read your class————?" Filling my office with exceptional books arranged in specific categories also makes it easy for me to recommend and lend a book to a substitute teacher, school volunteer, or parent.

These collections work especially well for those "real" substitute teachers who are hired for the day to replace an absent staff member. Over the years, we've developed our favorite regulars, but occasionally we do hire an unknown teacher whose name appears on a list of licensed substitutes. I've been known to frisk these newcomers for worksheets and ditto masters. Substitute teachers who have never taught in literature-based workshop settings have a hard time understanding what to do. They often have a hard time allowing students to talk, move around, make decisions, and work in small groups or independently. I try to encourage these teachers to read aloud a book that easily lends itself to classroom response and activity. It is the easiest way I've discovered to invite outsiders into our world and eliminate the possibility of passive coverage. When the right book is chosen (and the substitute teacher is asked to welcome responses), these read-alouds turn into active and interactive hour-long sessions, just right for children who are missing their teacher.

In addition to trade books, I also keep a handy file of newspaper clippings, particularly for our older students. It's a personal treat for me to read *The New York Times* at night with my antennae sticking out, always on the lookout for short, powerful articles to share with our upper-grade students. I've become quite good at selecting the hot topics. These include children's rights, pizza, or anything to do with animals. Our ten- and eleven-year-olds were eager to read the articles attached to such headlines as, "Birds Flee Wreckage as Bronx Aviary Falls" or "Ferrets Do Not Have Fido's Right." They also loved an article about sidewalk hieroglyphics that explained how the city cartographer of pavement defects uses different symbols on his map of the city to indicate such deformities as cracks, potholes, and uneven curbs.

Shared reading experiences are not just for early-childhood students; newspaper clippings make perfect choices for creating such moments with older students. The articles are short, timely, and often a bit of a stretch for students, which necessarily turns classroom conversation toward those strategies needed when the reading doesn't come easily. There is an additional benefit to sharing powerful newspaper articles. They encourage students to read the newspaper on their own. We're trying to plant very deep roots at the Manhattan New School, instilling lifelong literacy habits. Newspaper reading is, of course, one of the most important ones. Newspaper articles are also easy to duplicate—that is, if your copy machine is working. I always try to persuade our copier repairman to register his children in our school. That's the only way I know to guarantee the repairman will be there every day to fix the often-jammed machine.

Sometimes the short reading materials I choose for the older students surprise my colleagues when they turn into math lessons. I'm clearly seen as a language arts person. The students love the anonymously written poem entitled "The Surprising Number 37." They try to understand why it works.

> The number 37 has a special magic to it.
> If you multiply 37×3, you get 111.
> If you multiply 37×6, you get 222.
> If you multiply 37×9, you get 333.
> If you multiply 37×12, you get 444.
> If you multiply 37×15, you get 555.
> If you multiply 37×18, you get 666.
> If you multiply 37×21, you get 777.
> If you multiply 37×24, you get 888.
> If you multiply 37×27, you get 999.

I've also clipped graphs from the newspaper that reveal that the cost of a slice of pizza in New York City has for years correlated with the cost of a subway token, now around $1.50 each. I've duplicated perpetual calendars so that each student can find out the day of the week they will celebrate their birthdays on in the year 2001. I've also given them a copy of a key which enabled them to figure out the cross street in Manhattan when they only had an avenue address. (Manhattan is laid out in a grid; the numbered streets run east and west and the avenues run north and south. The key helped them discover, for example, that 1636 Second Avenue is near East Eighty-fourth Street.)

I've also taught mathematics by sharing true family stories. Fourth graders used a lot of creative thinking when I told them that my son recently informed me that he was ten thousand days old. It was great fun to eavesdrop on their plans to figure out how old he was in years. On another occasion, I told them that my sister had trouble finding just the right birthday card to send my son on his twenty-fifth birthday. So instead of just one, she sent him three, including a card for a six-, nine-, and ten-year-old. I then asked, "If you'd like to do the same for someone in your own family, how could you surprise them with a combination of three cards?" Children set off to figure out how to take their mother's age, for example, and divide it into three amounts that added up to her age. There are all kinds of ways to teach math, on the run.

When Joanne pulled her back out early one school year, I was suddenly in the position to teach social studies. Third graders study immigration, and so I quickly wrote up a few scenarios that would enable children to crystallize their thinking on what it means to move to a new country. For example, I composed the following passage and quickly made thirty copies.

> An eight-year-old boy named Joseph and his seven-year-old sister named Hannah are moving to Hungary from New York City. They want their lives in Budapest to be like their lives in Manhattan. What questions do you think they might ask their parents on the airplane flight?

Children worked in small groups and then returned to the meeting area to share their responses. Some responses were humorous, including, "Are we there yet?" and "Do they call Hungary, *Hungary* because everyone is hungry?" Other responses were more helpful in cracking open the life of an immigrant. These included, "Do they have good schools and big buildings like in New York?" and "Will we speak the same language?"

On the following day the children responded to the following:

> Joseph and Hannah and their parents have just landed at the Budapest airport. They collect their suitcases and get into a taxi cab. How do you think people start a new life in a new country? What things do they need to do?

Children's responses included such important beginnings as finding an apartment, getting a job, setting up a bank account, learning a new language, and finding good schools. I was delighted when several children included buying books, and I laughed when one child suggested that calling for a cable television hookup was a necessity!

When I create an effective teaching tool in one classroom, I always share it with other teachers who are studying the same curriculum area. Principals who teach and teach well are in a position to spread the wealth. Covering classes and reflecting on that work allows principals to live up to the title "instructional leader."

It's an awful Sunday afternoon for me when my desk is swamped with test security information, child abuse forms, and banking surveys. It's a glorious Sunday when I'm searching for or inventing materials to share whenever I'm on call. Some school districts do quite a talent search to find new principals who know curriculum and instruction. Then when these talented educators arrive at their new schools, they're called upon to be experts at administration alone. Principals must find ways to stay close to teaching.

Devoted Grandma

Principals, heads of schools, can't be the kind of grandparents who are only there for the birthday cupcakes and holiday celebrations. They also need to be the kind of grandparents who are willing to stay up all night with the feverish child. It's a great deal of fun to waltz into a classroom and join in a chorus of "If I had a Hammer . . ." and then go next door and dabble in collage, and then onto a choral reading, followed by sharing a snack or two, and then listen in on a great read-aloud. Participating in these joyous, social moments are definitely part of my job, but they are definitely not the heart of my job. I'm not the social director on the *Loveboat*. There is real serious work to be done and I need to be part of that work. There is a city billboard that reads *"Literacy—Pass it On."* Administrators need to be part of that passing it on.

I'm lucky. I came to this job with a strong background in literacy. Administrators who want to help children learn to read and write and who don't have the expertise need to take courses, read professional literature, attend conferences, and most of all hang out in the classrooms of teachers who do. When children are sent to the principal's office at the Manhattan New School, I'd prefer they were coming because they're stuck on a piece of writing or they want help with their reading. Public school teachers are responsible for too many children at once. Everyone needs to pitch in.

Students often track me down in the building, asking for a writing conference. Some just want to show off their latest finished work, and that's always a treat. Others need help. Some days, there are so many children waiting to talk to me, I wish I had one of those numbered ticket wheels that you see at a crowded New York deli or bakery. Joanne, at a summer institute, once showed a videotape of several writing conferences I had with students. A teacher in the audience asked if I were a split personality. "How could the principal talk to children in that nurturing way and also be the disciplinarian?" he continued. I told Joanne that the teacher missed the important point. I am a better disciplinarian, if I am called upon, because I know their stories. Knowing a child's story changes my relationships with them. They can't mess with me; I know them too well.

Tutorials   Children who are struggling with their reading can't sit around waiting. Their needs are too urgent. Several years ago, I began carving out time to work closely with third-grade students who needed extra help. Over the years, Joanne, Renay, Kevin, and later Amy and Pat, our third-grade teachers, each suggested students who might profit from some extra tutorial work. During the first year, clusters of students from each class crowded into my tiny office, twice a week at separate set times, for full-hour visits. Scheduling time for struggling students is a major concern. These students needed extra time on task. They don't need me instead of their classroom teacher. They need me (or any other reading teacher) in addition to their classroom teacher. I didn't want them to miss their regular reading workshop time, nor any subject, for that matter. For the most part, students joined me during their lunch hour, before school, or with some compromise during their regular reading time. In the best of all worlds, these tutorials must be before or after school. Children need to eat relaxed lunches and play with their friends after lunch and they need to live a full classroom life. Arriving early or staying late did not work for all children because of complicated transportation or daycare arrangements, not to mention my availability during these prime times.

The first year in which I ran tutorials, or "Shelley's book club," as they've come to be known, I met with Joanne's students separate from Renay's and Kevin's because dealing with each teacher separately made the scheduling easier. This matter of convenience should never take precedence over what offers the soundest instruction. Children need to be working together based on need, not on convenience. How else can my teaching make a difference? The students were not coming for individual conferences, they were coming for guided and shared reading experiences. My choice of materials and strategies would have been much more effective if I had been more thoughtful and flexible in inviting "guests" to these twice-weekly get-togethers. Don't get me wrong, the sessions were worthwhile, but not nearly as successful as they could have been. Revision needs to apply to our teaching as well as our writing.

I learned a great deal from these early tutorial experiences, in addition to the need for careful scheduling and flexible grouping. I learned how much these struggling students profited from predictability. Although I won't share specific techniques here, (see *Lifetime Guarantees* for details), each session had the same components, all the way from September through June. The children always knew what to expect from me and what was expected of them.

I also learned about the importance of close quarters for easily distracted children. My office is small, and although there are many things on the walls and shelves that could distract students, this small group sat so close to me, I could easily and gently touch every student whose thoughts appeared to be roaming and bring them back to the task at hand. We also sat so close to the makeshift screen and the light from the projector that it was hard *not* to pay attention. It was easy to imagine that classroom teachers were working overtime trying to keep these easily distracted children on task during whole group instruction.

In addition, I learned a great deal about the reading materials that are available in our school for struggling children. If for no other reason than to become wiser about purchasing, principals need to put some of these materials to use. I recommend that all faculties spend time reading the so-called easy-reads with a critical eye. Many are not so easy, nor worth reading.

Of course, I learned a great deal about our students and their strengths and weaknesses. The work pushed me to go back to these students' second-grade teachers and figure out their growth in a larger context. One year an epileptic child was having seizures about once a week. I telephoned his doctor to ask if he might need a change in medication. The doctor responded, "Once a week? That's great, he used to have fifteen seizures a day." Whenever we have concerns about a child, we have to remember where the child is coming from and how far they have come.

In addition, I never seemed to find convenient times to give regular feedback to the children's classroom teachers. That problem still exists today. Much of our sharing remains quite informal, and I probably never remember all there is to say. This weakness has helped me realize that lack of articulation probably effects many other situations in our school. Does the resource-room teacher have enough time to share her concerns with classroom teachers? Does the science teacher have enough time to share her objectives with classroom teachers? Does the ESL teacher have enough time to make suggestions to classroom teachers? Of course not, and this situation is yet to be remedied.

Spending regularly scheduled time with struggling students also had some building-wide impact. It helped me to realize that as a faculty we needed to spend time clarifying our expectations for students throughout the grades. When I asked teachers to recommend struggling students for these tutorials, I never expected the range of students who arrived in my office. We have recently devoted many hours to conversations about our hopes, expectations, and goals throughout the grades. (See Chapter 6, "Talking Curriculum and Assessment.")

Classroom teachers appreciated my help, as did the students and parents. Several teachers and student teachers stopped by to observe. Processing what I was doing and why with the teachers who stopped by always helped me to clarify my thinking and in the end improve my teaching. Sharon Taberski, for example, reminded me how crucial it was for children to read silently when I guided them through a text. (We all anxiously await the publication of her forthcoming book, *Standing on Solid Ground: Teaching Reading in the Primary Grades.*)

Several principals from other elementary schools in our district also observed these reading sessions. Afterward, we spoke about how to carve out time and how to prevent interruptions. I shared one simple rule I had learned from a neighboring principal, "Don't do paperwork when children are in the building." That was very good advice. If I wasn't filling my days filling out forms, I could be teaching. As for interruptions, they end when you refuse to acknowledge the person standing in your doorway. "Either don't look up," I said, "or if you do, your face has to say, 'Can't you see I'm teaching!'" Interruptions will end when people understand that teaching is a top priority. (Of course, real emergencies are the exceptions to any rules principals make.)

Interior Decorator

One year the co-presidents of the PTA, Ellen and Robyn, attended our annual end-of-the-year celebration at my house. As they wandered through the rooms, they commented that the house reminded them of our school. I had never thought of the similarities. It's true, they were both built at the turn of the century and therefore were equally marked by high ceilings, brass fixtures, oak trim, and lots of nooks and crannies, but Ellen and Robyn were talking about different similarities. They were referring to the decorative touches, the things that were added after the house was built. The house reminded them of my office, as well as the poetry room, the stairwells, the hallways, and the other common areas of the school. They said both places had the same look and feel.

After visiting our school, Tom Newkirk, acclaimed University of New Hampshire professor wrote, "I began to feel that space in the school was sacred like in a church where every niche, every window, every doorway had to be claimed and made beautiful. Leaving the school pushing through those copper doors left me with a feeling of loss—the exact opposite of the feeling I usually have in a school where the outside is always more appealing."

Laura Benson, a literacy expert from Denver, Colorado, home of the beautiful Tattered Cover bookstore, also helped me to see the impact of our physical setting through a visitor's eyes. She published the following in the *Colorado Reading Council Journal*:

> Shelley's office is in what was previously the nurse's office, next to two doors, one labeled "DENTIST" and another "DOCTOR." I enter her office by going through a very small lounge with an old moss sofa and a table of bagels and cream cheese. (Now I know I'm in New York!) Shelley's office looks like a marriage of The Metropolitan Museum of Art, the Tattered Cover, and FAO Schwartz. An army of cartoon figures tops the filing cabinets. An old Rolodex the size of a small car, fished from the trash, sits at the ready for additions and readings of poetry. The walls are collaged with T-shirts ("Book Woman"), awards, photographs, and art, mostly children's pictures of thick tempera paint and hope.

Laura then described our common living spaces:

> Hallways are used as art galleries, libraries and think tanks. Folk art decorates the bathrooms. Antique stained glass gardens top the ceilings of the first floors. Tiles of self portraits and patches of poetry authored by the children cover every wall. Social studies research and exploration is shared in the language of the students at the front door. Science experiments of tadpoles and planets narrow pathways in classrooms and corridors. What a difference to simply add tablecloths and chintz and fat-bottomed chairs.

I really do care about creating a stunning school environment, but I am not alone. All the classroom teachers working alongside their students and parents work hard to turn our school into one of the most beautiful buildings in the neighborhood. Our classrooms and our hallways are thoughtfully planned and carefully decorated. One teacher's idea often inspires another. One parent's contribution brings about others. One mother mixes custom colors for our walls, others create enormous wall hangings and meaningful quilts. Others donate a wicker settee, handcrafted cabinets, and handmade curtains. A school aide's husband paints a bouquet of roses to hang in the principal's office. The custodian, using old window poles and some brass hooks, creates an imaginative way to hang murals in a first-grade classroom. You can stand in any doorway and see warm, welcoming living areas. Those rugs, round tables, and rocking chairs announce that something different is happening here. They do not represent superficial changes. Our classrooms look different because we value beautiful and interesting spaces over bland rooms filled with row after row of desks. We have high standards not only for our work, but for our surroundings as well.

The teachers on staff not only take care of their own corner of the world, but their ideas enhance our common areas as well. Paula, her students, and their families paint African Kente cloth patterns onto hallway tabletops. Joanne's students create beautiful two-sided mobiles to dangle from the corridor ceilings and add depth to our long hallways. Isabel's kindergartners create the kind of murals that reach out and touch passersby. Lorraine's wall of black-and-white photographs helps us understand the life of a first grader. Karen and Diana fill bookcase display units outside their classroom doors with carefully chosen picture books. Scenery from Layne and Kevin's plays are permanently displayed on large expanses of corridor walls. Judy and Kathy turn long stretches of wall into galleries for fifth-grade student artwork and writing. Pam Saturday and her students create stained glass to light up our ballroom windows and create permanent sculptures that turn dreary landings into museum exhibits. Kevin and his students paint the walls of the fifth floor, our penthouse, to look like the outside of a city building. They dip sponges into crimson paint to create the effect of a red brick building.

I too spend a considerable amount of time thinking about the aesthetics of our common areas. I recently spent an evening in a quaint old inn in Cambridge, Massachusetts. One row of tiles in the charming bathroom had been artistically replaced. Instead of shiny white squares, there was a mosaic of broken pieces from colorfully patterned cups and saucers. Studded throughout were also small ceramic dolls, clock faces, and antique buttons. There were even delicate cup handles jutting out of the wall at the most pleasing places. I couldn't help but think about our school. The missing tiles along the staircase walls have always disturbed me. What fun it would be to fill those squares with a cemented collage of broken bits of crayons, pencil stubs, sharpeners, erasers, and tiny toys. I'd love to see a few Power Rangers grounded in concrete! I delight in challenging the givens of what public schools look like. I think my colleagues would agree with the following deep-held beliefs about how to create inviting places for people to live scholarly lives. (See Appendix 3 for a worksheet on making schools more beautiful.)

"Stuff" Holds Stories   I have a lot of stuff in my house, "chatchkas" as we call them in New York. Each decorative item tells a story. Each says where we have been, who cares about us, and what we value. Every item is worth talking about. They're "story starters" in the best sense of the term. The items displayed say that we are proud of our shared history together. The same is true in our school. In our poetry reading room we keep a beautiful blueberry-trimmed china platter. It was given to us, along with a special edition of Robert McCloskey's *Blueberries for Sal*, by the teachers from the Center for Teaching and Learning in Edgecomb, Maine, when they came for a visit. There is a restroom on every landing in our staircases. In each, we've hung a beautiful nature photograph, taken by Roberta, our resource room/learning disabilities teacher. A model of the classic ship *Queen Elizabeth II* sits on the window sill in our staff room. It was a gift from Blair and her family when they moved out of town. Of course, every classroom is also filled with carefully selected and displayed gifts, souvenirs, and memorabilia. A visiting teacher from Ohio named Julie Maruskin told me that all of her third

graders lined the borders of their classroom with framed photographs of their ances-
tors. The children dedicated their year to the memory of those beloved relatives and
when they had a difficult day, they recalled the hard times of those who came before.
When school settings include items like these, the messages are clear, "People live here.
We care about one another. This is our home away from home."

My own home is filled with lots of old things. They're not very expensive antiques, more like flea market and yard sale treasures. But I do love my nut grinders,
inkwells, and musician figurines. It's not hard to say what attracts me to these items.
Besides their color, design, and purpose (I do love nuts, writing, and music), I'm also
fascinated by the stories I imagine are attached to these collector's items. At school, we
have several antiques attached to the early life of our school. We have brass doorknobs
elaborately etched with the words "Public School—City of New York." We have an iron
plaque that pays tribute to the first principal of this school building. It reads, "Sarah
Goldie. First Principal. 1904–1931." We have an old oak file cabinet, filled with the
registration cards of children born in 1899, the first children to attend what was then
P.S. 190. We have old classroom photographs hanging, with an invitation to guess in
whose room the snapshots were taken. It's not so difficult for us to imagine the stories
attached to these collectibles—after all, we spend class time studying what life was like
in old New York. We've also acquired some additional old-fashioned school things.
Hindy List, our good friend and mentor, who spends time supervising student teachers
in our school and helping neighboring teachers make the most of visits to our school,
has given us unusual antique bookstands. I've added old brass school bells and an old
slate board. These old school things remind us that we are part of a rich history of public education in this country. We have an important legacy to care for.

Teachers, friends, and family members have also given our place a homey, old-
fashioned feel by donating well-worn crocheted blankets, vases, homemade pillows,
and dishes from their mother's cabinet. Along with these goodies, of course, come real
stories, not invented ones. People's stories always create fertile ground for writers, but
perhaps more important, when people give us touches of their family life, not only
does our school look more welcoming, but our friends are saying they trust us.

Sometimes educator friends drop over after school hours, when almost everyone
has gone home. I used to worry that they wouldn't be able to appreciate our place
when it is empty. I've discovered, though, that our school still feels warm and inviting
even when people aren't there. Visitors sense the life of our school, because it emanates
from the special items we've gathered there.

The Pleasure of Collections I adore collections. I think they elevate beautiful
things, adding drama and richness. At home I have a collection of photographs of
doors, all with the number 65 on them. Whenever I travel, I search for beautiful doors
with the same house number as mine. If I only hung up one of these, it wouldn't be
very effective, but my vestibule is becoming lined with these and they make quite a

welcoming statement. At school, I've framed a collection of black-and-white postcards of children and hung them in our hallways, at eye level, so that children can appreciate them. I've brought in several empty pretzel barrels. These see-through containers are now home to several collections. One is filled to the brim with broken crayons, another with lost toys—small trucks, dolls, Lego parts, and the like. They sit atop my highest bookshelf and it doesn't take long for young visitors to ask about them. I also have collections of books about birthdays and baseball. I even have a permanent display of four children's books with the word *serendipity* in the title. They pay tribute to the joy of accidental discovery and to this day I can't believe I found all four.

Teachers too use collections to add richness and drama to their classrooms. Julie collects hats and sits them atop her cabinets. Judy's students line their cabinet tops with a row of handcrafted stained glass bottles filled with paper flowers. Sharon Taberski's bulletin boards are bordered with her collection of New York City postcards.

Frame Surprising Things   I don't have much white space on my walls at home. I love a carefully arranged yet cluttered look. In addition to the usual paintings, posters, and photographs, I have wall arrangements that contain mounted, matted, and framed sheet music, covers of children's books, linen souvenir towels, and postage stamps, among other surprising things. All in one way or another are deeply connected to my life. In addition to the black-and-white picture postcards of children previously mentioned, our walls at school are also beautifully cluttered and meaningful. And all things displayed are connected to our life as a social yet scholarly community.

We spend a lot of money on Lucite box frames. They're inexpensive, come in many sizes, and it's so very easy to slip things in and out. Every once in a while I come across a line or two in a student's writer's notebook that is stunningly inspirational. Rather than buy any commercial posters to decorate our walls, I ask students if they'd be willing to illustrate their words and turn them into our homegrown sources of inspiration. If you visit, you'd see the following individually framed and illustrated messages, all of which give credence to the expression, "Out of the mouths of babes."

> It's better to help someone than to give them a present.
> Why don't people get together and make New York a better place to live?
> Teachers shouldn't give grades, it makes some people feel bad.
> People change quick, you have to get them while they're hot or you'll miss a lot.
> I hate when people tell you not to do something and then they do it.
> Sometimes life stinks, but when I least expect it, life gets better.
> If life didn't have dreams, life would be boring; you'd have nothing to look forward to.
> I wish I could grow up but stay the same age; stay eight forever but grow up.
> The thing I hate about life is that wherever I go, I miss something.

By honoring and elevating these student thoughts, we go a long way toward creating the kind of social tone we are interested in. (More on this in Chapter 4, "Making the Social Tone Top Priority.") These young students' comments also remind us what a privilege it is to be around children and to be able to appreciate the world from their points of view.

Student artwork, crafted pieces of writing, published poems, notes from visitors, as well as newspaper clippings about members of our community, are also temporarily housed in these easy display containers. Over the years we've paid tribute, in this way, to teachers who've published, children who've performed publicly, and families who have been newsworthy. These have included the family that takes children to their summer home as part of the city's Fresh Air Fund, the children who lead successful latchkey lives, the mother who weaves synthetic braids into peoples hair as well as into hats, rugs, and clothes, and the divorced father who has rebuilt his tiny apartment to make comfortable space for his daughter to spend weekends. We've also invested in permanent frames, especially when our students have become cover girls and boys. We loved when our students appeared on the cover of *Scholastic News* (January 1996), voicing strong opinions about the English-only issue (see *Teaching Pre K–8's* (May 1994) cover story on our school with the title, "In New York City There Are Schools that Work." Hanging appropriate items on corridor walls make it easy to fill our school with celebratory moments.

Unifying Threads   I love random acts of kindness; in fact, they are the only random acts I can tolerate in a school. I have a hard time with random field trips, random skills lessons, random auditorium specials. I believe people learn better when things are well planned for, connected and integrated. I apply a similar belief to creating a beautiful setting. I'm very fussy about elements of design in our physical environment. Each winter I even take the unpaired mittens and gloves that are inevitably found on sidewalks and staircases and collage them into an appealing arrangement on a bulletin board in a display cabinet. Not only is it colorful and attractive, but it's easy for owners to spot their missing items. In the months of January and February, it doesn't take long for me to replace my works of art.

I don't like stray articles of clothing nor do I like stray furniture. If there is a round table in the hall, you'll probably find three matching chairs around it. If there is a lopsided sketch, totally disconnected to its surroundings, I'd probably ask permission to find it a better home.

One way I've discovered of eliminating that hodgepodge feeling of random decorations is to create unifying threads that run through the school. Jerry Harste, renowned professor from the University of Indiana, once introduced me by suggesting that although we don't have many thematic studies sweeping our school, I serve as a unifying thread. I doubt if I deserve such attention, but I do think I add an "all-of-a-piece" presence to the building, by encouraging people to visually pay tribute to things we love. There are several interests that reappear throughout our school. The minute you walk in you know that we love New York City, alphabets, and playing with language.

We also create a satisfying sense of unity and cohesiveness by highlighting architectural elements that reappear throughout the building. Children's finger-painted handprints cover all the slop-sink doors in the building. Older students painted detailed city scenes on radiator covers, stairwell overhangs, and custodial storage areas. Our art teacher Pam Saturday, working with small clusters of students, has graphically designed all our restroom doors. One door boasts climbing lizards, another crawling bugs, and another tropical fish. Many of the swinging doors in our old school contain five rectangular panels. If we decorate these panels on each of the doors throughout this building, we create an aesthetically pleasing thread that unites the five floors of the school.

Eliminate Eyesores   I have visited several residential communities that have built tasteful wooden sheds to conceal residents' unsightly garbage cans. There are places in schools as well that require clever thinking to eliminate unattractive eyesores. We now have a lost-and-found clothesline instead of an overflowing box. The clothesline hangs against an alcove wall in our cafeteria, guaranteeing that all the students will clearly see the unclaimed treasures every day. All the sweaters, scarves, and jackets that are found about the school grounds are hung on the line, but I claim the mittens and gloves for my own version of found art. I do the same in the spring with the baseball caps left unattended in the playground, cafeteria, or hallways. When life gives you lemons, make lemonade.

When children are taken out of school early, we are required by law to have the parent or guardian sign the child out. The adults file their departure information in a big book that sits on the table in the main office. There's no reason for this very institutional book not to be beautifully adorned with student artwork. The same holds true for visitor guest books, attendance books, or any other school records. We are living with many joyful artists. We need to put them to work. Students wait on line in our cafeteria. They often lean against the cafeteria wall. Isabel's friend and co-worker Dilta, together with a group of five-year-old students, have assumed responsibility for turning this drab waiting wall into a beautiful gallery with new murals each month. We have wallpapered the girls restroom on the second floor with bright book jackets. I think the children may spend a few extra moments on each visit, but the restroom certainly looks more beautiful than most.

Align Design with Purpose   How we arrange our living room furniture can determine whether or not a Saturday night get-together will be successful. When seats are clustered in friendly groupings and placed strategically throughout the room, people will talk to one another. Teachers along with their students think long and hard about how to arrange classroom furniture. They not only think about creating conversation areas, but also quiet areas for study and ample workspace for messy projects. If I intended for my office to be a place to work with children, then the design implications would be clear. I'd need to have a place for children to sit, to store their books, to work on a tabletop. I'd need to have books, markers, and a supply of writing papers.

So, too, if we expect a rich corridor life in a school building, allowing students to gather in areas other than their classrooms as well as encouraging colleagues to always be talking to one another, we also need to think carefully about hallway and office furniture and design.

It's very important to me to have lots of places to stop and chat in a school building. Everywhere you look in our school you'll find the kind of furniture arrangements that make this possible. We've tucked donated couches into hallway alcoves. (One of our parents, Bill, owns a moving company and we count on him to bring us the sofas he is often asked to get rid of. It always pays to put out a call for donations and to know your community resources.) We've also placed narrow homemade benches along corridor walls. (Robert, another father, built these Shaker-type benches for Joan, one of our fourth-grade teachers. She uses the hollow space below the seats as hidden storage areas.) We even asked our custodian to bolt down old auditorium folding seats in our hallways to guarantee that everywhere you look, there will always be a place to really listen to a child, a colleague, a parent, or a visitor. If we want supportive, nurturing schools, we need to make it possible for people to really pull in close and listen to one another. Sometimes, I think the presence of these inviting seating areas pushes people to do more sharing, right on the spur of the moment.

The same is true for creating workspaces. We are always looking for donations of tables as well as chairs, so that people can find the space they need away from their classrooms. A teacher can set up shop at the beautiful oak table in the main office or at the large oval conference table in the staff room. For the teacher who prefers to spread out her things on a couch and coffee table, the staff room is also an easy place to work. A ring of four overstuffed couches with an occasional plush velvet high-back chair form a huge square with a simple low coffee table in the center. Each of our reading rooms is also equipped with assorted tables and chairs for the teachers or students who use these rooms as workspace getaways. The low round table in the poetry room is often home to a cluster of mathematicians. The loft in the fiction reading room is always filled with young readers. The carpeted area in the nonfiction reading room is often used by young dramatists to practice a play or as a space for teachers to run tutorials for struggling students. Hallway alcoves are also dotted with all kinds of tables and chairs so that students can work in small collaborative groups or independently away from the hubbub of their classes. Hallway walk spaces remain broad and clear, however. We have toured the building with fire marshals and we do think seriously about issues of safety. Besides, we need big expanses of floor space when kindergarten students want to trace their body images or older students want to create large graphs, murals, and posters.

I have one other *major* decorating suggestion for educators intent on creating inviting settings for readers and writers. Not surprisingly it concerns the use of letters, words, and books. Books really do breathe life into a school and they are more than mere items of decoration. Many literary art projects will be addressed in *Lifetime Guarantees*, Chapter 1, "Designing the Literary Landscape."

Housekeeper

If you walked into my office, you wouldn't think that I'm concerned with neatness. My desk is always swamped with paper. Frequently, days go by before I see the wood grain again. I can offer a simple explanation, excusing my apparent lack of orderliness. I could spend all day, every day, going through all the memorandum that come my way. I choose not to. I choose to let that stuff pile up all week. Otherwise, I'd never work with a child, teacher, or parent. I could spend entire days reading memos, responding to memos, and filing memos. Of course, I'd never leave the office. I choose to scoop up the stack, shovel the papers into an empty tote bag, and sort through it on Sunday mornings, when I have no interruptions, no emergencies, and no enticing students and teachers around who are too good to miss. What I can do in an hour of intense work time at home would probably take me all week to do at school. Even if I chose to sit at my desk and work during school hours, the constant phone calls, visitors, and day-to-day happenings would prevent me from getting very much done. No, I prefer to devote an hour or two of weekend time to my administrative life. Knowing that I'm not going to even try to be efficient also eliminates any stress, guilt, or frustration when I look at my swamped desk. Besides, my office has that homey lived-in look.

The stacks of books on the floor, in every corner of the room, and those balancing on the arms of the sofa and spilling onto the cushioned seats, also add to the cluttered, disorganized look. But these too are easy to explain. Since those of us at the Manhattan New School have taken over as the book review editors for *The New Advocate*, lots of review copies come our way. Their first stop is my office, and I'm responsible for unpacking, sorting, categorizing, and distributing them to students, parents, and teachers. It's a wonderful way to create a messy office. (Even before we took on this review role, we had lots of books, because we worked hard on encouraging donations.)

Books purchased with our limited funds never enter my office. These were requested by specific teachers, and Rachele, our hard-working school aide, is responsible for all the paperwork connected to these orders and the distribution of these texts. In fact, nothing to do with purchasing ever enters my office. The financial role in schools can also take over the principal's life. Instead, I've used some flexible funds to hire Tara as my administrative assistant. Tara, one of our original staff members now on maternity leave, comes in two days a week to help me with administrative chores. She is totally responsible for money issues, and it doesn't surprise me that this one administrative area can take up almost two full days a week. Tara and Rachele share the former dentist's office next door to mine and their presence helps relieve the stress attached to trying to handle every aspect of school life. (Our school is too small to warrant having an assistant principal, and so finding kindhearted, hardworking, and efficient assistants is essential.)

I've now explained why I don't have a very neat office, but there is no denying that, I adore building-wide cleanliness. I love spring-cleaning, as well as cleaning in the dead of winter, the fall, and in the summer. There is a big difference, I think, between works in progress and sheer sloppiness. I have zero tolerance for the latter. Although I expect classrooms to have clarity in their arrangements, organization, and decorations, I do appreciate all the messy works in progress you would expect to find in a hands-on, process-oriented work space. But for me, there is no place for sloppiness, disorder, and lack of concern for others, especially in our common living spaces. Robert Ful-gham's *All I Really Need to Know I Learned in Kindergarten* was a big hit several years back in staff rooms across this country. His advice, "Clean up your own mess," rings particularly true for me. Isabel Beaton, when asked by parents what her kindergarten curriculum was all about, replied, "Gracious living." Gracious living is not just for five-year-olds, of course. The grown-ups, as well as students throughout the grades, need to learn to clean up after themselves. There is no excuse for teachers to leave a sticky tabletop in the staff room. Likewise, it is unacceptable for students to leave dirty paintbrushes in the slop sink or for parents to leave coffee cups in the poetry reading room.

I realize, of course, that in the hectic life of a busy school, it is sometimes impossible to live up to all your good intentions. You run out of the staff room to take an emergency call. The school bus comes before you have time to rinse the brushes. Your child arrives to show off his work and you forget about dumping out that cup of coffee. I truly believe that the folks in our community never mean to leave a mess.

All this requires, then, that we are all willing to pitch in to get the job done. I used to think of myself as the solo housekeeper, feeling totally responsible for the common areas of the school—the hallways, offices, reading rooms, restrooms, and the like. Someone once joked that I should wear one of those handyman aprons, the ones with all those pockets. Then I could easily reach for a stapler, scissors, tape, tacks, and the like, as I make my way through the building, repairing all the frayed hangings. I finally learned that caring for the physical community is up to all of us. I'm not the solo housekeeper, perhaps just the senior one.

Isabel's comment that school life is a chorus, not a solo performance, must apply to housekeeping as well. If we walk down the hall and spot a mess on the floor and ask a student to help with the cleanup, we'd be stunned if the student replied, "But I didn't do it." How many times have you heard yourself say, "I didn't ask if you did it, I asked you to help me clean it up"? The same thinking applies to the adults in the community. It's a lot easier to clean out a refrigerator when several people pitch in. I think it also changes relationships between people when we clean up a mess together.

Schoolwide Housekeeping Structures   There are several ways we involve all members of the community in the housekeeping of our school.

Visible Reminders   I remember becoming discouraged one day when I opened the refrigerator door in our staff room. The shelves were bulging with leftover birthday cakes, bags of stale bagels, containers of sour milk, and assorted trays of half-eaten lunches. The mess not only looked bad, it smelled bad. I decided to empty the entire refrigerator. Rather than tossing the contents into the wastebasket, I covered the large conference table with mounds of the moldy food. I then propped up a sign that read, "You know how crashed cars are sometimes left on the side of the road to remind us to be careful . . . ?" My colleagues got the point.

I once hung a sign near the coffeepot that read, "Shelley brought in eight white mugs with gold trim. Now she has only one. How many are missing?" My colleagues got the point once again. One day, I propped up a letter on the oak table in our main office that read as follows:

1/24/95

Dear friends,

This table makes a wonderful workplace for parents and teachers. But please do not leave unfinished projects spread out here, along with extra copies, unwanted mail, coffee cups, etc.

Each morning, I have to clean this common area and I'm feeling a bit exasperated. When we leave messes, it's hard to teach children about good work habits. If you're here at the end of the day, please leave this area as you would hope to find it each morning. Common work spaces belong to all of us. Please look around and pitch in throughout the building.

Thanks,
Shelley

I frequently send brief housekeeping notes to all staff members. One began, "Just a reminder, we do not have a cleaning service to pick up after ourselves. What's the point in creating a beautiful setting if we don't take care of it?" Another began, "Let's do some spring-cleaning please. Let's take a hard look at classrooms, hallways, and bulletin boards and eliminate outdated, worn-out, random stuff, or anything that doesn't show what we value . . . " Yet another read, "How's this for a schoolwide New Year's resolution? We will return the things we borrow, in a timely fashion, in good working order, to their appropriate homes?" I once sent a note listing all my housekeeping pet peeves, leaving plenty of white space for others to add theirs. (See Appendix 4 for a reproducible housekeeper worksheet.) Mine included:

- Leaving chairs upside down, on top of tables, after the school day has begun (Custodians ask us to put the chairs up at the end of the day to facilitate sweeping.)
- Using common areas as if they were attics meant for storage
- Leaving dirty coffee cups around
- Leaving dirty plastic containers around
- Using expensive copier paper for artwork or scrap
- Using expensive permanent markers when regular ones would do
- Leaving one copy of a title from a set of multiple copies in a random place

- Laminating things that really need not be forever
- Leaving tabletops sticky and stained
- Mistreating any book
- Leaving food out overnight (We do have big roaches and mice in New York.)
- Letting wastebaskets overflow, without stamping down their contents
- Leaving wastebaskets at the entrance to a classroom, not a very welcoming sight
- Letting bulletin board displays grow faded, tattered, and worn
- Keeping announcements up after the event has passed

Teachers added their own, including the following:

- Not replacing the toilet paper when the roll is empty
- Not returning the vacuum cleaner to its expected storage spot
- Borrowing the heavy-duty stapler and not returning it
- Taking up excess space when parking in front of the school (We don't have sufficient parking spots for staff.)
- Not replacing water in empty ice trays
- Adults smoking anywhere near the school grounds

Joanne even left the following sign above the copy machine:

Okay guys—
   What's the deal? If you're Xeroxing, and the tray runs out of paper, (even if you manage to complete your job), please be considerate and replenish it. It won't take you any longer than it would the next person who wants to use it.

Our custodians have never added any pet peeves to our list, but I'm sure they have several. James Smith, our assistant custodian, has frequently complained to me about children leaving the cafeteria, carrying their trays of hot food upstairs, and spilling things on the staircases. (He was particularly concerned about the tomato sauce because he noticed it removed the paint off the floor. I, of course, wondered what it did to the insides of our students!) Nonetheless, it is important to listen to the custodians' concerns. Likewise, every once in awhile, we need to ask our secretary, school aide, paraprofessional, security guard, and kitchen worker, "So, what's bugging you?" I've sometimes thought it would be worth our while to incorporate all these honest requests into a handbook on housekeeping. That's how crucial I think it is to keep striving for "gracious living." I can imagine that the chapter headings for such a handbook would include "Proper Care of Machines," "Replacement of Supplies," "Food Issues," "Storage Concerns," "Security," and so on. The person asked to compile such a handbook should be someone who can write with a light touch and sense of humor. Otherwise, we might start to sound like "P.S. Anywhere."

Frequent Discussion   It not only helps to put things in writing, but it sometimes helps to talk about these hard issues face to face. We don't want staff meetings to turn into gripe sessions, but it helps to always have a few minutes set aside for business issues. Housekeeping falls under that heading. Just as classroom teachers know the value of devoting class time to management issues, communities of adults need to have peaceful, professional discussions about house rules. Of course, all these conversations need to be shared with children, parents, and the other folks who spend time in the school.

At staff meetings, it also helps to have people share the strategies they've come up with to ease the housekeeping headaches. I can easily imagine Joanne talking about the importance of requiring children to keep the coat closet door closed. No one needs to look at jackets, book bags, and stored items all day. She might also talk about the importance of standing in the classroom doorway and paying attention to your line of vision. "What's the first thing you notice?" she may ask, and "Is it good enough?" Joanne would probably also kindly suggest we camouflage messy work areas and not use the tops of our high cabinets to store shopping bags and cartons filled with the kind of supplies that are only needed every once in a while. "Those high areas are still visible," she'd probably advise. "Why not use that space to display something beautiful?" Joan could share how she and her students decorated empty copier boxes so that stored items are hidden in beautiful containers atop the highest cabinets in her classroom. Isabel could share how she bags her garbage at the end of the day and leaves these neatly tied up packages for the custodian to discard. Sharon could easily talk about her end-of-the-day cleanup ritual, when every child is responsible for straightening up the room and preparing all supplies for the next day. I always know where to go when I need a sharp pencil or a marker that is not dried up.

Consciousness-raising Among Students   Students play an equally important role in school housekeeping. When my children were toddlers, well-meaning friends used to suggest that my husband and I clear all fragile things from low tabletops and shelves. It made more sense to us to teach our son and daughter not to touch easily breakable things, and as they grew older to teach them how to handle such things with care. The same holds true for life in our schools. I've worked in too many schools where bulletin board displays were draped in thick plastic sheets to guarantee that no vandals would destroy other students' hard work. For me, this scene is always a heartbreaking one. As I'll describe in an upcoming chapter on social tone, nothing is more important than having people treat one another and one another's property with respect. Occasionally, someone will violate our walls and our work, but we will never cover our work the way nervous homemakers put plastic on their sofas. No, we just need to keep the conversation about respecting school property and other people's work on the front burner.

When our school first opened, I used to walk the school filling a bright red tote bag. When I walked into classrooms carrying that bag, the children used to say, "Uh-oh, here comes Shelley with the red bag." The bag contained damaged goods, school stuff that had been mistreated. I would gather the children near and then very dramatically, with deep, heart-felt sighs, I would pull each item out, one by one. "My heart breaks," I would tell the students, "when I see pages folded and crumpled in a beautiful book, book jackets with no books, blocks covered with streaks of colored marker, posters marked with crayon scribbles, or pencils broken into little pieces. I can't believe anyone would knowingly do these things." The message was clear—"I don't expect it to happen again." It seems to me that incidents of disrespect to personal property happen less frequently as each school year goes on, as newcomers get to know what we value and the way we live our lives together.

In the early years of our school, I also used to regularly walk the building with a small crew of student representatives. Our mission was to look for problems in the environment and then try to solve them. At the time, some of our early-childhood students kept their coats in hallway cubbies. Inevitably the slippery nylon jackets would fall off their hooks and wind up on the floor. Ben, a second grader at the time, decided to help solve the problem by innovating on a penny rhyme he knew. He hung signs all over the building that read, "See a coat, pick it up. All the day, you'll have good luck." His signs were charming, but they didn't influence our kindergartners, who hadn't learned to read yet. The signs did, however, motivate the older students and adults to occasionally bend down and pick up misplaced items.

We also noticed that one of the restrooms was always particularly untidy. We decided to require students to fill out brief surveys when they entered and when they left. In one such survey, (see Figure 2.1), Leah wrote in her best six-year-old spelling: "I saw toilet paper stuck to the ground. I did not clean it." I am always delighted with students' honesty.

Since our school has grown, this small crew has turned into a more formal student council. We meet every other Friday afternoon. Students frequently bring up housekeeping responsibilities. They share stories about gum getting stuck on rugs, graffiti on walls, drinking straws stuffed in sink drains, and the awful sport of wadding up wet toilet tissue and attempting to get it to stick on restroom ceilings. We take these matters very seriously and design plans of action to prevent their reoccurrence. All student council representatives report back to their classmates.

This year we added an extra challenge for our student council representatives. I read aloud Ifeoma Onyefulu's picture book *Ogbo: Sharing Life in an African Village*. In it, the author introduces the concept of ogbo, a Nigerian belief that people who are born during the same time period are spiritually bound together for life. Each ogbo takes on a village responsibility. We talked about having an ogbo spirit in our own school. We brainstormed all the school responsibilities that students of different ages could assume. Student council representatives, for example, thought that kindergarten children could continue to take care of the lost and found; first graders could remove litter from

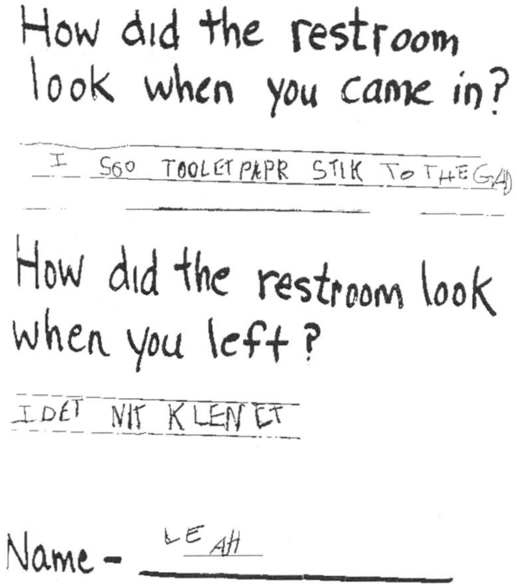

How did the restroom
look when you came in?

I SOO TOOLET PAPR STIK TO THE GA)

How did the restroom look
when you left?

I DET NIT KLEN ET

Name - LEAH

Figure 2.1

staircase floors; second graders could check the condition of restrooms and report problems to the custodians as well as dust in low places; third graders could host visitors on tours of the school and be lunch monitors; fourth graders can make sure all books were treated with respect, and they could make needed changes on our language board; fifth graders could repair bulletin boards, keep the birthday charts up to date, and clean in high places.

Additional schoolwide structures include individual community service commitments. Our upper-grade teachers, in fact, require older students to perform community service regularly. These students take on such responsibilities as helping kindergarten teachers put on students' snowsuits, boots, and gloves in winter weather, tutoring younger students in reading and math, updating the school map, or stamping new books. The list of possible community service chores includes many housekeeping ones as well.

We also need to pay attention to and honor those students who volunteer to help with housekeeping chores when they are not doing it for community service credit but because they genuinely want to take care of the school. I love when students take it upon themselves to hang cleanup reminders all over the school. I've spotted "No gum in the sink!" "Clean your table in the cafeteria!" "Stop messing up the Loft!," and the inevitable, "Remember to Flush!" I also appreciate receiving notes from concerned students. Brittany and Tina sent me an apology after they'd made a mess that they were unable to take care of (see Figure 2.2). It was comforting to know that they had tried to clean up after themselves. Some students send letters informing me of problems to be aware of. The thoughts of one second grader, Darryn,

Dear Shelley,
We couldn't get the
paper masha off the
walls. We tried. and tried
but it wouldn't come
off.
　　　　Love,
　　Brittany & Tina

Figure 2.2

4|22|96
Dear Shelly, kids are writing
Words on the bathroom Walls
that are bad influences for
kidnergarten, 1st grade, and
2nd grade. Since it's earth day
It Would be nice if you could
talk to the student Council
about pollution! I hope all
this works out!

　　　　Love

Darryn

Figure 2.3

were well received and I loved her spelling. She put the "kid" back in kindergarten (see Figure 2.3). Syed, a new student from Pakistan who had been learning British English, wrote me a letter volunteering to help solve the problem of gum chewers (see Figure 2.4). I didn't invite Syed to become a member of any "gum police" force, as his letter indicated he wanted to be, but I did welcome his help at the kindergarten lunch. He continued to send me notes periodically, including an apology he wrote when he couldn't live up to his obligation (see Figure 2.5). The last line of this note—"I hope you respect me"—was startling to read. You can be sure I asked his permission to talk about this kind letter in front of his classmates. It's an example not just of Literacy—Pass it On, but of Consideration—Pass it On. (More on this in Chapter 4, "Making the Social Tone Top Priority.")

```
To,
     Ms. Shelley,                              NOV-28-1993
     Director,
     M.N.School,
     New York.



     Dear  madam,

     I want to become cleaner helper, in my school.
     Because I see every boy and girl is chew and
     Peter say to them throw your gum in dustbin.
     and they throw it but, is not the way to throw
     1st roll in napkin and throw it.Is this the
     way to throw, I am right, I see more child do
     like this take gum from his moth and stick on
     carpet is this the way to use gum? and if you
     see  any child chew please take him/her to office
     or principal." DO NOT USE GUM IN THIS SCHOOL"
     I hate gum because it's not good.Tank's to do this
     job and please make me cleaner helperTANK'S SOMUCH
```
               I hope you accept my request

               FROM YOUR STUDEN

                         syed mohammed nazir hussain
                         grade:four'th joan's class
```
                    I tipe
                 This Latter
                  By Myself
```
Figure 2.4

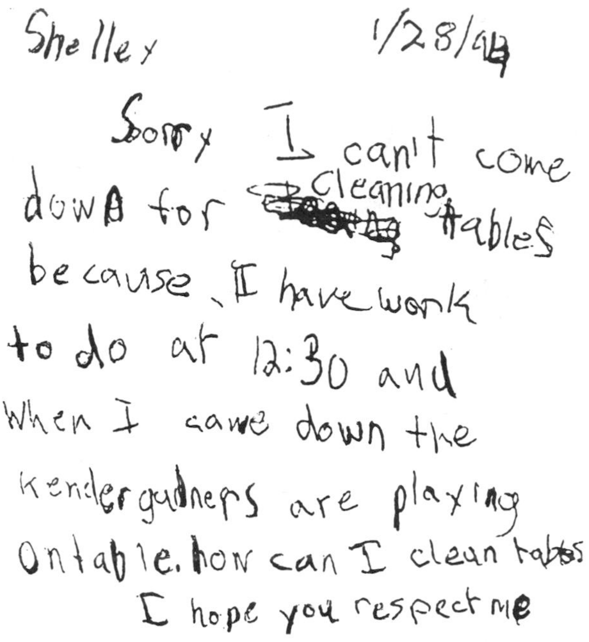

Shelley   1/28/94

Sorry I can't come
dowா for ~~cleaning~~ cleaning tables
because I have work
to do at 12:30 and
When I came down the
kendergudners are playing
Ontable. how can I clean tabs
          I hope you respect me

Figure 2.5

Sometimes students really surprise me with their offers to help. One year, each of Cindy's fifth graders, as a present for the New Year, gave me a coupon entitling me to some very personal gifts. They included the following:

- This is a coupon entitling Shelley to have the loft cleaned by Abby every Friday for one month.
- This coupon is worth: Me telling you an animal fact every Friday
- This coupon is for two weeks cleaning the fridge
- This coupon is for three weeks cleaning the staircase
- This coupon is worth one manicure for Shelley
- This coupon is for reading you your favorite picture book
- The use of this certificate grants Shelley one hour of computer training
- This coupon is for cleaning your coffee maker every afternoon for one week
- This coupon means I'll clean the cafeteria for a month
- This coupon means I'll be picking up garbage on the stairs
- This coupon means I'm willing to keep up the pictures in the lunchroom
- This coupon means I'll answer the phones for a day during lunchtime
- This coupon is worth help in unpacking books
- This coupon means I will help out in the recess yard
- This coupon means Gina will organize Shelley's office

Classes have also adopted community spaces, much the way businesses adopt a highway and design ways to beautify and maintain stretches of the road. One year Pam's kindergarten class was responsible for hanging those lost-and-found items on our clothesline, Sungho Pak's fourth graders took care of our ballroom, Sharon's second graders cleaned the poetry room, Joan's fourth graders organized the books in the fiction reading room, Cindy's fifth graders designed and updated our birthday wall, and Judy's sixth graders regularly cleaned our non-fiction reading room.

As a staff, we have also toyed with the idea of creating a Friday afternoon school-wide scrubdown. No special visits to Spanish, art, music, science, or physical education would be assigned at 2:15 on Fridays, and in addition to thorough classroom cleanups, corridor bookshelves and picture frames would be dusted, hallway sinks would be scoured, door windows shined, and wastebaskets rinsed. The custodial staff in many schools performs some of these jobs. No doubt, our wonderful custodians would do whatever we asked. But there is something very significant about all of us taking responsibility for the messes we make. Besides, we ask our custodians to do many jobs that other custodians probably don't do, like hanging paintings, moving couches, rearranging rugs, and reading to children. The least we can do in return is help out with the ordinary cleanup tasks.

Provide Necessary Tools   If people are to take housekeeping seriously, we must ensure that they have the right tools. Below is a list of requested donations that Kevin, a former third- and fourth-grade teacher, sent home to his students' families.

A List of Much Needed, Very Appreciated Donations . . . (If possible)

- sponges
- spray cleaner
- Band-Aids
- tissues (runny noses run rampant through the third grade—say this three times fast)
- plants (and green thumbs)
- Post-its (all sizes)
- dishwashing soap
- Xerox paper
- empty containers with lids (yogurt cups, glass jars, coffee cans)
- broom and dust pan
- markers
- tickets to Giants game
- a house in the Hamptons
- theater tickets

Kevin is, of course, kidding about the last three items, but he is quite serious about the other supplies. We can't keep schools neat and clean if we don't have adequate vacuum cleaners, dust rags, glass cleaners, soaps, brooms, and the like. If there is no money in the budget for such items, we must ask the community to help.

I remember with surprising vividness a next-door neighbor stopping by unannounced on a Friday night when I was a child. Our family had just finished eating dinner and my mother brought out a fantastic dessert. It was fresh from the local bakery and it was called a brown derby. The cake was piled high with bananas, peaches, strawberries, chocolate, and lots of luscious cream. Our neighbor was stunned that my mother had such a luxurious cake for no apparent special occasion. "Why would you buy such a cake when you don't even have company?" she asked. "It's for my family," my mother answered. "Who could be more special?" My mother taught me well. Family always comes first. I like to think the same is true in our school. The people who live here every day come before the visitors.

We don't keep our school clean, orderly, and attractive because company is coming. We do it for ourselves. We deserve to spend our long days in a beautiful surrounding. Yes, I admit, we might do an extra special cleanup when we know a large group of visitors will be spending a big block of time with us, but our school looks more than presentable any day of the week.

We've also learned that taking care of the physical environment is important not just for the sake of aesthetics. Things last longer when they are well cared for. Certainly in this era of incredible budget cuts, we have to think seriously about making things last. "Waste not, want not," also has strong meaning for those of us trying to live environmentally conscious lives. In addition, when things are carefully placed and cared for in our environment, we can guarantee that more time is spent on tasks. Students and teachers shouldn't have to waste time scrounging for a book or searching for a clean sheet of chart paper. And finally, beautiful settings change behaviors. Visitors often ask us about our discipline strategy. I can't help believing that one of the reasons that our students seem so well behaved is that our setting inspires a calm and caring attitude. We know that our students would have more peaceful lunchtimes if we had the money to redesign our cafeteria. This challenge is next on our wish list.

Literacy Lover

I've saved one of the best roles of principal for last. Eve Mutchnick, one of our kindergarten teachers, reminded her student Jessica to stay calm in the playground. "Be a model for the others," she suggested. Jessica replied. "I can't be a model, I'm going to be a doctor!"

Principals, as well as teachers, can be models, in fact they *must* be models. How can we ask students to lead literate lives if we don't? Of course, I don't take care of my own literacy because I'm trying to inspire anyone, I do it because reading and writing are two of life's pleasures. I work hard; I deserve them.

A Principal's Passion   Everyone knows I care deeply about reading and writing. I have to admit that I do own pencil earrings, alphabet pendants, and several book pins, one even inscribed with the words "It was a dark and stormy night." I also have a button that reads, "So many books, so little time." But my jewelry has nothing to do with serving as a model for passionate literacy in our school. People know I care about reading and writing because they hear me talking about these wonderful pastimes, but especially because they see me reading and they see me writing. Even if I had never published a single piece of writing, the students, teachers, and parents would know that books are a very special part of my life. I make no excuse, as a principal, for staying true to the passion of my teaching life.

One January several years ago, on our first day back after the winter break, I sent the following letter to all the older students.

January 4, 1993

Dear girls and boys,

Welcome back to school. I hope that 1993 is a wonderful year for all of you. I can't wait to hear all your holiday stories.

One of the best things I did over the break was to read several biographies and autobiographies of famous writers. Below you'll find a passage from E. B. White: Some Writer. *This biography of the famous writer was written by Beverly Gherman.*

Did you know that Elwyn was E. B. White's first name? When I read the following passage I thought of all of you, young notebook keepers. The author writes,

> *When he was eight, Elwyn began writing daily in a diary. To make it sound more important, he called it his journal. He didn't waste words on what he had eaten for dinner or studied at school that day. Instead he began asking himself questions about life and about his relationships with his parents and his friends. He wrote about his fears of the dark cellar and the damp lavatory in the school basement. He told about his shyness toward girls. If he could not speak out, at least he could put his thoughts on paper.*

I'd love to hear your reactions to this passage. I'll stop by soon.

Love,
Shelley

P.S. I also cleaned out my basement. I found lots of old art projects from when I taught second grade. Maybe there will be time to show them to you.

Our students know that the adults around them care about reading and writing because we are always demonstrating that we do.

Jane Kearns, a powerful literacy educator from Manchester, New Hampshire, told me that when her nephew Zach was born, she gave him 365 carefully selected books as a birth gift. We want to educate students who, when they are grown and become aunts or uncles, would think of a gift like that. Or if they become parents, they would appreciate a gift like that. Or if they received 365 books for their seventh or seventeenth birthday, they would think it was the best present ever.

I recently read about Moe Berg, an unconventional baseball player from the 1930s who not only played baseball but also was a lawyer and a spy for the United States government. One of the reasons he loved baseball was that it was a job that gave him a lot of time to read. He, in fact, carried a little cardboard sign that read, "I would rather be a poor man in a garret with plenty of books than a king who did not love reading." We'd like our students to believe the same.

Informing Students About Our Own Literacy   Our work is cut out for us. We need to think of every minute we are with children as potential for demonstration. I wear blazers with deep pockets so I can always have paper and pencil handy. I sometimes tuck in a tiny book as well. I drink coffee out of a black mug made from slate that just begs to be covered with chalk messages. I open new boxes of books with gusto, gently caressing the pages and ever so carefully cracking open the spine, and I do so for all to see. The children have also seen me burst into their classrooms whenever I've found just the right book connected to one of their class studies. (There *are* some acceptable reasons to interrupt a class!) I also collect baseball literature and I make sure the children know about my collection. My office shelves are filled with baseball poetry, short stories, novels, as well as nonfiction baseball texts. I wish someone had told me when I was a child that when you are passionate about something, you collect books on the topic. I'd have an even more valuable collection by now.

One year, I looked down from our second-floor window to the small playground below. I noticed that the children had removed their jackets, even though on this early-spring day, it was still a bit nippy. I called down to the children to put on their coats, but the playground noise made it impossible for the children to hear my plea. I grabbed a sheet of paper and a marker and wrote my message in large bold letters. Eventually one child looked up and noticed my sign. Quickly, the word spread, "Shelley's in the window writing messages." The children thought I was more interested in getting them to read than to put on their warm clothes. They, in fact, stood waiting for me to write even more messages. And so I did. Over the next few days, I held up such signs as, "No climbing on the walls," "Stop running so fast," and "No sucking lollipops while you are playing," each connected to playground concerns I was spotting. Children know that I care about health and safety, but they suspect that I especially care about literacy.

There are signs everywhere that the adults in this community care about their own literacy. On the door to the main office, I always list the monthly books we are reading in our adult reading groups. The titles are up to remind the teachers, but to inform the children as well. We need to be very public learners. Students also see the enlarged crossword puzzles that our staff members work on together. I use the poster printer machine to occasionally enlarge a puzzle from *The New York Times*. Playing with language is another way people delight in literacy. They see the literary cartoons we post, the book reviews we swap, and the journals we read.

Perhaps most important of all, they see our books everywhere. Our staff room bookcases are filled with lots of donated books. (In my son's apartment building in Manhattan, there is a bookcase near the wall of mailboxes. Residents informally swap books. That's a nice image for a staff room library, don't you think?) My office is home to our professional library. The students know we spend school funds on books for the grown-ups and we borrow these books, just like they borrow from the library. Perhaps the most dramatic demonstration of all is in our poetry reading room. One entire wall is filled with poetry books for the adults; the children's collections are housed across the room.

Students also know that books are an important part of gift giving in our lives. They know we spend lots of money at our local bookstores, buying books for ourselves as well as for our family, friends, and colleagues. We make sure to share with them the thrill of finding just the right book.

I also share with students when colleagues and visitors present our school with books. They know that Maureen Barbieri brought us a copy of Pablo Neruda's *Odes*, Georgia Heard brought us Naomi Nye's *This Same Sky*, and our friends at the Center for Teaching and Learning sent us *Mother Gave a Shout: Poems by Women and Girls*.

I tell students that Regie Routman sent me Daniel Pennac's *Better than Life,* and my literature-passionate friend Irene Tully handed me Edward O. Wilson's *Naturalist,* suggesting I read his passage about ants carefully. I let students know how excited I was when a visiting teacher, Doris Meyer, gave me an autographed copy of Billy Collins's adult poetry collection, *Questions About Angels.*

People who care about literacy introduce their friends to new writers and new titles. The children know that the silver notepad dangling on a silver chain that I frequently wear around my neck is the place I record recommended titles. When the students ask to look through the pages of that little pad, they know that they won't spot any of the writers that they care about. No, they realize that those titles and those authors are for me and for my adult friends. Many children have asked me where they can buy such a novelty necklace. If children admire us, they will want to do what we do. A child who doesn't love books in our school is as rare as a child who would turn down a long, cool drink on a hot afternoon.

Each September, I ask returning students what they read over the summer. I'm always delighted when they can rattle off several titles. I'm even more delighted when they in turn ask me, "And what did *you* read this summer?" The same holds true for writing. In November of 1995, an article appeared in *The New Yorker* about our school district and our superintendent. Tony Alvarado, quite proud of our schools, said, "I think we really do the finest work in literacy in the country. Our teachers are authors. Our principals are authors." It's wonderful to have such a confident superintendent. It's even more wonderful that adult writing is so closely connected with literacy work.

In a past life, I used to be known quite simply as the "writing lady." When my children were little and I'd attend open school nights, I could almost hear the teachers whisper, "Uh-oh, here comes the writing lady." I suppose I did have a one-track mind back in those days, the early 1980s, when I was just learning about the writing process approach. I was absolutely consumed with this new way to think about children and their composing processes. Occasionally, colleagues in the elementary school where I worked would leave the staff room when they saw me coming. They couldn't bear to hear one more thing about the writing process. And at first I didn't even couple the teaching of writing with the teaching of reading. It took me a few years to realize that you couldn't teach one well without the other.

And then I spent seven years at the Teachers College Writing Project, again wearing blinders. I was exclusively thinking about reading, writing, and literacy. And then eight years ago, we opened this school and I was in for a rude awakening. We couldn't think about literacy alone. There was social studies, science, and mathematics. There were parents, standardized tests, and head lice. Sometimes we get dizzy thinking about all we are expected to be good at. It was a much simpler life when I was known as the "writing lady."

Today, I still make time to do a lot of writing and thinking about the teaching of writing. I am able to be an effective literacy model for students, parents, and teachers, because I continue to take my own writing very seriously. I have several reasons for keeping writing on my front burner.

- First, I suppose I'm trying to show that you don't need to be at a university to lead a scholarly life. Schools at all levels need to take adult learning seriously. Educators need to read, write, and research to lead a more professionally satisfying and successful life. (More on adult learning in Chapter 7, "Turning Schools into Centers for Professional Study.")

- Second, I deeply believe in Donald Graves's profound comment, "If it is not for us, why should it be for them?" How can I ask 500 students and their teachers to read and write if I don't value reading and writing in my own life?

- Third, I want to be sure that all the suggestions I make to students to help them become better readers and writers are effective. What better way than to try these suggestions ourselves? Our own reading and writing are the wells we draw from.

- Fourth, I've discovered that writing can actually enrich and improve the quality of life in a school building, particularly if everyone's writing is put to good use. (More on this in *Lifetime Guarantees*.)

- Fifth is the selfish reason I referred to earlier. Reading and writing are two of life's pleasures. I work hard. I deserve them. I need to make time in my life to take care of my own literacy.

Classroom teachers have myriad ways of letting children know they value reading and writing in their own lives. They read aloud from their own writer's notebooks and talk about their own bedtime reading. They share drafts of their own writing and they complain to their students about the cost of hard-covered books. They share their attempts at writing for publication and gossip about how heated the discussion got at their adult book-talk group. Principals, too, need to devise ways to make sure that the students in their care know that they value literacy, just as their teachers do. Perhaps heads of schools might try any of the following joyful activities:

- Send regular letters to the entire student population commenting on your own reading. These can be similar to my "after-holiday-break" letter on page 61.
- Select a few students to keep dialogue journals with. Set up an easy schedule for passing the journal back and forth.
- Begin a reading/writing club based on a passion you have. (My baseball club meets at lunchtime once a week during the baseball season.)
- Ask students for recommendations for weekend reads. Borrow the books and give feedback on their choices. Make recommendations yourself.
- Share a draft of a letter you are writing to the PTA. Let your seniors offer suggestions.
- Sit in regularly on reading/writing workshops. Bring your real "stuff" to work on.
- Begin a ritual of opening your daily mail in a classroom during a reading/writing workshop. Give away any appropriate tasks to the curious student onlookers.

James Baldwin once said, "Children have never been very good at listening to their elders, but they have never failed to imitate them." Let them imitate us as we curl up with a good book or reach for our journal to capture a passing thought.

One June, knowing I'd be leaving for the summer to work on this book, I wondered if all the children knew how much I value reading and writing. I had an opportunity to find out when Judy needed some extra time to work on her students' middle school applications. When I covered her class, I asked the students to help me with my research. "Would you take a few minutes and jot down the things you think I really care about in this school?" Some of their answers appear below. Although there were a few surprising ones, for the most part their answers indicated they know me well. Everyone mentioned reading and writing.

Jessie	*Carmen*
kids	cleanliness
writing	reading
teachers	kids
neighborhood	different cultures
reading	fun

kids	teachers
teaching	learning
teaching about different kinds of kids	writing
relaxing	classes
first names	being comfortable

Gina	*Grady*
how kids behave	children
being happy	strangers entering the building
making sure things look nice	education
books, materials	kids' problems
kids	being comfortable in class
having visitors	writing
writing	books
teachers	health
paychecks	safety
teaching	rights, fairness

Another way that I could have gotten at the same information would have been to list the things I value and ask the students to rank them. Joanne and I devised a simple method to find out how much her students knew about her teaching priorities. We came up with a survey form that asks students to grade a list of descriptors on a scale of 1 to 3, 1 being "very important" and 3 being "not that important." (See Appendix 5 for a reproducible form.)

We could use a similar form to evaluate the priorities of our colleagues (see Appendix 6). After all, we serve as literacy models for each other as well as for the children. Teachers are not surprised to receive letters from me that begin,

> *Dear friends,*
> *What an incredible spring break, matzo balls, snowballs, and of course chocolate Easter eggs. Quite an unlikely combination. I spent my days off, mostly at home, indoors—my favorite place to unwind. Of course, I did very little unwinding. Lots of cooking, reading, and especially writing. I spent several days trying to figure out how best to edit the new column for The New Advocate. Reviewers, we must meet!! I loved reading the contributions, but most were too long and most people forgot to refer to the format guidelines. Reviewers, can we please meet as soon as you dismiss your students on Thursday's half-day? That way, you'll still have time for lunch before our staff meeting. I also spent several days rereading my files for this new book I'm about to write. So far I've got an annotated table of contents and an introduction. That may not sound like much, but it really feels like a major achievement to me, since I'm finally working on a word processor . . .*

Sometimes my welcome-back-to-school letters deal more with my life as a reader.

Dear friends,

Welcome back. Rather than greet you with standard memos and endless reminders, I thought I'd share some of the reading materials that made me laugh, cry, question, and wonder this summer.

Fortunately, I had lots of time to catch up on my reading—on very long flights and during a two-week dormitory stay at Oxford. No phone, no fax, no interruptions—just evening hours for reading the books I had been meaning to read all winter. Of course, I can't include the thick reads here—Penelope Lively's Moon Tiger, *Erdrich and Dorris's* Crown of Columbus, *several new books published by Heinemann including ones by Kathy Short and Nigel Hall, a few feminist titles given to me by my daughter, and a great baseball anthology entitled* Yankee Reader. *Instead, I've attached some poems and some worthwhile newspaper clippings. Let me know what you think. Do share your summer finds.*

Here's to a great year!
Love, Shelley

Letters like these help teachers know who I am and what I value. If I trust that every moment has potential for demonstration, then my school life and what I prize should be clearly visible to both students and teachers.

The Roles Not Mentioned

Throughout this chapter, I have been sharing a few unexpected principal roles that I carry out with much pleasure. I have not been all-inclusive. I haven't mentioned how happy I've been to show a young visually impaired student how to wear contact lenses, to light a candle at a graduate's bat mitzvah party, or to nudge teachers to write for publication. I haven't mentioned that Isabel Beaton paid me the highest of compliments when she told me that I make her feel as if her class is the only one in the building. She says my role is to *kvell,* a Yiddish word meaning to beam with pride.

I wish my main job was to kvell. It's so easy to beam with pride when I look at the work our students and teachers are doing. But when I look at my own work, there are several roles I don't perform very well. I am no where near ready to put these aspects of my job in a principal's portfolio. I have yet to write a successful grant. I am still learning how to keep my appointments and paperwork in order. I don't hang out on the fifth floor, our penthouse, nearly as much as I'd like to. My morning notes to the staff in our logbook are frequently illegible. I am not nearly as up-to-date as my colleagues in the teaching of math and science. I have yet to master scheduling, the Risograph machine, or anything beyond the rudimentary use of the computer. Beyond the cognitive domain, there are several affective issues I know I need to work on. My friend Hindy teases me about "pushing the Shelley button." I know she admires my ability to come up with ideas quickly and to carry them out quickly as well. Of course, our strengths are also our weaknesses: I speak too quickly, throw out suggestions to others too quickly, and expect change too quickly. I also need to learn to say hard things to people and to assure others in the community that it's okay to say hard things to me. Nothing frustrates me more than finding out that someone in the community is upset about something and that I had no idea about it. The intensity of this job has helped me to discover a lot of new truths about myself. (Everyone should write about their work, it yields mounds of New Year's resolutions.) There is a lot of work to be done, but dealing with the above deficiencies feels manageable because they are all within my control.

Our custodian once asked me if I had pushed the principal's panic button. I thought he was kidding or using a figure of speech. "No," he said, "the alarm is registering downtown." I didn't even know that there *was* such a button. I suppose it is intended for real emergencies—intruders, bomb scares, snipers, and the like, but I couldn't help but think about the everyday things that make me want to push the panic button.

A friend once sent me a framed sketch depicting the administrator's life. The room was cluttered with stacks labeled "disciplinary problems," "attendance records," "curriculum issues," "requests for supplies," "textbooks for review," and so on. Scattered about was also a bottle of antacid, headache medicine, and a bucket for pulled hair. That office is not mine. The School Construction Authority, the main office responsible for making repairs in the city schools, recently visited our building. One of the workers asked me, "What do you think is the most frequent request we get from principals?" "Window guards," I naively guessed. "No" he said, "Bullet-proof windows for their office." That concern is not mine. The things that drive me wild, the ones that make me feel I need to press a panic button, are the ones I feel I have no control over.

Inevitable Obstacles

For years, I was never given keys to the front door. I suppose city officials were afraid that school workers would enter the building on the weekends and set off the elaborate burglar alarm installed to protect city property. I have finally been given a set of keys and the code to shut off the alarm. Of course, for safety as well as security reasons, we are still not permitted to be in the building if a custodian is not present.

I used to complain about not having keys to the front door of our school and I meant it in a literal as well as a metaphorical sense. Even though I now have a set of keys, I am still not in control of who or what enters our building. Of course, I am not referring to children or their parents. They're always welcome.

But there are many things that come through our front door that really could keep us from doing all the splendid things we'd like to do with children. Thankfully, some of those things we can choose to ignore. We don't have to use, for example, every curriculum guidebook that comes our way or pay tribute to every special event sanctioned by the central office. If we did, we would never get to our regularly scheduled work. We would have to stop everything to celebrate Geography Awareness Week, Career Development Month, Better Speech and Hearing Month, Fire Safety Week, and so on. We'd also have to stop to enter all the contests that come our way, including Mayor for a Day Essay Contest, Paint the Town Red Contest, and Child Abuse Prevention Poster Contest. I haven't even mentioned all the memos on heritage studies we receive: Jamaican Heritage Week, Italian Heritage Week, Asian Pacific American Heritage Week, and Celebration of Native American Month, to name just a few. Our answer to all these specials can be summed up by a banner Paula has hung outside her classroom door. It reads, "Black History Month Is All Year Long." We don't go in much for specials; instead, we like to think that issues that are important are woven in to everything we do. Luckily, our district places no demands on us to take part in all these events. Instead, the information is there for us to use if we want.

Other problems are not so easy for us to solve. There are many obstacles, interruptions, and special programs over which I have no control. I would, for example, appreciate some help in rethinking special education models, particularly ones that corral children with severe emotional handicaps into one self-contained classroom. I'd also like the teachers' union to continue its movement toward allowing teachers to be part of the process of choosing their own colleagues. It's hard to have an effective school when teachers with different philosophical beliefs about teaching and learning arrive on your doorstep, without any professional discussion as to whether they are a good match for the school. The following two issues offer especially big challenges.

The Plague of Standardized Testing

It's late April or early May in New York City and those familiar cartons come right through that front door, occasionally followed by inspectors whose job it is to make sure that the boxes remain sealed until the big moment arrives. The inspectors really don't have to check on us—we *never* want to open those cartons of standardized tests!

Several years ago in *Whole Language: The Debate*, I wrote,

> Not too long ago at an airport gift store, I noticed a schoolhouse music box. I couldn't resist turning the key. It played, "School days, school days, dear old golden rule days. Reading and writing and arithmetic, taught to the tune of a hickory stick . . . " We may not have actual hickory sticks in our school anymore, but standardized tests are serving the same purposes. In some schools in this country, those tests continue to dictate teaching practices, and there is as much pain and punishment attached to them as to those old hickory sticks. Even in our school where we downplay the yearly plague of tests, we have children who in the not-so-merry-month of May complain of stomach cramps and develop asthmatic attacks from which they do not suffer at nontesting times. The teachers who have to administer these exams to children who have only been on this planet seven, eight, or nine years, wince as much as if they were witnessing a child being physically abused.

Several pieces of student writing bear witness to students' negative reactions to the standardized tests they must endure. Gina wrote her thoughts on a math test in her writer's notebook (see Figure 2.6). Sari wrote about a reading test (see Figure 2.7, p. 71).

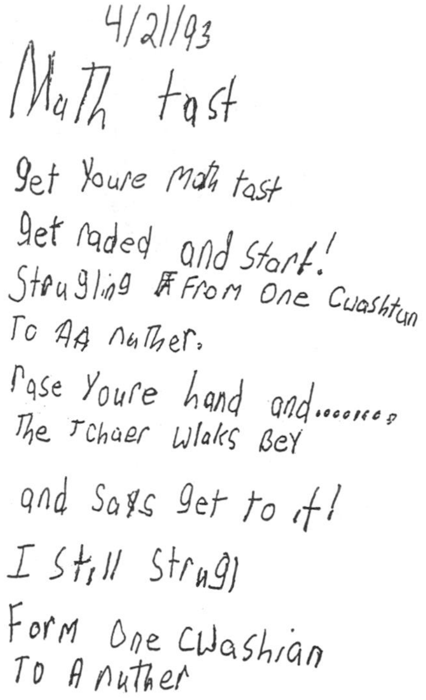

4/21/93

Math tast

Get Youre math tast
Get raded and start!
Strugling From One Cuashtun
To AA nuther.
rase Youre hand and.........,
The Tchaer Wlaks Bey

and Says get to it!

I Still Strugl

Form One CWashian
To A nuther

Figure 2.6

There are no sour grapes growing on this issue. I don't dislike standardized tests because our children don't do well on them. Quite the contrary, our students do very well on these tests. A computer printout tells me that last spring, 90 percent of our students were reading at or above grade level, and 91 percent were performing at or above grade level in mathematics. (They do well for several reasons. As a staff, we spend a lot of time carefully and rigorously teaching children how to read and how to solve mathematical problems. We spend thoughtful, although limited, time helping students learn how to take these tests. And thankfully, our state does not test isolated skills, so the testing situation is not as removed from our teaching as it could be.) I dislike the tests for several other reasons. I dislike them because they interrupt our school lives—we have better things to do. I dislike the tests because they make young children nervous and competitive. I dislike the tests because parents get anxious over them. I dislike the tests because those in charge don't realize that not all second language learners acquire English at the same pace. If you have been living in this country two years prior to the date of the exams, you must take them. (Imagine yourself living in Bulgaria for two years and being asked to take a standardized test in Bulgarian.) I dislike the tests because children who don't do well are often in settings in which they get quickly labeled for their struggles. Most of all, I dislike the tests because they don't tell me anything I need to know. (I'm much more interested in reading tastes, for example, than reading tests.)

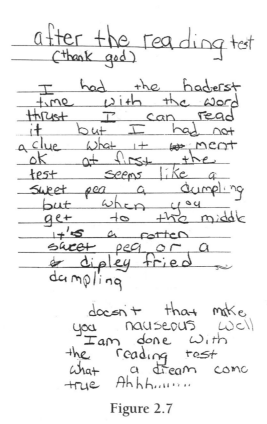

Figure 2.7

I often administer the tests to children who are allowed to have special testing conditions, including a separate location and unlimited time. I was watching Stephanie struggle through a math test. It seemed as if she hadn't turned the page in a long time. When I approached I was stunned to see Stephanie working on a sketch (see Figure 2.8). She explained that the problem was about four clowns who each had two balloons. Stephanie was doing what she knows best to solve this math problem. How could the blacken-the-circle answer sheet, sent off to a strange place to be scored, ever reveal what we as a community know about Stephanie? (See additional thoughts on standardized testing in Chapter 6, "Talking Curriculum and Assessment.")

The Nightmare of Scheduling Pullout Programs

Notice, please, that I didn't say "the nightmare of pullout programs," but rather "the nightmare of *scheduling* pullout programs." When we have a wonderful resource room teacher, speech teacher, English as a second language teacher, teacher of the hearing impaired, teacher of the visually impaired, and teacher specializing in early intervention, our educators are willing to send their students off into the hands of another caring colleague. Problems occur, of course, if students, teachers, parents, and administrators don't have confidence in the specialist. This problem falls into the

Figure 2.8

principal's hands as well as the hands of the district office staff. We must do whatever it takes to ensure that all instruction is of the highest quality. We need to be as fussy about our specialists as we are about our classroom teachers.

Assuming that all teachers are personally and philosophically in tune, the problem of scheduling remains a real one. Earlier, I shared my displeasure with pulling children out of class for reading tutorials in my office. I repeat this concern here. It's near to impossible to do whole language if you never have your whole class together. This has implications not just for the scheduling of the support services described previously but also for the scheduling of such things as chorus, band, or chess club. Yes, children need opportunities for one-on-one and small-group instruction, but they also deserve to take part in all aspects of their classroom life. Our young inspirational writer was correct when she said, "The thing I hate about life is, wherever I go I miss something." What is a day like for the child who receives two or three of those special services? How does he ever feel like one of the guys?

I appreciate that some students do need special services. But I also appreciate that all teachers need their doors to stop opening and closing constantly. To that end, perhaps school communities need to consider any one of the following options:

- Utilizing more push-in programs in which the specialist works within the regular classroom rather than pullout ones.
- Staggering work hours for specialist teachers—perhaps they can start early or stay late, so that some children are serviced before or after school.

- Capping the number of special services that any one child can receive during a set time frame, creating an off-again, on-again system.
- Scheduling pullout programs so that students aren't missing the same class work all the time.
- Clustering services, so that a child may leave for support that has been chunked rather than spread out over each day. In other words, a child might receive English as a second language help only three mornings a week, for longer periods, rather than miss class every single day.
- Coordinating the work of all specialists in the building so that they are taking clusters of children from the same room at the same time, thereby allowing the classroom teacher to remain with a small group of students. The classroom teacher would then be able to provide her own regularly scheduled small-group instruction. (This could be thought of as the "If you can't beat them, join them," school of scheduling.)

Earlier, I complained that I was not in control of who or what enters our school. It's also true that I have no control over who does *not* enter our building. It would be wonderful to have a full-time administrative assistant, nurse, librarian, and guidance counselor. Years ago, I shared with our superintendent a very short wish list that I had for our school. My list contained only three items. First, I'd love a full-time secretary. (In the early years of our school, we weren't big enough to warrant a full-time secretary. Then, due to budget cuts, we couldn't afford one for awhile.) Next, I'd love a full-time parent educator. I'm not referring to a social worker, but rather someone who could help parents understand our way of teaching and at the same time help parents discover important ways to help their children at home. If graduate schools offered master's degrees in parent education, I know a lot of teachers who would apply. Of course, there are no funds for such a "luxury." The last item on my list takes into account the "baker's dozen" concept. For example, in New York, when you buy a dozen bagels, you get one free. I think the same principle should apply to our schools. For every twelve teachers you need to hire, you're allotted one more free of charge. Imagine how different our school lives would be if there were someone on staff who could give teachers the occasional white space they need. A deeper look at what teachers really need is the subject of the chapter that follows, "Honoring Teachers."

The Role of Principal Rethought

Not too long ago, in a lead for our column in *The New Advocate*, I commented on the image of the school principal in pop culture, and the myth that children hate going to school. In part, I wrote,

Perhaps my current role makes me overly sensitive, but I don't think I would be laughing as hard today if I were to watch the incompetent principals in reruns of *Our Miss Brooks* or *Welcome Back Kotter*. Today's *Faculty Lounge* also presents silly people doing trivial things. I'd hate school too, if the grown-ups acted in these ridiculous ways. It's easy to imagine a school as a setting for a situation comedy, but not because the people who work there are idiots.

I continue by noting that children's writers as well often feed into this unfortunate treatment of schools and the grown-ups who work there. I state, "Several current and popular picture books also describe children who feel the need to sneak by the principal's office, out of fear of bumping into the dreaded leader of the school." In my next life, when I retire from this role of principal, I have sketchy plans for a series of children's books whose heroes are teachers and their principal. These kinds of stories will be seen as realistic to most students, and I think they are long overdue.

RELATED READINGS IN COMPANION VOLUMES

Lifetime Guarantees (Heinemann, forthcoming), will be abbreviated as LG.
Writing Through Childhood (Heinemann, forthcoming), will be abbreviated as WC.

Needing a primer on writing process	**WC**: Ch. 1-11.
	LG: Ch. 2-5.
Understanding alternative assessment	**WC**: Ch. 8.
	LG: Ch. 8.
Learning to read	**LG**: Ch. 6, Ch. 7, Ch. 8, and Ch. 9.
Understanding invented spelling	**WC**: Ch. 6.
Pronouncing names accurately	**LG**: Ch. 10.
Creating interactive bulletin boards	**WC**: Ch. 9.
Sharing areas of expertise	**LG**: Ch. 4.
Enriching students' drafts	**WC**: Ch. 4, Ch. 5.
Writing about the lost and found	**LG**: Ch. 3.
Expecting principals to teach	**WC**: Ch. 5, Ch. 7.
Covering classes by sharing literature	**WC**: Ch. 5.
Tapping students' interests in animals	**LG**: Ch. 3, Ch. 4.
Reading the newspaper	**LG**: Ch. 3, Ch. 4.
Tutoring struggling children	**LG**: Ch. 9.
Selecting reading materials	**LG**: Ch. 9.
Decorating ideas based on literacy	**LG**: Ch. 1.
Learning a second language	**LG**: Ch. 10.
Writing to improve school-life	**LG**: Ch. 3.

Reporting on student council	**LG**: Ch. 3.
Serving as literacy model	**WC**: Ch. 3, Ch. 4.
Demonstrating adult literacy	**WC**: Ch. 3.
	LG: Ch. 6, Ch. 9.
Playing with language	**LG**: Ch. 1, Ch. 10.
Decorating with books	**LG**: Ch. 1.
Keeping writing on the front burner	**WC**: Ch. 11.
	LG: Ch. 7.
Understanding standardized testing	**WC**: Ch. 8.
	LG: Ch. 8.

CHAPTER 3

HONORING TEACHERS

Priorities

- Keep the focus on what teachers really need—compliments, respect for their differences, tranquility, professional colleagues, and opportunities to lead scholarly lives.
- Remember that there is no one way to run a successful classroom and that, in a context of commonly held, broad beliefs, it is important to value idiosyncrasies and diversity.

Practice

- On students and parents paying tribute to teachers
- On writing formal teacher observations
- On viewing differences as a strength, not a weakness
- On talking to parents about teacher differences
- On providing teachers with emotional support
- On providing teachers with an environment condusive to teaching and learning
- On going to the source and finding out what staff members need

Our friend Hindy List has an unusual name. Several years ago a children's book was published entitled *Miss Hindy's Cats*. Hindy was terribly excited and bought several copies of the book as gifts to give to family and close friends. She still keeps one propped up on her piano at home. One evening, Hindy called me to share a startling phone call she had received. She had been leading a workshop at Teachers College, and a woman noticed her named in the institute brochure. The woman had known a Hindy List in her childhood. She looked up her telephone number in the Manhattan directory. She called to ask, "Are you the Hindy List who used to work in a dentist's office in Brooklyn when you were a teenager?" Sure enough, it was our Hindy. The woman went on to explain how she always remembered Hindy because she was so nice to the children that came to the dentist. "I was around eight, you were around eighteen," the woman, named Helena Pittman, continued. "I never forgot you." Hindy and Helena chatted for a while and finally Hindy asked, "What do you do today?" "I'm a children's book writer," Helena answered, "In fact several year's ago, I wrote a book called *Miss Hindy's Cats*. Of course, I was thinking about you."

Hindy was working in a dentist's office and had a lifelong effect on someone she hardly knew. How many other young people has she touched through all her years working in schools? How much greater the potential is for all of us working in schools to touch the lives of children who spend so much time with us. Sometimes teachers are lucky enough to hear from former students, and they are always thrilled to find out that they made a difference. No doubt, there are many stories teachers never get to hear. Teachers, in fact, rarely get paid the tributes they deserve.

What Teachers Need

Several years ago, I found myself doing a crossword puzzle in one of those airline magazines. The clue for sixty-seven across, a five-letter word, read, "What teachers need." Many times, I've challenged audiences to guess the answer. The most frequent response I get is "Money!" That is a good response. In Fannie Flagg's book, *Fried Green Tomatoes at the Whistle Stop Café,* the character Evelyn Couch, when taking on her Towanda personality, "dreams of the day when teachers and nurses would make as much as professional ball players." I wonder how many educators clipped and displayed the Esprit ad that appeared in magazines years go. People were asked what they would do to make a better world. Laura Griffith, a New Yorker, responded, "I'd reverse the economic status of celebrities and educators." Money, of course, was not the answer the puzzle creator had in mind. In fact, the answer was "chalk." In the six years that our school has been in existence, no teacher has asked me for chalk. It's the kind of thing that seems to re-generate in our tote bags; we're always able to find a little stub when we need one. Of course, wipe-off boards and dry erase markers have eliminated the use of chalk in our school almost entirely. (The children who want to draw on our concrete playgrounds occasionally ask me for thick pastels). It doesn't surprise me that someone would think teachers need chalk. People are often mistaken about what teachers need.

I once attended a meeting in which the chair asked those attending, "What do your reading teachers need?" One woman responded, "A thing box. You know, like if they're teaching *The Pearl*, there would be an oyster shell or a rubber scorpion in the box." Teachers don't need props. They don't need principals willing to sit in vats of Jell-O or wear their pajamas to work in order to motivate students to read. They don't need teachers' manuals filled with red-lettered scripts telling them what to say and how to say it. They don't need bureaucratic memos and statistical reports informing them whether or not outsiders think their students are growing as readers, writers, and mathematicians. They don't need lots of "feel-good" gifts and jingles. I once began a school newsletter column with the following thought:

> Every once in a while I receive in the mail an announcement for some Teacher's Recognition Day contest or a brochure of gift items for celebrating such an event. The advertisement is filled with cheery, pro-teacher "goodies"—badges, notepads, bumper stickers, and other decorative items covered with the inevitable apples, alphabets, and rulers. I've never understood how these gifts can ever say what needs to be said to teachers. There is no profession I admire more. There is no profession I would prefer to call my own.

There are lots of things that teachers don't need; likewise, there are lots of important things they do. (See summary worksheet in Appendix 7.)

Compliments

Teachers do need compliments. They do need to know they're valued and appreciated. One year, our local Seattle Bean coffee shop paid tribute to teachers by announcing on their September calendar, on the very first day of school, "Welcome Back! Teachers drink free today." We were all so touched, and it was just a cup of coffee. Good coffee, but nonetheless, just a cup of coffee.

One year, I received an invitation to attend an award ceremony for the children's writer Karen Hesse. I passed the invitation on to Pat Werner, then a part-time teacher in our school. After attending the celebration, Pat sent me the following gracious letter.

3/20/98

Dear Shelley,

Thank you for inviting me to attend the presentation to Karen Hesse. I walked into a sun-filled many-windowed Penthouse room with five round tables outfitted with cloth and flowers and napkins with ribbons around them. I felt like I was the award winner!

We were fed quiche and sausages and fruit and French toast and croissants and . . . I even had my seat pulled out for me and my tea poured! We drank champagne in honor of Karen. It was quite magical to be part of it.

I sat with a woman who asked if I'd written any books and she predicted I would . . . in time.

Karen Hesse brought tears to my eyes when she spoke of Scott O'Dell's influence on her. She hadn't prepared a speech and was "terrified" because authors are used to revising what they say.

She was disarming in her honesty (she admitted that she went shopping instead of attending the recording of her book), and charming in her humility. She reminded us that although she wrote of utterly desperate times, there was life ever hopeful. There was Ma's apple trees and Pa's pond—from dust we come—out of the dust comes life.

Gratefully,
Pat

If only I could pay tribute to all the teachers on staff by providing occasions to have their seat pulled out and their tea poured! Don't they all deserve to feel like award winners? Don't they all need to hear from students, parents, and administrators just how much they are valued?

Tributes from Students and Parents   Teachers benefit immensely from receiving fan mail from their students (see Figures 3.1 and 3.2).

Parents, too, need to pay tribute to teachers. At our school, parents show their appreciation for teachers in lots of ways. They bring in homemade delicacies, they invite teachers to celebrations in their homes, they handmake gifts, they stop in to thank them for taking such fine care of their children. At the end of each year, our parents also host an outdoor reception in our teachers' honor. They organize a potluck dinner, toast all the teachers, and usually create a song parody in their honor.

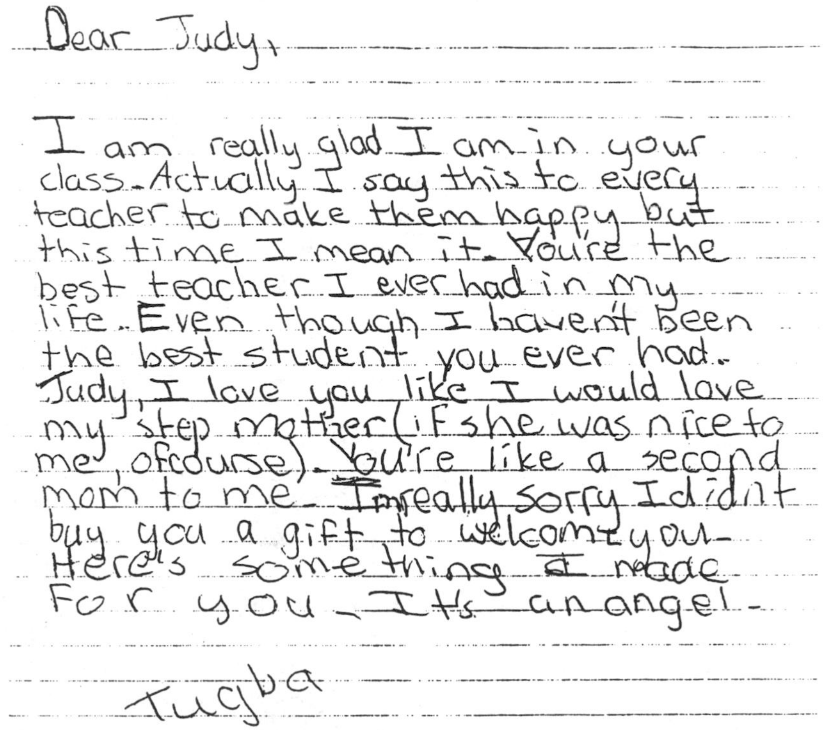

> Dear Judy,
>
> I am really glad I am in your class. Actually I say this to every teacher to make them happy but this time I mean it. You're the best teacher I ever had in my life. Even though I haven't been the best student you ever had. Judy, I love you like I would love my step mother (if she was nice to me, ofcourse). You're like a second mom to me. I'm really sorry I didn't buy you a gift to welcome you. Here's something I made. For you. It's an angel.
>
> Tugba

Figure 3.1

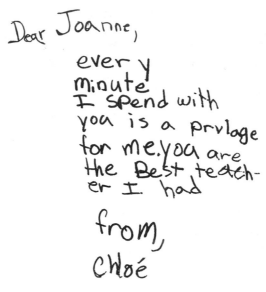

Dear Joanne,
every minute I spend with you is a prvloge for me. you are the Best teach-er I had

from,
Chloé

Figure 3.2

In addition, just as Tugba and Chloé have done, they send notes and letters thanking teachers for a job well done. Last year, we received a six-page letter addressed to the Manhattan New School from Kathy Hipple, mother of Samantha, who was join-ing Lorraine Shapiro's class as a first-grader. In part, Kathy writes,

> Having left a school infused with a moral responsibility to the larger world, I expected to feel the loss. Instead, Lorraine's Old World Testament sense of justice and right and wrong infused the classroom with profound respect and compassion for each student. Meetings between students taught six-year-olds how to resolve conflict. Once while ice-skating af-ter school, Samantha, Isabelle, and Riri began to bicker about who could skate the best. They called a brief meeting, huddled. Then returned to the ice, their argument settled . . .
>
> Respect for all children from other cultures starts with Lorraine. At a parents' meeting Lorraine consoled a Polish father who was unable to help his daughter learn to read Eng-lish because his own is so limited. "Is Paulina learning Polish at home?" asked Lorraine. "Then you are giving her the greatest gift. Leave the English to me. This is what America is all about."
>
> Lorraine honestly believes that each child's growth and achievement in the classroom is earth-shattering, awesome, or at least deserving of a pat on the back (which she teaches the children to do to themselves). Her enthusiasm and her genuine belief that children have special gifts caught me by surprise. Often she seemed more excited by Samantha's accomplishments than I was . . .
>
> Besides reading and writing, everything Samantha explores in first grade she enthusias-tically brings home. When she studied seeds, every single pot or pan was enlisted as a seed-growing container. When she studied architecture, every cardboard box became part of an elaborate house. When she learned chopstick weaving, she wanted to order Chinese food every night for the chopsticks. Which was good, because seeds were growing in all the pots . . .

Lucky for us, Kathy wrote this as an open letter to all the members of our school community. We all felt honored, not just to call Lorraine a colleague, but for the compliment Kathy was paying to the teaching profession.

Last year a parent, whose two daughters had had a wonderful year at our school, passed me in the hall and called out, "You're like a genius." She was referring to my ability to bring so many incredible educators together under one roof. In a similar way, I need to call out to teachers their genius-like talents and abilities. I need to find many ways to pay tribute to the talents of our teaching staff. Sometimes I attempt to honor my colleagues by tucking pro-teacher clippings and articles into their mailboxes. My all-time favorite compliment came from Natalie Babbitt, who in a *HornBook Magazine* article entitled "Beacons of Light" challenged the statement, "Those who can, do. Those who can't, teach." She writes, "I would like to correct the old saying which is long overdue for a rewrite. Let it read, 'Those who can, teach. Those who can't, be grateful for those who can.'"

Each year I receive appreciative letters from prospective parents after they have toured our school. Unfortunately, they are usually addressed to me, but of course they are not for my eyes only. They really deserve to be read by the entire staff, so I hang them publicly for all to see. What a shame it would be if every teacher didn't have the opportunity to bask in the following tribute crafted by a neighborhood parent, Jennifer Brown.

This morning you changed my mind about what public education could be.

I have passed your building for years now. First as an expectant mother, then with a baby carriage, and now as a prospective parent. I have peeked through the windows wondering what exactly was going on inside, listened to the playground buzz about the new school, and interviewed some moms I've met. This morning, as I pulled those doors open, I was immediately struck by your extraordinary school. I've always trusted my instincts, that little voice inside, and when making big decisions I've learned if there's no spark, if your heart kind of sinks, move on. But this morning I fell in love. The tremendous respect and concern for the children and the teachers was unlike any other school I have toured.

I saw a kindergarten class where a large wooden block hotel had just crashed to the floor leaving one lone tower with a sign "rooms 10$, fancy rooms 20$." When asked what a fancy room included I was informed that I'd get video games and a computer. Nice touch. Too late to book a room, a small boy approached the teacher, presenting her with a paper person he had taped to a block. We suggested his "guy" take a tour of the city while construction began again. I think my favorite moment was a pause in a second-grade science class (yes, I lost the tour) and an extensive conversation with Sam. He allowed me to read what he had observed when he looked through the jug of water on the table. He had written, "stars, fur" (a great combination, I thought). When I held up the jug in front of my face he jumped in, thanked me, and added "face" to the growing list. He then took me by the arm to show me a variety of materials under a magnifying glass, told me what he had recently learned about astronomy, and introduced me to the animals in the classroom. When I told him I had to leave he asked me to meet him there, same time and place, again. I considered a career change all the way back to work . . .

Nods from the Principal   My colleagues always appreciate articles and letters such as those, but they also need and deserve individual praise and attention.

I suppose I could compliment teachers individually, by telling them what I see in them each time I enter their rooms. I probably don't do this often enough. What principal does?

I hope I've told Eve Mutchnick how I love to watch her sing with her students, how I've never seen a teacher more at home dancing, clapping, whistling, and swaying with her students, and I don't know of any educator with as wide a repertoire of cool songs and chants. I hope I've told Kevin Tallat-Kelpsa that he is a master at creating a serene class environment, in which he gently but seriously nudges his students to do more than they themselves thought possible. I hope I've told Karen Ruzzo that it is a joy to watch her respond to children. No one has a more engaging smile or shares more genuine laughter. She has made it so easy for the children in room 401 to feel good about themselves. I hope I've told Paula Rogovin how much I'm awed by her ability to welcome the community into her classroom. It's no surprise that her first graders interview over forty people a year. I hope I've told Sharon Hill that her ability to create community shines through every moment of her teaching day. When anyone in her classroom speaks, everyone listens respectfully. I hope I've told Renay Sadis how good she is at putting two hands on her students' shoulders and telling them in honest and forthright ways how they need to tow the line and never settle for less than the best that they can do.

I hope Pam Mayer knows that I'm in awe of all the fresh thinking that is evident in her classroom. How did she think of asking families to include a bouquet of fresh flowers when it is their turn to bring weekly snacks to the kindergarten? How did she think of starting an exchange of outgrown winter coats with her students? How did she think of preparing a cassette recording of herself reading aloud all the children's favorite books, making twenty-five copies of it, and then giving them out as end-of-term gifts to her students? How did she begin the custom of sketching the outline of the children's snack portions on the butcher-block paper that covers her snack table and labeling each shape? Each day her students know just how many crackers, rice cakes, or carrot sticks they are welcome to eat. And all the while they're developing number sense, one-to-one correspondence as well as sight vocabulary.

Similarly, I wonder how Joan Backer thought of designing those perfect wooden boxes to hold paperbacks, face forward, on all her bookcase shelves, and then convinced the local cabinetmaker to size and cut slats so that her students could build these homemade book boxes? How did Regina Chiou think of putting on that floppy black velvet hat with the big daisy on the side whenever she wants her students to know that she can't be interrupted? How did Layne and Eve think of filling kindergarten sand tables with thousands of buttons from the garment center? How did Denise think to hang small bulletin boards on hinges over open storage shelves to hide classroom supplies?

I also pay tribute to teachers by taking pen in hand. Sometimes I do so in a light-hearted way, as in the following flier I sent to each faculty member.

Top Ten Visitor's Comments at the Manhattan New School

"Where did you get all these books?"

"Don't you have discipline problems?"

"The kids are so involved, they don't even look up when we walk in."

"Who does all the art?"

"The classrooms look like libraries."

"The classrooms look like living rooms."

"The teachers are all so wonderful."

"The kids seem so kind to each other."

"There's so much to look at."

"How can I get a job here?"

"How can I bring my child here?"

One morning, after listening to the morning news, a poem began to dance around in my head. I worked on it a bit and then shared it with my colleagues, as a means of congratulating them for the wise career choice they each had made.

Tribute to Teaching

"What wakes you up
in the morning?"
the survey read.
Is it really that
annoying drone
of the alarm clock?
Or do you depend on
a strong cup of coffee,
a stinging cold shower,
a can of caffeined Coke?
All of the above?

No, what jolts me—
what really gets me going
is the morning news.

A bombing in Jerusalem.
An abused child in Brooklyn.
Corruption in Washington.

A riot in South Africa.
A killing in Croatia.
A murder in our neighborhood.

I'm up now, really up.
Eager to go to work,
Eager to see the honest faces of children,
Eager to lose myself in the important work at hand—
Teaching children to make a better world.

Even when I am not trying to explicitly pay honor to the teaching profession, I try very hard, even in the most mundane correspondence, to let teachers know that I think they have chosen a worthy career. The following is a welcome-back-to-school letter that I sent after a summer break.

September 2, 1997

Dear friends,

As I write this brief welcome-back note, I cross my fingers that our school will not be in total disarray when you all return this morning. As many of you know, it has been a most turbulent summer for this beautiful old building. I have learned more than I really care to know about contractors, sub-contractors, and the School Construction Authority. I have even been accused of micro-managing this work. So be it. The work has been carried out without sufficient planning, communication, respect for property, security, and time management. I am composing quite an elaborate letter to the powers that be. Together with our very fine and funny custodian, Neil, we have our own version of a running record to share.

For now, know that there should be a dozen workers available to help all of us lift, place, dust, polish, hang, move, rearrange, carry, sweep, and otherwise make our rooms as inviting as we know they should be. Do not attempt to clean house yourselves. I will be sending workers to your rooms as soon as they arrive. I am most serious about not asking you to do these out-of-the-ordinary housekeeping tasks.

Do pay careful attention to any damaged, soiled, or missing items. Please give me a list of these and receipts if they are personal possessions. I will get them replaced or you will be reimbursed for new purchases. Also, please write down any concerns you have about the renovations (nails sticking up, damaged tiles, missing patches of paint on the walls, etc.)

I know that people have an inordinate amount of work to do, so we will meet briefly at 2:30, just to talk about a a few essential beginning-of-the-year details.

So a hearty welcome back. Despite the renovation craziness, I know we will have a splendid year. Do stop in to meet and greet the new members of our faculty. David is in 506, Sharon Hill is in 504, Kathy is in 507, and Jennifer is in 402.

There are bagels and coffee in ???? (I have no idea right now where I can set up. Look for a sign.)

Love,
Shelley

The contractors who lived in our schoolhouse during that summer showed no respect for the teachers who worked there. Personal belongings were moved willy-nilly, damaged, and stolen. School property was likewise mishandled. Decisions about color and design were made when no teachers were present. Classrooms were left in chaotic conditions, giving teachers only two days to re-create their beautiful classrooms before their students arrived. Would such things happen to doctors or lawyers who were on summer break? I don't think so, and I can't let such things happen to the professionals I know best. I became enraged and determined to right the wrongs. Teachers shouldn't have to scrape paint off their windows, scrub glue-stained floors, or move heavy bookcases. They have pedagogical things to tend to.

Formal Teacher Observations. I also pay tribute to teachers when I write up those formal observations I am required to do of untenured teachers. I wish I had the time to do this kind of close observation and give as frequent detailed feedback to all staff members. I know I see more in them than they see in themselves. The observation below was of Pam when she was a beginning teacher.

Dear Pam,

It was a real treat for me to sit back and observe a new kindergarten teacher in her first year of teaching. I'm always amazed by early-childhood teachers who can manage to not only succeed at living, learning, and teaching six hours a day in a room filled with twenty-five five-year-olds, but who at the same time seem to take pleasure in all they do. You are certainly just such a teacher.

Your room is so very beautiful. I appreciate the extreme care you take with every sign, poem, and chart you hang. I appreciate how thoughtful you are about room arrangements, curriculum plans, and children's emotional and social well-being. It's no wonder your classroom lights burn so frequently well into the night.

Above all, your teaching is so clear, consistent, and child centered. On the morning I visited, the children were engaged in self-chosen center-time activities. Some were making intricate collages. Some were wearing headsets and swaying to the songs in the listening center. Others were observing the newly arrived guinea pigs, taking part in dramatic play, building in the block area, and painting in carefully prepared cookie-tray workstations.

Several children were surrounding you, learning how to plant cuttings. It was clear that you worked hard to prepare the environment. The work space was lined with newspapers and the children had easy access to all the necessary tools—paper cups, spoons, soil, water, cuttings. I could tell from the calm, content look on your face and the simple, clear directions you offered that you put great trust in the children's ability to accept new challenges. When you left this work area to make your way around the room, I appreciated how easily you handled those children who were experiencing small moments of sadness or discomfort. Throughout, your gentle touch, eye contact, and comforting tone of voice helped children learn how to solve their own problems and to treat one another with respect and caring.

I was particularly enchanted with how you gathered a small group of children to help them get to know the recently arrived guinea pig. From the way you encouraged them to arrange their legs in order to corral the critter in to your instructions for holding the furry creature, "Like in a cup, close to your body," it was clear that you understand and adore five-year-olds.

Each comment you made said a lot about what you believe is important in the lives of young children. The room filled with

"What do you think you can do about it?"

"Ian, can you teach William about planting?"

"Oh Liana, you've never done that before."

"We're observing the guinea pig, finding out what he looks like and how he behaves, so we can pick the right name."

The rich, supportive community you've created has enabled your kindergarten students to take risks, to ask hard questions, to appreciate language and literacy. You've enveloped them in a spirit of learning.

I won't soon forget the smile on your face when Andrej, not realizing you had taken the guinea pig out of the cage, remarked, "Someone stole the Guinea pig!" or when Liam placed the guinea pig in his lap and Imer called out, "Liam is now Santa Claus!"

You are a wonderful asset to the Manhattan New School. I look forward to your participation in many collegial study groups, classroom-intervisitations, and all aspects of school life. Don't ever hesitate to share your struggles and your successes.

With respect for the work you do.

Love,
Shelley

With Pam's permission I've occasionally distributed this observation at workshops, asking participants to read through this letter and list the essential qualities of Pam's teaching that could apply to all teaching situations, no matter the age of the students. Elementary, middle school, and secondary educators, as well as college professors, talked about the need for all teachers to treat students with respect, prepare the environment, make it safe to take risks, follow students' leads, listen attentively to students, marvel at students' insights, create beautiful settings, and offer options in our classrooms.

Additional teacher observations appear in Appendix 8. Whenever I reread formal teacher observations, I realize that I not only want teachers to know their own strengths, but I also want to figure out ways for them to share their talents with the rest of the teaching and learning community.

I not only write to teachers to let them know the power of their teaching, I occasionally remind family members just how privileged I feel to be working alongside such a talented staff. In the fall of 1994, the year of the baseball strike, I wrote the following column for the first newsletter of the school year.

Dear families,

It's that time of year once again—lots of new shoes, new lunch boxes, and new backpacks. And here, at the Manhattan New School, we have lots of new students, new classrooms, and new teachers. All that is missing this September is the World Series. (We'll have to do a lot of reading, writing, and thinking about baseball to fill the void. Maybe even some playing!)

I hope that your summer was all that you hoped it would be, filled with recreation. I traveled quite a bit, working with teachers in England and Ecuador, and closer to home, in Denver, Colorado, and Shaker Heights, Ohio. In the midst of all that, I tucked in a two-week vacation in Alaska.

All those long flights gave me lots of time to read. I recommend Peter Hoeg's Miss Smilla's Sense of Snow, *William Trevor's* Two Lives, *and Frank Conroy's* Body and Soul. *The long flights also gave me time to think about my favorite subject, school. I thought about teaching and learning, of course, but mostly about teachers, our teachers.*

How lucky I felt to be returning to such an accomplished group of educators. Each time I checked in with a colleague, I heard wonderful stories about summertime collegiality, camaraderie, professional development, and our teachers simply enjoying one another's company during their time away from school. Our teachers taught courses together, took courses together, traveled together, planned the new year together, and even relaxed at the shore together. I feel privileged to be in the company of such good friends.

Recently I read a powerful anecdote about Joseph Campbell, the author of The Power of Myth, *which brought our teachers to mind. Campbell had been endlessly searching for a parking spot on the streets of New York City. Finally he found one and began to back in when he spotted a child standing rigid on the curb nearby. "You can't park here," the child called out. "Why not?" Campbell asked. "Can't you see I'm a fire hydrant?" the child responded. And Joseph Campbell drove off.*

No, our teachers would never give up a parking spot, but yes they do believe in children and they do respect their creative processes. Most of all, what marks the educators in our school is a shared belief that it is a privilege to be around children.

Parents have confidence in our teachers not because I send letters like this, but because their children are eager, productive, and successful. My letter just serves as a reminder to members of the community that we need to continually pay tribute to the teaching profession, not with contests, award ceremonies, and bumper stickers, but with the everyday awareness that teaching is a noble and rewarding profession and that exquisite and dedicated teachers deserve our heartfelt gratitude and admiration. It also serves as a reminder to families to be as proud of our teaching staff as we are of our students.

Respect for Differences

One of the biggest lessons I learned since opening this school I gained through rethinking the teaching of writing. It was a revelation to me that there is no *one* way to run a writing workshop. There are twenty-two classrooms in our school, each taught by a different teacher. Their writing workshops are equally successful and yet incredibly different. Our teachers share many common beliefs, but they clearly are not clones of one another. They have different tools, routines, and writing challenges. Each has a different way of conferring, editing, teaching spelling, publishing, and so on. I have learned to take great delight in seeing all the different ways teachers can create successful writing workshops. What cuts across them is that each teacher really listens to children, and the children are empowered to tell the truths of their lives. I've become incredibly tolerant in the teaching of writing. Teachers don't have to do it *my* way. (See companion volume *Writing Through Childhood.*)

Valuing Idiosyncrasies   In an earlier chapter I talked about substitute teachers who attempted to get their students' attention by blowing whistles and holding "quiet contests," pitting the boys against the girls. These teachers didn't have the big picture. We found their strategies to be unnatural, sexist, and competitive. Our regular crew of substitute teachers understands our ways of teaching and learning and would never choose such devices. There are over two dozen teachers in our building, including our five specialists, and each probably has their own way of controlling volume and their own way of getting their students' attention. (See page 122 for specifics). None insult our shared beliefs about how we want to live our lives.

Not too long ago I was listening to a Sunday-morning news program. The host was asking his guest panelists about the recent Arab-Israeli conflict over the opening of a tunnel at the Western Wall in Jerusalem. The host asked, "Why has the tunnel become such a big issue?" One of the guests, Pulitzer Prize–winning journalist Thomas Friedman offered an explanation. He suggested that when people don't agree on the big things, the little things take on enormous significance. With the previous Israeli leadership, the big understandings were in place and people were willing to ignore annoying loose ends. The controversy over the tunnel took on enormous proportions because the two sides were no longer clear on the big picture.

The same holds true in our teaching lives. I don't have to employ the exact same techniques my colleagues do, because the big understandings are in place. I can respect the differences in our teaching styles because we share broad beliefs about teaching and learning. This concept becomes crystal clear when we work with parents. Parents who have not yet understood the big picture continue to ask about spelling tests, workbook pages, and desks for every child. They can't let go of these requests because they don't yet understand and trust our ways of working.

Just as I have come to realize that there is no one way to run a writing workshop, I have also learned that there is no one way to live your life in a classroom. Isabel Beaton likes to think of our school as a garden in which each teacher is given an individual plot of land. Teachers are not handed an overall design and then assigned little jobs in order to achieve a predetermined effect. Instead, she believes, all the teachers are invited to create very individual gardens. What adds wholeness to our setting is that all of us are gazing in the same direction. We have a set of shared things we value, just as serious gardeners count on the quality of the soil, the sunshine, and abundant rain showers.

Isabel's thinking about our schoolhouse reminds me of the Japanese art form known as Renga. It is poetry composed by improvisation. A group of poets takes turns responding to one another with half stanzas, which, when complete, form a sequence of interlocking but separate poems. We are a sequence of interlocking but separate poems. We respond to one another. We improvise off of one another. We affect one another, but each of us remains true to who we are as human beings.

The wonderful sculptor and printmaker Elizabeth Catlett explains her artistic development by referring to two qualities. She writes, "We work alone but we also work with and for others, and it is expressed by two words: one is 'solitarity,' in which we create out of what is in us, from our innermost feelings, ideas, emotions, knowledge—

all of this combined in other elements; we also create from 'solidarity,' which is what we have gotten from our solidarity with other people." The teachers I know best are shining examples of this artist's beliefs. Each has their own way, and yet each grows and creates as members of a staff that shares a vision of what schools can be for all members of a community.

Some visitors to our school might argue that I can be so inviting of "nonconformity" because each teacher on staff is such an exquisite educator. I would suggest that each of these fine teachers has become so accomplished because they have positioned themselves, throughout their careers, in places where they have been allowed to be themselves in order to do their best work. (Several admit that they have made changes in their professional life because they felt stifled.) As hard as I might try, I can't have well-ordered files and a neat desk and still be the kind of principal that suits me best. It would take me all day every day to be an efficient paper person, and I'd probably have to forfeit my work in classrooms to even become remotely organized. I can't be anyone else. Becoming a very administrative type of principal would be as unnatural for me as straightening my hair, wearing pastels, or becoming an outdoors person. I would feel as if I was walking around in someone else's skin. The same, no doubt, applies to my colleagues.

I once delivered a speech entitled, "Embracing the Eccentric: Valuing Passions, Quirks, and Idiosyncrasies in Our Teaching." I've discovered that classrooms become better places when teachers are encouraged to bring their own personal ways of being into their teaching lives. Isabel lives a quiet, compassionate life, and it shows in her teaching. Paula lives a rich, multi-cultural life, and it shows in her teaching. Regina lives a peaceful, nurturing, scholarly life and it shows in her teaching. When people feel free to bring their personal selves into their classrooms, the sky is the limit. Students get to hang out with honest, open human beings. Students get to know people who have real interests, concerns, and priorities.

Valuing Diversity There is no way to describe the "average" teacher in our school. Several years ago I was asked to contribute to a discussion on teaching in *Whole Language: The Debate*. I wrote,

> Meet the teachers. Some are very new, just beginning their careers. Several have been teaching for over twenty-five years. A few were staff developers who decided to return to classrooms. Some are graduate students. Some attended community colleges; others Ivy League universities.
>
> They're Black, White, Asian-American, Latino.
> They're Catholic, Jewish, Protestant, atheist, and agnostic.
> They're conservative; they're liberal.
> They're meat-eaters; they're vegetarian.
> They have loud voices and soft.
> They have neat rooms and casual ones.
> And yet, they all call themselves Whole Language teachers.

As a school that offers a great deal of staff development to visiting teachers, it becomes important that each visitor find someone to identify with. Everyone can see themselves in this array of diverse teachers. When I hire new teachers I get the Casey Stenghal feel of trying to create a winning team. I am always looking for the wonderful teacher who can bring unique perspectives to our school. How much better schools become when members of the staff represent a mix of ages, backgrounds, strengths, styles, talents, and experiences.

Lorraine, Layne, and Paula are our first-grade teachers. They can't be any more different in teaching styles and interests. I wouldn't be surprised to hear that in one first-grade room the students were studying the work of Ezra Jack Keats, in another A. A. Milne, and in the third, Eloise Greenfield. And I could guess instantly in which rooms these studies were taking place. Similarly, if I received an early-childhood book on architecture, space travel, or civil rights, I'd know who would most appreciate adding each book to their classroom collections. Likewise, I'd know who to *especially* call upon if I had a student struggling with issues of self-esteem, HIV/AIDS, or racial prejudice. Teachers do follow their students' areas of interest, but they never leave who they are outside their classroom doors. They themselves have unique areas of interest. They are very different. And I wouldn't have it any other way.

The doors to the first-grade classrooms seem to announce the diversity in teacher styles. Layne's is covered with a bulletin board labeled, "Why is First Grade Cool?" followed by students' written responses to the question in engaging invented spelling. The remainder of the door is covered with student doodles in vibrant marker colors sketched directly on the wooden door. Lorraine's door has twenty-seven teacher-made balloon shapes filled with the name of each of her students. A sign announces the architects-in-residence that visit the class regularly. Paula's door has a welcome sign in both Spanish and English, a request for school workers to volunteer for class interviews, photographs of community scenes, and the names of her student teachers. Their daily agenda boards further confirm that although all children will be working in the same disciplines, their teachers' ways of organizing the day will be markedly different.

Even when it comes to the teaching of reading and writing, Lorraine, Layne, and Paula have very different methods. They all use real literature in their reading workshops and all their students participate in daily writing workshops, but their routines, materials, and ways of working with children are markedly different. That's okay too. Lorraine is fussy about commercially prepared emergent reader materials. There are publishers she appreciates, others she avoids. She uses very little whole class shared reading materials. Layne relies heavily on teaching reading through multiple copies of carefully selected trade books, with very little reliance on packaged sets. She relies heavily on creating original shared reading materials for use with the whole class. Paula's main source of reading material in her first-grade classroom are homemade books based on children's interview notes and duplicated for each student. She also relies heavily on poetry and song as shared reading experiences. These three first-grade teachers combined have over *seventy* years of teaching experience. Each has developed her own comfortable way of helping children learn to read and write and care about reading and writing. All their first graders leave prepared to meet the challenges of second-grade life. All three teachers are interesting, compassionate human beings, who may not do what one another does, but who respect and appreciate the diversity that exists. (See page 250, on "Airing Differences Respectfully.") Each is interested in visiting one another's classroom, allowing the solitarity that comes from within and the solidarity that comes from being part of a team to enrich and inform the work they do.

Our teachers' styles *throughout* the grades vary, but this need not imply a hodge-podge quality of teaching in our school. In the book *Whole Language: The Debate*, I explain,

> When I interview prospective teachers, I always ask them how they teach reading. If a teacher says, "I use what works, use whatever works," I quickly show them to the door.
>
> Workbooks work. Xerographed activity sheets work. Trivial questions at the end of chapters work. Story-starters work. They're all great behavior-management tools (weapons!) They all keep children at their seats, silent and busy.
>
> Not everything that works is good. Children who become hooked on phonics get a deceptive picture of what reading is. Children who read watered-down texts get used to them. Poor quality texts become the given. Children who must answer endless, inane questions after reading get a dangerous view of response to reading.
>
> If "eclectic" means using phonics kits, flash cards, and laminated fill-in-the-blank passages, alongside a shelf of library books, I'm not interested. Loving to read is a high priority in our school building. We can't risk mixed messages. We can't afford to allow even one child to get turned off. From the very first day of school, all students need to understand what it means to read.
>
> If, on the other hand, eclectic means pulling alongside a child, employing lots of ways to discover the student's strengths and weaknesses, having a wide range of high quality texts and genres, offering a multitude of reading strategies, and orchestrating flexible social groupings for reading response, then I'm all for it.

Talking to Parents About Teacher Differences   When staffs are filled with teachers representing a wide range of teaching styles, you would expect that my office each June becomes filled with parents making requests for their children's next year's class placement. Our parents have learned, however, that I don't ever take requests for students to be placed in specific teachers' rooms, nor do I ever make changes after the teachers make class placement decisions. I explain to family members when they first join our school that I trust that every teacher on staff is wonderful and that children will profit from living with all kinds of mentors during the six years in which they study with us. I further explain that I should not, can not, and will not mandate that teachers teach in exactly the same way. Some teachers love to sing, work with volunteers, tell funny jokes, do messy projects, and others simply do not. I remind incoming parents of the obvious—"Teachers are people and people have different tastes, interests, talents, preferences, and personalities." And we do not match students to our teachers' personalities. Instead, each June our teachers create new class rosters, making sure that every class has a mosaic of students with varying interests, needs, strengths, cultural backgrounds, and languages. As they fill these new rooms, teachers also take into account social relationships, making sure that every child will be with a few old friends in the year ahead.

Tranquility

In *Lasting Impressions: Weaving Literature into the Writing Workshop*, I suggested that after selecting the finest teachers, my work would continue with building in many areas of support. That support includes caring for one another emotionally. Since our school has opened we have helped one another through the death of a parent, the breakup of a marriage, serious surgery, as well as the hospitalization of a child. Of course, we have also been there for such joyous occasions as engagements, weddings, births of new sons and daughters, grandsons and granddaughters. Schools have to be places where teachers can live their personal lives as well as their professional ones. We spend too many hours together for us not to take care of one another. Several years ago, Gretel Ehrlich wrote a wonderful book called *The Solace of Open Spaces*. Teachers should be able to write a book called *The Solace of Scholarly Spaces*.

Providing Emotional Support   Of course we are there for each other during big, life-changing times, but we are also there for each other for everyday upsets and sorrows. When our car gets towed, our mortgage falls through, or our wallet gets stolen, we know someone will be there with a warm hug, some friendly advice, and probably a bouquet of fresh flowers. This holds true for school-related sorrows. We need to be there for one another when we're helping a student and his family through a crisis, when we have to report a family to the child welfare offices, or when we have disappointments with students, their families, or with our colleagues.

There is no one on staff who wouldn't help a struggling colleague. When teachers have real emergencies, they need to know that their colleagues will make it possible for them to walk out the door and that their students will be well cared for. No questions asked, no proof required. Teachers work hard. They deserve tranquil settings. Students work hard. They deserve calm, stress-free teachers.

I like to think that the way we live our life at school enables and encourages people to be there for one another. I also like to think that I have a role in setting the emotional tone. Although I don't see myself at the top of any pyramid of authority or influence around our school, I have been in schools where negative elements in an administrator's personality affect the way people treat one another. Principals who don't trust teachers create teachers who need to look over their shoulders. Principals who pit one group of teachers against another create social cliques marked by competition and tension. The reverse must also be true. When principals have unconditional love, trust, and respect for their colleagues, it becomes much easier to create calm, peaceful settings.

Administrators have to be willing to make it possible for teachers to make important calls to doctors in the middle of the day, run out to take care of banking mishaps, or bring their failing car in to be serviced. When we meet a student at the supermarket on the weekend and they look up at us with disbelief in their eyes, we know that they just don't conceive of us actually having a life outside of school. Well we do, and just like everyone else, every once in awhile we need to tie up our loose ends. Teaching is the only profession in which we are "on" every minute we are at work. Lawyers are not in the courtroom all day, every day; surgeons are not wearing sterile gowns every minute they are at work. Occasionally and legitimately, teachers need to step away from their classrooms during school hours. Life happens.

When my son was younger, depending on whether or not the Yankees won that day's ball game, I knew whether we would have joyful or somber talk at dinner. Baseball outcomes were a barometer in our home. This kind of moodiness has no place in a school. Administrators can't blow hot, then cold. They can't be mellow, then maniacal.

I make a deliberate effort not to seem overwhelmed. When teachers come to me with concerns, I often suggest, "Don't worry, we'll take care of it." I try not to raise my voice or lose my temper. Even though I speak and act quickly, I try not to demonstrate a lot of frenetic energy. (My peak time of obvious overload is standardized testing time.) Then too, administrators must retain enough emotional energy to take part in all the hugging, advising, and giving of flowers. (See related thoughts in Chapter 4, "Making the Social Tone Top Priority.")

Professional Colleagues

New York City teachers don't make very much money. In fact, if they were to move to some of the wealthier suburban districts, a half hour away, they would bring home up to twenty thousand dollars more each year in salary, plus they would have only twenty children in their classes instead of the usual thirty. City schools must be offering something very special. Otherwise, more and more wonderful educators would be ready to give up the commuting headaches, the parking nightmares, the security precautions, and the layers of big-city bureaucratic red tape. We do offer special things. At the Manhattan New School, teachers appreciate the diversity of our student population, the easy access to the city's cultural resources, and the energy and vitality of city kids' lives. Some, no doubt, stay because they want to give back to the public school system that has been so good to them and to their own children. Most of all, I think our teachers stay because they are thrilled to be working alongside their chosen colleagues.

Several wonderful teachers have left our school. Elizabeth Servidio married and moved out of state. Julie Liebersohn moved to the suburbs to start her own family. Dawn Harris Martine left to work wonders, teaching young adults. Kevin Tallat-Kelpsa became a staff developer in mathematics. Only one teacher left because we asked her to. She wasn't the right choice to work with our very special youngsters, and I spent six months writing reports, making sure those students would get the kind of high-quality teacher they deserved. We have also been through a revolving door of part-time specialists, partly because our school had been too small to warrant full-time English as a second language or resource room teachers. (It is comforting to now have wonderful permanent teachers in place.) We've also hired lots of part-time subject specialists over the years—music, storytelling, science, physical education, art, computer teachers, and the like. Today, the teachers who become full-time are the teachers we fall in love with. They're not only brilliant educators, but they understand our way of living as a school community. We're very fussy about who joins our community. We have to be. Not only do our students and parents deserve fabulous teachers, so do we. It's the professional community that keeps our colleagues from packing their bags and heading for the rolling hills of Westchester.

In addition, two teachers chose to leave our school because they didn't feel ready to be here at that point in their personal and professional lives. When Jeanne Francis decided to take a leave of absence after only one year in our school, she eloquently explained her decision to me. She and her family had just moved to the suburbs and the commute from eastern Long Island into the city each day was too much for her. "With the new house, new job, new commute, I couldn't give it my all," she said. "I couldn't get here early and I couldn't stay late. This place is very special. I'm sorry this wasn't the time in my life to be a full participant in the life of the school." Some people have admiringly called our school "teacher heaven." Jeanne reminds us just how exhausting teacher heaven can be. Jeanne's honesty and integrity pushed her to make this important professional decision. It's clear that our community makes public that we not only have high standards for our students, we have high standards for each other.

Jamie Chaet left for a very different reason. This new young teacher wasn't sure that she wanted to stick with teaching, and she felt sure that she wasn't ready to teach in the company of such an overwhelming cluster of experienced and dedicated teachers. Although we have supported several beginning teachers through their first years of teaching, Jamie felt she needed to work her way up to teaching in such a successful setting. She sent us the following thank-you note.

Dear Shelley and everyone,

I wanted to send you a little note of appreciation to thank you all for all that you taught me in my first year of teaching. After starting out this school year in a "great job" not related to teaching, it wasn't long before I realized how much I missed working with children. I quit my job and now I'm back in the classroom, working almost every day as a substitute teacher at a school in the Bronx. The school is in a difficult neighborhood but the kids are the best and I do really like it there!

I am sure you all know from past teaching experiences what some schools are like compared to the Manhattan New School. It's sad to see broken windows in classrooms, children sitting at name-tagged desks, no integrated curriculum, no listening, math, or other centers in the classrooms, few big books or nonfiction, classrooms with barely enough books to fill a bookcase, textbooks and whole-class readers instead of good literature, a pretty bad school library, not nearly enough math manipulatives etc.

I want to tell you how glad I am that I was given the chance to learn from all of you be-cause I feel like I am bringing so many great teaching ideas into the classrooms. If I hadn't been so fortunate to learn from all of you, I would not know how to make such a difference with children in a traditional school. (I hope I am, I mean.) Maybe this sounds a little con-ceited (but I mean it not in an arrogant way, just in a sort of proud-of-myself-as-a-teacher way), but I feel like I'm doing a great thing for these children, which makes me feel great. I have all of you to thank for this.

When I go into those traditional classrooms, I have the children push back the desks so we can all sit together on the floor. I give them time to just read for enjoyment. I have them work in groups, write about math, and make classroom books where they are all the au-thors. (I am hoping I won't get into trouble for teaching this way, but the absent teacher or preps I cover don't leave me any plans anyway. Plus, if it turns into a full-time regular teaching position, I hope I can teach like this.) Also I read aloud to them constantly and it feels like they just can't get enough of hearing stories. (You taught me the importance of constantly reading to children.)

I know I still have so much to learn about teaching, but I honestly would not be the teacher I am today without all of the teachers at the Manhattan New School. I always knew your school was special, but I think I am able to appreciate it more. I am able to now compare it with other schools and other ways of teaching. The students at the Manhattan New School are incredibly lucky.

Again, thanks a million for everything. As I pass through the next twenty or thirty years teaching, I will never ever forget where I got started and how much knowledge I took with me from my first year of teaching.

I wish you and the school many, many years of continued support and success!

Thanks again.

With sincere appreciation,
Jamie

Jamie's letter moved us all. Although we wished we could have convinced her to stay, we were delighted to see that she had returned to teaching. And she returned with very strong convictions in her heart.

An Environment Conducive to Teaching—And Learning   Early in my teaching ca-reer when I ran a reading/writing workshop with special education youngsters, some visitors would say, "Sure you can do it, you only have eight students." Later, when I taught a room filled with thirty-four children labeled "gifted and talented," some visi-tors would say, "Sure you can do it, the kids are all gifted and talented." Likewise, some visitors to our school say, "Sure you can do it, look who is teaching there."

As previously noted, I make no apologies for having wonderful teachers. My main responsibility as a building administrator is to fill that building with the best teachers I can hire and work toward improving or removing teachers who do not meet our high standards. (If I were the principal of a school whose staff had a more uneven ability to teach effectively, joyfully, and exquisitely, I would have to spend a great deal more of my time gently coaching teachers into change or gently encouraging teachers to move on to different settings or different careers.) Most of our teachers were hired because they were wonderful to begin with; some grew up with us and became wonderful because they were wrapped in support. All principals hire new teachers, and they all need to search for the best. But just as filling classrooms with wonderful books doesn't guarantee that all children will read, filling schools with talented teachers is not the end of our responsibility. If we want to keep our carefully chosen colleagues happy, we need to invent ways for them to continually learn from one another. I wouldn't be upset if visitors to our school would say, "Sure you can do it, look who is teaching there," if only they would add, "Look who is teaching and learning there."

Scholarly Lives

Sixty-seven across, a five-letter word—What teachers need. I didn't guess "money." My answer was "space." I used to work in a university setting. And what made that setting an especially enticing one for the teachers who left their classrooms to work as staff developers was, first of all, the physical space. There, teachers had a room with a desk and a file cabinet, a word processor and a Xerox machine that worked all the time. They had easy access to journal articles and a Rolodex filled with experts' phone numbers. In addition to this scholarly physical space, teachers had a bit of white space in their busy lives. There was a simple structure built in, so that once a week, people got together to reflect on what they were teaching and learning.

Now that I'm back in an elementary school full time, I know that classroom teachers don't have to be in university settings to lead scholarly lives. All schools can be settings of scholarship. I tell prospective parents, "If this is a good place for teachers, it will be a good place for students. If the adults in this building feel alive and growing, so will your children." I once heard a radio commercial for Mercedes-Benz. The announcer was listing oxymorons, and included "student-teacher." He couldn't have been more wrong. Aren't we all students and teachers at the same time? And if we are not, shouldn't we aim for this noble goal?

In *Lasting Impressions: Weaving Literature into the Writing Workshop,* I describe the business card I give to all members of our staff. On it is a quote from Maimonides. It reads, "I've learned much from my teachers, more from my colleagues, but most from my students." The truth is, it takes time, space, and a real commitment to adult learning to guarantee that we will continue to learn from our teachers, our colleagues, and our students. Attention to adult learning is especially difficult to provide in times of severe budget cuts. It is much easier to create moments of white space in teachers' lives when you have some money to spare. Several years ago, I heard Robert Spillane, the superintendent of schools in Fairfax, Virginia, say, "The main thing is to keep the main thing the main thing." Adult learning needs to be our main thing. Teachers need professional company. Staffs need to give top priority to creating physical space as well as white space for teachers to take care of their own scholarly pursuits. Staffs need to continually work to create simple rituals and structures to ensure that the grown-ups in a school are alive and growing. Staffs need to continually ask, "Can we lead literate, scholarly lives in this school? (Specific suggestions for professional study appear in Chapter 7, "Turning Schools into Centers for Professional Study.")

Going to the Source   One year, on the last day of school in June, I sent the following short note to my colleagues,

> *Dear friends,*
>
> *In another week from today, many of you will be lounging by a pool, "leaving on a jet plane," sleeping until noon, sticking close to the air conditioner with a good book, sunbathing at the beach, and finding lots of other ways to delight in your summer break.*
>
> *I'll be leaving on the fourth of July for a three-week spree in Prague, Budapest, and Vienna. When I return I'll be home for a month attempting to write a new book. Don't hesitate to call or visit during the month of August. I have a great sea breeze, and I usually only write from the crack of dawn until 2 P.M.*
>
> *This has been a wonderful school year. We have much to be proud of. Leisure time, though, always gives me a chance to pause and look back. I know I'll be thinking about the things I think I did well, and the things I know need improvement. The summertime white space allows me to reflect and then revise my hopes and plans for the new school year.*
>
> *I hope you'll find time to think about your school year and let me know if there's anything I can do to make your next year at the Manhattan New School the best ever.*
>
> *I hope we all return in September with new energy and with renewed commitments to our very special setting. I thank you all for your efforts in creating this beautiful, joyful, rigorous, and scholarly school. My hope is that next year it will be even more so.*
>
> *To a healthy and carefree summer,*
>
> *Love,*
> *Shelley*

This letter stands out for me, not because I love reminiscing about my trip to Eastern Europe, nor my summer plans to write and reflect. It seems to me that the most important part of this letter is my request for teachers to tell me what they need to have the best school year ever. It's a question that all principals might think about asking their staffs: "What do you need to have a great year?" I think many administrators would be surprised by their teachers' answers.

If this chapter sounds very proud and in awe of the teaching profession, I've done my job. More principals need to let the world know how hard their teachers work, how successful they are, and how they serve as the heartbeat of our schools. The school photographer hired to take photographs of our students last year gave me a photo album filled with each of the class pictures. He called it my "principal's brag book." Yes, I could share class photos the way grandmothers exchange snapshots of their grandchildren, but a principal's brag book brings a different image to my mind. My album would be filled with portraits of my colleagues.

Related Readings in Companion Volumes

Lifetime Guarantees (Heinemann, forthcoming), will be abbreviated as LG.
Writing Through Childhood (Heinemann, forthcoming), will be abbreviated as WC.

Respecting differences	**WC**: Ch. 11.
Running varied writing workshops	**WC**: Ch. 2.
	LG: Ch. 2.
Sharing broad beliefs about teaching	**LG**: Ch. 2.
Teaching first grade readers and writers	**WC**: Ch. 6.
	LG: Ch. 6.
Asking prospective teachers about how they teach reading	**LG**: Ch. 6, Ch. 7.
Having professional colleagues	**LG**: Ch. 7.
	WC: Ch. 11.
Leading scholarly lives	**LG**: Ch. 7.
	WC: Ch. 11.

CHAPTER 4

MAKING THE SOCIAL TONE TOP PRIORITY

Priorities

- We must foster a spirit of generosity in our school communities and create a curriculum of caring.
- We can transform schools when we carefully watch how we talk to and about students, parents, and our colleagues.
- Literature must be viewed as a humanizing tool in our schools.
- We must be mindful of the ways in which generosity and the extending of gracious invitations can change relationships.
- We must allow for an environment that welcomes hearty laughter and a joyful social tone.
- We should work to increase the possibilities for multigrade moments, which add to the nurturing feel of a school.
- We should hold celebrations that remind us how lucky we are to be together.

Practice

- On employing schoolwide strategies to create a caring social tone, including student discussions, the sharing of relevant writing, modeling of behaviors, environmental reminders, schoolwide meetings, letters home, staff reminders, and student council
- On humane ways to bring a class to attention
- On treating colleagues and other adults cordially
- On building community through literacy
- On crafting invitations to achieve community participation
- On fostering community through humor
- On creating more opportunities for multigrade interactions
- On creating celebratory rituals

When my friend Lesley Gordon became principal of her school, I was honored to speak on her behalf at the school board's appointment ceremony. I carefully chose an appropriate story to tell. It was about a woman who was lucky enough to see both heaven and hell during her lifetime. She took a look at hell first. It was an incredible scene—a beautiful banquet hall with tables piled high with wonderful delicacies. Beautifully dressed people surrounded the tables, but the people were moaning and groaning and ever so miserable. The woman looked down and understood why the people were so unhappy. Their eating utensils, their forks ands spoons, had such long handles that they couldn't bring any food to their mouths. Then she checked out heaven. The scene was exactly the same. The people had the same food, the same long-handled utensils, but here, the people were incredibly happy. They were singing and laughing. The reason became clear to the woman. Instead of trying to feed themselves, the people in heaven were reaching across the table with their long-handled utensils and feeding each other. It was an appropriate story to tell because Lesley is a kind and caring human being. She always takes care of other people. I've shared this story on only one other occasion—at one of our fifth-grade graduations. (Mind you, I told the story without the reference to heaven and hell. After all, we are a public school.) "If there is anything I'd like you to remember about your years with us at the Manhattan New School," I advised our graduates, "It's to be kind and caring, to take care of other people."

A Spirit of Generosity

After one of his visits, Don Graves sent me a letter that included the following surprising observation. "I'm realizing that there is a spiritual quality to the school, a sense of oneness and support, a sense of otherness that makes it so special. I laugh, you may yet transcend the separation of church and state. You are a church! Don't tell anyone." We of course teach no religion, nor do we celebrate religious holidays at our school, and yet people feel something special in the air. Those of us who are fortunate enough to call the Manhattan New School home know what accounts for that very special feeling. We come to work filled with joy and compassion, as well as devotion to the work we do and the people we work alongside of.

A prospective parent touring our school was surprised that our children were working so hard. She had heard that our school was "crunchy granola." I had never heard that term used to describe a school before and had to ask her to explain. She was referring to an environment of politically correct congeniality. I then told her that being compassionate doesn't negate the fact that we are rigorous in our educational aims. Another parent heard our school described as the "free" Ethical Culture, a private school in New York that aims to live up to its lovely name. That was a better description of our setting. Deborah Meier, grandmother of two of our students, Daniel and Lilli, gave me a copy of Ron Berger's essay, "A Culture of Quality," published by the Annenberg Institute for School Reform. In it, Berger describes a school setting marked by trust, respect, common vision, and a sense of privilege. His is a school culture of quality. Deborah inscribed the slim volume with the words, "It feels like the Manhattan New School." That was a great compliment.

Educators everywhere are talking about reaching new heights. Everyone is calling for high test scores, high standards, and high levels of community involvement. The children at our school do have high test scores, our teachers have always had high standards for themselves and their students, and our parents and community members have high levels of energy and commitment. But I have discovered that in order for a school to be truly successful, the children, teachers, family members, and administrators must consider yet another factor. We need to create schools in which peoples' spirits are on high. There is a Ladino proverb that reads, "It's not how many commandments you fulfill but the spirit in which you fulfill them." So too, it's not how many books a student reads in a semester, or how many summer institutes a teacher attends, or how many committees a parent joins. What really matters is the spirit in which we carry out these tasks.

The Manhattan New School is a place where people teach and learn with gusto and a generosity of spirit. One parent, Kate Manning, calls us "a fired-up, gentle school." After touring our school, a prospective parent sent me a letter in which she observed, "You spoke about social tone and I have to admit that it is as tangible as the colors of your painted walls. The children were cooperative, alert, and happy. What more could a parent want?" We expect our classrooms and corridors to be filled with soft voices, gentle footsteps, calm and respectful interactions, and people reaching out to help one another.

I learned a long time ago that it doesn't matter what curriculum decisions we make, what instructional strategies we try, or what assessment tools we select, if students and teachers don't care about each other. It doesn't matter how brilliant our minilessons are or how clever our conferences are if children make fun of each other's handwriting, dialect, or choice of topic. These things don't matter at all if the really important stuff isn't in place. Children will not share significant stories, take risks as spellers, or accept new challenges if the classroom is not secure or supportive. The tone of the classroom can make or break your writing workshop. Similarly, experienced staff developers who are attempting to make change in a school know that they must begin by establishing trust and building collegial relationships before they make suggestions for turning classrooms into reading and writing workshops. If the first is not in place, the second will never take place. At the risk of sounding "touchy-feely" (or "crunchy-granola"), we must give top priority to creating a caring school culture.

I recently read that *alma mater* can be roughly translated as nourishing mother. We hope our graduates will think of us as a source of nourishment. One year, a parent of one of our kindergarten students brought in an old end-of-the-year report from his primary school education in Montevideo, Uruguay (see Figure 4.1).

It translates, "I was a student in the kindergarten class at Practice School #12, "Cervantes." Miss Libertad was my first teacher, my kind and understanding friend. All the teachers in my school expect a great deal from me. In the years to come, I will be an exemplary student at this house where everyone loves me."

I hope *all* the children in our school feel that everyone loves them. I hope the adults feel likewise. School faculties need to be thought of as an ensemble, one that works in caring and kind ways. Gary David Goldberg, the producer of the television shows *Family Ties* and *Spin City,* who is known for running friendly and stress-free sets, once explained, "If something goes wrong on this set, it's because I was not able to communicate to people how much I care about them and how much I respect them. Somehow I let them down by letting that slide, because otherwise this would be the safest place they've ever been, the place they are more loved than any place in the world. People only behave badly out of fear and out of neglect." I couldn't craft a better description of what schools have the potential to be.

Both students and teachers need to think of schools as the safest place they've ever been and the most joyful. I read with interest news reports about one phase of the peace negotiations between the Israelis and the Palestinians. They were held in a diplomat's home in Norway. The diplomat said that what really helped lead to conviviality between the two opposing sides was the presence of his four-year-old son. People

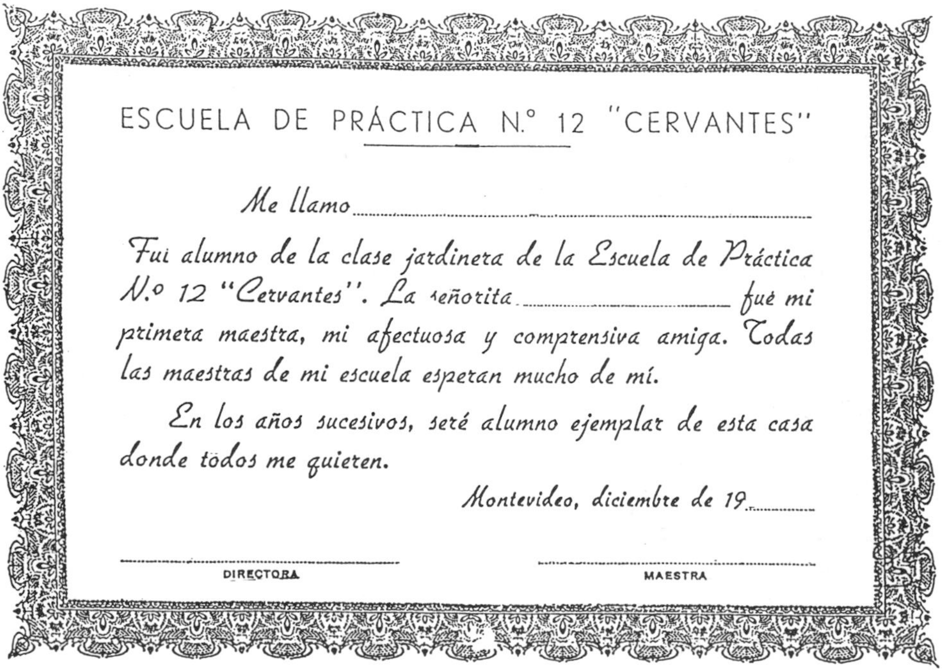

ESCUELA DE PRÁCTICA N.º 12 "CERVANTES"

Me llamo

Fui alumno de la clase jardinera de la Escuela de Práctica N.º 12 "Cervantes". La señorita _____ fue mi primera maestra, mi afectuosa y comprensiva amiga. Todas las maestras de mi escuela esperan mucho de mí.

En los años sucesivos, seré alumno ejemplar de esta casa donde todos me quieren.

Montevideo, diciembre de 19____

DIRECTORA   MAESTRA

Figure 4.1

become joyful around children. If this is true, then schools should be the most joyful settings in the neighborhood.

This entire chapter is devoted to creating a caring social tone, and yet I have more than hinted at the importance of this in all the preceding chapters. I have already shared how we have learned to not be exclusionary, to be willing to trade places, to value knowing one another's names and stories. I have shared such in-house understandings as "gracious living," *ogbo* responsibilities, and the all important question, "So what's bugging you?" I have talked about the need for compliments, tranquility, and respect for differences. All of these play significant roles in achieving the supportive, nurturing, stress-free zone we are after. And yet, there are other important tools in our toolbox. All of the following beliefs and practices have helped us create the kind of school in which young and old feel loved and cared for. (See Appendix 9 for a worksheet on Rethinking Social Tone.)

Curriculum of Caring

I heard Robert Coles speak at Harvard. He was addressing the families of the incoming freshmen class. He told these proud parents and their children, "If you're smart, you're not necessarily good." He continued by advising his audience, "Character is how you behave when no one is looking." He then added, "But someone is always looking."

I recently flew to Canada and a young Japanese man was seated next to me on the plane. He spoke very little English. When the flight attendant asked if he'd like a beverage, he referred to his Japanese-English dictionary. A little while later the flight attendant returned, this time handing out customs cards. I could sense the man's frustration with the very detailed questions, and as best I could, I explained the card to him. He was very grateful for the help. I'm not sure why, but on that flight I began thinking about our students. I guessed that most of our older students could easily read that customs card. What I wondered about, however, was, "Would all of them turn to help a struggling neighbor?" That, too, must be part of our curriculum. Character is how you behave when no one is looking.

Children's scores on standardized reading tests don't keep me up at night; children that do not turn to help a neighbor do. Likewise, children sneaking off with someone else's snack, stuffing toilets for fun, or walking by rubbish without thinking of picking it up, do cause me to lose sleep. We spend a great deal of time at school talking about treating people and property kindly and respectfully. I tell children all the time, "I don't know if my neighbors are good spellers, but I know if they are caring citizens." It's no surprise that when children misbehave, when they take away from community, they are expected to provide community service and give back to community. We have as rigorous expectations for students in their social lives as we do in their academic pursuits. A visiting superintendent from Texas commented that she saw no, "Ay pobrecita!" attitude in our school. She was right. We don't coddle our students. We hold our students and ourselves to high standards when we read and write as well as when we play, break bread, sing, and dance together. Other visitors have commented that the social tone brings to mind the concept of "smart love." So be it. We must be as thoughtful and demanding about relationships as we are about reading.

When new student teachers arrive in our building, I often ask them to begin their stay with us by spending a half hour just hanging out in the hallway, observing and eavesdropping. You can learn a great deal about a place by being a fly on the wall. At the end of their thirty minutes I ask, "What have you learned so far?" Their responses help me open up the conversation about the social tone of our school. They usually notice how calm and friendly the children and the adults seem. I suggest that if they had spotted anxious and unfriendly folks we would have our work cut out for us. For example, if they had noticed children passing by our security guard without saying good morning, we would need to talk to those children. If they had overheard folks in the office gossiping about a child, we would need to talk to those people. If they had noticed children bad-mouthing another child, we would have serious work to do.

It's very typical for people to talk about social relationships and responsibilities during the first few weeks of school. That's the time when teachers and children establish class procedures, priorities, and protocols. That's the time when everyone is still thinking about having the best year ever. But talk about social tone needs to continue well into the autumn, winter, and right on into the spring.

Schoolwide Strategies to Create a Caring Social Tone

Create Occasions for Student Discussions

Teachers bring up important social concerns at regular, whole-class gatherings and encourage students to do likewise. Lorraine's first graders request special meetings when they've been offended or have witnessed an injustice to others. Regina and her students develop their own peace compact, sort of a classroom bill of rights. It hangs prominently in their classroom all year. One year it read, "You have a right to be yourself in this room. This means I will not treat you unfairly because you are black or white or any color; fat or thin, tall or short, boy or girl, rich or poor. You have a right to feel safe in this room. This means I will not kick, push, pinch, or hurt you. You have a right to be respected and treated kindly in this room. This means I will not laugh at you or hurt your feelings. You have a right to hear and be heard in this room. This means I will not yell, scream, shout, or make loud noises. You have a right to learn about yourself in this room. This means you will be free to express your feelings and opinions without interruptions or punishment." These rights apply to teacher and students. Joanne's third graders sing with enthusiasm the simple song their student teacher Sandra taught them. "Everybody ought to know . . . Everybody ought to know . . . what *freedom* is, what *freedom* is . . . " They eagerly substitute other school-life essentials for the word *freedom* when they begin innovating on this repeated refrain. I have heard them insert such essential elements as justice, friendship, peace, nonviolence, caring, family, and kindness. It's clear that they have been talking about how they want to live their lives together in room 205.

Share Relevant Writing

Individual pieces of student or teacher writing can also be shared in ways that promote important class conversations about appropriate ways of living our lives together. Children often focus on schoolhouse injustices when they write in their writer's notebook. With the writers' permission, I have shared carefully selected notebook entries with whole classes in order to spark conversations about the ways we want to live together. I simply ask, "So, what do you think?" after sharing student jottings. I include several of these here.

Richard wrote about teasing (see Figure 4.2). Lindsay admitted that she didn't clean up the classroom because she didn't think she had contributed to the mess! (See Figure 4.3, with the following translation.)

> One day of school we had two meetings and one of them was about cleaning and our class was a little messy. But I didn't do it so I just sat there. I know I should of done something but remember that I didn't do it.

Students are always eager to respond to heartfelt pieces written by real classmates. Productive talk can also occur when entries have positive sentiments, as in the entry titled "Natalie" (see Figure 4.4).

Students' letters to friends, teachers, and to me also frequently serve to change relationships in the school building. A letter from Daniella, a third grader in Joanne's

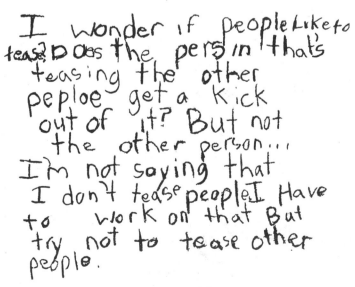

Figure 4.2

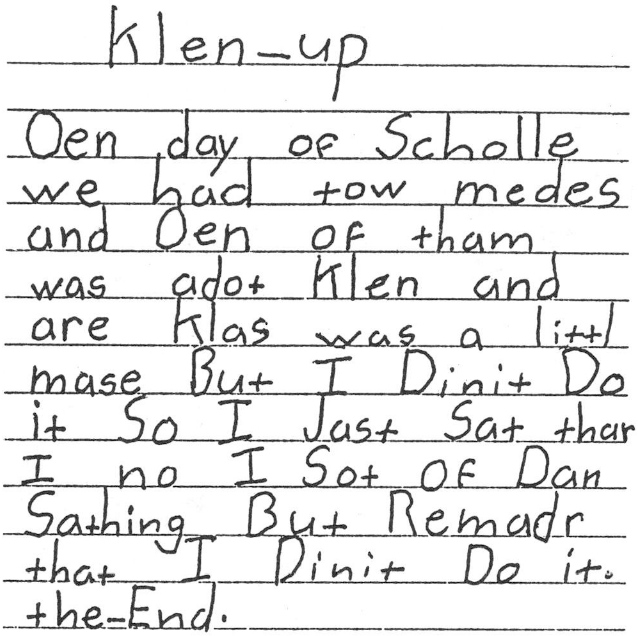

Klen-up

Oen day of Scholle
we had tow medes
and Oen of tham
was adot Klen and
are Klas was a littl
mase But I Dinit Do
it So I Jast Sat thar
I no I Sot of Dan
Sathing But Remadr
that I Dinit Do it.
the-End.

Figure 4.3

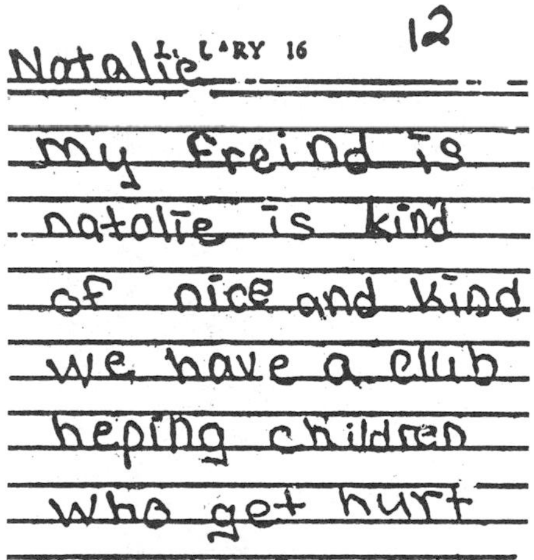

Natalie FEBRUARY 16   12

my freind is
natalie is kind
of nice and kind
we have a club
heping children
who get hurt
Sometimes we help
each other, when
we get hurt.

Figure 4.4

class, boldly asserted the wrongs she felt she had been done in a communication she sent to a classmate, with copies to Joanne, myself, and the classmate's mother! (See Figure 4.5.) You can be sure that Joanne took the accusations most seriously and made sure that the young girls worked out their differences.

Letters containing positive sentiments can also be put to good use, spreading the spirit of camaraderie if they are given recognition and children are shown that kind thoughts are appreciated. One kindergarten child wrote to her upper-grade reading buddy expressing gratitude for help and friendship. This note deserved to be publicly recognized (see Figure 4.6).

Two second graders wrote to me requesting a special day to honor siblings (see Figure 4.7). We have never set aside a day to honor sisters and brothers—too many children without siblings wouldn't be able to take part—but it is not surprising to see sisters and brothers invited to one another's classrooms, particularly during writing time. (All our children take part in a writer's workshops, and so it is easy for them to feel at home in one another's rooms.)

We also have a sign posted that encourages students to write to friends who have moved away. We keep a running list of the names of children who unfortunately had to

I Hope you know that "foureyed" is a mean word to use when you have broken up with your friend ... anyway if you think I,m a foureyed mabe you are not seeing well, bcause I do not have four eyes!!!!!!!!!!!!!!!!!!
You made me feel that you didn't care about my feelings the day before yesterday, when you embarassed me when I was humming.
I somtimes I can,t help humming you know!!!!!!!!!!!!!!! It helps me concentrate on my work better, and I don't even know I'm doing it sometimes. Lately you have been very mean to me and I don't think you should be mean to people.

                                                          Daniella

P.S. I will give a copy of this letter to

Joanne,Shelly and your mother.

Figure 4.5

Figure 4.6

Dear Shelley,
Emma and I where thinking that
Friday the 21 could be brother sister
day? get back to us today
please.

From
Ben and Emma

Figure 4.7

leave our school. The message is clear for our students: "We take our friendships very seriously. People should keep in touch with people they care about."

I also thank people who are willing to admit that they have mistreated a friend, as Jasmin did when he took responsibility for hurting his classmate Eric's feelings (see Figure 4.8).

I thank children who write kind messages to staff members. When Ben wrote to our science teacher offering to lend her a book about plants that he found in his house, I was sure to let him know that his thoughtfulness was appreciated. When Josh wrote a note welcoming all teachers back to school and placed a copy in everyone's mailbox attached to a school key-chain purchased by the PTA, everyone thanked Josh. When Stephanie wrote a welcome-back-to-school message in huge chalk letters on the sidewalk in front of school, and even sprayed it with hairspray to make it more durable, we all thanked Stephanie. When Alexei wrote to the kitchen workers thanking for the good food they prepared, we posted a copy for all to see. When our custodian John was leaving to work in another school we all talked about the kind letter that Natalie sent (see Figure 4.9).

I've also written some texts that invite social tone discussions. This simple poem is entitled "School Rules."

> No screaming, just dreaming.
> No tugging, just hugging
> No poking, just joking.
> No scaring, just sharing.
> No cussing, just discussing.
> No slapping, just clapping.
> No competing, just reading.
> No teasing, just pleasing.
> No screeching, just teaching.
> No yelling, just spelling.
> No shoving, just loving.
> No jeering, just cheering.
> No fighting, just writing
> No cursing, just rehearsing.
> No yelping, just helping.
> No lying, just trying.
> No berating, just celebrating.
> No hitting, just sitting and listening to a good story.

Students easily and willingly talk about the reasons for the rules contained in this verse and frequently add their own rhyming bits of advice, such as no dissing, just kissing; no mugging, just hugging; no stealing, just healing, etc.

Dear Shelly
I really wasn't acting
grown up when I wanted
to throw Eric in the
garabe. I wasn't thinking
I should have just
told him not to
Crise And to go upstairs.
But I was just Jokheing
but they didnt Know.

from Jasmin

Figure 4.8

Dear John

I'llwill miss your songs and
your key ringing when you walk
I'll will miss you going to
classes and fixing things and
reading
And its sad that your leaving
I'll miss you alot.

Love
Natalie
Rodroquez
P.s don't forget
us and good luck

Figure 4.9

When Pam asked me to write a page for an end-of-the-year kindergarten anthology, I highlighted the kind and caring aspects of curriculum and used several refrains to support these young readers. My letter read,

Dear children,

I hope you will always remember the important things you learned in kindergarten, like . . .

When you have a snack, share it with a friend.
When you read a book, share it with a friend.
When you write a story, share it with a friend.

When you play a game, enjoy taking turns.
When you talk with friends, enjoy taking turns.
When a leader is needed, enjoy taking turns.

When you see someone crying, ask how you can help.
When you see someone in pain, ask how you can help.
When you see someone frightened, ask how you can help.

When you sing, sing from the heart.
When you paint, paint from the heart.
When you dance, dance from the heart.

And when you are all grown up, I hope you will close your eyes every once in a while and picture Pam,

and all those morning meetings
and all those wonderful songs
and all those trips to the park
and all those center times
and all those books you read
and all those stories you wrote.

Please remember us.
We will remember all of you.

Love,
Shelley

Serve as Models

Perhaps the most important way we invite students to become part of our caring community is to continually serve as models. The late Garth Boomer reminded us that some things can be learned through language, but some things must be learned through demonstration. When Joanne heard that her colleague Eve had her very first Christmas tree and yet had no ornaments for it, she bought over two dozen clear hanging balls and invited her students to hand paint these tree trimmings. The children individually wrapped their creations, and squealed in delight each time Eve opened another of these surprise gifts that were offered in the spirit of friendship and from the goodness of their hearts. There could not have been a more powerful lesson in how people can take care of one another.

The children also know that we worry about our elderly next-door neighbor, Ellen, who occasionally forgets to take care of herself. They see the custodian buy her a sandwich and a cup of coffee. They see her wearing the PTA co-president's donated warm winter coat. They've seen me rummage through her bag looking for the name of her social worker or the nurse that occasionally visits. They know Eve won't use popcorn or marshmallows for art collage or macaroni as math manipulatives, not when there are hungry people on the streets. They see teachers launch campaigns to collect toys for children in homeless shelters, canned goods for a nearby food pantry, clothing for hurricane victims in the Caribbean, and books to send to a rural library in Puerto Rico. They know that Layne participates every year in the AIDS walkathon, Judy marches to raise money for cancer research, and Mike encourages all his classes to jump rope to raise funds for heart research. They also see adults rally around the child or the colleague who has lost a parent, is worried about a sick relative, or whose family has broken up. (I wonder if anyone at school knows that I keep a little slip of paper in my pocket with the names of children I am especially worried about. The little slip of paper reminds me to stop in and talk to these children each day.)

Compassion is contagious. It comes as no surprise to me that Madeline has started a very determined third-grade effort to save endangered animals (see Figure 4.10), or that Paula's former students accompany her each year to a candlelight vigil to protest child labor.

And every day, the students have opportunities to eavesdrop on caring conversations between staff members. They hear me say to their teacher, "Let's figure out a way for you to go home. You look sick." or, "Leave early, the roads are icy." They hear all of us asking one another, "How is your father feeling?" "Is your cat any better?" "Do you need anything? I'm going out." They hear lots of friendly chatter as well—"Your haircut looks great," or "Your outfit is beautiful." They hear us wishing one another "Happy Birthday" and making plans for get-togethers. Children are not the only ones in our school who have sleepovers and play dates.

Provide Environmental Reminders

In my office hangs a framed copy of that popular slogan, "Practice random acts of kindness and senseless acts of beauty." On Sharon Taberski's door hangs the question, "How can I help?" A parent gave the school a framed plaque that reads, "It's wonderful to know someone who makes the earth a better place to live." These are not mere decorative items. They are words to live by. (The inspirational student one-liners described earlier on page 45 are as important as those listed here.)

Although these wall hangings announce to all who enter that we care about one another, they are also helpful in getting people to interact. For example, after having read Mark Grashow's book, *How to Make New York a Better Place to Live: A Handbook for Resident Angels*, I hung a long sheet of mural paper labeled, "What Have You Done Lately to Make the Manhattan New School a Better Place to Live?" There was plenty of

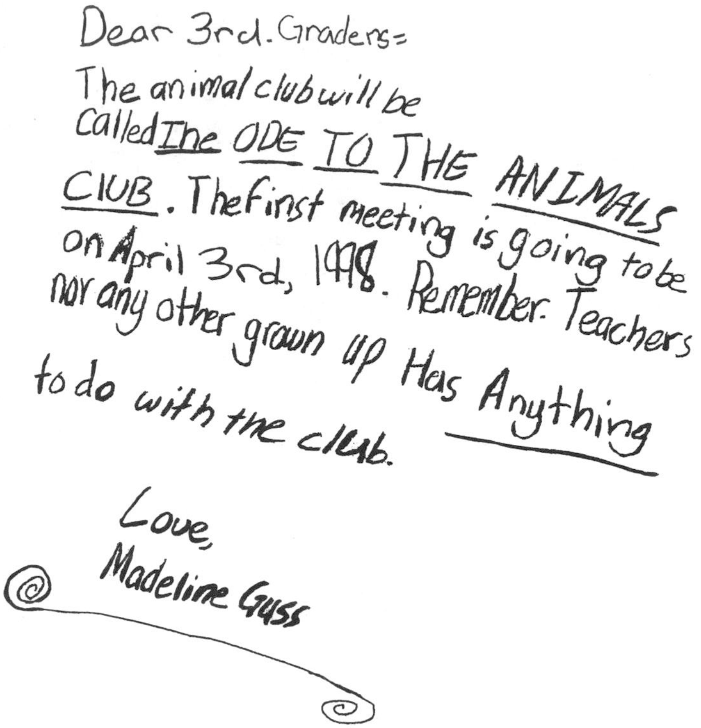

Dear 3rd. Graders =
The animal club will be
called The ODE TO THE ANIMALS
CLUB. The first meeting is going to be
on April 3rd, 1998. Remember. Teachers
nor any other grown up Has Anything
to do with the club.

Love,
Madeline Guss

Figure 4.10

space for passers-by to fill in their do-gooder acts. Among my favorites were—"Flushed someone else's toilet," "Showed a visitor how to get out of here," and "Scraped off my cupcake that dropped onto the radiator."

I've also gathered newspaper stories of New York acts of kindness, creating an ongoing display of wonderful ways people in our community have treated one another. One headline read, "Police Offer Baseball-Like Trading Cards, but of Themselves." Officers gave these cards as collector's items to students, hoping they would encourage children to feel more comfortable with their local police. Another read, "Enjoy the Silence," describing a window manufacturer who is donating a special windowpane to city schools to cut down on the sounds of traffic, sirens, construction, and garbage pickups. A third headline read, "Triangle Tragedy Burns in Memory," and described our own teacher Paula and her first graders placing flowers at the site of the historic Triangle Shirt Factory fire in memory of those who died. I also hung the obituary of a Greenwich Village resident, who for thirty years handed out gloves to poor and homeless New Yorkers, and an article suggesting the need to highlight cooperation in our physical education programs and eliminate competition and humiliation.

Of course, we post newspaper articles dealing with the charitable acts of those outside New York City too. Children need to know that the world's richest man, Bill

Gates, donated one hundred million dollars to provide immunizations for children all over the world, and Colorado school children have raised money to liberate slaves in Sudan, and Oseola McCarty, an elderly laundress, donated her life savings of $150,000 to enrich students' lives at the University of Southern Mississippi.

Alongside these clippings I hang slips of paper for reader response, as well as an invitation for students and teachers to add related clippings.

Call for Schoolwide Meetings

I receive many letters from our superintendent and his staff. Some are announcements for our monthly administrator get-togethers, descriptions of a wide range of professional development opportunities, or thank-you notes for our school's participation in one or another staff development initiative. All are well received; they are worth reading. Thankfully, our district staff doesn't waste paper and doesn't waste our time. Several years ago, I received a letter from the superintendent calling for an out-of-the-ordinary early-morning meeting. His unusual letter began,

> *Dear Colleague:*
>
> *As school leaders and as a district professional community, we have made great strides enriching our educational work. There is much we have to be proud of.*
>
> *Over the recent past, however, the very intensity of our work has created questions about what it is we deeply believe in, about the nature of our philosophical underpinnings, about our responsibilities for how we behave toward each other and how we support one another. Essentially, we need to revisit the character of our organization . . .*

In other words, the district had decided it was time to have an honest conversation about how the adults in this teaching/learning community were treating one another. I can't imagine any meeting being more risky and gutsy, nor any being more worthwhile. (It's much easier to create a supportive social tone when there is a chain of trust and compassion in a school district. When principals feel trusted and supported, it's more likely teachers will feel the same, as well as parents and students.)

Just as our superintendent had done, those of us in school-based leadership positions need to call for special meetings. As a staff, we also need to talk about treating one another respectfully, with compassion and humanity. One time I announced an emergency meeting with the words, "I think we need a heart-to-heart at lunch. There are some hurt feelings in the building. Please let's clear the air before the weekend." Grown-ups need to create their own curriculum of caring.

Out-of-the-ordinary meetings with students also elevate their importance. Students know we are serious when we call for a special large group meeting in the ballroom. They know we rarely interrupt their regular classroom studies. This dramatic gathering announces that we have serious concerns. We use these get-togethers to talk about responsible and respectful behavior in the cafeteria, hallways, stairwells, specialists' classrooms, playgrounds, and play street. (We close our street to traffic at lunch in order to make a place for the older children to play. We actually drag police barricades across the gutter and roll out a heavy official metal sign to prevent cars from entering. There is a lot of street etiquette to be learned.) We can add even more drama to these meetings by inviting guest speakers. I can easily imagine asking our custodian to speak. He gets very tired of cleaning unnecessary messes. I can easily imagine asking our security guard to speak. She gets really tired of children using their hands to solve differences. I can easily imagine inviting our next-door neighbor to speak. She gets really tired of asking students not to leave lunch residue on her front stoop. These meetings provide the perfect opportunity to air our concerns and to invite students in on the solution to these problems.

Send Letters Home

Parents need to know that caring is part of the curriculum. They need to be invited into these conversations. Occasionally my letters to families address these issues. One read, in part,

> I've decided to periodically celebrate small moments of kindness in our schoolhouse. I recently read *Tell Me a Mitzvah— Little and Big Ways to Repair the World*, by Danny Siegel. The author defines the Yiddish word *mitzvah* as a "synonym for personal acts of goodness." Here, then, are some personal acts of goodness that have been noted with a great deal of pleasure around our school. I think you'll agree they demonstrate little ways to repair our world.
>
> - Billy Sage was home sick on his student teacher Sondra Lee's last day at school. Billy called the school, asking to speak to Sondra. He wanted to thank her for her help, wish her well, and say good-bye.
> - On AIDS Awareness Day, Sarah Shelzi read aloud a book she had written on AIDS and brought in a bagful of red ribbons to teach her class how to make this important symbol.
> - When a new student Samreen Jadmani entered her class, Sarah Norum Gross wrote the following kind letter:
>
>> *Samreen,*
>> *I like how you write. Welcome to the class. I hope you like it here and I know you will get used to being in this school. I would also like to be your friend.*
>>
>> *Sarah*

Teachers and family members were delighted to hear good things about their children, and were always willing to pass on more good deeds. It would probably help to post a permanent envelope, appropriately labeled so that people could always slip in the story of other mitzvahs. This would make my periodic column easier to write and would remind people to pay attention to these wonderful moments. Of course, parents deserve to hear about them at teacher conferences and to talk about related issues at PTA meetings.

Provide Staff Reminders

Each year our staff works on several initiatives. Over the years, we have focused our attention on such issues as the struggling reader, teaching spelling, or portfolio assessment. Sometimes I think we need to add a quality-of-life initiative. Imagine putting all of our attention for awhile into improving social concerns around the school. No doubt this kind of study would have a very different feel.

I remember in the earliest days of our school we were asked by the district to submit a required, "Policy on Student Conduct and Discipline." We didn't know where to begin or what language to use. We did what we know best. We told stories. We compiled a list of situations to help us think about what was really important to us under the institutional phrase "student conduct and discipline." We came up with our own set of absolutes. For example, if anyone was seen crying, we would expect any passerby, child or adult, to stop and ask what was wrong and if they could help. If a visitor was in the building we would expect anyone, child or adult, to make eye contact, be welcoming, enter into conversations. If rubbish was on the floor, we would expect anyone, child or adult, to not pass it by, but help in the cleanup. Then of course we covered scenarios involving physical harm to people or property, offensive language, and acts of prejudice. These vignettes helped us flesh out what we believed in.

Occasionally, I put social tone reminders into staff letters. Some of them refer to the adults in our community, others are meant to share with the children. The following were culled from various letters written over the last several years. They didn't ever appear all at the same time.

> Please remember not to discuss concerns about children in front of strangers, parents, visitors, support staff, or other children.

> Let's remember to not have side conversations at staff meetings. People have important things to say to the whole group. Everyone's ideas deserve to be heard. I'm concerned too that people are bringing work to the meetings. If you're feeling overwhelmed, just skip the meeting. We really need to have everyone's undivided attention.

> No one wants to be interrupted. We all need to think about softening our voices in the hallways and lightening our footsteps.

> Please don't initiate anything that might be interpreted as a schoolwide policy or ritual without bringing it up to the whole staff.

> We need to talk about all those children with all those surveys. Perhaps we need a time for them to enter classrooms or an unofficial rule about conducting surveys in the hallways.

> Again, we need to establish some hallway etiquette for classes arriving and leaving the fifth floor, penthouse, specials. (Here I'm referring to art, science, music, and Spanish). Renay, Kevin, and Sungho are being very patient with those disturbances.

The custodians take a lot of pride in those newly waxed floors. Please lift, not drag, furniture. Keep scrapes to a minimum.

Please have a heart-to-heart again about lunchroom "loveliness."

Do invite new faculty members in to meet your kids, so that no one remains a stranger very long. Everyone should probably stop in to be introduced to the new kindergarten students. Meet our new special students as well.

Please remind children not to lean on hallway displays. Their friends work too hard for their projects to be mistreated.

Uh, oh!! Smashed apples in the stairwells. Enough said.

On another occasion I included the following thoughts in a letter to the staff:

> I hope we can all do a better job of talking to people when we are upset. I think that oc-casionally events occur that unsettle people, and instead of going directly to the source in a timely fashion, people often keep their unhappiness inside, add hearsay to the events, or make erroneous assumptions. In other words, if my words or actions have of-fended you, please tell me directly. If someone else is involved please don't hesitate to ap-proach your colleague. I'm sure that no one wants anyone to feel that they are being treated unfairly or inequitably. Sometimes, we are not even aware that someone is upset. And when we find out, people often have incomplete understandings of the situation and need more information. Disagreements are inevitable in a thinking community. Dis-trust is not. I look forward to a new school year with more honest and direct communi-cation.

In every school community, no matter how philosophically, politically, or socially in-tune the members are, every once in a while, people (including administrators), will speak before thinking, misinterpret actions and conversations, or show poor judgment. These are not the times to simply sweep these misunderstandings under the rug. Clear-ing the air is essential if we are to ensure a nurturing social tone for all, grown-ups in-cluded.

Create a Student Council

The student council is my way of sharing leadership with students. (See related infor-mation in Chapter 2, "Rethinking the Role of Principal," page 54.) Below is an excerpt of a letter I sent to families, explaining the work we do.

> Every other Friday afternoon, I meet in the poetry reading room with this enthusiastic group, made up of one representative from each class. The children with clipboard, notepad, and pencil in hand, talk about schoolwide issues. They first share moments and trends worth celebrating, then discuss ongoing problems and their possible solutions. Each representative returns to their classrooms to share the key points discussed.
>
> Of course, I find it very worthwhile to hear the students discuss school life, the things they're proud of, as well as the things that aren't quite good enough yet (I've included a summary of these at the end of this letter). But for me, the most joyful part of each meet-ing is the opportunity to observe the interactions between the children. The youngest

members seem so proud to be sitting alongside such big kids, being asked to do the same job. They listen intently when an older child speaks, their eyes riveted on those "grown-up" looking kids. And it is just as wonderful to watch the older students. Evan, a fifth grader, is such a serious listener and often tries to make a younger child's concerns more clear with a polite, "What I think she's trying to say is . . . " Allie, a fourth grader, often gives me a knowing smile when a kindergarten child begins to tell a too long or too detailed story, but graciously never interrupts. Older students help younger ones take notes at the meetings, encouraging them to spell as best they can or draw the key points so they'll be able to report back to their classmates. Big guys and little ones listen to one another, support one another, and show admiration and appreciation for the different perspectives such a multigrade group offers. Below is a sampler of the kinds of things the students bring up at up meetings.

Worthy of Celebration

We finally have a nurse

Everyone has a wall tile to decorate

Lots of trips have been scheduled

Winter solstice was a hit

Students were chosen for Reading Rainbow

Students were on cover of Scholastic News

Everyone received *Jar of Tiny Stars*

We now have a music and an art teacher

We get new books all the time

We have push-button phones now

No more wet wads of toilet paper being thrown on restroom ceilings

Student council reps attending all meetings on time

Work to be Done

People writing on school stuff

Play-fighting getting out of hand

Snowball throwing is dangerous

Sharing hats a No-No, spreads lice

Gum and candy wrappers on stairs

Hurtful words said or written

Everyone needs to arrive on time

Rainy day boxes need to be brought

Entering and exiting through main door only

Decisions need to be made concerning emergency use of a public address system and the place of sports teams in our school

The challenge in schools is for more students to have opportunities to take on leadership roles. Other ways include:

Establishing buddy relationships with new or younger students

Serving as escorts for visitors

Participating in school committees (e.g. establishing discipline codes, safety plans, etc.)

Participating in curriculum presentations

Hosting parent-teacher conferences

Getting involved in public presentations (e.g. school board meetings)

Extending "help-wanted" calls to all students

Valuing school business as part of the curriculum

Celebrating student initiative (e.g. beginning lunchtime clubs, literary magazines, etc.)

Watching Our Language

When our school first opened, I suggested that teachers imagine that everything they say to their students is somehow broadcast throughout the entire building on a public-address system. "We shouldn't say anything, in any tone, that would embarrass us if our colleagues overheard," I added. That's a pretty good filter. My son, Michael, graduated from Harvard Business School. He was taught to live as if every action he takes and every decision he makes would be on the cover of tomorrow's *New York Times*. Likewise, his friend Lara, who attends Harvard Medical School, was taught to treat every patient as if a relative of that patient were in the room watching her. These are very fine filters. Robert Coles's notion that, "Character is how you behave when no one is looking, but someone is always looking," applies to grown-ups as well as children.

Language can hurt. When everyone, all the time, speaks with respect, humanity, and compassion, we do transform our classrooms, as well as our staff rooms, parent rooms, offices, playgrounds, hallways, and principals' offices. Recently, my twenty-six-year-old daughter recalled a most unpleasant second-grade memory. Her teacher asked her to distribute books, stating, "Please give one to every other child." My daughter had never heard the expression "every other" before and proceeded to give a book to every child except herself, assuming that that is what her teacher meant. Of course, she ran out of books halfway through. The teacher scolded her publicly saying, "Didn't I tell you to give one to every other child?" That's exactly what my daughter thought she had been doing. She never forgot what it felt like to be publicly humiliated in front of her class. My daughter's misunderstanding of language didn't hurt anyone, but her teacher's use of language did.

After Karen Ernst visited our school, she wrote, "Copper doors, stained glass windows, blue framed window, bright yellow walls, and appropriately enough a red carpet rolled out for all those who enter. I guess Shelley thinks of children as visiting dignitaries, heads of state, or royalty." Wouldn't that be another amazing filter on our language if we imagined all our students, their parents, and our colleagues as visiting dignitaries? Why not?

There are many city educators and politicians who believe we would transform schools if we put our students in uniforms. I prefer to put my trust in language. We transform schools when we carefully watch how we talk *to* and *about* students, parents, and our colleagues.

Humanely Bringing a Class to Attention

If we zoom in on just the everyday ways that teachers get their students' attention, we can note a world of difference. In some settings teachers seem to bark at their students, screaming above the class chatter to bring the class to attention. Others blow harsh whistles or endlessly repeat, "I'm waiting, I'm waiting," or barrage the students with a string of "Sh, sh, sh, sh!" What a difference to walk into Paula's first grade and hear her calmly say the Swahili word *Ago,* (AH go), roughly translated as, "I want you to look at me," to which her first graders respond, *Ame* (AH may), meaning, "I am paying attention." Or to walk into Jenn's room and hear her announce, "And a hush fell over the room," to which the children softly respond in unison, "Hush." Or to walk into Eve's room and hear her announce, "I see," to which all her five-year-olds respond, "I see what?" with Eve perhaps announcing, "I see all the children sitting in a circle on the rug." Or to hear Karen sing, "Two hands, two hands up," and watch all her second graders stop what they are doing, lift their hands to the sky, and look at the teacher for her announcement. Similarly, Regina's students know that it is time to come together when she starts singing her version of "The Name Game." What student wouldn't want to join in on, "Quiet, quiet, bo bi-et, bana fana, fo fi-et, quiet!"? (Even the teachers who choose sounds over words make sure to choose pleasing ones, such as wind chimes, rhythmic claps, and classical music.)

My friend Alicia recently visited from Buenos Aires. In her notebook she had copied down a quote from the local newspaper. It read, "No puede haber cultura sin el uso cuidado del lenguaje," which translates, "You can't have culture without the careful use of language." I would change this slightly to read, "You can't have a healthy *school* culture without the careful use of language."

Cordiality Among Adults

I took all the required administration and supervision courses to become a licensed New York City principal. At the time, I remember feeling the need for information that was very specific and very practical. I found it helpful, for example, when one professor suggested we leave our buildings, disguise our voices, and call our schools. "Find out how you are treated," he added. Language counts.

At the opening of school a few years ago, I panicked the night before. There was so much to think about. To alleviate my anxiety, I quickly jotted off a note to my colleagues. Thankfully, when I got to the copier machine at school, I stopped to reread my hurried words. The letter began:

> *PLEASE READ TODAY*
>
> *9/12/94*
>
> *Dear friends,*
>
> *A few quick reminders and requests:*
>
>> *Send list of no-shows ASAP.*
>> *Chairs up at the end of Mondays, Wednesdays, and Fridays.*
>> *Send down children who take bus promptly at 2:45.*
>> *New folks' please label a box in the main office.*
>> *Note lunch procedures on Ida's desk.*

My words were so cold and institutional, certainly not appropriate for the first day of school, especially for someone who talks so much about good writing. Language counts. That note was revised as follows:

9/12/94

Dear friends,

Here's to a great first day of school. Slow down. Read a great book. Sing a happy song. Recite a beautiful poem. Swap wild stories. Share snacks. Make some plans. Decorate some walls. Tell funny jokes. Learn new names. Ask real questions. Smell the roses.

Then too, please tend to these very "school" tasks . . .

After this gentler, welcoming opening, I then listed all those necessary beginning-of-school chores, but I was more careful with my language. For example, the first request now read, "Please send me a list of children who never showed up." The second read, "Please help the custodians by placing chairs atop desks on Mondays, Wednesdays, and Fridays." My tone was much more cordial and civilized. I'm not the only educator who needs to watch her language. I once received letter from another school district. In part, it suggested a theme involving "Child-Centered, Progressive/Collaborative, Multicultural/Language Studies." The district suggested that our school is funded with this theme.

Well, our school is not funded with such a theme, nor do we fully understand their descriptors. As educators, we too better watch our language. It comes as no surprise that parents are confused by changes in classrooms when they are subjected to a barrage of educational labels intended to describe them.

It's not only helpful for me to watch my language at school, it's also enlightening to watch the language of others—not in the sense of monitoring it, but in the sense of paying attention to it. I have discovered, for example, that close-knit communities develop a language all their own. Just as families coin their own personal expressions and language short cuts, so do schools. We all know what Joanne means by the phrase "P.S. Anywhere," and we understand when Isabel talks about "gracious living." The sign on Eve's classroom door, "Come in We're Open," has come to serve as a reminder that the walls need to come tumbling down between school and community. Our students need to go out into the community and the community needs to feel welcome inside our school. All of our kindergarten students understand their teachers' refrain, "That's too casual for school," when the kids begin stretching out on the rug during meeting time or removing their sweatshirts to reveal just their undergarments. Many students are also familiar with the line "Simultaneous talk is selfish." We use it to remind students that one person at a time talks during whole-class meetings. To avoid being exclusionary, we do not use the phrase "teacher's lounge"; our "staff room" is open to all the grown-ups in the building. We never call children who are having difficulty with their studies "slow" children in "bottom" classes. We prefer Don Holdoway's notion of "extra-time" kids, or we might describe a child as "struggling with work habits," or "struggling with reading." We don't write, "Dear parents," on our letters home, but were taught by our former colleague, Elizabeth Servidio, to write, "Dear families." Not everyone lives with their parents. Language counts.

The language we choose says a lot about what we value. I hope readers have realized that throughout this text I have never said "My school," or "My teachers." After all, it is "Our school" and "Our teachers." I always correct people who call the Manhattan New School, "Shelley's school." It's not. It belongs to all of us. Language counts.

We think we are creating a very special place. Surprising language reminds us to keep it that way. We don't have a fifth floor, we have a penthouse. We don't have an auditorium, we have a ballroom. We don't have a dance festival, we go dancing in the streets. Perhaps we shouldn't have a lunchroom or a cafeteria. Children might behave differently if they referred to the place where they had their meals as the "dining hall." (I doubt it, but perhaps it's worth a try.)

Polite Teachers Make For Polite Students

We are also interested in teaching children to speak politely to one another. Visitors seem startled if a child says "Excuse me" when they need to pass someone in the hall, "I beg your pardon" when they need a comment repeated, or "Thanks for visiting" when guests leave. Visitors shouldn't be so surprised. When grown-ups talk politely, children learn what is expected. We can explicitly teach children how language changes relationships. When our friend Steph Harvey visited one year, I recall introducing her to lots of children as we made our way in and out of classrooms throughout the school. At one point Steph suggested to a small group of children how valuable it is when you are introduced to a new person to really try to remember the person's name so that you can use the name when you say goodbye. When we left and the children called out, "Bye Steph!" I knew she had taught those children a lifelong lesson.

Valuing Literature as a Humanizing Tool

I was working in Oxford, England, on the occasion of the two hundredth anniversary of Percy Bysshe Shelley's birth. One of the many newspaper captions celebrating this event read, "Shelley's remarkable belief in the power of poetry to effect social change is the secret of his lasting appeal." I would hope that reporters would say the same thing about the "Shelley" that leads a school on East Eighty-second Street in Manhattan. I too, believe in the power of poetry (as well as fairy tales, fables, newspaper articles, political speeches, and the like) to effect social change. In fact, I count on it. Literature is one of the handiest and most powerful tools we have to add humanity and compassion to our schools.

In *Lasting Impressions*, I quote former secretary of education William Bennett, who said, "The teaching of humanity begins with 'Once upon a time.'" We do need to humanize our schools. We need tender moments in schools, and carefully chosen literature gives us those moments. When Susan Cheever, one of our parents, learned of our fifth-grade parent/child reading club, she wrote, "Reading together is, if you ask me, the best way to establish common ground and understanding between two people. It's like going into couple's therapy with Charles Dickens or Charlotte Bronte or Rudyard

Kipling; a brilliant third party is there to field ideas and generate imaginative solutions." (See page 176 for more information on parent/child bookclubs).

Several years ago there was a big celebration in New York on the occasion of the publication of *Anne Frank's The Diary of a Young Girl: The Definitive Edition*. The gala tribute, a read-aloud by very famous people including actors and actresses, as well as Miep Gies, the Dutch woman who hid the diary, took place at the Fifth Avenue Presbyterian Church. A few fifth-grade girls who had just read the diary made me an offer I couldn't refuse. We hopped into a cab and spent our lunch hour listening to incredible passages read aloud by incredible voices. We were different people in the cab ride back to school. Literature changes relationships. It humanizes the world.

Percy Bysshe Shelley was right. Poetry can effect social change. There are days when I wish I had published *Lasting Impressions* in a three-ring-binder format, so I could easily slip in newly discovered literary treasures. The following poems would be perfect additions to the chapter titled "The Camaraderie of Language and Literature," as they each speak to quality-of-life issues.

Paul Engle's "Together" can serve to remind teachers and children how lucky they are to be together.

Together

Because we do
All things together
All things improve,
Even weather.
Our daily meat
And bread taste better,
Trees are greener,
Rain is wetter.

Lillian Morrison's "Daily Violence" announces the only kind of violence we can tolerate in or near schoolhouses.

Dawn cracked;
    the sun stole through.
Day broke;
    the sun climbed over rooftops.
Clouds chased the sun,
    then burst.
Night fell.
The clock struck midnight.

Other poems that can be used in similar ways include Oscar Hammerstein's "You've Got to Be Taught," which of course is sung in the musical *South Pacific*, and

Christina Rossetti's classic poem, "Hurt No Living Thing." Anthologies such as Gary Soto's *Neighborhood Odes* can also inspire students to craft their own poems in tribute to deserving things in their own environment. Michael J. Rosen's collection *Food Fight* can help children understand the need to fight hunger in the world.

Many literature selections inspire children to talk about how important it is to treat people with respect, humanity, and compassion. Some of my favorite picture books to use in this way include Mem Fox's *Whoever You Are*, Marjorie Barker Yoshi's *Magical Hands*, Mary Ann Hoberman's *One of Each*, Peter Golenbach's *Teammates*, and Sheila Hamanaka's *All the Colors of the Earth*.

Eight-year-old Vyonna's postscript to a letter she sent to her third-grade teacher Renay (see Figure 4.11) demonstrates that literature does get children thinking about improving their relationships with other people. Renay had recently read aloud Robert Kimmel Smith's *The War with Grandpa*.

Adults too need to be surrounded by texts that move them to think and talk about social justice. I frequently clip and post newspaper articles that get adults thinking about the human condition. Likewise, I include carefully selected poems when I create "Welcome back to school" packets for my colleagues. You look at children differently when you read and respond to Molly Peacock's "Our Room," Gary Soto's "Stars," and Linda Pastan's "Recess," from *Realms of Gold*.

Ways Literacy Builds Community at the Manhattan New School

The major ways that literature and literacy improve the social tone in our school are included in the list below.

1. We share carefully selected literature, the kind that turns the conversation toward a caring social tone at school.

2. We design classroom and school-wide rituals, structures, and events that bring the community together. See *Lifetime Guarantees*.

3. We design everyday literacy displays that invite community interaction. See *Lifetime Guarantees*.

4. We encourage students to do the kind of writing that can improve the quality of school life by paying tribute to members of the community. See *Lifetime Guarantees*.

5. We encourage students to do the kind of writing that can improve the quality of school life by accomplishing real-world goals.

6. We encourage students to do the kind of reading and writing that connects them to the world outside of school. See *Lifetime Guarantees* and *Writing Through Childhood*.

7. We encourage students to use their literacies to make the world outside of school a better place. See *Lifetime Guarantees*.

8. We pay tribute to the language and literature of many diverse cultures. See *Lifetime Guarantees.*

9. We pay attention to family literacy. (See Chapter 5, "Reaching Out to Families.")

10. We use literate acts to strengthen professional growth and relationships. (See Chapter 7, "Turning Schools into Centers for Professional Study.")

Dear Renay,

I am very sorry for being rood.

I am sorry for all of the things I did wrong. My mom might come in to speak with you But I don't want her to know that I have been being disrespecketfull because my godmother said that if there are know problems I can stay in Puto Rko. I have been very exited too. So please just keep that between me and you ok. If you have a problem with it just let me know and we can work something out ok. Just give me one more chance and If I don't behave you can tell my mom ok!

Thanks,
Vyenna

P.S. Remember it's a deal.
P.S This Reminds me of the war with Grandpa

Figure 4.11

Gift-Giving and the Gracious Invitation

One evening I was leaving the building late and I met one of our families, a mother and her daughter. They were recently in a car accident and little Julianna's eye was black and blue and bloodshot. As we stood there on the corner talking, along came Tina, another student, with her mother, Elizabeth. They had heard about the accident and were on their way to Julianna's to cheer her up. Their arms were filled with goodies. Tina was bringing her kitten because she knew that her friend loved cats. They also had a stack of cheerful drawings and a home-baked cake. The next day I met Tina's mother, Elizabeth, and I told her how touched I was by their thoughtfulness. "We're Hungarian," she said, "that's what we do." "We're New Yorkers," I thought, "that's what we *should* do."

The very sad follow-up to this story is that Elizabeth, Tina's mother, passed away recently, after battling a serious illness for a long time. So many people from our school community rallied around Elizabeth in her hospital bed. We were all there for her—a parent who is a hospital administrator looked into medical procedures; a parent who is a lawyer took care of her will; Cindy, Tina's teacher, and I served as bedside witnesses; and innumerable moms and dads contributed to Tina's well-being, in small ways and big. We were New Yorkers. That's what we should do.

Gift giving in a school need not refer only to offering packages wrapped in shiny paper and tied with a silky ribbon. Gift giving can have a much richer connotation. I'm referring to the student notion previously quoted: "It's better to help someone than to give them a present." This student needs to know that helping someone *is* giving a present. Thoughtfulness and lending a hand are very precious gifts.

Crafting Invitations

Gift giving begins with sincere invitations to participate in the life of a school. Lisa, our science specialist, sent the following note home to our families:

Fall 1994

Dear families,

Welcome to another year of hands-on science. We will be working "the way scientists do" as much as possible. This is an active, exciting, sometimes messy process. If your job gives you access to any materials or equipment you think we might be able to use, please contact me! Anything we don't have to buy is a help.

I am also delighted to have help in the classroom. If any of you have time to help out, even on an occasional basis, please speak to me. If you are a scientist or work in a science-related field and would be willing to come speak to any of the classes or do any projects with them, PLEASE let me know. I think that the connections between what we do in the classroom and what happens in the "real world" are extremely important.

If you have any questions, problems, or suggestions, do not hesitate to get in touch with me. Thank you for your assistance.

Lisa Siegman

I can't imagine any parent or family member not feeling welcome after receiving such an invitation, unless of course the letter is not translated into the language that our families understand. (More on this challenge in Chapter 5, "Reaching Out to Families.") The same holds true for the following request I made of children and their families right before one summer break. My letter began,

Dear families,

Even though we're apart in July and August, it doesn't mean we stop thinking about all of you. We hope that you won't stop thinking about us. In fact, I've put together the following list of challenges and projects that will keep the Manhattan New School on your minds all summer long.

The letter continued with the following practical requests:

- We're planning to do an in-depth study across the grades of our one city block, East Eighty-second to East Eighty-third Streets, between First and Second Avenue. We're in need of resources—maps, photographs, news articles, historical documents, etc. We'd also like contacts with city agencies to help us explore the phone lines, gas lines, etc. We'd like people to interview—residents, shopkeepers, etc. We'd like to study architecture, immigration, plants, etc. Any information gathered will be put to good use in the fall, and all through the year.

- I have a huge basket of school photographs that need to be organized, captioned, and slipped into photo albums. Volunteers are welcome.

- How about designing a *Welcome to the Manhattan New School Activity Book* to be given out to new kindergarten students in the fall?

- Our School Beautification Committee will meet early in the school year. Any suggestions for backyard murals, alleyway designs, front door logos, etc. will be helpful.

- We'd love to have a set of Reading Rainbow tapes for long, snowy lunchtimes in the winter. Anyone able to provide them?

- Those of you who kindly volunteer to care for our plants and animals over the summer, how about a photo journal to let us know what we missed?

- We're looking for caricatures of famous people as well as *New Yorker* magazine covers for some autumn murals. Please clip and save for us.

- We always love alphabets. How about designing a Manhattan New School alphabet book? Perhaps the pages could be framed and hung in our hallway in the fall.

- Are you interested in letter writing? Over the years, many children have moved away. See me for addresses if you would like to reestablish a friendship and write to an old friend over the summer.

- How about writing to a student who will be taking your place in your old classroom this year? If you're leaving second grade, you could write to a student who is entering grade two. You might tell the child what to expect in your former classroom.

- Get an early start on our Welcome Back to School Parade. Make sign, hats, banners, chants, etc. We will parade again at the beginning of the second week back.

- Gather words to songs you'd like your friends to sing with you next year. We can duplicate them in the fall.

- Study Spanish. Take out some Spanish books from the library. Share what you have learned when we come back to school.

- Visit the public library often. Keep a list of books, "Too Good to Miss." Share them with your teacher and classmates in September.

- Keep a log of important news events that happen when we're apart. We can swap stories in September.

- Prepare a course of study for the fall. This year, children set up lunch courses and taught one another origami, hockey, French, and even taught zippering and shoe-tying to kindergarten children.

- Design Manhattan New School birthday cards and thank-you notes. We're always looking for a steady supply of these.

- Prepare a guide for animal care in our building. Include all the pets we have, including bunnies, hamsters, snakes, gerbils, etc.

- Collect New York City scenes from magazines and newspapers, as well as postcards and photographs. We never have enough when we create collages, murals, and bulletin board displays.

- Prepare "Do Not Disturb," or "Enter Quietly—We're Working" signs to hang on classroom doors. You might want to make the hotel kind that slip over doorknobs. You might think of using heavy stock cardboard or even more permanent wood.

- Talk to your teachers about sending postcards or letters to them at their summer addresses. You might also pen pal with a classmate who is leaving town for the summer.

- Design a monthly calendar to be used by your class next year. The illustrations could remind your classmates of the events that take place during the school year.

- Gather poems appropriate for each season to be hung in the display cabinet next to Ida's desk.

- Reorganize and update the contents of your rainy day boxes. Let's keep them neater and sturdier next fall.

Sincere invitations to participate fully in the life of the school apply to teachers as well. Earlier, I suggested the importance of trading places within a school community (see "Walking a Mile in One Another's Shoes," p. 9). Many teachers are more than willing to take on appropriate administrative tasks, if they are kindly asked, acknowledged, and appreciated.

One year I was asked to attend a working lunch at New York University focusing on NYU's student-teacher program. It seemed more important for a cooperating teacher to attend rather than myself. I passed the invitation on to my colleagues in my weekly ramblings. I wrote, "It makes much more sense for someone who works closely with student teachers to attend. Let me know if you'd like to be covered at midday. I'll call the university to let them know you are representing the school and to find out about parking downtown." Just because a letter is addressed to the school principal, doesn't mean the principal is the best person for the job.

Another year, during an autumn Jewish holiday, I wrote the following note to staff, knowing that our then secretary Hadasa, as well as our first-grade teacher Lorraine, would be absent in order to observe the holiday. The letter, I think, clearly demonstrates how much confidence I have in my colleagues, how much trust I have in shared leadership, and how much I depend on my co-workers' input in many aspects of school life.

> *October 19*
>
> *Dear friends,*
>
> *I won't be in on Thursday due to a principal's conference at the Cooper Hewitt museum. I'd really appreciate it if you spent any free moments in the main office, keeping an eye on things. (This will be an especially difficult day since Hadasa will be absent as well as Lorraine). Don't hesitate to pop in to room 207 to support whoever is subbing.*
>
> *In preparation for our Wednesday staff meeting, won't you think about a visitor's day policy, ways to make our staff room and restrooms more inviting, and any conferences you're hoping to attend. I've left the district professional development calendar on my desk.*
>
> *In addition, on Thursday evening, I was asked to host a booth about our school at the Ninety-second Street Y. I'd be delighted if anyone is free and can join me. I could also use any "show and tell" materials about our school.*
>
> *By the way, have we confirmed Monday November 23 (my forty-fifth birthday) as the day we will be taking school pictures? Will everyone be here? No trips? I'll bring birthday bagels!!*
>
> *I'll miss you and the children.*
>
> *Love, Shelley*
>
> *P.S. If you have any wonderful student writing samples, I'd love to highlight them at a Board of Education keynote I'm doing on the 26th. Thanks again.*

The teachers I know best are more than willing to give their time and expertise when they know their opinions are valued, their plans carried out, and their contributions acknowledged.

Of course there are many moments of gift-giving that are completely unsolicited. Some of these involve gifts that could actually be tied with a silky ribbon. We know it is Isabel who fills our mailboxes with chocolate kisses whenever special occasions roll around. Paula brings wildflowers from her garden to adorn Ida's security desk. Meggan leaves pastries on the table in the main office. Pat hangs carefully chosen poems and poignant letters on the office board whenever the spirit moves her.

Then there are all those important gifts that can never be wrapped. Judy gives hugs to her old friends and just as easily to new ones, always at just the right moment. Lorraine is so filled with compliments for others, seeing more in us than we see in ourselves. Eve has the biggest heart, never turning down a friend in need. In addition, there are all those wonderful moments when teachers ask, "How can I help?" Lisa is ready to type, Layne to write an extra book review or two, Joanne to decorate another hallway, Karen to assess a struggling reader, Sharon Taberski to demonstrate guided reading, and Joan to stay for a late-night meeting. It is also a gift that all the teachers on staff open their doors so willingly and graciously to all the visitors that make their way to the Big Apple.

When school environments are warm and inviting, there is no limit to the amount of teacher and parent gift-giving that takes place.

In the writing workshop, we teach many genres because we realize that students need many ways to shine. The child who struggles with poetry may excel at journalism. The student who is bored with narrative writing may become engaged in crafting informational texts. So too, parents and community members need a wide range of ways to contribute to the school community. Schools are transformed when adults are not afraid to enter and contribute, in whatever ways they know best. (See related information in Chapter 5, "Reaching Out to Families.")

We are a better place because we have volunteers who know how to mix paint, cook, sew, do carpentry, juggle, sing opera, design playgrounds, move furniture, run auctions, play the piano, tell jokes, test hearing, translate texts into Braille, Spanish, Serbo-Croatian, etc.

We are a better place because parents walk in carrying stacks of leftover daily menus from the restaurants where they work, to be sure we have scrap paper for writing rough drafts and figuring out math problems. They walk in with cartons of fabric swatches to be sure we have material for collages. They walk in with packages of photocopy paper to be sure we never run out.

We are a better place because Joseph and Ben's grandmother walked in with a Braille translation of Paul's favorite story so that his blind mother could read it to him. And a Polish immigrant father presented the school, upon his son Sam's graduation, with an oil painting of Sam's class photograph. It hangs in our main lobby along with a note stating, "This is my gift for you for this seed you gave to my son Samuel." And Stephanie's father took a photograph of our entire school community with a special panoramic-lens camera. And Maia's mother Judy designed our school logo, which has an open book carving out the *M* in Manhattan. How perfect for us!

We are a better place because Lorraine's husband, Herb, takes beautiful black-and-white photographs of our students. And Debby's sister, Rachel, brings a beehive to share with special education students. And Joanne's Aunt Cathy writes students' names on their graduation diplomas with her fancy calligraphy pen. And Pam's father, Bob, reads to her class every year and tops it off with a pizza party. And Paula's son, David, plays the guitar at evening celebrations. And Sharon Taberski's husband, Ted, builds bookcases. And Eve's dad donates shopping bags filled with paper. And Pat's husband, Eric, knows how to take apart our loft and rebuild it in a new location.

We are a better place because all members of our community are invited to be full participants in the life of the school. When people met John D'Antonio, the wonderful founding custodian of the Manhattan New School, they asked me if it was simply luck or had I done a lot of searching to find someone like him. "No," I say, "It was the gracious invitation." John not only carried out his custodial obligations well, he read aloud to children, gave the children guided tours of the boiler room, wrote a children's book to help children understand how that room works, and most of all he taught us, through his writing and his friendly chatter, how lucky we all were to be together.

John was able to challenge that exlusionary pro-teacher inscription on my coffee mug because the social tone made it safe for him to do so. He could drink coffee with the principal. He could safely voice a strong opinion. When the school first opened, I gave every teacher a stack of business cards. On each was a quote from Maimonides. It read, "I have learned much from my teachers, more from my colleagues, but most from my students." I could easily add "custodian" to that list.

He once told me that he divided people into two groups according to which kind of mustard they'd be. Some belong to the everyday French's group, and then there is the Grey Poupon crowd. He thought that teachers belonged to the more elegant category, and he was part of the down-to-earth variety. I hope we proved him wrong. John wrote more than any adult in the building during those early years. He teased me that someday he would publish a book entitled, *Notes from the Slop Sink*. I wish he were serious.

The letters included here (Figures 4.12, 4.13, and 4.14) reveal John's compassionate spirit. How could our school not be a caring place when a guy like him is able to make his presence felt?

John's words always reminded us how privileged we were to work alongside each other and what a treat it was to be surrounded by children. Some of his notes were the heart-warming kind like those on pages 135–137. More often than not, they were incredibly funny. John's sense of humor was a gift to us all. He taught us that laughter is another tool for transforming schools.

Hearty Laughter

In the novel *Chapters and Verse*, the fictional account of the life of a bookstore owner, author Joel Barr begins many of his chapters with questions that were asked by children in a bookstore. They include, "Do you have any books with ducks in them and the ducks are real smart?" "Where's anything about my guinea pig and how fast does a spider bite?" and "I used to like books about rockets and old presidents but not anymore. Do you have any just stories?" Those of us in education don't have to read books to appreciate children's thinking. We have stories to tell all day, every day.

Some days I feel like Art Linkletter, agreeing wholeheartedly that "*Kids Say the Darndest Things*." I wish the cameras were rolling the day a kindergartner entered my

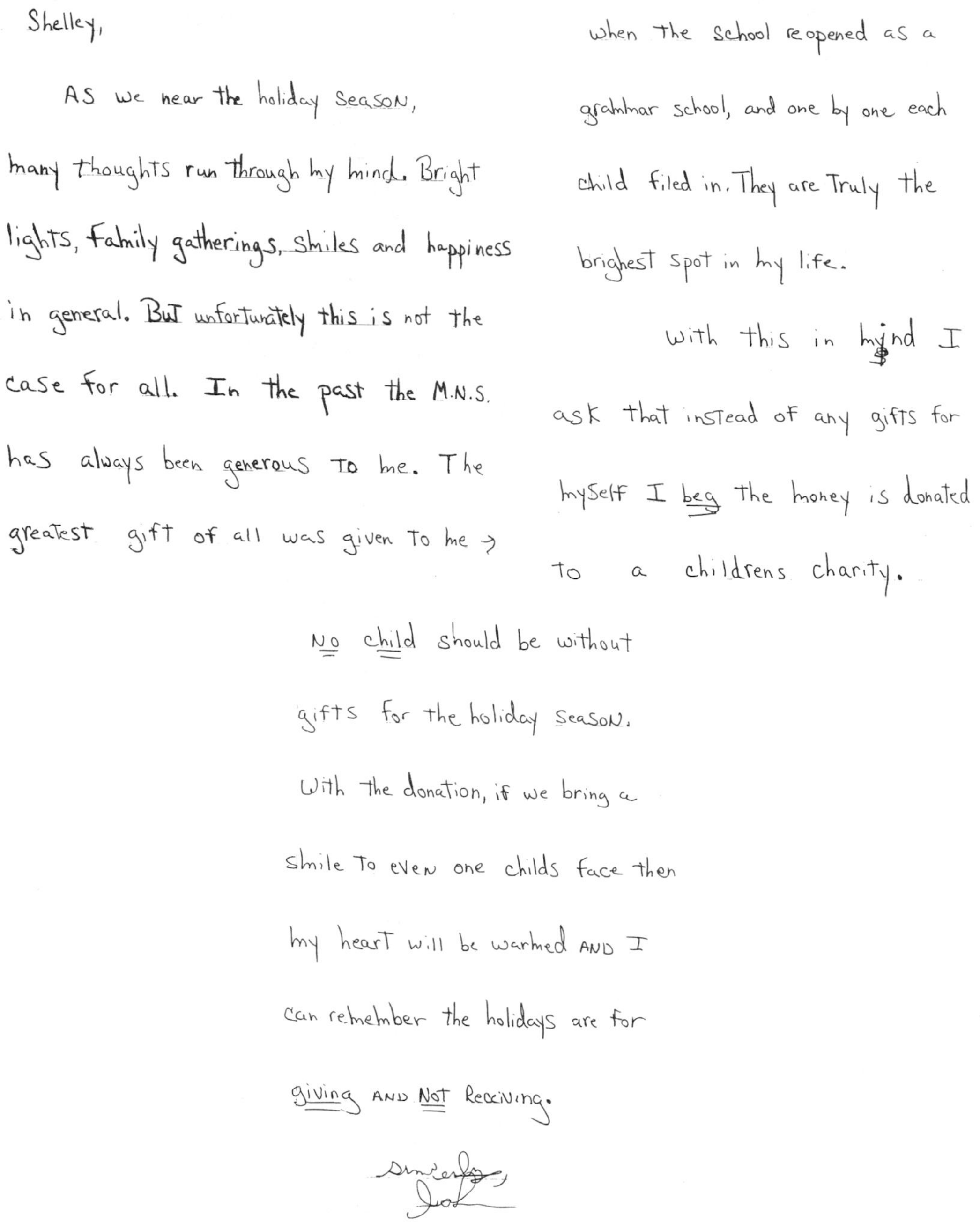

Shelley,

AS we near the holiday SeasoN, many thoughts run through my mind. Bright lights, family gatherings, smiles and happiness in general. But unfortunately this is not the case for all. In the past the M.N.S. has always been generous To me. The greatest gift of all was given To me →

when the school reopened as a grammar school, and one by one each child filed in. They are Truly the brightest spot in my life.

With this in mind I ask that instead of any gifts for myself I beg the money is donated to a childrens charity.

No child should be without gifts for the holiday SeasoN. With the donation, if we bring a smile To eveN one childs face then my heart will be warmed AND I can remember the holidays are for giving AND Not Receiving.

Sincerely,
Joe

Figure 4.12

office to share a serious problem she was having. "Static cling!" she said. Or the day Vanessa, a fourth grader, asked if she could call her grandma. "Of course," I told her. When she got off the phone, I asked if Grandma were picking her up. "No," she said, "my grandma lives in California!" The phone bill was a little higher that month.

If children are in places where they are allowed to ask real questions, make honest observations, and offer heartfelt responses, then those classrooms and corridors

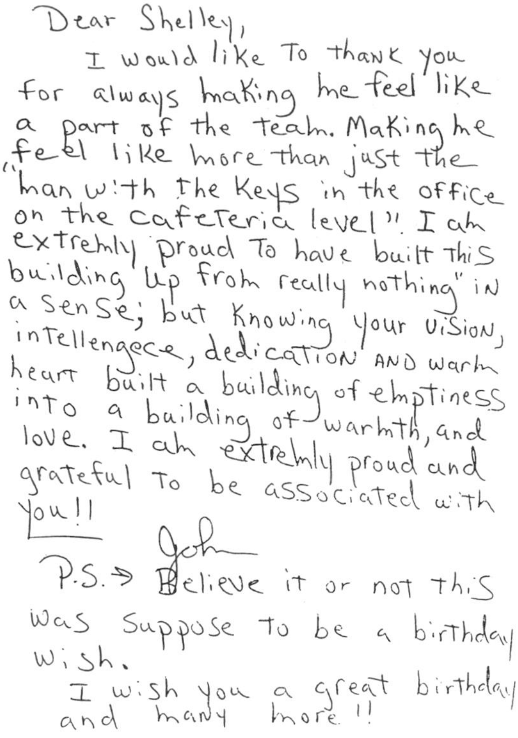

> Dear Shelley,
>   I would like to thank you for always making me feel like a part of the team. Making me feel like more than just the "man with the keys in the office on the cafeteria level". I am extremly proud to have built this building up from really nothing" in a sense; but knowing your vision, intellengece, dedication AND warm heart built a building of emptiness into a building of warmth, and love. I am extrelmly proud and grateful to be associated with you!!
>   John
>   P.S.⇒ Believe it or not this was suppose to be a birthday wish.
>   I wish you a great birthday and many more!!

Figure 4.13

must resound with laughter. Of course, we are not laughing at our children's expense. More times than not, we are laughing because their innocence has touched us. We are laughing because they have reminded us what a fascinating place this world really is. More times than not, we are laughing because our students have invented surprising ways to use language. We often begin conversations with, "Did you hear what so and so said?"

"Did you hear what Sari said about those prospective parents waiting to see Shelley?" many of my colleagues asked each other the day the folks in the office didn't know where I was. Sari was asked to find me and she ran all over the building. When she finally spotted me on the top floor, she called out, "Quick Shelley, there are customers downstairs!" Sari is also the student who, upon discovering that there were so many *Goosebumps* books, asked, "Shelley, is that a franchise?"

Joanne's class had been studying idiomatic expressions. Among many others, she taught the class the meaning of the expression "like a bull in a china shop." Later that day, Matt tripped over his own feet, "I know," he said, "I'm like a cow in a Chinese restaurant!"

Judy and I accompanied the sixth graders on a graduation trip to Washington, D.C. On the long bus ride back to school, Judy teased the children that she was going to quiz them on what they had learned. "Like what kind of questions would you ask?"

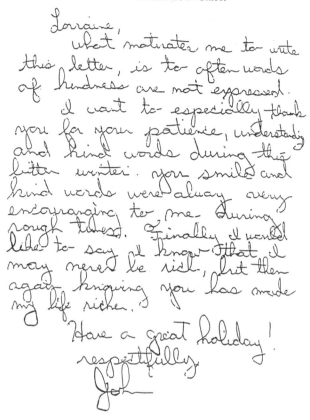

From the desk of :

JOHN D'ANTONIO
Custodian
Manhattan New School

Lorraine,
what motivates me to write this letter, is to often words of kindness are not expressed.
I want to especially thank you for your patience, understanding and kind words during the bitter winter. your smile and kind words were always very encouraging to me during rough times. Finally I would like to say I know that I may never be rich, but then again knowing you has made my life richer.
Have a great holiday!
respectfully,
John

Figure 4.14

Tugba wanted to know. Judy responded, "Well, I might ask you what D.C. stands for." Tugba quickly answered, "That's easy—Da Capital."

Isabel overheard her kindergartners talking. "Andrew, can I borrow some sharp crayons?" a five-year-old asked her friend." Sorry," said Andrew, "I only have gentle ones."

On a class trip to the Empire State Building, Rachel pointed out the Port Authority to her young students. Chris then asked, "Where's Puerto Rico?"

Tammy's kindergartner Mikel noticed that Mindy, his science teacher, was wearing slacks with a single stripe down each leg. He asked her, "You're a doorman also?" City kids, city sensibilities.

When Renay discovered some five-year-olds wandering in the penthouse stairwell, she asked them what grade they were in. "No grade," they replied, "we're in kindergarten." Then Shayla added, "Yeah, we're freshmen!"

How Humor Brings Us Together

Because it is a New York City school, you might expect there to be a few children of famous folks in attendance. After all, lots of writers, artists, actors, and politicians live in New York. And many of them do, I'm proud to say, send their children to public schools. You can meet Susan Cheever's son in our school, Faith Ringgold's grandaughter, Leo Lionni's great-grandchildren, and Ring Lardner's great-granddaughter. We're delighted that such literary folks have confidence in us, but equally as important is that Sharon Hill, Lorraine Shapiro, Lisa Siegman, Pat Werner, Tara Fishman, Dawn Harris Martine, and Carmen Colon have confidence in us. These women are teachers on our staff, and they pay us the biggest compliment when they trust us with their children and grandchildren. In addition, they are a great source of information. They offer a rich perspective on how we are doing. One summer, before Carmen's daughter Maia was about to enter kindergarten, we asked her to tell us what makes the experience of sending a child off to school for the first time so hard on parents. Carmen admitted that she couldn't bear to miss the clever things her daughter says all day. Carmen reminds us that we must remember to share the humorous, insightful remarks children make all day. The families of Sari, Matt, Tugba, Andrew, Chris, and Shayla deserve to know that their children make us laugh.

Paying attention to children's language provides more than just amusement, however. When we really listen to children we are reminded of what a privilege it is to be around them all day; we are given the opportunity to keep tabs on their language growth; and we acquire mirrors on their thinking.

There are lots of things in our school building that make us laugh and lots of reasons we value that laughter. We transform our schools when we realize as a community how important it is to have a good time. Every once in a while a hearty belly laugh keeps us from becoming overwhelmed or stressed out. When our friend Hindy visits, she says she feels the positive environment embrace her the minute she walks in the door. It could be the soft voices, the gentle language, or the slower pace attached to our big blocks of study, but I think the good atmosphere comes from our sense of humor as well. Funny things make us shift gears, respond to one another in different ways, and appreciate the moment. I would put laughing together, alongside breaking bread, sharing literature, and watching our language, on my list of tools that have the power to transform communities.

It doesn't surprise me that folks are always mounting cartoons on our restroom walls and hallway bulletins. Many of the jokes relate to schools and literacy. We laugh when we see the one where the child approaches a librarian looking for a book whose title he has forgotten, saying that he remembers the story began with "Once upon a time." Or the one of the child sitting in Santa's lap, having no real request but just wanting the experience so that she could write about it. Or the one of the child crossing the street where the street lights read, "Walk, Dick, Walk." A word of warning is due. We must be careful that the cartoons we mount will not offend. I'm sure many educators clipped the recent *New Yorker* cartoon in which a teacher bluntly announces at a parent-teacher conference, "Your daughter is a pain in the ass!" Teachers may laugh when they read it; many parents and students would not.

Not all our humor stems from school-related topics. Educators do live real lives and have stories to tell apart from school. At last year's NCTE conference, six members of our faculty presented together. Joanne had the idea of introducing ourselves with a quick trivia game. We challenged the audience to guess which member of the panel was the first runner up in a beauty pageant, can eat the same exact lunch for at least two months straight, moonlights as a ski instructor, is the only member of her family not to have an Ivy League degree, played both the male and female lead in the *Pirates of Penzance*, and played the sugarplum fairy in a school performance of *The Nutcracker*. We are a playful staff, enjoying fun and games as much as our students do.

Occasionally we laugh about things that are for our eyes only, not for the little ones. Sometimes staff members play practical jokes on me, wondering how long it will take me to notice their handiwork. It took me about a week to realize that among the finger puppets standing on a high shelf in my office were some fancy European condoms with brightly painted faces. It took me about a day to see that someone had added newspaper photographs of some very unsavory characters to my collage of student faces. It took me months to realize that someone had been showcasing poetry collections on the bookcase outside my office door, selecting personally meaningful titles. (Among these were Mary Ann Hoberman's *A Fine Fat Pig* and William Coles's *I'm Mad at You!*)

Practical jokes are also played on the entire staff. Below is the invitation to a winter holiday party, distributed one year by our social committee. The front cover of this neatly folded page read quite appropriately, "Manhattan New School Celebrates the Season." But the inside page read,

Date
December 25, 1995

Time
6:00 A.M. to 6:02 A.M.

Location
Burger King

Menu
French Toast Sticks
Pocahontas Happy Meal
Diet Coke

Everyone had a great laugh and the actual details of the event were then orally announced. The pranksters wouldn't dare waste paper to reissue the invitation. (We do try to live environmentally conscious lives.) Any walk through the building reveals the wit and wisdom of the people who live there. In front of several classroom doors sit chart pads filled with interesting facts and questions that just beckon on-lookers to respond. Each day, Joanne's students post intriguing questions on a sheet outside the classroom door that's titled "Come in and ask us about . . ." One day they challenged passersby to guess the weight of the largest ice cream sundae in the world. Someone circled one of the choices given and in the margins wrote, "And Shelley ate it!" (You have to have a thick skin around this place.) Near Judy's door the students keep a pad filled with trivia. For example, one day a student wrote an interesting fact about latex, namely that both bubble gum and boots were made from this same product. An anonymous adult scribbled across the page, "I just love the taste of boots!"

One time, I hung up a clothesline filled with cardboard tee shirts. On each was a frequently asked question at school including, "Has anyone seen Shelley's keys?" (I'm always misplacing them), and "Has anyone called Errol?" He's our photocopier repair-man and our machine is always broken. If we didn't laugh about such everyday annoy-ances, we'd probably cry.

Parents too make us laugh. Fred, one of our very sociable dads, sent me a one-line fax. It read, "Do people in the Swiss cheese industry use "hole" language?" His jokes also get told and retold around our school. One of our favorites goes this way: Did you hear the one about the chicken that kept on taking out books from the li-brary? The chicken would borrow a book from the librarian and then return a few minutes later asking for another book. This continued with several return trips to the library. Finally the librarian decided to follow the chicken. The chicken left the li-brary with book in beak and made its way out to a lake. There in the middle of the lake sat a frog on a lily pad. The librarian watched as the chicken gave the book to the frog, who responded in the past tense, "READ IT, READ IT!!!" Fred shared this joke at our PTA meeting and then teachers told it to their students. All kinds of hu-mor (except for sarcasm directed at children) belong in our classrooms. Children too need to have a good belly laugh to relieve any stress and tension that might be com-ing their way.

And then of course there's our clever custodian John, a very serious Elvis (the "Big E") fan. In one letter (Figure 4.15), he advises me how best to select new students for the school. He wants to make sure our students turn out to be "real people," not the "stuffed-shirt" types he dramatically calls mannequins.

There are restrooms on all our staircase landings. Unfortunately, each has a floor-to-ceiling window, with no window guards. These rooms must be kept locked in order to prevent children from entering these potentially dangerous settings. Much to our frustration, the locks sometimes jam. John said they worked. I said they didn't. We made a bet and John checked the locks, after which he sent me a humorous note (see Figure 4.16). John was also responsible for any rodent problems we might encounter at the school. He met this challenge with humor as well (see Figure 4.17). Sometimes John has taken on different personas in his notes to me (see Figure 4.18).

Shelley,

I feel it is my duty as a parent To inform you That admissions (new) is a great responsibility. It is *extremely important That you realize this (age (4-9) is Manequin busting years. I feel 'extremely* obligated To help out. So please remember the important qualities To look for.

1) Must listen to the "Big E"
2) Must have Sang doo-wop music under the street light with at least 4 other people. (No other music can be substituted) Especially DISCO Listening To disco is a violation Application rejected on spot. Disco is a true form of ManequiniSM!
3) Have To love AND Respect The janitor!

OVER

* Please note I spelled extremly (extremely) to 2 different ways, ~~top~~ praying I spelled it right once.)

GOOD LUCK AND Happy Manequin BUSTiNG.

Sincerly,
J.D.

P.S. ANY problems busting Manequins, who you gonna Call,
CALL ☎ 1-800-Manequin BuSTER
OR 772-0460
Toll free Manequin 24 hour hot liNE

Figure 4.15

In one of my favorite short notes from John, he teases me that he is going to be leaving the Manhattan New School for a time (see Figure 4.19).

Unfortunately, John did leave us after four wonderful years. He moved on to take care of a high school closer to home. We still miss him, but appreciate the legacy he left. He taught us to not take ourselves too seriously, to be willing to laugh at ourselves, and most of all he reminded us to take care of one another and to delight in one another's company. Another custodian, Neil Donovan, took his place and arrived right before our building was to undergo major renovations. During the summer Neil sent me a calendar of the scheduled work from the subcontractor. There was a list of jobs to be done as well as the anticipated dates for completion of this work. For example, next to "Interior floor tiles," the contractor filled in "Third week in July." He then anticipated the work schedule for the chimney replacement and the new roof. At the bottom of the list, Neil added one more job. It read, "Provide ulcers," and the calendar indicated that this phase would last the entire summer. Once again we are fortunate and grateful to have a custodian with a grand sense of humor. Additionally, every time an anxious staff member greets Neil with a barage of requests first thing in the morning, he responds with a "Good morning. How are you?" reminding us that common etiquette goes a long way and that each of us deserves to be treated with respect. Once again we need to extend that gracious invitation for our new custodian to participate fully in the life of our school.

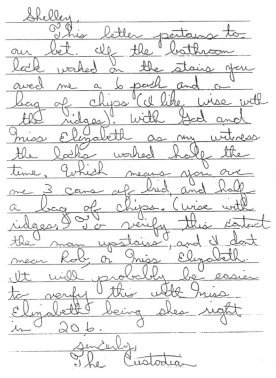

Figure 4.16

Multigrade Moments

When our school first opened, we had many multigrade classrooms. As the years went on, teachers requested fewer and fewer of these options. Among their many reasons for opting out of the multigrade class arrangements were the increasingly high registers and the increasing number of different languages spoken in their classrooms. Teachers were concerned that they weren't meeting all their students' needs in the best ways they knew how. Multigrade responsibilities felt like just one more thing to think about. Teachers were well aware of all the advantages of multiage grouping, including a nurturing family feel and the absence of competition between students at different places in their learning. They knew that multigrade classrooms meant no labeling of children and no comparison of children to other children the same age. They pointed out, however, that these conditions already existed in our school. Our teachers thought a multigrade tone already existed in our school, and they were right.

Opportunities for Multigrade Interaction

Currently, we do have several multigrade classrooms, but the majority of our classes contain children of approximately the same age. All students, however, have lots of reasons and opportunities to work and play alongside children younger and older than

Mrs. Harwayne,

This morning I was informed That The Teacher in 205, had a visitor.

She Then Told me, "Either the visitor goes or I go". With that in mind, I was wondering when is The farewell party for The Teacher? The visitor is here To stay. As a matter of. fact im sure The visitor will be bringing company eventually.

Sincerly,
John D (custodian)

P.S. If I miss The party, Tell Jo Anne it was nice Knowing her. ☺

P.S. P.S Ask Jo Anne for details about This mousey situation

Figure 4.17

To Mrs Harwayne,

over the summer Time, we were stripped and waxed. Dont we look shiny + happy? You know what would make us unhappy? If your Teachers scraped us with Their furniture. ouch! Please ask the custodian To bring up a hand Truck To move The furniture. This will keep us shiny + happy.

Many Thanks,
The 2ND floor Floor.

Figure 4.18

Shelley,
   I have news for you.
There's a new program out
called "FROM Your SlopSINK to our
SlopSiNK" (I have been Selected
for This eliTe program) IT's a
janitors Sabittacal. I'll be in
Europe Six months to learn The
latest in janiTorAl Techniques.
          SincerelY YouRS JANiTOR — John

Figure 4.19

themselves. A family feel does exist in our school community. Our students feel like they belong to a school, not just a class (and they feel like they belong to a community, not just to a school). Children feel at home in one another's classrooms and in the corridors not near their home classrooms. Children of different ages frequently work and play together. In all of the following arrangements, children are not gathered in size-place order or by their birth dates, but rather like adults in the real world, who have opportunities to meet with a wide range of people who share common needs, interests and commitments.

All of our students have opportunities to:

• Serve as guest speakers in one another's classrooms

• Share books and other materials from one another's classrooms

• Serve as interview resources for one another

• Join one another's reader-response groups

• Take part in one another's math workshops

• Read to children in different classes

• Share their writing with new audiences

• Teach one another how to keep writer's notebooks

• Make teaching appointments to share areas of expertise

• Serve as tutors for one another

• Read the same school anthologies and perform poetry together

• Sing together in the school chorus

• Perform together in the school orchestra

• Serve as translators for one another

- Go on field trips together
- Visit siblings' writing workshops
- Serve on the student council together
- Join clubs across grade level, playing chess, talking baseball, etc.
- Travel on the school buses together
- Attend after-school programs together
- Play in the yards together
- Attend English as a second language and resource room classes together
- Offer computer guidance to friends of many ages
- Perform community service alongside older and younger children
- Participate in joint workshops with other whole classes
- Spend time in classrooms engaged in similar content studies (see checklist in Appendix 10)

When children of different ages get together in these supportive settings, to work, play, engage in serious conversations, or carry out significant projects, they are learning incredibly important life-skills and they are strengthening the nurturing social tone in our building. I recently hosted a long-term author study with a second-grade class coupled with a fifth-grade class. Working alongside one another, there were absolutely no hints of competition, impatience, or intolerance. The older children seemed to naturally bring to center stage their respect for individual differences, their ability to understand other people's opinions and points of view, and their understanding of the need for gracious response and patient collaboration. The younger children approached the older students with pride, awe, and gratitude. The more across-grade projects, rituals, and events we can weave into our everyday school lives, the better our social tone will continue to grow.

Celebrations

When our families hold a street festival, Fest with Zest, each spring, they advertise it as a celebration of school and community. What we've learned is that celebrating our life together cannot be reserved for one Saturday in May. When the social tone in a school is supportive and nurturing, every day is a day of celebration. But there are several times during the year when we do get together to publicly acknowledge how grateful we are to be together.

Our celebrations begin immediately following the first week of school, when our five-year-olds have worked their way up to staying full days. We hold a Welcome Back to School Parade. It's very rare for us to hold "specials" on school time, but this brief, half-hour one is worth it. Children and their teachers simply walk around the block, just once, carrying handmade signs, wearing homemade hats, and sometimes singing or chanting appropriate tunes. They are announcing, "We are happy to be back." They are stating Eve's familiar line, "Come in, we're open!" This event is important to me for several reasons. It lets the community, the merchants and residents, know that they have nothing to fear. We are a respectful, joyful, diverse group of learners who would very much like to see the walls come tumbling down between school and community. When our neighbors meet us early on, it's more likely that the chefs and the shopkeepers, the museum curators and the custodians, the greengrocers and the gardeners, will say, "Yes, I'd be delighted!" when we ask them to be guest speakers, to let us visit their job sites, or to donate goods and services. The parade also gives our mamas and papas and grandmas and grandpas the chance to officially acknowledge that summer is over, that their children will now spend their weekdays in the hands of energetic, joyful people who care about children. Lots of cameras click and videos whir on the sidewalks that September morning.

The parade also does something very important for our children. Years ago, when the opening day of school was postponed for several weeks due to an asbestos problem in some locations, our children, much to the public's surprise, were not celebrating. Contrary to popular belief, they wanted to get back into the building. They missed their friends, their teachers, their books, their projects. They even missed school lunches. When we send out our Welcome Back to School letters each fall, I try to find an appropriate poem to soften the letter, which is filled with all the necessary nitty-gritty details of scheduling and class assignments. Unfortunately, it is a lot easier to find negative poems about the return to school than positive ones. We need to change the public's ideas about children's attitudes toward school.

Not too long ago, a school volunteer named Marie Faust Evitt published a column in the "My Turn" section of *Newsweek* magazine. In it, she suggests that the public stop acting "as though school is a holding tank rather than a launching pad." She astutely points out that in June, children are frequently asked if they are happy that school is almost over, but no one would think to ask them if they are happy that Little League is over. The wonderful writer Robert Lipsyte writes a "Coping" column for *The New York Times*. Several years ago he described the return of teachers to a middle school in Brooklyn. He notes, "School can be such fun before the students arrive." True, it is fun on those first few days back when the adults are able to give undivided attention to one another and swap summer stories, but school must continue to be fun after the students arrive. Our parade lets the public know that we are all happy to be back together. It lets our students know that it is not nerdy to like school. (See Chapter 8, "Sing About It!").

Our Turkish students have told me that there is a Children's Day celebration in Turkey. On this very special day, children participate in running the national government, and kids throughout the country receive free ice cream, free transportation, and free entrance to movies. My friend Kerstin Palmqvist is a principal of a school in Gothenberg, Sweden. One year I visited with her on the first day of school. I was stunned by the beautiful bouquets of flowers that filled the building in honor of the first day back. So although some of our teachers joke about putting paper bags over their heads when they are asked to march around the block, we will keep parading. When schools are kind and caring places, students, teachers, and administrators love school. That's cause for celebration.

Classrooms are, of course, filled with celebrations. Teachers and students celebrate birthdays, change of seasons, the work of volunteers and student teachers, the arrival of class pets, the launching of particular courses of study, (see Figure 4.20) as well as the greatly anticipated hundredth day of school. (Children and teachers bring in their "hundreds" collections for these special days. My favorite one over the years has been Paul Filippini's. He brought in one hundred silver clips, each etched with the name of a color. They were used by his blind mother Elizabeth to make sure that Paul left for school each day with a matching outfit.) Dilta, Isabel's friend and a classroom volunteer, celebrates her own birthday each June by treating the kindergartners to a visit by a professional clown or a magician. Paula Rogovin and her first graders end all their content studies with a bigger-than-life family celebration.

It's A Picnic!!!

JUNE 9, 1997

DEAR K-206 & 3-508 FAMILIES,

ON FRIDAY, JUNE 13, PAM'S CLASS AND RENAY'S CLASS WILL CELEBRATE OUR STORY PARTNER FRIENDSHIP IN CENTRAL PARK. WE WILL ENJOY A PICNIC LUNCH TOGETHER. PLEASE SEND YOUR CHILD'S LUNCH IN A DISPOSABLE BAG. (NO GLASS PLEASE.) IF YOUR CHILD USUALLY EATS SCHOOL LUNCH, A BAGGED LUNCH WILL BE PROVIDED.

WE ARE PLANNING A STORY PARTNER POETRY ANTHOLOGY CELEBRATION WITH FAMILIES FROM BOTH CLASSES ON FRIDAY, JUNE 20. BE ON THE LOOKOUT FOR INVITATIONS VERY SOON!

SINCERELY,

Pam & Renay

PAM MAYER AND RENAY SADIS

Figure 4.20

Celebrations are not just for young children. Renay Sadis's students and their families celebrate their yearlong immigration study with an international luncheon. Joan Backer celebrates every return to school after a vacation or holiday break by providing a bagel breakfast for her students. Judy Davis, a masterful teacher of fifth and sixth graders really does Byrd Baylor's title proud. She really is "in charge of celebrations." She not only orchestrates wonderful graduations, she also creates surprising moments of celebration all through the year. The best part of Judy's classroom celebrations is that they involve parents.

As noted earlier, we don't celebrate any religious holidays in our school. We even downplay Halloween. (Most of the early-childhood teachers, in fact, leave the building on this last day of October, taking their students apple picking. Trick-or-treating has become too dangerous a tradition for us to promote in the big city. Besides, it's hard to read and write with a roomful of costumed children filled with sweets. The holiday is, as well, rooted in religious beliefs.) We do, however, celebrate the change of seasons. Several weeks before their autumn celebration, Judy and her students begin collecting bits and pieces of autumnal collage materials. They fill a carton with photographs, fabric swatches, magazine clippings, greeting cards, gift wrappings, and the like, each covered with leaves, pumpkins, and other harvest scenes, in shades of orange, brown, and green. The invitations are sent home, announcing an autumn celebration. I'm not sure what the families expect, but they are always surprised. Judy puts them to work. Every adult is assigned a cluster of children and challenged to create a collaborative autumn collage. The adult touches make the works of art very distinctive and the collages light up our hallways for many weeks. Joyful parent participation is the added benefit to this celebration. All parents can participate. You don't need to speak English well, or read any directions. It is a very inclusive celebration of community. In the weeks that follow, Judy invites students to create titles for each work of art and to craft original poems to accompany them. If we ever think to include these masterpieces in our annual school auction, we would probably raise significant amounts of money.

Judy's classroom poetry performance is also a wonderful celebration of community. When they respond to the invitations, family members no doubt expect to hear poetry read aloud by their children. Instead, Judy once again puts them to work. As each adult arrives, they are given a sheet of poems carefully chosen for their choral reading potential, and they are assigned a cluster of students to work with. Judy sends them all off to choose one poem and prepare a choral reading of it. The students help the parents understand the performance of poetry. When they return we are always bowled over by their clever arrangements. Again, the adult touches make these performances very memorable. Parents who love to sing, dance, or play music add interesting twists to the choral performances, and the contrast of sweet youthful voices and deep adult ones adds even more texture to these choral reads. (For more ways on helping parents appreciate the work we do, see Chapter 5, "Reaching Out to Families.")

We have several additional annual schoolwide celebrations. Most are held during the evenings or on the weekends. They include an International Potluck Dinner, a Saturday Morning Ice-Skating Get-Together, a Winter Solstice Music Celebration (see Figure 4.21), and our annual Family Picnic in Central Park. Just recently, I invited two sisters to begin an annual children's concert, a talent show of sorts. Colby and Haden had just beautifully sung "Don't Fence Me In," complete with verses that the teachers gathered had never even heard of. When they were done, Isabel remarked, "Way to go, Colby and Haden!" "Perfect name for a children's performance," I thought, "The Way to Go concert." After each student performs, I could imagine the audience responding, "Way to go!" (If the children arrange such an annual event, it will give the entire community yet another way to observe our children's special gifts.)

As noted earlier, we also host an open house of sorts, Grand People's Day, for grandparents and other significant family members or friends, on the Monday following the Thanksgiving holiday break. So many guests are in town, that we invite them in to see where their favorite children spend so much time. The morning is business as usual. We don't put on any shows; it's a nonspecial special. Our favorite kind.

Throughout the school year, the central board of education schedules periodic half-days so that teachers can participate in professional development activities during school hours. The children leave at lunchtime. Last year, rather than trying to pretend that these very short days were just like any other, our music teacher Diane suggested that we use one of these June mornings for our annual "Dancing in the Street" celebration. We blocked off traffic, brought speakers out to the sidewalk, and entertained our neighbors and each other with a wide range of dances. The children who had studied ballroom dancing danced the merengue, the tango, and the cha-cha. Children who had been studying colonial America performed the Virginia reel. Students who had been studying the Native Americans in the New York area taught us a dance that paid tribute to corn. Almost everyone joined in on the hard-to-resist macarena. This year our "Dancing in the Street" morning will be devoted to rock and roll. Children will dance the twist, mashed potato, stroll, bunny hop, and lindy too. Diane had the right idea. These halfday mornings are perfect for special gatherings and celebrations. (See Chapter 6, "Talking Curriculum and Assessment," for half-day portfolio assessment tasks.)

Not all of our school celebrations involve children. Some are for adults only, like class cocktail parties held in family apartments, Saturday evening dances, and the end-of-the-year Teacher's Recognition party hosted by the parents. Then too, there are a few staff-only get-togethers, like the annual end-of-year faculty barbecue at my home and the December holiday dinner in a local restaurant. Perhaps the get-togethers that are even more important are the spur-of-the-moment ones, when staff members decide to go around the corner to the Easy Street happy hour and share rum runners, bowls of popcorn, and good conversations after school. These kinds of celebrations remind us how lucky we are to be working alongside one another.

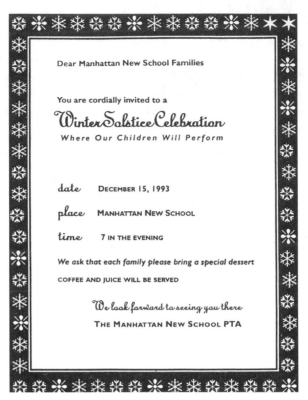

Dear Manhattan New School Families

You are cordially invited to a

Winter Solstice Celebration

Where Our Children Will Perform

date   DECEMBER 15, 1993

place   MANHATTAN NEW SCHOOL

time   7 IN THE EVENING

We ask that each family please bring a special dessert
COFFEE AND JUICE WILL BE SERVED

We look forward to seeing you there
THE MANHATTAN NEW SCHOOL PTA

Figure 4.21

The Importance of a Supportive Social Tone

It is essential for students, teachers, parents, administrators, support staff, and community members to treat one another with respect, dignity, and humanity in all schools, but particularly in whole language schools. A supportive social tone must be a top priority when there are so many occasions for social interaction. When children sit in rows and must ask permission to move, speak, or turn to the next page, there are many fewer opportunities to interact with neighboring children. Not so in whole language schools.

After her visit to our school, Mary Ellen Giacobbe sent me a copy of Doris Kearns Goodwin's memoir, *Wait Till Next Year*, along with a gracious letter. In part, she wrote,

> It wasn't until I read Doris Kearns Goodwin's memoir, *Wait Till Next Year*, that I realized what I wanted and needed to say to you. As a child she had the opportunity to acquire and develop so many of her passions. For her, it all started with baseball. But her curiosity, her devotion to her subject, her opportunities to share it with others, her sense of belonging in her neighborhood (and being important)—all this helped to develop her strong narrative voice and to shape who she is—a wonderful historian and human being.
>
>   I think this is what I saw at MNS. Teachers and students acquiring and developing pas-

sions, sharing with one another, and such a strong sense of belonging to something very important. MNS is the neighborhood that Goodwin was so fortunate to belong to as a child but so many children miss today.

No doubt Mary Ellen's kind and insightful words were inspired by the social tone she recognized. The Manhattan New School does bring to my mind the Brooklyn neighborhood in which I grew up, with all the mothers and grandmothers hanging out of their apartment house windows, keeping an eye on *all* the children, not just their own. So too, teachers, paraprofessionals, and school aides keep an eye on *all* the children. They work in a school, not just in a classroom. Similarly, our children are expected to care for the entire community, not just their classroom and not just their classmates. We are all in this together. Adults and children alike believe we belong to something very important. And it is this feeling of being members of the Manhattan New School community that inspires children and teachers to work their hardest and do their best. After all, they know that everyone in the "neighborhood" will take pride in their accomplishments.

RELATED READINGS IN COMPANION VOLUMES

Lifetime Guarantees (Heinemann, forthcoming), will be abbreviated as LG.
Writing Through Childhood (Heinemann, forthcoming), will be abbreviated as WC.

Putting student writing to good use	**LG**: Ch. 3.
	WC: Ch. 9.
Writing letters	**LG**: Ch. 3.
	WC: Ch. 7.
Watching our language	**LG**: Ch. 10.
Appreciating literature as a humanizing tool	**LG**: Ch. 1, Ch. 6.
Using poetry to enrich school life	**LG**: Ch. 5.
Having many ways to excel in the writing workshop	**WC**: Ch. 4, Ch. 7. **LG**: Ch. 3, Ch. 4, Ch. 5.
Paying attention to children's language	**LG**: Ch. 10.
Valuing custodians who write	**LG**: Ch. 3.
Honoring the performance of poetry	**LG**: Ch. 5.

CHAPTER 5

REACHING OUT TO FAMILIES

Priorities

- We must trust that family members have a great deal to teach staff members about their children and will do so if we extend gracious invitations and present important ways and opportunities for them to share.

- When classrooms and teaching techniques differ from the ways family members were taught, we must discover effective and engaging ways to help them understand alternate approaches to teaching and learning.

- We must have as high standards about the materials we send home to families as we do about the material we put in students' hands.

- Schools must work hard to involve as many parents and family members as possible in the life of the school.

Practice

- On inventing structures to help family members keep staff members informed, including background letters and family literacy portfolios.

- On discovering day and evening structures to educate family members about teaching and learning, including narrated tours, parent writing workshops, and courses of study.

- On using engaging techniques for family involvement, including slide shows and video presentations, student speakers, and reading aloud from appropriate literature.

- On sending worthwhile materials home, including newsletters, photo albums, and poetry for adults.

- On finding ways for all family members to contribute to the life of the school, including volunteer programs, fund-raising, and political activism.

- On ways to get more parents involved.

REACHING OUT TO FAMILIES

Photo Credit: Tammy DiPaolo

A teacher from Denver, Colorado, sent me the following Elizabeth Stone quote. "The decision to have a child . . . it's momentous. It is to decide forever to have your heart go walking outside your body." I have had this quote hanging over my desk at work for many years. It reminds me to take our students' parents very seriously. I may see things differently than they do at times, but I've learned to pay close attention to their requests, questions, and concerns. That doesn't mean that I honor all their requests, but I do take them seriously. After all, that child is their heart walking outside their body. The quote reminds me that parents deserve patience, tolerance, and kindness.

In my previous professional life as a university-based staff developer, I did not have to deal with many of the issues school-based educators face. I was never in schools, for example, during standardized testing weeks. Professional development activities are usually put on hold during those agonizing times. Fortunately, and to the best of my memory, I was also never in schools during an outbreak of head lice. Then too, I don't ever recall being in schools at the same time parents were there. I never sat in on parent-teacher conferences, never eavesdropped on parents talking to administrators, never attended PTA meetings, never attended fund-raisers. I have no regrets about missing out on the frenzy of standardized tests or outbreaks of head lice, but I do regret never having spent time with parents. Of course, I'm making up for it now.

In an earlier chapter, I described my wish for a full-time parent educator. I could easily imagine having someone on staff who is ever on call to help new family members understand why their child's homework looks so very different from the kind they remember getting, why there are no weekly spelling tests covered with happy-face stickers, or why there are no textbooks, workbooks, or basal readers. I could easily imagine having someone on staff who has big blocks of time to teach parents how best to help their child at home when they come across a difficult word in their reading or struggle with spelling in their writing. I could get very used to having someone on staff who can speak to parents in Maltese, Macedonian, Burmese, and Albanian, or translate letters home into Portuguese, Serbo-Croatian, Spanish, French, and Urdu. But of course, we have no parent educator and all of the above challenges are up to us.

Some principals complain that parents take up too much of their time at school. I don't have that problem. Our parents don't have many complaints. And when they do, they voice their concerns in appropriate ways at appropriate times. Our parents don't hang out. They are very present, active, and essential to the life of our school, but they don't live there. If they have time to give, they are helpful and productive. Our parents don't expect to unilaterally set school policies. They contribute to these policies in many ways, but they don't seek to control decision making at our school. Over the years and much to my delight, I discovered that I like spending time with parents because our moments together add up. In the remainder of this chapter I describe the structures, activities, and school policies that invite worthwhile parental interactions in the school, as well as those which are still on our list of "Good Ideas, Yet to Happen."

Extending the Gracious Invitation

Carmen, our teacher of Spanish, is also an accomplished early-childhood teacher, and in her first year at our school she taught kindergarten. As is common in kindergarten, Carmen asked families to rotate the responsibility of bringing in a week's worth of snacks for the entire class. What a surprise when Henry's dad, Gary, walked in with a snack he had prepared himself. This professional chef had carved an exact replica of a hansom cab (a horse and buggy with a driver, used to take visitors on tours of Manhattan) out of cantaloupe and cheese. The children couldn't wait to pull it apart and eat it; the grown-ups needed to marvel awhile and capture this "Kodak moment." Everyone at school appreciated how much this one talented parent had to offer, and we trust this is true for all our parents. Although each parent has a different specialty, they are all willing to share if invited. (The PTA, in fact, asks each family to fill out a home survey and has recently compiled the responses in a database. We can now scroll down the computer screen when we need a guest speaker on a particular topic, or someone to help with a specialized project or provide a field trip connection.)

Structures for Family Involvement

Besides their hobbies and vocations, parents and families can also offer us what we need most—information about their children. I listened in awe several years ago when Denny Taylor, acclaimed researcher and professor at Hofstra University, spoke at NCTE, making a passionate plea for educators *not* to rely on what she called bureaucratic literacy. We must find lots of real ways to learn about our students. Tapping parents is a good place to begin. The following structures enable parents to make the educators in the building their students for awhile.

Occasions for Informal Talk

Teachers frequently gather important information about their students in very surprising places. Not everything is contained in cumulative records, health cards, or student portfolios. Our teachers gain some of their most helpful insights when they bump into parents as they shop at the corner deli, stand in line for coffee at Starbucks, or wait for the Second Avenue bus. Then too, teachers learn a great deal of useful information when the culture of the building says it's okay for a concerned parent to stop by before class begins, or grab a teacher en route to the cafeteria, or linger with the teacher in the playground at dismissal. Several years ago, Isabel Beaton wrote an article eloquently entitled "Chit Chat." In it, she elevates what we learn about each other through informal conversation, what she describes as "hanging out on the back fence." Isabel is a master at listening to parents' stories, and she remains incredibly protective of these occasions for casual dialogue. She warns us not to take away the spontaneity of these moments when she says, "I'm going to keep calling it chit-chat because in education if you change the language of something to make it more academic, there soon appears a chit-chat specialist, a chit-chat supervisor, a chit-chat coordinator, and before you know it, here I am—a chit-chat consultant." The principle of chit-chat applies as well to building administrators. As mentioned earlier, I deliberately place cozy seating areas in convenient locations so that people will be encouraged to stop and say, "Can I talk to you for a minute?"

Accommodating Appointment Times

Parents (and I'm using the term liberally now to refer to all legal guardians and people who are significant in the lives of our students) also need opportunities for regularly scheduled and arranged appointments. According to Board of Education regulations, our teachers must meet with parents every November and March. Half days of school are provided as well as evening conference times. These rushed moments are never enough, especially when parents are now poring over student portfolios and listening to their students describe their own growth and goals. If we allowed only the ten-minute sessions allotted to parents, we wouldn't learn very much from them. In fact, they would hardly have a moment to talk. Instead, we try to be much more generous and creative in our scheduling. We are determined to carve out half-hour blocks of time to meet with families. In the months of November and March, it's not surprising to see a teacher sitting right outside her classroom door, meeting with a child and his parent while a student teacher looks after the class. Teachers also schedule family meetings before school, after school, and during their preparation times. Teachers are also very accessible during the other months of the year to meet with parents. All they have to do is ask, and appointments are easily made. Parents and teachers frequently talk on the telephone at night or e-mail one another, particularly if there is a crisis brewing. Some parents prefer in person meetings, particularly folks who aren't comfortable speaking English and want to bring along a bilingual neighbor, friend, or relative.

Occasionally, parents ask to meet with me because they have *special* concerns about their child's well-being. Most of the time, parents go directly to their children's teachers with their concerns about academics, peer relationships, and matters of health. It's not unusual on an open-school evening for me to sit alone in my office, with only an occasional parent stopping in to say hello. (When you hire brilliant teachers, it is not surprising that few parents ask for meetings with the principal.) I am always happy to meet with parents. Just as Paul's mother, Elizabeth, taught me so much about the teaching of reading, so too all family members have lessons to teach. My only rule for appointments is that they must be scheduled before school or after school, so I can spend as much time as possible in classrooms with students and teachers. Parents understand this preference. In fact, I think they admire it. (Of course, I must break this rule for any family or community emergency.)

Accessible Mailboxes

I hung mailboxes on classroom doors primarily to cut down the number of interruptions, but I think they also serve as invitations to parents to keep us informed. There's a mailbox with my name on it hanging on the door of the poetry reading room, my favorite hang-out. Parents frequently let me know what they are thinking by taking pen to paper.

Sometimes, they write to tell me just how wonderful they think their child's teacher is. Clive's parents appreciated Paula's social studies curriculum, which revolves around the cultural backgrounds of her students. They wrote a long letter describing their son's experiences in first grade. In part it reads, "For Paula, multiculturalism is not a pandering to political correctness. . . . It's the way she coaxed every child into participating in the class, every day, and her way of unifying the class. It also encouraged phenomenal class participation from parents." I appreciated that Clive's parents sent this acknowledgment to me as well as to the mayor of New York City.

Frequently, parents send me notes asking for advice or my opinion. These too help me to understand what is going on in our students' lives. Some days, the questions are easy to answer like, "What do you think of Hooked on Phonics?" or "How do you think a 'gifted' program would be different from our school?" or "What happens if children hear 'bad' language in the playground?" Other times, the questions are more complex and I don't feel wise enough to respond. One mother wonders if her son is old enough to hear about the Holocaust. Another asks if I think her son is too young to read Stephen King's books. A father asks what I would do with a child who seems to being growing closer each day to an imaginary friend. The parents seem to trust my opinions; I only wish I had all the right answers. When I'm really stumped, I ask permission to bring up the question at our weekly staff meeting. Parental concerns often lead to interesting conversations, and thirty good thinkers inevitably hit on helpful insights.

At-Home Assignments

Besides all the kinds of correspondence described above, when we are in need of specific kinds of information, we "assign" topics. For example, Joanne Hindley Salch asks parents to write reflective pages on their child's portfolio. (See her book, *In the Company of Children*.) Regina asks parents to take part in a class family journal. The book is filled with a photograph of each child, and family members are encouraged to write about their son or daughter, sister or brother. The book gets passed around from one family to another. Other teachers ask family members to comment on their own reading habits and to compile lists of the kinds of writing they do every day. In preparation for last year's graduation ceremonies, Cindy and Judy asked the parents of the graduates to write down images from their own graduation days. We wove these into a short speech to be delivered at graduation. It was filled with memories of bad hairdos, hot auditoriums, endless speeches, out-of-tune instruments, champagne toasts, loud kisses, tight hugs, and pink lace dresses.

Background Letters   As principal, I also ask parents to accept a few written assignments. Whenever a new student joins our school I send the following letter to families.

Dear families,

We have a tradition at the Manhattan New School. We ask families to write to us about their children.

Nine years ago, when my son was about to leave home for Harvard University, I was asked by the housing directors to write an honest letter about Michael in order that they find just the right roommates for him. I found their request incredibly challenging and at the same time very rewarding. I discovered that I had so much to say.

Won't you please take some time this summer and share with us any information you think would help us work with your children in ways that are wise and rewarding. Feel free to include family stories, anecdotes, memorable conversations, as well as descriptions of strengths, weaknesses, likes, dislikes, fears, and passions. We'd also be interested to learn the story behind their names.

Although we won't be using this information to find roommates for your children (they really do have to leave us at three o'clock), we will put any information you offer to good use. To this day, my son remains close friends with his very first college roommates. They were a perfect match.

Thanks for helping us get to know your child in really important ways.

Sincerely,
Shelley

Of course, not all parents respond to my request, but many do. I have hundreds of background letters on file. The one that I include here (see Figure 5.1) demonstrates clearly how valuable it is to tap parents as informants about their own children. In addition, the letter by Riri's mother brings up the need to translate our letters into many languages. As an undergraduate, I was a Spanish literature major. I always knew that studying Spanish was more than a life pleasure. Indeed, it has come in very handy at work. But of course, our parents speak so many different languages that we must depend on members of the community to serve as translators.

Not only must we make every attempt to translate the letters we send home, we must also graciously invite parents to respond in the best way they can. Some ask friends or relatives to translate their words into English. Some respond in person, preferring to talk rather than attempt to write in English. Others bring translators to their meetings. Some respond in their first language, knowing that, with their permission, I will find someone to translate their letter. Riri's mother explained to me that a friend helped her to write her exquisite response.

After reading letters like Atsuko's, we wonder how we can teach well without knowing all that fills our students' minds. Inviting parents to teach us about their children has the added benefit of encouraging otherwise-reserved parents to share.

Dear Ms. Shelley Harwayne

    I write down about my daughter, Riri NAGAO, in response to your request. It is so hard for me to do it. Because my English is no good. But I try to do it.

    We have met with the death of two acquaintances in this summer. One of them is Riri's playmate. Riri asked me on the return way after we went to his memorial service.

Riri : Did Julius die ?

I : Yes

Riri : After the person died, where does he go ? Where did Julius go ?

I : He returned to the universe. But he will come back soon, he will be born again soon.

Riri : When ?

I : I cannot say when. But if we pray a lot for him he will come back soon.

Riri : Yes ? Same to me ? Even if I will die, I will be able to be born again soon ?

I : Yes. Although Riri is born as my daughter in this lifetime, you had died in the past life.

Riri : Had I been in the universe before ?

I : Yes. Your father and I wish Riri would be born as our child, so we prayed a lot for that. And you were born to us.

Riri : Did father and mother pray very much ?

I : Yes, we did.

She asked me the death many times before. When she saw that a pigeon had died in the park. When she saw that a mouse had died on the street. And she asked why the petals of cherry blossoms fell. why leaves of the trees died and fell in autumn. I cannot tell how she feels and thinks for the death, if she has the obscure fear and anxiety for it. But after this conversation, she sometimes asked me "Will you die some day ? And father ? I will also get old and die ? But I can be born again ? "

    When I think about what her strengths is, I recall last summer. She likes to play monkey bar, but she couldn't do it at the beginning of July. She tried and practiced many times. She got blisters and broken them on her palms. She cried and cried for pain and not being able to do it, but didn't stop practicing. And finally she could do it toward the end of August. Also she tried to push swing by herself this summer. and accomplished it. I think she really challenges and makes an effort for her likes.

    About her weaknesses. She is short-tempered and stubborn, I think. And she is likely to be possessed by a preconceived idea and her own thinking. She is weak in thinking and judging the situations cool from various angles.

    She likes Anpanman and Melonpanna, which are popular animation characters in Japan. She likes Power Ranger. She likes painting, cooking, singing, dancing, ridding on a bicycle, putting on a cute and pretty dress.

    She dislikes putting on a pants. When she is catching a cold, I always ask her to do it. But she never gives a nod at first. When she must do it unwillingly, she is hurt her feelings.

    About the passion, I cannot grasp that meaning very well. But if I do it as a desire, Riri is eager to fly in the sky like a Superman, a fairy or a bird. She asked me to make a cape before, so I made it for her. She always puts on it in home, in the park or on the street. She said, "I want to fly." ..... "But I cannot fly by this cape that mother made." She was disappointed so much. However, she still has this dream of flying in the sky freely.

Sincerely,

Atsuko NAGAO

Figure 5.1

Some day I would love to invite parents to inform us in the following additional ways:

- Send in a videotape of a bedtime read-aloud.
- Prepare a bibliography with your child of their at-home libraries.
- Keep a journal recording real-world occasions in which your child thought like a mathematician.
- Send in a photograph of yourself reading to your child along with a written description of the scene. (This would make a great wall display and when taken down would form a wonderful school anthology.)
- Send in reading material used by your child when they were attending school in another country or another city. Comment how this material was used.

Family Literacy Portfolios Last year I began a very new tradition at school. I decided to invite parents in on the fun that all our students were having keeping portfolios. I wrote the following letter to our families:

Dear families,

As you know by now, our students have begun to keep portfolios in order to share proud learning moments across the curriculum. They're filling these portfolios with artifacts which demonstrate their breakthroughs, reflections on their learning processes, as well as their hopes for future studies.

At this time, I'd like to invite each of you to create a very special family literacy portfolio. It is my hope that this unique collection will document all the ways you've helped your children learn to read and write as well as the ways you've instilled a love of lifelong literacy in your children.

Years ago, the summer before my daughter was to leave for college, I made a quilt for her dormitory bed. It was made up of squares cut from her favorite tee shirts. Each patch contained a logo from the schools she attended, the cities she visited, the clubs she belonged to, as well as her favorite teams, bands, and movie stars. Throughout her childhood, I had saved all the tee shirts that had deep personal connections for her. Whenever I tell this story, people comment, "I wish I had heard that idea years ago, I would have saved all those tee shirts."

Similarly, twenty years ago when my children were just starting their literacy journeys, I wish someone had suggested a family literacy portfolio. I would now be able to tenderly turn the pages of a scrapbook (binder, photo album, journal) to recall those literacy moments. I probably would have slipped in copies of little notes I tucked into my children's lunch boxes, instructions for playing Probe and Boggle, book covers from their favorite read-alouds, ranging from Peggy Parish's Amelia Bedelia *to C. S. Lewis's* The Lion, the Witch and the Wardrobe. *I would have also copied in my children's favorite poems from our dog-eared copy of Wendy and Clyde Watson's* Father Fox's Pennyrhymes.

I probably would have also tried to capture in writing our weekly visits to the bookmobile when we lived in a rural neighborhood, and our delight when our children began to read street signs from the backseat of the family car, and the look of those bedroom bookcases before grown-up novels replaced picture-books, pop-up books, and the scratch-and-sniff books that became so popular in the 1970s. Most likely, I would have included a letter to the editor my son wrote about Soviet Jewry that was published in the Staten Island Advance *in the early 1980s and a letter my daughter wrote to a young Native American boy she saw a picture of in Newsweek magazine when they were both eight years old. Little Sun Bordeaux made the news because he was a Jewish Native American. My daughter was intrigued by his background and by his cute photograph and wrote him a very friendly letter. She never heard from him—that is, not until fourteen years later. When she was about to leave for law school, she finally received a response. Had I kept a portfolio, Little Sun's "better late than never" response would be a great addition.*

And if I had kept this portfolio current, I would have slipped in copies of all the news clippings, miss-you cards, and captioned family photographs I have continued to mail to my son and daughter as they moved from college to graduate school.

If only someone had suggested saving all these treasured things in one special container, my literacy memory bank would be much fuller and richer today. And I could imagine the thrill of sharing the collection every once in a while with my own grown children and someday with my children's children.

Just this past Thanksgiving holiday break, Judy shared with me a letter she wrote to her beautiful daughter Meredith. Our sixth graders know that as a birthday surprise, Judy restored Meredith's favorite childhood doll, a classic Holly Hobby. Along with this incredible re-creation, Judy attached a loving letter supposedly written by Holly herself. When Judy shared the letter with me, I quickly asked her permission to reprint it in this column. Judy reminds us all just how precious our childhood memories and family stories are. And she reminds us to take delight in shared family moments of music, play, drama, and of course, literature.

Enjoy Judy's letter and do begin to gather your own family literacy treasures. After the holiday break, I'll invite you to share your collection at a school gathering in order to celebrate your role in your child's literacy growth, as well as to inspire one another to try a few new family rituals and activities.

To a joyful holiday season,

Shelley

Judy's love letter to her daughter follows:

Dear Meredith,

I know I've been gone for a long time. I've kept our times together in a very special place in my heart. I remember when we used to listen to Really Rosie and The Point together and Sylvester and the Magic Pebble is still my favorite book (although I also love Big Dog, Little Dog too!). I've missed those tents made out of blankets and snuggling inside with you and the Smurfs.

How are your bones? I've been so worried because you used to hide all those vitamins in that brown couch. Do you still play the guitar? I loved to listen to you make up songs. I really loved watching Little House on the Prairie. I always thought I looked a lot like Laura when she wore her bonnet. What do you think?

But honestly, now that you're older, I can tell you truthfully what I miss most of all. It's your mother, singing us to sleep at night. When she used to sing that lullaby she wrote, "Sweet Meredith Paige," I couldn't believe someone could have such a sweet voice. I haven't had a good night's sleep since.

Well anyway, I'm so happy to be back with you. I can't wait to meet Pudge and Steve. While your mom was helping me get back into shape, she updated me on the past ten to fifteen years or so. I know you're an actress now. I always knew you had talent way back when we played those pretend games together. I was sort of stiff, but you were all life and vitality.

Oh let's not forget why I came back so suddenly. I've missed so many birthdays that I couldn't bear to miss any more.

So here we are. Together again. I love you. Happy 24th birthday

Love,
Holly

The family literacy portfolio was a very good idea, but as I continue to discover, good ideas are like a dime a dozen in schools, particularly when you are in a setting where people find everything to do with teaching and learning so very fascinating. I did send this invitational letter home in early December, but I did very little else to ensure the success of the portfolio idea. We never got together after the holidays. In fact, I almost put the entire project out of my mind entirely, getting so involved with other things as the school year went by. Finally in June, I realized I better bring some closure to this invitation. I offered to host a family portfolio display at the last PTA meeting of the year. Only a few people showed up with literacy artifacts to share. At first I was disappointed, but then realized that I did nothing in six months to guide this work or keep it on the parents' front burners. I would never have neglected a student project as I had this parent one. I would never have taken a "come what may" attitude with students, nor should I have with adults. But the other lesson I learned is that even a few engaged parents can make a difference in the life of a school. Parents tell parents. Word spreads. Next year, twice as many families will begin to save their family literacy treasures and eventually many will come to school ready to flip the pages of albums brimming with tooth fairy letters, lunch box notes, and lists of books bought for birthdays and holidays. I will, though, make a concerted effort to improve my parenting of this project. More frequent meetings. More modeling of possible ways to collect items. More telling of stories that demonstrate the value of such an undertaking. More inviting children in on the collecting. More attention paid to this valuable pursuit.

Educating Parents About Alternative Approaches to Teaching and Learning

When I was visiting the West Coast, I had dinner with a family whose child attended public school. "How are things in the schools?" I naturally asked. "Oh," she responded, "there's all this whole earth stuff going on." I knew just what she was referring to (whole language), and I also knew that her son's school hadn't made a strong enough effort to ensure that the parent body understood their ways of teaching. When parents understand and appreciate a school's ways of working, they become its strongest allies and supporters.

Prospective parents visiting from other schools, in other districts, usually ask an inordinate number of questions about homework assignments, spelling tests, and reading scores. These seem to be the criterion upon which many parents judge schools. It is rare for parents of enrolled students to ask for appointments to discuss such matters with me. Yes, our parents want their children to have reasonable amounts of worthwhile work to do at home, and yes, they want their children to go off to middle school knowing standard spelling, and yes, they want their children to do well on the entire battery of standardized tests we are required to administer, and so do we. But our parents are able to keep these things in perspective for two reasons. First, parents trust that as a staff we take these issues seriously. They know that we think long and hard about how best to assign homework, teach spelling, and help students take standardized tests. Secondly, our parents understand and appreciate *what* makes our teaching and learning effective, because we work hard at making sure this kind of information is available.

Many of the parents of our students were schooled in Eastern Europe or South America. They come with a very different image of what schools should look and sound like. If we want parents to understand and support our ways of working with children, we must take parent education very seriously. Alternate ways of teaching require alternate ways of communicating with parents. It's not enough that parents help *us* to understand their children; we have to be equally determined to find ways to help *them* understand our work with children. A teacher in Virginia commented to me that a parent complained that her classroom seemed like a birthday party all year long. We can't let even one parent believe that if children seem happy, the classroom isn't rigorous enough. Parent education merits priority status in the life of all our schools.

When I teach at summer institutes, I often ask teachers to think through the different kinds of information they'd like students, colleagues, administrators, *and* parents to understand about the teaching of writing. I use a form (see Figure 5.2) that lists particular categories of information. The same kind of form can be developed for the teaching of reading. When teachers fill out these forms, they are inevitably surprised at which information overlaps for the different groups of people and which information is particular to certain audiences. What strikes me as essential about these brainstorming sessions is that we do not neglect parents. We must figure out what is essential for them to understand and then design ways to effectively deliver that information.

I also use forms with the following headings: GENRES, GRAMMAR, GOOD WRITING, HANDWRITING, LITERATURE, PUBLISHING, NOTEBOOKS, ASSESSMENT, DRAWING, and RECORD KEEPING. (See Appendix 11 for reproducible worksheets.)

The following structures, for helping parents understand our work, have been divided into those that take place during the school day and those that occur in the evenings. They are followed by some strategies for presenting information that we have found particularly helpful.

What you'd like them to understand about	TOPIC CHOICE	SPELLING	CONFERRING	PUNCTUATION	SHARING
STUDENTS					
ADMINISTRATORS					
COLLEAGUES					
PARENTS					

Figure 5.2   Educators' Worksheet for Determining Knowledge Base

Daytime Structures for Family Education

Before-School Workshops

Sharon Taberski runs a series of parent workshops at 8:00 in the morning, forty minutes before the children's day begins. Occasionally, she extends those periods into full hours, by asking a school aide to keep her class, with books in hand, in the cafeteria for an extra twenty minutes. During that big block of time Sharon can convey to parents exactly how her classroom runs, her expectations for the year, as well as offer specific suggestions for helping their children grow as readers. Similarly, Regina hosts early-morning family meetings to discuss a range of curriculum areas as well as child development concerns.

The turnouts are always large for these early-morning meetings. Family members appreciate receiving all that information, particularly at such an early hour. For many folks it seems easier to concentrate when you are not tired and worrying about baby-sitters, evening travel, and who will be cooking dinner.

Starting the Day Together

Whenever parents have opportunities to volunteer in classrooms, they develop an understanding of how and why we do what we do. Whenever parents get lost in the work of the classroom, they are exposed to our beliefs about teaching and learning. Whether they are making autumn collages, performing poetry, taking care of pets, leading a first-grade research project, or helping kindergartners keep journals, they are acquiring knowledge about what we value.

Periodically, Joanne invites her students and their parents to begin their weekday mornings the same way people the world over begin a luxurious weekend morning, with a favorite beverage and a favorite daily newspaper. Joanne invites parents to linger awhile, first thing in the morning. She puts up a pot of coffee and provides juice for the children. Families are encouraged to bring their daily newspaper, sit down alongside students who are reading their own, and just do what people naturally do. The room fills with soft chatter. "Look at the picture on page two!" "Can you believe the story on page nine?" "Just where is Angola anyway?" A handful of different parents attend each morning for the brief twenty minutes of newspaper reading, but they come to appreciate natural talk about reading and the need to plant deep roots if we want children to make reading the newspaper a lifelong habit. They get to spend time in their child's classroom, placing faces with names they've heard, appreciating the diverse backgrounds of the students, and learning why comfortable reading areas are so valuable. They also come to appreciate all the reading strategies the children have been taught to use in order to make sense of the often challenging text. Parents frequently take on the role of teacher, pointing out a country on a map, explaining a difficult concept, or translating a phrase or two. Over the years, Joanne has invited parents to browse dictionaries and atlases with children. The results are the same. Parents appreciate the invitation, and children are inspired to learn how to handle these grown-up materials on their own.

Guided Tours

Several times a month we offer guided tours of our school to prospective parents. Since there is so much choice in the New York City public schools, parents can virtually select any school for their child as long as there is a spot available. (Of course, transportation is not always easily available, which limits the choices for many families.) Parents who understand how the system works sign up to tour all the schools they have heard about. (The underlying message here is that not all parents in the city know their options. Community organizations are working hard to spread the word. Choice cannot be for a privileged few.) Usually upwards of sixty parents attend each of these Tuesday-morning tours. I begin with a little talk about the history, philosophy, and teaching practice of the school. I make sure prospective parents understand what we believe about how children learn to read and write and warn them not to believe everything they read in the newspaper about the "phonics versus whole language debate." Years after their initial tours, parents tell me that they can still recall some of the "quotable quotes" I shared during these introductory meetings. For example, time and again I tell prospective parents that we are offering them lifetime guarantees (hence the title of the companion volume to this book, *Lifetime Guarantees*). I also suggest that we are "planting very deep roots," that we encourage children to "become obsessed with topics," that "language transforms schools," that we "don't ask children to do anything that we ourselves don't do," that "reading and writing are two of life's pleasures," that our children feel like "they belong to a school not just a class," that I'm interested in hiring teachers "who consider it a privilege to be around children," that we are interested in creating a "strikingly beautiful school," and so on—all key phrases that appear throughout this book.

A few parents of enrolled students accompany me on these Tuesday-morning gatherings. They answer questions and offer advice to the prospective parents. With the experienced Manhattan New School parents at the back of the line, shepherding the crowd as we go, I then escort the visiting parents on a brisk tour of the entire school. Walking through the corridors, briefly stopping in every classroom, and eavesdropping on conversations and teaching moments helps parents to decide if this might be the right setting for their child.

Below is an excerpt of a letter sent by Kate Manning after her initial tour. Her daughter Carey and son Oliver now attend our school.

> If we could find the "perfect" school for Carey, it would be part of the public school system, which we wish to support, and which we believe can offer things the private schools cannot. Namely, diversity. But we also hope that our daughter's school will be a place that is creative, where imagination is a learning tool. We hope that the school will be rigorous, with high expectations for its students, and also progressive, using many different ways of teaching and engaging children. The Manhattan New School's expressed philosophy of using whole language methods, of exploring the city and capitalizing on its resources, of "workshop" approaches to individual students, with attention to each child's abilities and skills, seems to us ideal.

Jean Kundherdt Hershkowitz also sent a note after her first visit. Her daughter Eliza is a graduate and Susannah still attends. Her observations included the following:

> One can see it and feel it the moment you walk in those fantastic brass doors—the way you value your students—their thoughts, their art, their writing—all so carefully and aesthetically bedecking the hallway walls. A table with a vase of flowers in a hallway niche set out for reading, conversation, or a quiet time out. The books available over the water fountain—all the little touches that say a lot about the school's respect for its kids.
>
> There was such a wonderfully focused and relaxed hubbub of learning going on in each of the classrooms we entered. The teachers seemed like masters, yet masters who continue to have excitement for and love of their jobs.

These letters remind me how much parents can learn in a two-hour visit to our school. It has occurred to me, however, that these narrated tours should not be reserved for *prospective* parents. I can hear my mother asking, as she serves that brown derby cake, "Who is more special than my own family?" Likewise, no parents should be more special than the parents of our currently enrolled students. It occurred to me that I should, in fact, be leading tours for the parents I know best, particularly for parents of children about to end their early-childhood years with us. Parents usually feel comfortable with our kindergarten, first, and second-grade classrooms. After all, most of them have just left child-centered, gregarious nursery and day care programs. They can imagine an easy transition when they see happy, talkative children having a grand time choosing all those hands-on centers of interest in brightly decorated classrooms. Somewhere toward the end of second grade, some parents start to wonder. It's as if they ask themselves, "The children are so happy, can they really be learning all they'll need to know to do well in middle school and high school? Is this manner of teaching really going to prepare them for rigorous, competitive futures?" I could merely point to the students' standardized test scores, but in so doing I'm giving those scores much more credit than they deserve. No, the best way I know to relieve parents' anxieties is to help them get to know our upper-grade classrooms. Just as one shouldn't select a puppy without taking a look at the full-grown breed, so too parents need to see our seniors at work to fully understand how what we practice throughout the grades prepares students to become scholars. When I walk in and out of these third-, fourth-, and fifth-grade rooms, I can point out the sustained blocks of time for rigorous work, the skills taught in context, the attention to spelling, handwriting, and punctuation, the long-term projects, and the rich background knowledge our students are acquiring as they pursue interests in science, social studies, mathematics, and the arts. Giving our students' parents narrated tours is one of the supreme ways of sharing our beliefs and practices with them.

Close Observation

New York City traditionally announces an Open School Week every November. Parents are encouraged to spend time in their childrens' classrooms. When you live in a school like ours, that week feels no different from any other week. All year long, parents ask teachers if they can visit. Sometimes parents are interested in observing their child's participation or socialization. I'm particularly delighted when parents ask to visit because they are trying to understand how we go about teaching reading, writing, and mathematics. When parents observe with their interests focused, they get a great deal out of their observations.

Over the years, parents have even asked to watch me at work. Kate Lardner wanted to better understand how her daughter Maud was being taught to write. What better way to accomplish this than to invite Kate to pull up alongside me and eavesdrop as I confer with children about their writer's notebooks, rough drafts, and edited work. I chose not to work in Maud's room, so that our visiting mother could give undivided attention to the teaching of writing. I also invite parents to sit in on the small tutorial sessions I run with third graders in my office. It's most helpful to process the sessions with parents, highlighting those strategies that could be used with their children at home.

Coffee Chats

The more varied our structures for holding parent meetings, the more likely we will reach a wide range of parents. Parents who work at night, live great distances away from the school, or who have very young children at home often are unable to attend our monthly Wednesday-evening PTA meetings. We do offer baby-sitting service for the families, but the meetings often last too long for very young children, especially if families have to travel great distances late at night. We have begun putting "Coffee with Shelley" meetings on the school calendar on a regular basis. These informal gatherings, held first thing in the morning from 8:15 to 9:15, attract an audience that is very different from the one that attends our evening meetings. Attendees are primarily family members who travel great distances to our school and stop by after dropping their children off, as well as family members who work very long days and can't make it to evening meetings on time. The tone is very different from that of the more formal PTA meetings, because we have no set agenda. Folks simply gather in a corner of our ballroom and ask me questions. Sometimes we jump from topic to topic, other times we stick with one hot issue. It feels more like a college seminar than a meeting. The joke of it is that we never even serve coffee at these billed "coffee chats."

Language Forums

Carmen Colon carved out weekly time to reach out to our Spanish-speaking parents, especially those who do not feel comfortable talking about school issues in English and who usually do not attend school meetings for fear they will not understand all that is said. Carmen's gracious invitation for parents to attend occasional meetings appears below, followed by an English translation.

> *Queridas Familias,*
>
> *Bienvenidos a otro año escolar en Manhattan New School. El proposito de esta carta es invitarles a una reunion informal donde discutira lo que nuestra escuela provee; las polizas y practicas educativas de nuestra escuela. Favor de venir con sus inquietudes, preguntas y sugerencias de como proveer a nuestros ninos un mejor ambiente educativo.*
>
> *Quremos formar un "forum" donde podamos discutir problemas, ideas, y sugerencias de como poder ayudar a nuestros ninos en las casa. Quremos reuniros o varias veces al mes o solo una vez al mes. Esto se discutira con mas detalles en la primera reunion.*
>
> *Esta primera reunion se llevara acabo el jueves,19 de octubre de 2:15 a 3:00 p.m. Favor de indicar en el cupon al final de esta carta si podra asistir a la reunion. Favor de venir a apoyar a nuestros ninos. Su voz y su presenciaes sumsmente importante para la comunidad de la escuela.*
>
> *Atentamente,*
>
> *Carmen Colon*
> *maestra*

> *Dear families,*
>
> *Welcome to another year at the Manhattan New School. The purpose of this letter is to invite you to an informal meeting in which we will discuss what our school offers; the policies and educational practices of our school. Please come with your worries, questions, and suggestions for how to provide a better educational environment for our children.*
>
> *We would like to create a "forum" where we can discuss problems, ideas, and suggestions for how to help our children at home. We would like to meet several times a month or even once a month. We will discuss this with more detail at our first meeting.*

The first meeting will be held on Thursday October 19th from 2:15 to 3:00 P.M. Please indicate on the attached tear-off slip if you will be able to attend. Please come to support our children. Your voice and your presence is extremely important for the school community.

With caring attention,

Carmen Colon
Teacher

Carmen's letter reminds me once again of how important it would be to have bilingual members of the community meeting with clusters of Albanian, Turkish, French, Portuguese, and other nonnative mothers and fathers, extending the same invitation. I could imagine Carmen offering a leadership course for these bilingual hosts, enabling them to pull more families into the life of our school. This sounds like an idea worth putting at the top of our list. I could imagine our bilingual hosts also becoming our reliable translators at PTA meetings as well as providing written translations of letters sent home.

In their ongoing effort to reach out to non-English-speaking parents, our PTA once sent the following request to all teachers on staff.

Dear teacher,
*   We are interested in creating a way for non-English-speaking parents to feel more included in the activities of the school. We are compiling a list of both non-English-speaking parents and of bilingual parents. Our intention is to offer contact for non-English-speaking parents with a parent who speaks both their language and English.*
*   Are there parents whom you believe might be interested in receiving the name and phone number of a Manhattan New School parent who speaks their language and also English? Also, are there parents who are bilingual whom you believe might be willing to help by being a contact person for people who speak their language? Please give us this information on the back of this page and return it to the PTA mailbox.*

Evening Structures for Family Education

PTA Meetings (Of Course)

Not all PTA meetings are intended to fill parents with information on reading, 'riting, and 'rithmetic. Police officers, child psychologists, conflict-resolution specialists, and health care workers are also invited to present important information to parents. When we are talking about major areas of curriculum and instruction, however, some of our most effective and best-attended meetings are those presented in a panel format. Teachers across the grades, for example, might volunteer to make short presentations about the teaching of mathematics and then field questions from interested parents. Family members know that this is not the time to voice individual concerns about their child, but to make broader inquiries. The added bonus to having such a format is that staff members have the opportunity to hear one another present. We leave those meetings reminded of how lucky we are to have one another as colleagues.

Over the years, we have arranged for panels to discuss the teaching of writing, reading, social studies, technology, and spelling as well as such controversial issues as homework, assessment, and standardized testing. Once parents have a rich, broad background in such issues, their questions become more focused and detailed during curriculum nights (see below), and parent-teacher conferences.

Another effective strategy for sharing information is for an individual teacher to volunteer to help parents understand how math, social studies, reading, or writing is taught at a particular grade. Parents appreciate meeting in actual classrooms and seeing how the room arrangements and materials facilitate the teaching and learning of different curriculum areas. They're also able to see actual student work samples. An added benefit, one that brings many parents out, is the chance to hang out in another teacher's room. Parents are always eager to get to know another staff member. Parents of students in the classroom where the meeting is being held always beam with pride, happy to show off their child's learning environment.

Our family members are also eager to attend PTA meetings in which we show videotapes, both professionally produced and homegrown. We have shown video clips of the teachers in our school, as well as those created by educators around the country. (See Chapter 7, p. 247, for titles.) Even though these tapes were intended for teacher audiences, they offer valuable information for parents, and the remote control enables us to freeze-frame moments in order to highlight techniques, clarify points, and answer questions.

I have also spoken to principal colleagues of neighboring schools about sharing our resources and/or combining our meetings. I could easily imagine inviting Tanya Kaufman to our building to share her thoughts on multiage groupings, alternative assessments, and meaningful science instruction. Likewise, I'd be happy to address her PTA on a wide range of literacy issues. Similarly, Tanya's PTA and the members of ours could combine meetings occasionally when guest speakers are of interest to both parent bodies.

Parent Writing Workshop

At one regularly scheduled PTA meeting in the early years of our school, I volunteered to explain the writing process approach. A parent had attached an invitation in our daily logbook. The note read, "Can anyone talk about writing process at the next parent meeting?" I jumped at the chance to be the writing lady again. We met in the cafeteria, with the tables arranged in a U-shape, and I stood center stage. In the audience was a very diverse group of parents, including a housekeeper, a locksmith, a librarian, a seamstress, a cook, a bus driver, a butcher, a lawyer, a dentist, a handyman, and a mother living in a Ronald McDonald house with two young children. The people came from all over the world, including big and small towns in Albania, Croatia, Hungary, Turkey, Malta, Myanmar, Haiti, Trinidad, Chile, and Puerto Rico.

What I said was fairly predictable. I began by contrasting the process approach with the product approach. I showed the family members a very old and worn report my son had written many years before when he had been in elementary school. It was entitled, "My Life," and it was divided into such chapters as, "My Family," "My School," and "My Hobbies." Each chapter was accompanied by just the right photograph and it was impeccably correct. His grammar, spelling, punctuation, and handwriting were flawless. His teacher had written the obligatory word, "Excellent," across the red construction paper cover. I explained to the parents gathered that this work represented the product approach to the teaching of writing. The teacher had a neat, precise finished product in mind when she handed out the assignment. The students' job was to come up with the perfect match. Their writing had to match the image of the finished work that their teacher had in mind.

"The problem," I explained to the audience, "is that his writing was not very good. Yes, it is mechanically correct, but if you read the words, you'd be disappointed." "The words," I continued, "are rather flat. They do not match the way my son shared his life at the dinner table, filled with stories, humor, and passion. Michael had in fact taken much of the information he used in the report from a padded baby book I kept in the attic."

I then presented the process approach, and rather than talk about it, I attempted to get the parents involved. I began by proving to them that they had important stories to tell. I began telling my own family stories, sharing strong images and memories from my childhood. Then I read some evocative poems and passages. The cafeteria filled with talk that night. Parents were laughing, crying, commiserating with, and comforting one another. Finally, I invited them to take the writing of those stories, images, and memories seriously, and I announced a six-week parent writing workshop, open to all.

Some very important things happened in that cafeteria that night. First, our relationships changed. Parents who have attended my writing workshops relate to me on a different level. When I know how your brother died and you know about mine, our communication is more intimate and more immediate. Secondly, parents began caring deeply about reading, writing, and literature. And finally, they began to understand, firsthand, what we were asking their children to do.

I passed around a sign-up sheet and what began as a six-week course lasted for several months (see Figure 5.3). Parents didn't want to stop. We met for a couple of hours each Monday evening. I often began these get-togethers by sharing stories of adults who appreciate the role of writing in their lives. I shared an article about a woman who realized she had been writing a kind of memoir in the margins of her favorite cookbook, recording notes on all her important family dinners. I shared a newspaper clipping about a custom in Thailand, where people compose a small cookbook before their deaths, describing their favorite meals. The book is distributed as a keepsake to the mourners who attend their funerals.

Not all my stories involved food, although they all dealt with everyday events. I

Figure 5.3

often shared accessible poetry with parents, ones that would inspire adults to think, "I wonder if I could do that!" like this poem, by Lewis Gardner, which I came across in the Metropolitan Diary section of *The New York Times*.

Morning Strangers

There are people I've seen for years
As they buy a buttered roll at the deli,
Walk a spaniel at the corner,
Board the 8:06 bus.
There's the girl who reads hardcover books,
The man who stares intently,
The woman who does the Sunday crossword
With a purple felt-tipped pen.

As they move through the morning routine,
Are they remembering scenes of passion,
Worrying about symptoms or their children,
Or planning the morning's phone calls?
And what do they think about me
When they see me in the morning?

Likewise Doris Klein, grandmother of our student Kimberly, published this poem in the same section of *The New York Times*.

New Neighbor Across the Street

> I see you in the morning.
> yawning,
> striped pajamas
> rummaging the fridge.
> Later,
> at a bridge table,
> hear the Fred Astaire sound
> of typewriter keys
> tapping across the way.
> A budding Bronte?
> Edna St. Vincent Millay?

When the parents read poems like these, they seem to relax. They begin to think that writing is a possibility in their lives. After all, they see scenes like the ones these poets have captured, they pay attention to their surroundings, and they have surprising thoughts to share. I then suggest that they begin to keep a writer's notebook, just as their children are asked to do. I have proven to them that their lives are worth writing about. They are ready to write and ready to share. A Filipino mother writes of her grandmother, who lived to be 120 years old; how when she approached these very late years a second set of baby teeth began to grow in her mouth. A German mother, a hairdresser by trade, describes her boredom at work, and how she has begun asking her clients to read poetry aloud as she clips and styles their hair. A newly arrived mother from Ecuador describes her frustration when dealing with customers in her shoe repair shop, because her English isn't fluent.

Parents did lots of first-draft jottings in their writer's notebooks and they revised, edited, and published finished pieces to be shared in our school newsletter. The power of their writing did not surprise me. For several summers, I ran a writing workshop for Swedish teachers held at Merton College at Oxford University in England. One morning, a colleague pointed out a waiter named Frank Cairns. "He's a writer," my friend said. "Ask him to show you his writing." And I did. My request to read his work was the beginning of a lovely friendship and a reinforcement of the lesson that John, our custodian, had been teaching me. Lots of people who are not professional educators, English literature majors, or college graduates care about reading and writing. Frank was a short story writer. Each day he would slip me another story to read, but he refused to come to class to talk about his writing. He seemed to believe in John's mustard theory and could not believe that he had anything to teach teachers. That was too bad, but his stories spoke for themselves. My favorite story is a most mysterious one, entitled "The Watcher." In this story, Frank has the reader believe that a resident of the neighborhood he describes is a keen observer of all that happens on this seemingly dull block. The narrator describes all the passersby, including the milkman, the paperboys, the lovers who rendezvous, burglars, and police officers. It is not until the absolute last line of this detailed, gossipy piece that we realize the watcher is a dog. It comes as a marvelous surprise. Frank prepared me for the talent in room 203. Each week, I met with the parents in Joan's fourth-grade classroom and each week we sat in awe as parents shared their finished pieces. We learned how a mother who works in a doctor's office allows the names of patients to bring back memories of her childhood in Liverpool. We learn from a father his vivid memory of accidentally jamming the point of a pencil into the palm of his hand at the exact moment the principal announced over the school loudspeaker that President Kennedy had been shot. Another father invites us to believe in the homeless man on his corner who asks for money by calling out, "Make a wish, only twenty-five cents!" It doesn't surprise me that each year parents ask me to lead another writing workshop. The word is out in our school. We all have stories to tell.

Strategies for Holding Parent Writing Workshops

- Work hard at outreach. The writing group becomes more interesting when members of the group come from different backgrounds, and even speak different languages. Don't fret if only a half dozen people show up. Walls really do have ears in a school. Word will spread. Be grateful for small circles in the beginning.

- Keep the meetings structured. It's easy for any group of adults to spend time talking about the day's events. Not that this kind of talk isn't important for writers, but it becomes easy *not* to write. It's also helpful to have clear amounts of time devoted to the different components of your writing workshop. The structures that work for students and teachers at summer institutes also work for parents. If you meet from six to eight P.M., for example, you might devote the first few minutes to talking about the ways people made time for writing during the week, and then spend a half hour reading and talking about good writing. (I always select short essays and poems that I think will resonate for the assembled group. Most are taken from newspapers and magazines.) Then parents can have a full hour to write and almost a half hour to share at the end of the evening.

- Make sure parents know this is a serious commitment, *not* a "drop-in whenever you can make it" kind of experience. Let parents know that the group counts on them to be there every week for the full workshop.

- At all cost, avoid talking about their children and their children's teachers, even if the conversation is about the teaching of writing. This is the time for the adults to think about themselves as writers. Nothing else.

- Carefully chosen supplies add dignity and seriousness of purpose to the meetings. Talk to parents about choosing a notebook or daybook carefully and about creating a system to save all the literature handouts so that they are available for rereading.

- Place no restraints on genres. Some adults have unfinished novels in their dresser drawers, steamy love stories they've been meaning to tell, or screenplays they're hoping to sell. I don't claim to be an expert at conferring on any of these genres, but I'm a good listener and I give honest feedback. I have to admit that I was relieved when some parents just wanted to get in the habit of keeping a journal or attempt to record their childhood memories as a family keepsake.

- Let students know how happy you are to be working with their parents. Invite the parent/writers to share appropriate work in their children's classrooms. I can't imagine a more powerful model of literacy.

- Be prepared for the workshops to extend past eight weeks. The parents won't want to stop, and your "customers" are always right.

Curriculum Meetings

Early in the school year it becomes important to share with parents our hopes for the year. Parents are not only curious to find out what the curriculum involves as they and their child move to a new grade, they also want to get to know the teacher and check out the new classroom. They want to be able to imagine where their child is spending six hours and twenty minutes a day, 5 days a week, 180 days a year. Creating a curriculum evening early in October, every year, is the least we can do. Knowing that many teachers commute great distances to and from school, the parents have begun a lovely tradition to thank teachers for putting in such a late night. On curriculum night, they provide dinner for all members of the staff. We always have these evenings on Wednesdays, our traditional faculty meeting days. In lieu of our afternoon meeting, teachers use the time to get ready for their evening presentations, then meet to have dinner before welcoming their guests into their rooms. We encourage one parent who attends each meeting to serve as secretary, either tape-recording the proceedings or preparing notes to distribute to parents unable to attend.

Reading Get-togethers

Every once in a while Judy Davis invites parents of her students to join in the reading of a novel. Usually eight to ten parents accept her invitation. A book is chosen, a date is scheduled, and pizzas are ordered. I can't resist being part of these get-togethers. Not only do I get to read such books as Susan Creech's *Walk Two Moons* or Gary Paulsen's *Monument,* but I also get to take part in the most serious of multiage book talks. When mothers and daughters, fathers and daughters, mothers and sons, or fathers and sons read the same book, the conversations take on additional layers of meaning. People discover new things about people they thought they knew very well. Additionally, the parents get to experience what is meant by "reader response," "book clubs," and the notion of employing strategies to get at deeper meanings. We need to expand our invitations to form parent/child book talks to many more grades, and we probably should think about starting one for our Spanish-speaking parents. (If we could find appropriate material in other languages, we'd really pay tribute to our multilingual setting).

Parent Book Club

Each month I publicly post the title of the book our staff book club is reading (see page 258 for details). Members of our parent body were inspired to begin their own, asking me to launch a parent's reading group. Their title, as well as the date and time of their next meeting, is now posted next to the staff choice. They usually get together in the evening at a local coffee shop to share responses to the novel chosen. After the first meeting, the parents realized that they didn't need my leadership, although I am eager to be a participant whenever I can. There is a limit to how many books one can read at the same time, as well as how many late work nights I can manage. This parent book club addresses the literacy needs of only a small percentage of our parent body. The challenge lies ahead to design ways for more parents to gather to talk about improving their abilities as readers, making time for reading in their lives, finding authors that are appealing, taking advantage of public libraries, and discovering sources of books, magazines, and newspapers in other languages.

Courses of Study

Just as my presentation of the writing process approach turned into a six-week writing workshop for parents, I can imagine following up whole-group presentations with a workshop series on "hot topics." After the initial presentation to all, I could imagine passing around a sign-up sheet, inviting parents to do even closer study on such issues as:

- Working with the struggling reader at home
- Choosing books for at-home read-alouds
- Learning to read aloud well
- How to respond when they ask, "How do you spell . . . ?"
- Notebook writing: A tool for use at school, at home, and in the doctor's waiting room
- Unpacking our labels: What's meant by genres, manipulatives, and inquiry studies
- Have you met . . . ? Authors for all ages
- Phonics taught wisely and well
- How reading informs writing
- How writing informs reading
- Family rituals for writing at home
- Feeling at home in bookstores and libraries
- Making a place for nonfiction reading at home

These series could be offered right after school or in the evenings, depending on the participants' availability as well as mine. I could easily imagine hosting these and inviting teachers to be the occasional guest speakers, so that no one person is totally responsible for the entire course. (Thinking through these topics and outlining the content for a course of study would also be a worthwhile staff meeting activity. See additional staff-meeting activities in Chapter 7, "Turning Schools into Centers for Professional Study.")

Engaging Techniques for Family Involvement

Whatever the structure for communicating with parents, there are certain techniques we have found to be particularly effective in helping parents understand our ways of working with their children. (Of course, humor, good snacks, and an attractive and comfortable setting also go a long way in helping to make meetings inviting.)

Presentations and Demonstrations

We have found it helpful to take the familiar writing process suggestion and remember to "Show, don't tell." We rarely do a presentation without an overhead projector, a slide show, or a demonstration video. Then too, parents always have a deeper understanding when they are asked to roll up their sleeves and do as we ask their children to do. I've asked parents to spell *hors-d'oeuvres* to demonstrate to them what it means to study a spelling word. I've asked parents to figure out and jot down their explanation of why the number 37 has a special magic (see poem on page 37) in order to demonstrate the value of writing to clarify mathematical thinking. I've also asked parents to do what we *don't* ask their children to do, in order to help them understand the choices we make. When I ask parents to fill in the blanks on a phonics workbook page, they understand the ambiguity, isolation, and boredom attached to these activities.

Student Participation

Inviting students to speak at parent meetings is another effective tool. One year Joanne, Judy, and Joan invited family members to an author's celebration. In preparation for their visit, the teachers taught their students how to lead a workshop, and then the children taught their parents about how their finished pieces came to be. They planned inspirational leads to their workshops, showed overheads to illustrate their points, and allowed time for questions and answers. Students can also be invited to parent get-togethers not as workshop leaders but rather to enable teachers, or principals, to publicly demonstrate teaching techniques. Frequently when I lead out-of-town summer institutes, I request that "real-live" students attend so that I can publicly confer with them. There is no more effective way for participants to understand teaching and learning techniques than to have a front-row seat at live teaching/learning moments.

Reading Aloud

Carefully chosen literature also comes in handy at parent presentations. Not only does it whet parents appetite to keep up with children's literature, it frequently can serve as metaphor for the points we want to make, and as inspiration for the parenting responsibilities participants have assumed. The following list contains some of the picture books that I have shared at recent parent gatherings, along with the topics of conversations they inspired.

> James Stevenson's *I Meant to Tell You* (We need to find ways to record and share memories with our children about their growing up years.)
>
> Henri Sorensen's *Your First Step* (We need to find ways to hold onto those breakthrough moments. As the years pass, they're surprisingly easy to forget.)
>
> Margaret Park Bridges' *Will You Take Care of Me?* (We need to make sure that our children know that parent devotion lasts forever.)
>
> Rosemary Wells's *Read to Your Bunny* (Reading aloud is the best way that we can help our children to become readers.)
>
> Lynn Reiser's *Cherry Pies and Lullabies* and *Tortillas and Lullabies,* and *Tortillas y Cancioncitas* (Do we have family customs that our children will remember forever?)
>
> Rebecca C. Jones's *Great Aunt Martha* (Do we have realistic rules and regulations for company behavior?)
>
> Bethany Roberts's *A Mouse Told His Mother* (Are we encouraging our children's imagination? Do we support their spirit of adventure? Do we have bedtime rituals?)
>
> Debra Frasier's *Out of the Ocean* (Do we have important life secrets to share with our children?)
>
> Rachel Coyne's *Daughter, Have I Told You?* (Do our daughters have strong female role-models in their lives? In the books they read? In the television shows they watch?)
>
> Jennifer Owings Dewey's *Faces Only a Mother Could Love* (How do we talk about appearances to children? Do we share enough nonfiction with our children? Why are children so interested in animals?)

Send Worthwhile Stuff Home

Parents who are new to literature-based, language-rich classrooms taught in a workshop approach often long to have the old familiar stuff sent home. They wonder about the workbook pages, ditto masters, basal readers, and social studies, science, and mathematics textbooks. They feel the need to have weekly graded spellings tests, handwriting exercises covered with happy-face stickers, and cleverly completed story-starters to hang with magnets on their refrigerator doors. Somehow these things prove to parents that their children are working hard in school and doing well. Our parents and family members come to understand that these items will not be coming to their homes from our school. Instead, they come to expect other things.

Several years ago, the wonderful children's literature expert Bee Cullinan heard me share a dream I had for the Manhattan New School. I envisioned being able to buy a poetry anthology every year, for every child in our school, ones they would keep forever. When the children graduated, they would own six anthologies that they knew very well. What a gift for life. Bee Cullinan made our dream come true and donated five hundred copies of *A Jar of Tiny Stars: Poems by Award-Winning NCTE Poets.* (Details on how this text was used across the grades appear in Chapter 1, "Designing the Literary Landscape," and in *Lifetime Guarantees.*) When the cartons of books arrived, a parent volunteered to inscribe them all in beautiful calligraphy with Bee's name as the donor and each child's name as the proud owner. Parents were thrilled when the children brought these anthologies home (as opposed to basal readers). They have come to expect the truely meaningful stuff that tumbles out of their children's book bags. Stuff like the following:

Content-Rich School Newsletters

For several years, our parents worked very hard in publishing a school newsletter several times a year. This mini-magazine contained student writing samples, interviews with staff members, news about upcoming events, and reports about completed ones. The parents also invited me to add a lengthy letter to each issue. I valued this as an opportunity to talk about things that really matter. Throughout this text, I have included excerpts from these letters. Their topics so far have included social tone, summer volunteer options, and teacher respect. In forthcoming chapters, as well as in the companion text *Lifetime Guarantees*, I will be referring to additional letters home that deal with the place of playing with language, taking reading tests, and the teaching of skills in context. I know that there are many parents whose work schedules and family obligations make it impossible for them to visit during the day or attend meetings during the evening. Our correspondences with parents, therefore, take on great significance. We have to write letters that are engaging, clear, jargon-free, and packed with specific information. We also have to find translators in the community to ensure that all families have equal access to information. (Currently our parents publish a one-page "News Flash," which comes out quite regularly and is relatively easy to produce. Parents felt the need to simplify this publication in order to make timely announcements to the entire community. I miss crafting those long letters home and realize I need to find a new container for my content-rich ramblings.) (See Appendix 12, Manhattan New School Newsletter: Summer & Autumn Wish List.)

Highlighted Announcements and Articles

Everyone in a school gets too much mail. Teachers and parents both probably get too much mail, and it becomes hard to give every piece equal attention. It's a great relief when something worthy and practical comes along.

When wonderful things do appear, we need to share those things not only with teachers, but when appropriate, with parents. For example, it takes but a minute to skim all the professional announcements for upcoming conferences and conventions to find out if there are any parent strands. A handwritten note to the PTA across the top of relevant material can announce, "Take the time to read this one!" I wish someone would perform this screening service for me.

I also receive many district and central board memorandums related to parent education. These too deserve a quick once-over, to make sure we're not passing up any helpful ways to keep parents well-informed. I was impressed recently with a copy of the central board–sponsored publication *The Writing Initiative: A Parent Perspective*. The short document written by parents is filled with practical parent suggestions, well worth duplicating and distributing to families. This handout, which is available in Spanish, Chinese, Korean, Haitian, and soon Russian, includes such suggestions as using student writing as a family read-aloud, keeping a dialogue journal with your child's teacher, and inviting what they describe as "9 to 5" writers—local professionals—into schools to talk to students. It's wonderful to get handouts that are worth handing out.

In addition, the parent columns in professional journals are often worth passing on as well as some of the parent materials produced by the state departments of education and by the U.S. Department of Education. I also publicize appropriate newspaper clippings. At first I used to hope that parents wouldn't see the negative articles about whole language that appear periodically. They inevitably do, and I've found it helpful to duplicate the article, reducing it so that I have wide margins to write my response. I can either display my reaction on a parent bulletin board or copy and distribute the article to the entire parent body. I do the same with positive articles. I've discovered that parents are more likely to read these handouts if personal notes written by the educators they know best accompany them.

Classroom Correspondence

Teachers of course send lots of letters home. (See Appendixes 13 and 14 for letters sent home: handwriting and work habits.) They work just as hard to make them jargon-free, content rich, and translated into needed languages whenever possible. Some of their correspondence includes brief curriculum updates, invitations, or explanations of new teaching practices. Teachers also attach carefully chosen articles, bibliographies of popular classroom books, recipes of foods prepared in class, upcoming trip brochures, family homework packets, as well as lists of required supplies and desired donations.

Some teachers also send home periodic classroom newsletters, in addition to the school-wide one that the PTA sponsors. Teachers who have the time and enjoy playing with their word processors often put these together themselves. Others share the responsibility with parents and students. Pam asks her five-year-olds to keep journals about their school experiences. Their jottings become the content for her family newsletter (see Appendix 15, Pam's Class Newsletter). In the upper grades, students can assume full responsibility for classroom newsletters and bilingual students can be asked to translate these newsletters for their families.

Pictures That are Worth a Few Thousand Words

I frequently joke about the reason that I think children have short necks—it's from all the shrugging of their shoulders when they say, "I dunno!" Parents find this response especially frustrating when they ask the inevitable, "What did you do at school today?" In the early days of our school, Elizabeth Servidio conducted a workshop for parents on how to get the children to respond in richer ways at home. Her main suggestion involved asking the right questions. Not "What did you do in school?" but "What did the teacher read aloud today?" Not, "So how was school today? but "What are you talking about in science class?"

Joanne has found yet another way to help parents understand their child's school day and at the same time encourage rich talk at home. Joanne keeps a photo album filled with snapshots of the children at work. She and her students always reach for the camera to capture memorable moments. The album is sent home with a different student each night and Joanne includes a section for the parents to write a response to the photos as well as to the experience of sharing them with their child. No child ever says, "I dunno!" when a parent asks, "What's happening in this picture?"

Poetry for Adults

Many teachers preserve all the poems shared with the students over the course of a year in individual and personalized poetry binders. These go home at set intervals to be shared with parents. Parents marvel when children can read these poems aloud as well as when they've memorized them by heart. Sharing poems at home gives parents a real feel for one activity that takes place regularly at school. But there can be more benefits to these poetry collections. I've encouraged teachers to include an additional section of poems in their poetry binders, ones chosen deliberately for parents. I keep my own binder, filled with poems that speak particularly well to parents, on a shelf in the poetry room. Whenever I come across an appropriate poem, I tuck it into this big red binder and I encourage others to do the same. Isabel handed me this short, powerful poem and I knew just where to save and savor it. It probably should be read by many principals as well as by parents. It was written by Christine Lamb Parker.

Four-Year-Old's First Test

You do a graceless swan dive
off the couch
when the new woman appears
to test you for kindergarten.
After you have shown her
your hockey trophy, your sister's photograph,

she begins
with authority:
"How are a pencil and a crayon similar?"
You say, "They are both skinny."
She checks the box marked wrong.
"Fill-in the blank-red, white, and . . ."
"Green." Wrong again.
"Where does ham come from?"
You think and think,
then say, "God."
Wrong.
"What would someone who is brave do?"
You answer quickly,
"Walk through rose bushes."

Poems like this one help parents appreciate our setting and remind them to appreciate their child's original and nonconforming thoughts. They know there is plenty of time later in life to learn about the one right answer.

Also contained in my parent's poetry folder is a poem I wrote about my own kindergarten experience. It follows:

September, 1952

First lunch box—
Howdy Doody I think.
New pair of shoes—
Red with laces.
Freshly starched dress—
With plaid apron bib.
First look at Mrs. Barmatz,
My kindergarten teacher.
I hope she asks me my A-B-C's
I practiced all night.

(See Appendix 16 for additional poems for parents.)

Library Materials

We have as yet to formalize a parent lending library, but passing around books, articles, and videos to interested parents happens informally all the time. Perhaps this will be our year to get the parent library off the ground. All we need is space, some donated volumes, some starter funds for new books and magazine subscriptions, and a family member with the time and passion for creating a family resource library. I'd be happy to donate my small collection of parent books to a larger, more organized library.

Putting Parents to Work

A friend of mine assumed that when I mentioned putting parents to work, I wanted to help them get jobs so they would be "out of our hair." Quite the contrary, when parents are well informed and we have a shared vision for what is possible in a public elementary school, they become our best supporters. In fact, we wouldn't be able to run a very effective school if parent contributions weren't woven into our everyday lives. In addition to their roles as informants about their own children, I have already alluded to several other essential roles parents play. Clearly they are part of all the celebrating, gift-giving, donating, decorating, political action taking, and teaching in specialty areas. They are also part of the decision making in the school. Their ideas are shared and their opinions are counted when they serve on PTA executive boards and committees, as well as on hiring committees and district advisory councils. In New York, parent involvement is also mandated in the state commissioner's regulations. All schools must invite parents to take part in decision making regarding school policy, procedures, goals, and budgeting.

Parents do much of their good deeds as part of their commitment to the school's very active PTA, but some parents carve out roles on their own. Either way, it comes as no surprise that parents take part in such varied tasks. After all, trading places is as important an activity for parents as it is for teachers and administrators. The following parent roles are deserving of some extra explanation and attention.

Media Hounds

Frequently, parents clip newspaper articles for me to read. They're usually about some innovative teaching practice that they think seems right for our setting. Topics have ranged from avoiding sex bias in schools to social studies texts written in a storyteller's voice. Rakheli's mother sent me a magazine article about the importance of appreciating nature as a teacher. She penciled in a request in the margin for the children to have opportunities to have outdoor playtime during our "magical, snow-covered," winter days. Ariella's parents sent in a stack of reprints of a *Reader's Digest* article entitled "Most Important Thing You Can Do for Your Child." It was about Jim Trelease and his message of reading aloud to children. The article reminded me of the importance of distributing jargon-free material to families. Parents who know our interests well always pass on very worthwhile material. Adar's mother sent in the following typewritten passage, given to her by a neighbor.

> As the old man walked the beach at dawn, he noticed a young man ahead of him picking up starfish and flinging them into the sea. Finally catching up with the youth, he asked him why he was doing this. The answer was that the stranded starfish would die if left until morning sun.
>
> "But the beach goes on for miles and there are millions of starfish," countered the other. "How can your effort make any difference?"

The young man looked at the starfish in his hand and then threw it to safety in the waves. "It makes a difference to this one," he said.

I posted the passage, gave copies to colleagues, and shared it with members of the student council. It sparked interesting conversation about social tone.

Gabe's mom, Lisa, sent a generous note to Joanne, part of which follows.

On tonight's news I saw a bit about an exhibit of photographs of African-American photo-journalists documenting African-American life. It's currently at the Museum of the City of New York. It will be going on national tour. If you're interested for a class trip, I'll find out how long it will be there. If you think enough is booked for now, I understand.

How much easier teachers' lives become when parents take on such time-consuming tasks as arranging class trips.

Donation Seekers

Throughout this book I have noted how important donations are to the life of this school. Parents stop by with Band-Aids, rubber gloves, fabric swatches, markers, scrap paper, and even photocopy paper. They donate unwanted microwaves, popcorn poppers, vacuum cleaners, coffeemakers, and mini refrigerators. Years ago, I saw a bumper sticker that read, "My money and my son go to Harvard." I could easily imagine our parents displaying bumper stickers that read, "Our children and our paper towels, tissues, sponges, and spray cleaners go to the Manhattan New School."

In addition, parents work hard at seeking donations from others. When visitors come, for example, the PTA often hands out a kind note describing the kinds of things we are always in need of. These include paper, markers, and all things related to keeping up with visitors. (See Chapter 7, "Turning Schools into Centers for Professional Study" and Appendix 17, donation letter from the PTA.)

Our ballroom has a beautifully crafted portable wooden stage because a parent presented our needs to the cabinetmaker down the block. The shelves in our nonfiction reading room are filled with reference books from a prestigious private school library because a parent made just the right connection. Our school has become a field test site for computer software that enables us to bar-code our library books because a parent made just the right connections. Our school is brimming with sofas, bookcases, and plush chairs because a parent with a moving company knows how to make all the right connections. Some parents have even begun a big fund-raising campaign looking for corporate benefactors. In a letter to staff, the parents described their plans to search for guardian angels to donate products and equipment. They asked teachers to help by providing concrete examples of what they might do with the needed "stuff," as well as any corporate connections teachers might have. They are particularly looking toward international corporations that might want to be part of educating our diverse student population. Schools with very little money can seem well endowed, if we tap the expertise of parents and community members.

Volunteers

I've already noted that I know who to call upon when different jobs around the school need to be done. I talked about the parents who are willing to cook, mend, paint, and move furniture. Parents also perform endless chores in our main office. They answer the telephone, run the copy machine, register students, translate letters, and handle all the thousand and one interruptions that keep our secretary from doing her regularly scheduled work. I really appreciate the parents I never have to call upon, those who somehow remember to do the things that I might easily forget. Nancy Gilston tests children's vision and hearing each year. Kas Wilson updates teachers' names on office mailboxes. Susan Geller-Ettenheim takes care of our computer needs. Volunteers are always welcome. They produce our newsletter, help out at lunchtime, and arrange class trips. Some, like Kas, Nancy, and Susan, become regular fixtures around the school. It's easy to forget that they receive no salary. We probably don't thank them enough. They have become "one of the guys," and we dread the day when their last child graduates.

Teachers also put out calls for help, some more than others. Each of us has a different way of working with parents and family members. Some teachers welcome parents at any time with open arms, others prefer more formal appointments and regularly scheduled commitments. As a school policy, I can insist that all educators treat parents with the respect they deserve; I can not mandate that parents be equally present in everyone's classroom. I must respect teacher's different styles of working. The following letter sent by Pam Mayer to her families illustrates a wide range of ways parents can be involved:

> *Dear families,*
>
> *Many of you have asked how you can get involved by either spending time in the classroom or from a distance. The following are some ways families can get involved:*
>
> - *Volunteer to help during lunch. We always appreciate all of the extra help you can offer. The kindergartners play in the yard and then eat lunch in the cafeteria.*
> - *Be a guest reader! We can arrange a time for you to come read a book to our class. Share a family favorite or choose a book from our room. Other ideas: share an oral tale, a family story, or read to us in another language!*
> - *If you're rushing off to work or if mornings are easier, join us for book partners (8:40–9:00).*
> - *Trips: You can help with the planning (making phone calls, arranging buses, etc.) and/or join us on trips.*
> - *Do you have a special interest or talent? Come in and share your expertise!*
> - *Work with a group of children during center time. Some suggestions include art projects, math games, origami, share a collection (a father who traveled around the world shared his coin collection, which the children were able to touch, sort, examine). Possibilities are limitless! We can work out the details.*
> - *Computer-literate adults might volunteer your time to work with children using the computer.*

- *Are you on-line? Help your child to send e-mail to a friend on the computer! I'll be sending my e-mail address home to the children. I promise to write back to all who write.*

- *Do you speak a language other than English? We'd love you to translate forms/letters into other languages.*

- *Come in and label our classroom in your family's language.*

- *Put stories on tape in our listening center. What a treat for the children to hear the voices of their families reading our favorite books on cassette.*

- *Collect poems or other seasonal things for different months of the year.*

- *Recreate the text of a story we know by writing the words on sentence strips. Let me know if you're interested so we can talk about it.*

- *Many MNS classes will be studying Eighty-second Street and the surrounding neighborhood. We'd love enlarged photos of the block and/or constructions.*

- *Who is your child's favorite author? Prepare an author packet.*

- *I have several "traveling briefcases" that need to be filled. The children will then sign them out to take home and enjoy. I'd love your ideas for filling the briefcases. Come pick one up and fill it with your child. (Some examples include: office supply briefcase, autumn briefcase, science briefcase, bug briefcase, music briefcase.) Choose one of these or share your original ideas.*

- *Make environmental print signs. See me for suggestions.*

- *Help organize and put together a class newsletter. Ideas include: interview me and/or the children. Type it on the computer. Does anyone have software that includes a newspaper layout?*

- *Be pattern detectives. Look for patterns around the house and in the neighborhood. (Bring in patterns on fabric, take pictures of architectural patterns, etc.)*

- *Share any writing you do at home with your child, name it, and talk about it. For example, include your child as you make a shopping list, take phone messages, write thank-you notes. When you read the newspaper, also think about the things you can point out to your child (headlines, etc.).*

- *Collect quotable quotes from your child. It would be great to compile a class scrapbook of language stories from home. Print the quote in large letters for beginning readers.*

- *Has your child become an expert on a certain topic through the media? Please send a note if your child has learned something from an educational program, a newspaper, etc.*

Pam ended her letter by including a few of the suggestions that appear in my letter home on pages 130–131. She then reiterated that the possibilities for parent involvement are endless and that the class would love to see many family members participate. I appreciate Pam's letter because she taps so many areas of expertise, and most of her suggestions do not require great amounts of time or money.

Each class, through the auspices of the PTA, also has someone designated as the class parent. When teachers need help, they need only make one phone call. This volunteer serves as telephone liaison with all parents, organizes parents for volunteer work on special class projects, initiates after-school and weekend social gatherings, and shares important information with grade delegates, another structure put in place by our PTA.

Some volunteers come from surprising places. Edith, a neighborhood senior citizen, helps out in the cafeteria. She is at home taking care of an infirm husband, and looks forward to this break in her demanding at-home schedule. Max's grandparents live in Connecticut and come to visit once a month, always on a Tuesday. They sent me a wonderful letter, informing me of all the things they are good at including woodworking, gardening, and painting. "Put us to work," they simply asked. Karen Feuer, a member of our school board whose youngest child recently graduated from our school, has offered to "adopt" a child who is in need of an adult advocate. She knows she could help a needy child, and she thinks the plan will alleviate her own separation anxiety from our school.

Isabel Beaton has a phenomenal knack for acquiring volunteers and then putting them to brilliant use. The children think of Dilta, Isabel's friend, as another teacher in the room. She attends several days a week, all year long. Isabel's children also get to know her other talented friends who have some free time. The children fall in love with and come to expect to learn from Doris, their poetry teacher, and Mary, their storyteller. Isabel also takes wonderful advantage of all the talents her parents have. Haden's mother taught the children how to build log cabins from little salty pretzel rods and sticky peanut butter and then eat their creations. Her father was invited to introduce the five-year-olds to the world of opera. The children stared in awe as he sang, "The Last Rose of Summer."

Paula Rogovin is also a master at putting family volunteers to work. She likes to describe parents as her coworkers. Dora, a student's grandmother, walked in and has never walked out, serving year after year as Paula's right hand. Family members are of course a part of Paula's extensive interview projects but they also read to children, help with all the class pets, teach songs and dances, and confer with children during reading, writing, and math workshops. When schools have a welcoming attitude toward volunteers, children can be well attended to, even during times of dire budget cuts.

A few volunteer "gigs" have turned into careers for members of our parent body. Kas spent so much time doing essential clerical jobs she has since become a licensed school secretary. Susan volunteered in our special education class and has since become a fully certified teacher of special education. Tamara, always ready to lend a helping hand, has been hired by the PTA to facilitate all the messy hands-on work in Lisa's science lab. Beatrice put in so many hours every day for so many years, helping children open their milk containers in the cafeteria and wiping up spills, she has been hired by the PTA to be an official lunchtime aide. (When Tamara left to start a family bakery, Beatrice moved to the fifth floor to become Lisa's science lab assistant.)

New York City also has several very well organized volunteer networks. The School Volunteers sends several adults each year who can spare a few hours a week to tutor a child. These folks are screened and trained to work in public schools. (We of course make sure that their work coincides with ours and we never expect volunteers to do the highly trained work of an experienced and skilled teacher.) We also host many high school interns. These teenagers attend an alternative high school, and receive course credit for working with children three full days a week. We've also hosted several "economically disadvantaged adults fifty-five and older," who are attending community colleges as part of a job recertification program as early-childcare specialists. They hope to obtain jobs in daycare centers. Student teachers from several universities play a major role in our school and they are discussed in Chapter 7, "Turning Schools into Centers for Professional Development."

Family Homework

Prospective parents always ask how much homework our teachers assign. We have no carved-in-stone schoolwide policy, other than that we would love children to do worthwhile things after school hours. We certainly don't want to give so much homework that the children have no time to play in the park, take sports or music lessons, or attend the cultural or religious classes some families take part in. And we don't want children to have the kind of homework that creates stressful moments between parents and children at the kitchen table. We want children, after school, to engage in some of the literate acts that adults engage in after their workday is done. Most teachers consider at-home reading and writing as the core foundation of nightly homework assignments. Additional assignments are also given in other curriculum areas depending on student and class needs (in math, science, spelling, social studies, Spanish, etc.). Some teachers also include what is called family homework, intended to be done around the kitchen table but deliberately designed not to become agonizing moments of family torture. We don't expect family members to introduce hard concepts in mathematics, correct students' handwriting problems, solve their spelling issues, or build big show-off science projects. Instead, some teachers assign work to be done at home that gently capitalizes on children being in a home environment, surrounded by grown people who know different things. In other words, it is not family homework if the child is doing it alone in his bedroom with the door closed.

Paula writes to the families of her first-graders:

> We did a lot of work with graphs last week and will continue this week. Please look in the newspaper (in any language) to see if there are any kinds of graphs. There may be bar graphs like the ones we have done, line graphs, or even pie charts. If you find some, please discuss them with your child, and send them to school so the whole class can see.

Paula included examples of the graphs listed and also attached a classroom graph of favorite read-alouds for the children to discuss with their families and a challenge to create a graph of kitchen items.

Regina included the following task in the family homework packet for her second-grade class.

Dear families,

We are making personal number books in school and would like you to help if you can.

Numbers are a part of our lives from the moment we're born. At the time we are born, a hospital may record our length and weight and the time and date of our birth. After starting our lives we soon have more personal numbers: age, street address, zip code, telephone number, and social security number. These are just a few!

We are going to fill our books with as many numbers that are part of our lives as we can. Thanks.

Do you know your child's
  birth weight?_____
  birth length?_____
  age when he/she first walked?_____
We will add these numbers to our books.

Joanne invites parents in on her third graders' social studies research. Her letter home begins,

Dear families,

Attached is the information regarding an important social studies project. As you know, the third-grade social studies curriculum is "Celebrating Diversity." What better environment to learn about that than in a school that represents a multitude of different cultures. . . . The students will each be doing an oral presentation for the class about his/her own cultural background. Some of the items listed are required for the project, and some are optional. I suggest that you and your child read it over together, and think about which optional ones he/she will have easiest access to the information needed to complete.

Much of the research will need to be done at home, as it requires interviewing family members, gathering photos, etc. We will have some time also to work on it at school, so your child may want to bring in books that they are gathering. . . .

Joanne's packet continues with a list of the required and optional tasks that were created by the students, with Joanne's help, of course. The required ones included indicating the country's location on a world map, describing a native festival or holiday, teaching words from the language, preparing a family tree, and conducting an interview with a member of the family. Optional items included preparing a typical food, reading a poem, showing money, or teaching a song or dance from the country.

It's no wonder family members need to be involved with eight-year-olds in this ambitious project. Parents often attend the student presentations, and it is obvious how joyfully engaged they have become in the assignment. Their participation in this family homework as well as all those described in this section are one of the methods we have for communicating with parents about our ways of teaching and learning.

Especially in the upper grades, the family's role in homework involves help with providing quiet spaces, appropriate tools, and time management. Upper-grade homework assignments often stretch out over days, weeks, or even months.

Administrators do not traditionally give homework, but every once in a while I ask all families to do a little extra work at home. The following brief notes illustrate this very special kind of "home" work.

> *Dear families,*
>
> *A small request—Won't you please do some spring cleaning for us? Please check through your child's treasures, looking for other people's possessions in their bookcases, toy chests, dresser drawers, shoeboxes, in their closets and under their beds. We are searching for books that belong to classroom libraries as well as to other children. We are also looking for other children's toys, games, and rainy day materials that may have been borrowed, mixed-up, or taken home by mistake.*
>
> *Thanks for the extra effort. Here's hoping we will all find our missing goodies.*
>
> *With respect,*
Shelley

The next note also talks about spring-cleaning, but my purpose in this one is to put an end to the wintry-weather slacking off in on-time arrivals and pickups. In other words, no more excuses, we want to begin the day on time, without interruptions by late-arriving students, and our teachers want to be able to begin their own after-school lives at three o'clock. Teachers love their children, but they have other personal and professional obligations. It's only fair that parents respect this. I try to begin my letter in the most gracious way I know how, leading up to a strong plea.

> *Dear families,*
>
> *Somehow the beautiful sights of spring—parks filled with children, yellow daffodils in bloom, birds returning to city perches—always remind us to do some spring cleaning at home. The cluttered closets and overflowing drawers begin to gnaw at us, begging to be straightened up. At school too, it feels like time to do some spring cleaning. We've begun to redecorate our classrooms and hallways, hanging up fresh posters and poems, student art and writing. We've begun to rearrange furniture, reorganize files, and rethink school routines.*
>
> *And with the weather finally warming up, the school routines that are most on my mind are the arrival and dismissal procedures. Please pitch in with our spring-cleaning efforts here at school and review the attached procedures with your children.*

I then remind parents about our rules for arrival and dismissal times. "Home" work also involves getting up for school on time, allotting appropriate times for travel to school, and arranging your adult life to make on-time pickups a reality. (Lots of teachers make individual arrangements for parents with pressing problems, but these are exceptions to the school rules.) When people honor one another's time schedules, it makes it possible for us to do our work well and at the same time live the personal lives we choose.

Fundraisers

I remember, as a kid, loving those bumper cars in Coney Island. Every way you turned, you got smashed by another kid in another little car. Each year, when the budget cuts get announced, I once again feel that every which way I turn, I'm getting smashed head-on. Only now it's no fun at all. Each year, we've come to depend on hardworking parents to fill the void. Prospective parents inevitably ask me how much our PTA raises each year. At first the question seemed so odd to me, like asking a new acquaintance his salary. I couldn't even understand why the amount even mattered. We were such a small school, with such a small parent body, that the funds raised were always minimal. Now that we've grown, this is no longer true. Parents are now raising greater amounts of money and their purchases are essential.

In an end-of-the-year note to the parents, the co-presidents of the PTA wrote the following public thank-you to the fundraisers among them.

> *Just this past week everyone who entered the cafeteria was greeted with ropes being hung for the gym program. Suzy Campbell was mixing luscious paint colors for Alfredo, our custodian, who is graciously painting our auditorium. Henry, our computer coordinator, was completing an order for even more computers and printers. The next day, all our wonderful children were dancing in the streets. The fifth and sixth graders were showing off their ballroom dancing skills and Diane, our music teacher, hosted the event with the help of a new, powerful public-address system. The same week, fans were being delivered to every classroom.*
>
> *These scenes are thrilling to us because we could really feel the impact our parents' organization has made on the Manhattan New School. Parents bought that gym equipment and are even paying part-time for our gym teacher. You bought the paint, in fact, paid and arranged for all the work in the old auditorium/ballroom, including the stage and chairs in that room. You have purchased almost all of the computers and printers in the school, in addition to the PA system and the fans. You even paid for the ballroom dancing. You should feel great to see how much you are giving back to the school and to all our incredible children. You are helping to create a comfortable, stimulating environment, in which children can learn and grow. It's a wonderful feeling to be able to make a difference and everyone should give themselves a giant pat on the back!!! Well-deserved!*
>
> *Have a wonderful summer!*
>
> *Ellen and Robyn*

I always listen with awe as I attend parent planning sessions for the fund-raising events to come. Yes, they want to raise a lot of money, but participants are very conscious that not every family has money to spare. They make sure that parents who can't be part of the spending can take part in the gathering of goods, organizing and decorating for events, or selling. They make sure that parents are not overwhelmed with too many opportunities to give. They make sure that no one is made to feel bad if they cannot afford to take part in fundraisers. They also make sure that there are lots of inexpensive moneymakers. They sell ice cream on the sidewalk in good weather. They hold the traditional bake sales periodically. They sell student-made craft items at sidewalk sales. Everyone can feel that they are adding to the school treasury. (No doubt the healthy social tone of the PTA adds to its success. Sure, there are occasional disagreements, but the grown-ups act grown up and disagreements are aired and resolved.)

Family members also have opportunities to buy basics at school, items they would most likely buy somewhere else. These include school tee shirts and sweatshirts, gift-wrapping, and photographs of their child. Parents have recently added school tote bags, book bags, and file folders emblazoned with the school logo to our PTA-operated school store. Parents can also buy books at school. Twice a year, a small group of hard-working parents organize a bookfair. They always arrange these during November and March, when parents have formal conferences with their children and their teachers. On their way in and out, they walk through aisles of books for sale. This event not only raises money for our PTA, but children can add books to their personal collections and teachers can receive books for their classroom libraries. The organizers of the fair ask all of the teachers to browse the tables and create a stack of books they'd love to have in their classrooms. Parents are encouraged to look at the teacher's dream stack and buy one as a donation. Parents beautifully inscribe the family's name in the book before presenting it to the teacher.

Then there are the big annual fund-raising events. These include our spring street fair, affectionately known as our Fest with Zest, our weekend walkathon to the Forty-second Street Library, and our auction, in which family members bid on goods and services donated by members of our school and community. (Each year, a barbecue in my backyard is raffled off, as well as play dates with all the teachers.) We also tap parent performance abilities. Parents organize an annual "All in the Family" concert in which parents, as well as a small group of teachers, share their singing and musical talents. These fundraisers could easily be called "fun-raisers," as they not only raise money but community spirit.

A final fund-raising method deserves special recognition. Last year I began to receive small donation checks made out to the school, written in what appeared to be elderly persons' handwriting. It wasn't until someone told me of the passing of first grader Jesse's grandmother that I understood how these donations came about. When Elyse Rothschild died, her son Charles, father of our student Jesse, suggested that in lieu of flowers, mourners send donations to her granddaughter's school. When I called the family to offer my condolences and my gratitude, Charles explained that nothing was more important to his almost one-hundred-year-old mother than her children and grandchildren's education. Later on, Jesse's mom Stephanie sent me an article that had been written several years ago about Elsye in *The New York Times*. We were especially proud to have been connected to this incredible neighborhood activist.

Political Activists

Parents become politically active in many ways. They remind one another to listen carefully to people's platforms before voting in school board elections or for city council, for assembly members, or in mayoralty elections. They encourage new citizens to register to vote. They nudge one another to sign petitions and write letters of protest. They even provide postcards and addresses. They attend rallies at city hall and at the state capital. They invite local politicians to visit our school so that they will make policy decisions based on real student needs.

Fan-Club Presidents

Some parents treat us as if they are presidents of our fan clubs. I doubt if they even realize how important this role is to us. As mentioned in an earlier chapter, all educators need compliments. Don't we all need to know that our good work is noticed and valued?

Our parents find so many little ways to show their appreciation and gratitude. They stop by with iced coffee and electric fans on hot days, they pop in with beautiful bouquets, and they also take the time to send thank-you notes. Teachers love receiving these notes and so do I. I especially love when parents thank me for the tiniest of things. Karen Feuer, president of our school board, drops me a line to say, "Thanks for those sports books Noah came home with. He's been reading fast and furiously. It's amazing and wonderful." Susan, mother of Rosie and Mattie, writes, "I know you can't be everywhere—nor should you feel that pressure—yet since school has started you have been—shaking hands with Mattie the first morning, appearing to help Rosie with a lunch box problem the first week, and then today "rescuing" Mattie. . . . Your caring is appreciated." That's the way to start a day. Susan reminds me that it's so easy to make children happy. It's no surprise that I love my work. Another mom named Karen, this one belonging to Vanesa and Sebastian, sent me a generous and much appreciated note (see Figure 5.4). Another mom, Susan, mother of Nico, wrote, "I am constantly amazed that despite the growth of the school and your busy schedule, you are always accessible and easy to talk to. When I was upset, your undefensive, level-headed attitude and willingness to listen calmed me down. Also your shrug. It's one of your defining gestures and practically says, relax . . . this is normal."

More great ways to start the day. I didn't know I *had* any defining gestures. These letters make me stop and think. I know I should take lessons from these parents. They are so good at noticing the tiniest of things and they seem so comfortable letting people know what's in their hearts. Those are very important qualities to have, especially when you're in a leadership role.

"Love letters" like these occasionally arrive at my door; more often they arrive at teachers' doors. If more parents knew how much they mean to us, no doubt, more would write. Hardworking educators need to be recognized, not with competitive award ceremonies but with messages from the heart, from the people who they care most about.

Getting More Parents Involved

I have worked in schools in which it was sometimes difficult to establish strong working relationships with family members. The first step is always to make parents feel

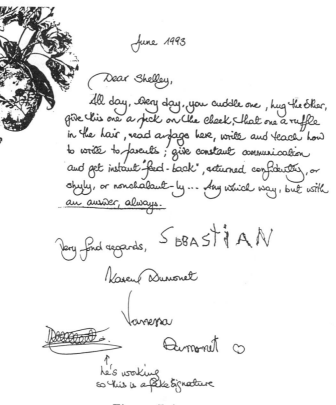

June 1993

Dear Shelley,

All day, every day, you cuddle one, hug the other, give this one a peck on the cheek, that one a ruffle in the hair, read a page here, write and teach how to write to parents; give constant communication and get instant "feed-back", returned confidently, or shyly, or nonchalant-ly ... Any which way, but with an answer, always.

Very fond regards,   S EBA ST i A N

Karen Dumonet

Vanessa

Dumonet ♡

↑
he's working
so this is a fake signature

Figure 5.4

welcome and comfortable inside the building. It helps to have an easily accessible parent room that is baby-carriage friendly (no steps!), one with a coffeepot going, a place for toddlers to play, and workspace for the many tasks that parents can perform.

If a parent feels intimidated, incompetent, or ill at ease, there is no chance that he or she will be an active participant in the life of a school. I was therefore delighted when a group of Asian parents asked to meet with me periodically to talk about school practice and discuss the best ways to support their children at home. The group, made up of Chinese-, Korean-, and Japanese-speaking mothers, explained that the talk at our general PTA meetings was too fast and that they hesitated to ask their questions at whole-group meetings. They much preferred the intimate gatherings in my office, where they could take the time to make their meaning clear and seek any clarification needed. I'm only sorry that no one had thought to arrange these meetings sooner.

I was equally delighted when our PTA began a buddy program for in-coming parents, much the way colleges have Big Brother and Big Sister programs for incoming freshmen. (Their invitation appears in Appendix 18.) The buddy project, which is available to new families in grades one through five, was easy to implement and maintain, since relatively few families enroll after kindergarten. But it makes sense. No doubt, when newcomers are taken by the hand, there is a greater likelihood that they will get involved sooner and stay involved in the life of the school.

I have also worked in schools in which parents' frustration at feeling voiceless resulted in angry confrontations and tension at PTA meetings. Pretty soon, no one wants to attend these uncomfortable meetings. It is therefore essential that parent organizers remain especially sensitive to the needs of family members who do not ordinarily make phone calls, write letters, or join committees.

Parent leaders also need to remain conscious of families with differing financial capabilities. Ours is a well-integrated community, in which children of rich families and those of poor families work and play alongside one another. Years ago, the parents organized a Friday-night dance for our older students. The children from the Bronx and Upper Manhattan, who traveled very far to attend our school, admitted that they could not attend the dance because it would be too hard for them to travel home safely at night by public transportation. To avoid canceling the event, children were invited to sleep at neighborhood children's homes. In this instance, the community thought of a gracious way to avoid being exclusionary. Sometimes solutions cannot be found and the community must rethink their plans. I was pleased when parent leaders turned down an expensive lunchtime language course because the costs would be prohibitive for many families, and chose not to create a computerized network for parents to contact one another because it would exclude so many families.

Likewise, parent organizers need to be very conscious that the members of the audience at our parent meetings and school celebrations should be as diverse as our student body. If not, parent leaders need to design gracious ways of extending invitations, making everyone feel welcome and removing any possible obstacles so that all members of the school community can be full participants in the life of the school. Last year's organizers of one of our weekend fundraisers, the All in the Family concert, wondered if the ten-dollar tickets were preventing many families from attending this joyful Sunday-afternoon soiree. Teachers were, therefore, given free tickets to distribute privately as they saw fit. In addition, structures were put in place for more financially able families to sponsor others to attend. All of this was carried out anonymously and with great sensitivity.

If parents are treated with respect and their opinions are sought and valued, most will become involved with their child's school, especially if there are many entrance ramps to participation. Not everyone has to run for president of the PTA nor become a member of its executive board. Years ago, I heard a speaker explain the difference between involvement and commitment, by describing the difference between bacon and eggs. The hen is involved, the pig is committed. Schools need both kinds of participants. Following are a few suggestions for encouraging more parents to attend school meetings. Once parents attend, and the meetings are calm, interesting, nonexclusionary, and joyful, more parents will join committees, volunteer, and take part in school-wide events.

- Invite children to perform at school meetings. Everyone wants to see his or her child sing, dance, act, or play a musical instrument.

- Announce slide shows of students at work. Everyone wants to see his or her beautiful child on a larger-than-life screen. Allow parents to borrow slides to turn them into wallet-size photographs.

- Provide school calendars with meeting dates listed well in advance.

- If translators are not available, allow for what the Swedes call a "Swedish pause." (Swedish teachers, when confused at my English presentations, hold up their hands and ask for a time out so that they can huddle together and discuss in Swedish the confusing parts.)

- Encourage parents in buddy relationships to bring new parents to meetings.

- Encourage classroom teachers to attend. It's hard to resist the chance to spend time with your child's teacher.

- Add a few comforts—baby-sitting service, early-evening meeting times, and a few good snacks.

- Personal invitations, extended by teachers and administrators to a few key parents, may also work wonders.

The Swedish pause explained above is not all that I learned in Sweden. I was always struck by how many young immigrants hung out in the Gothenberg public library. The attraction included the availability of daily newspapers from the newcomers' home countries as well as plush, comfortable chairs arranged in wide aisles, making it possible, for instance, to park a baby carriage alongside your seat. When you really want people to feel welcome, you take thoughtful and deliberate actions, whether in a library, school auditorium, parent meeting room, or the corridors and classrooms of your school.

RELATED READINGS IN COMPANION VOLUMES ────────────

Lifetime Guarantees (Heinemann, forthcoming), will be abbreviated as LG.
Writing Through Childhood (Heinemann, forthcoming), will be abbreviated as WC.

Noting family reading habits	**LG**: Ch. 8.
Inviting family members to write about their children	**LG**: Ch. 8. **WC**: Ch. 8.
Photographing at-home readers	**LG**: Ch. 8.
Keeping family literacy portfolios	**LG**: Ch. 8.
Informing families about writing	**WC**: Ch. 8.
Offering early morning parent workshops	**LG**: Ch. 8.

Noting newspaper habits	**LG**: Ch. 4, Ch. 8.
Inviting family members to visit writing workshops	**WC**: Ch. 8.
Holding language forums	**LG**: Ch. 10.
Offering parent writing workshops	**WC**: Ch. 3, Ch. 8.
Connecting poetry to notebook keeping	**WC**: Ch. 3. **LG**: Ch. 5.
Arranging a parent/child reading group	**LG**: Ch. 8.
Arranging a reading group for parents	**LG**: Ch. 8.
Selecting literacy topics for parent workshops	**LG**: Ch. 8.
Designing staff meeting activities	**WC**: Ch. 11. **LG**: Ch. 7.
Arranging author celebrations	**WC**: Ch. 9.
Selecting picture books for parents	**WC**: Ch. 8. **LG**: Ch. 8.
Promoting the reading of poetry	**LG**: Ch. 5, Ch. 9.
Offering suggestions for at-home writing	**WC**: Ch. 8.
Asking kindergartners to keep journals	**WC**: Ch. 6.
Distributing school-wide poetry anthologies	**LG**: Ch. 1.

CHAPTER 6

TALKING CURRICULUM AND ASSESSMENT

Priorities

- Curriculum decisions must be guided by social tone and controlled by the educational community.
- In developing curriculum, we must choose what is valuable; our decisions must be influenced by our desire to help children see the richness of their world and use their literacies to improve the quality of their lives, in school and out.
- People's genuine passions must be invited into our classrooms.
- We must understand that studying issues deeply and meaningfully requires time.
- The principal's role in curriculum should include maintaining the organizing vision, creating structures to push thinking, fulfilling district obligations, writing grants, working with parents, and gathering resources.
- We must design assessment tools and systems that meet the needs of the entire community

Practice

- On sifting through curriculum choices to arrive at what is valuable
- On discovering social studies non-negotiables
- On selecting and designing thematic studies
- On creating structures to push thinking about curriculum, including weekly staff meetings, grade-level meetings, joint teaching sessions, informal study groups, and summer planning meetings.
- On working directly with parents on issues of curriculum
- On designing meaningful assessment tools; such as student portfolios
- On involving family members in student assessment
- On informing parents about the standards movement

The comedian Steven Wright reminds us that we can't have everything we want, by asking the question, "Where would you put it?" When we think about curriculum, a similar thought applies. We can't teach everything we want, because, "Where would we put it?" There is so much to teach and learn, and the days go by so quickly. On any one day, walking in and out of classrooms in our five-story building, I can learn about the history of Wall Street, the contributions of Native Americans to the founding of New York City, the names of local trees, the importance of recycling, patterns in local architecture, varieties of breads, and reasons for immigration to the United States. I can join children as they weave, do woodworking, and water their plants. I can help children replicate colonial toys, make dyes from natural plants, churn their own butter, estimate the number of raisins in a box, build a life-size skeleton from toilet paper rolls, design their own version of the chunnel connecting England and France, or create realistic giraffes from empty pretzel barrels, papier mâché and paint. I can bump into park rangers from Central Park, curators from the Metropolitan Museum of Art, and chefs from the American Wine and Food Institute. I can peek over children's shoulders as they devour nonfiction books, the more mysterious the topic the better. I can marvel as I watch children search the Internet for information to enrich the topics they are studying in their science workshops. I can wave goodbye to classes leaving to visit the Empire State Building, Yankee Stadium, or the local construction site. I can stand in awe as ballroom dance instructors demonstrate the merengue and the macarena, as Jacques d'Amboise teaches children to lift their knees higher than they ever thought possible, or as Rachel Robinson answers questions asked by first-graders about her beloved husband Jackie.

The dedication in Betsy Bowen's book *Gathering: A Northwoods Counting Book* reads, "In honor of teachers, enthusiastic and caring, in particular Miss Glixon, who taught me to measure the sun passing across the floor through the seasons of fourth grade." I'd like to think that the teachers at the Manhattan New School are developing the kinds of curriculum that will create lifetime memories for children.

We do not have a schoolwide curriculum that is set in stone. And though our curriculum is rich, varied, and dynamic, it is not the result of a helter-skelter, come-what-may, hodgepodge of ideas. Although teachers and students have ample flexibility in choosing, negotiating, and developing curriculum, and our classes may at times study very different issues, there are several umbrella beliefs that guide our choice and development of curriculum. These schoolwide beliefs, coupled with consistent views on how children learn, make Isabel's notion of each teacher having an individual plot add up to an aesthetically pleasing garden of curriculum.

Attitudes and Beliefs that Guide Curriculum Choices

Social Tone as Prime Curriculum

Throughout this book I have argued for the importance of a supportive social tone. In the introduction, I suggested that our school's social tone is an integral feature of our curriculum. Later, I shared Isabel's belief that her kindergarten curriculum is easily summed up by her phrase "gracious living." I noted how all of us, throughout the grades, have come to appreciate the wisdom of her words. In Chapter 4 I explored in detail our curriculum of caring. I learned a long time ago that if students don't care about one another, it doesn't really matter what materials we order, what assessment systems we design, or what instructional strategies we try. Donald Graves suggested to us that we have allowed love to become the antenna of our curriculum. Those are powerful words, worth living up to. Not only do teachers devote a great deal of classroom time to reading, writing, thinking, and talking about treating one another with kindness and respect, teachers also highlight connections between topics studied in social studies and science to the vision of creating a more just and peaceful world. This one aspect of curriculum, having a caring social tone, reminds us of the importance of having a curriculum that informs the way you live your life at school. What would be the point of teaching environmental studies if we didn't recycle? What would be the point of teaching Spanish if we didn't try to use it in our everyday lives? What would be the point of teaching mathematical problem solving if we didn't invite students in on the everyday math problems that arise? What would be the point of teaching tolerance, respect, and humanity if these qualities were not present in our social interactions with one another?

Community Control of Curriculum

Several years ago, I was struck by a list of kindergarten teaching "tips" published in a local newsletter. The writer suggested that teachers plan reinforcement activities for children prior to the morning Pledge of Allegiance. These included setting up coloring and cutting tasks so that the teacher could take attendance and collect absence notes. The writer suggested that early-childhood teachers seek the help of upper-grade students to mark and staple homework sheets and PTA notices into younger students' notebooks, and invite kindergartners to tutor ESL peers, allowing the young children to give out stickers and stars to students who do well. The writer also suggested that kindergarten teachers give prizes to students who raise their hands, tie their shoes, et cetera. I'm sure these suggestions work in the classroom of the teacher who wrote them. I am equally as sure that they would have no relevance for the kindergarten teachers in our school. In fact, the assumptions behind each of these management tips would be totally wrong in our setting. Our teachers would argue against each and every one of them. For example, in our school we do teach our older students about the meaning of the Pledge and the role the flag has played in the history of our country, but we do not have a daily morning Pledge of Allegiance. Secondly, if children needed "reinforcement" of a skill, we would stand alongside them and coach them. We would not use valuable teaching time to do our own paperwork. Besides, our teachers would prefer to invite students to participate in the taking of attendance and the collecting of absence notes. Then too, these tips wouldn't work in our community because we don't give homework to our five-year-olds and we certainly don't grade any student's homework. Nor would we attach PTA notices to students' notebooks. We also wouldn't ask a five-year-old to formally "tutor" another child who doesn't speak English. Hang out together, help one another, work on projects together, yes, but we certainly wouldn't call it "tutoring," nor invite a five-year-old to decide if a classmate is deserving of a sticker. In fact, we don't believe that stickers, stars, and prizes should be used to reward students or to convince them to follow rules. All in all, these teaching suggestions make absolutely no sense in our community. Such crucial school issues as management techniques, choice of materials, school routines, and especially curriculum decisions must be made by the people whose lives are touched by those decisions. It doesn't surprise me that what works in one school community may not work in another community, even in the same city.

Several years ago, there was no pot of gold at the end of the very controversial Rainbow Curriculum in our city. Mandating this curriculum citywide in part cost the chancellor his job. This curriculum guide suggested that teachers present different aspects of alternate lifestyles to students throughout the grades. Our one city district covers such diverse settings as Chinatown, Greenwich Village, Governor's Island, Chelsea, Hell's Kitchen, Tribeca, and the Upper East Side. How can such diverse cultural, economic, and ethnic enclaves all agree on any one social curriculum? The reaction of different neighborhoods to the Rainbow Curriculum brought to mind Goldilocks's reaction to the three bears' bowls of porridge. In some parts of our district, the curriculum was too avant-garde; in others, it didn't go far enough; in a few, it would have been just right. Curriculum decisions need to be made by the people whose lives are touched by those decisions. All the curriculum guides that come our way, and many do, are seen as resource material, not prescribed mandates.

Choosing What Is Valuable

Prospective parents always ask me about curriculum. "What makes your school different?" they ask. I used to begin answering such questions by sharing a few of the teaching priorities in the school. I'd attempt to describe the meaning of whole language teaching, using all the key phrases, including "learner-centered," "process approach," and "literature-based." I'd then warn parents that so much comes at us in the name of whole language, we need a way to filter out what is really valuable. Publishers often send us prepackaged 'whole language' thematic studies, covered with cute teddy-bears and colorful rainbows. I make sure that parents understand that "cute and colorful" is not the criterion we use when we choose and develop curriculum.

In the very first chapter of this book, I suggested that educators need to believe in something. I explained how I used the notion of authenticity as a means of sifting through all the curriculum suggestions that make their way into our bulging mailboxes. Parents seem to appreciate that we never ask children to do things inside school that people outside school do not do. Parents understand why we don't ask children to write pretend letters that never get mailed, or answer endless questions at the end of every chapter read, or fill-in the blanks on insufferable phonics sheets. They understand why children are invited to talk or write in response to books read, to fill portfolios with their important achievements, to keep journals, read newspapers, and to take pride in public speaking. Our children not only have mentors in school, they can find mentors outside of school because we ask them to do the kinds of things that people really do in the real world.

In that same early chapter (see "Believe in Something" in Chapter 1, "Sharing the Secrets of our Success"), I reveal what has become the heart of our curriculum, throughout the grades. I suggest that we are raising activists at the Manhattan New School. We want to raise wide-awake children who pay attention to and take responsibility for their world. Alexandra asks in her writer's notebook, "Why don't people get together and make New York a better place to live?" We have framed Alexandra's words and they hang in our main lobby, serving as a rallying cry for us all.

I always suggest to parents that we are offering them lifetime guarantees. Their children will not just know how to read and write, they will choose to read and write. I can make such a bold promise because we continually demonstrate and prove to students just how powerful it is to become literate. The essence of our curriculum is twofold. First, we desperately want to help children see the richness of their lives. Second, we want them to use their literacies to improve the quality of their lives.

The following is a recent New York City fact sheet released in a report entitled *Keeping Track of New York City's Children* published by the Citizens' Committee for Children of New York, Inc.

Fact One	One out of every 4 people in New York is a child.
Fact Two	Every day 340 babies are born.
Fact Three	Every day 4 babies die before their first birthdays.
Fact Four	Every day babies are born at risk:
	150 babies are born into poverty.
	35 babies born to teen parents.
	57 babies born to mothers with inadequate prenatal care.
	33 babies born with low birthweight.
Fact Five	Every day 762,000 children live in poverty.
Fact Six	Every day 9700 children are homeless.
Fact Seven	Every 14 hours a young person under 25 is murdered.
Fact Eight	Every day 477,700 students read below grade level.
Fact Nine	Every week 11,393 children use mental health services.
Fact Ten	Every day 77 children are reported abused or neglected.

Unfortunately, I don't doubt these statistics. Just ask any New York City educator who has tried to call the child abuse hotline. The line is always busy, especially during school hours. We've learned to carry the necessary information home with us, so that we can call at dawn or dusk, when the lines are less busy. New York is not an easy place to grow up. That's why our organizing vision, our filtering question, must become, "How can we improve the quality of our lives?" Several years ago, I wrote in *Whole Language: The Debate*:

As the director of a New York City public school, I am *not* looking for systematic investigations, improved evaluative research, valid measures of worthiness, or quantitative paradigms. Instead, I'm looking for ways to make every minute in our building count. I'm looking for that "community of learners," the right book for the right child, and ways not just to teach children *how* to read and write but ways of living that will make them *choose* to read and write. I'm looking for ways to make everyone who enters our school passionate about their own literacies. I'm looking for ways to make our schoolhouse the most beautiful, the most nourishing building in the neighborhood. I'm looking for ways to teach reading and writing that will enable children to use their literacies to improve the quality of their inner-city lives.

No matter where our school was located, I think my big curriculum goals would be the same. I want children to lead wide-awake lives and to use their literacies to improve the quality of their lives. This would be true if our school were on the Zuni reservation in New Mexico, or on a quiet tree-lined street in Shaker Heights, Ohio, or in downtown Denver, Colorado. We ask children to read the daily newspaper, write letters, interview community members, personally respond to books, sketch street scenes, visit museums, parks, and libraries, and fill their writer's notebooks with observations, wonderings, questions, suggestions, plans, hopes, and dreams. All these authentic acts in which students engage can be valued as tools that help them see the richness of their lives and tools that help them improve the quality of those lives. Eight-year-old Alexandra was right. Our job, as educators, is to get together and make our communities better places to live. Our job is to provide hopefulness. Our job is to offer children the tools and the confidence to fully live as citizens in their classrooms, communities, and the world.

The New York Times offers a "Newspaper in Education" service. Last year the service sent a list of conversation starters to help students take more from their reading of the news. For example, they suggested that teachers ask students, "Are things getting better or worse in New York City? What news about New York City makes you feel optimistic, which pessimistic, which cheerful, which gloomy, which admiring, which scornful? Which stories . . . do you think have the potential to help promote a feeling of togetherness among New York's varied communities or cultures, if they were to read them?" These are important questions teachers in any city can ask students who read the local newspaper. We want all students to pay attention to their world and use their literacies to make it a better place.

Each year, the New York City schools are closed for one week in February designated as a midwinter school recess. Each year, the New York City Board of Education publishes and distributes to every student a calendar of weeklong cultural activities. The calendar, which is available in English, Chinese, Haitian, Russian, and Spanish, offers fifteen pages of mostly free events during the week that school is closed. All of New York City's public agencies and several private ones offer special programs and services during this winter week. This handout has always been one of my favorites. It's incredibly thoughtful and informative, and it serves to remind our children how lucky they are to live in our city.

When my colleagues ask me if I think a certain topic is worthy of a big block of time for individual, small-group, whole-class or schoolwide study, I suggest that they ask themselves two broad questions. First, "Will this study help students see the richness of their world?" Second, "Will this study provide students with opportunities to use their literacies and talents to improve the quality of their world?" (Students know that we work hard at letter writing, newspaper reading, public speaking, dramatic performances, and creating works of art because we want to enrich and improve our lives.) These questions not only provide a means of selecting areas to study but they can also influence the kinds of invitations extended and the experiences provided.

Several years ago, I met with two young women from the Association for a Better New York. They had designed a curriculum on New York City's infrastructure for school children in grades three through five. I couldn't imagine a more worthwhile project. Students would gain an understanding of the workings of all the utilities they use every day, including electric, gas, telephone, and sewage, as well as become familiar with the subways, tunnels, and bridges of our city. Such in-depth study would no doubt make students marvel at the complexity of their hometown, its underground worlds and colossal structures, and at the same time encourage students to identify problems and play with possible solutions. Similarly, I've always kept the Board of Education curriculum guide entitled *Operation New York* in a safe place in my office. This guide to using the natural environment of the city as a curriculum resource is filled with information on the materials used to create sidewalks, playgrounds, and school buildings, and helps students identify the trees and plants growing on those city sidewalks. Likewise, I always offer a thumbs-up when I hear that a teacher is planning to research the Broadway theater, the construction of a skyscraper, our city's animal life, or the mayoral election. I was especially thrilled the year our fourth graders danced the history of New York City with Jacques d'Amboise's National Dance Institute. What better way to understand how our city grew than to create dances to explore the Dutch colony, immigration, and the Harlem Renaissance?

To accompany my button that reads "So many books, so little time," we can create one that says, "So many topics, so little time." We need to spend time on those issues that really engage students and help them lead enriched lives.

Social Studies Non-negotiables   I read that Russian fairy tales often begin with the words, "There was and there was not. . ." We do have a prescribed curriculum and we do not have a prescribed curriculum. In the area of social studies, we do take a look at all the curriculum suggestions offered in city, state, and district handbooks, sifting through these to discover the things that really matter for our community. Kindergarten and first-grade handbooks suggest that our youngest children study the meaning of family and the workings of their local community. It's no surprise to find our youngest children interviewing family members, writing captions for family photo albums, visiting local shopkeepers, sketching their neighborhoods, and so on. In second grade, we begin more formal studies of our city. All of our second-grade teachers invite children to choose areas of interest connected to a study of New York. The study of our city remains a thread throughout the grades, but our exploration begins in grade two. We want children early on to know their hometown. Appreciating all that New York has to offer is a major part of seeing the richness of their lives. Second-grade teachers and students select from a wide range of possibilities, taking such perspectives as historical, geographical, environmental, and cultural. Our third graders research their cultural backgrounds and examine how their personal family stories are part of the bigger story of immigration in our city and our country. Our fourth and fifth graders are invited to explore several important stories and documents in American history. Teachers think long and hard about which stories to tell and which documents to share. They can't teach every moment on the timeline of American history and so they must select key moments. Fourth-grade teachers usually begin with colonial settlements and move through the American Revolution and on through westward expansion. Fifth-grade teachers lead children through the story of the Industrial Revolution and examine the history of the United States through the wars that have so influenced the development of our country. Our students come to understand that we study history to better understand what is happening on the streets of our city today.

Throughout the teaching of social studies, current events hold a revered place in curriculum development. We have learned to drop everything and pay attention to a "fast-breaking" story, whether it comes from *The New York Times*, the six o'clock evening news, or out of the mouth of Jameelah, Adriatik, Priscilla, or Kyaw Saw. We are also determined to help students make connections between what they are studying about the history of New York City, the reasons for immigration, the causes of wars in the United States, the Constitution and the Bill of Rights, and what is happening every day on the streets of their neighborhood and in towns and cities throughout the country and the world. The newspaper always provides worthwhile companion reading. Our job is to help students understand how their understanding of history feeds their reading of the daily news and how their reading of the newspaper both informs their day-to-day lives and inspires their study of what came before. We want to raise the kind of students who can't imagine starting their day without the morning paper. We want to raise the kind of students who wouldn't think of voting for a candidate without reading where the candidate stands on crucial issues. We want to raise the kind of students who acquire lifelong newspaper-reading habits.

Our social studies curriculum is also greatly influenced by the specific issues members of our community are currently facing. How can we not talk about the crisis in Yugoslavia and the Balkans when so many of our students come from that part of the world? How can we not discuss immigration laws, green cards, and visas when so many of our students are the primary speakers of English in their families and are called upon to interpret and fill out U.S. government documents? How can we not teach children about the procedures and politics involved in school board elections when a school board member is a parent in our school? How can we not attend to the plight of the homeless in our city when our next-door neighbor, Ellen, periodically wanders into our building hungry, cold, and disoriented? How can we not challenge our fifth graders to understand how people like Ellen, with dwindling resources, few family contacts, and poor health, often do become homeless, if we don't provide a safety net before she falls?

In addition to current events, teachers throughout the grades also take the teaching of geography very seriously. We want all students to feel at home reading maps. We want them to see browsing atlases as an enjoyable pastime. We want them to take delight in identifying major landforms and in understanding the role geography plays in the development of towns, cities, states, and countries. We want them to be in awe of mountain ranges, stretches of desert, and bodies of water. We want them to take pride in knowing the precise names of these natural formations. We love maps and map reading so much, if we had adequate space we would create a map room, exclusively devoted to this one area of study. We would line the walls with the most current world maps, but also with subway, bus, and street maps. For now, we need to make sure that these lifelong tools are sought-after items of choice in every classroom library.

Thematic Studies

Celebrating the Passions of Teachers and Students   In addition to the social studies topics described previously, other content studies are primarily based on the needs, interests, and passions of teachers and students, coupled with a belief in developmentally appropriate study. Again, we are greatly influenced by community issues. How can we not research pigeons when these unofficial city mascots sit on our window ledges all day long? How can we not involve our students in the study of playgrounds when we received a grant to reconstruct our turn-of-the-century park? How can the study of museums not become a major focus when our school is within walking distance of some of the grandest museums in the world?

Lorraine loves architecture. Each summer, she attends architectural courses and reads related books. This past school year her first graders worked with several area architects. Together they constructed a replica of our one city block. Have you ever seen children construct a building using a half-gallon orange juice container covered with colored construction paper? They usually draw a zillion little odd-shaped windows irregularly placed across the entire façade. Not Lorraine's six-year-olds. Not children who have been studying with real live architects. Each floor of their juice-container buildings is covered with a different color strip of construction paper. This very graphic device helped them to easily understand the concept of stories in a building. Then they were able to understand why you can only have one band of windows on each story, not a collage of random windows placed haphazardly. They even learned that the windows have to be placed at just the right height in a wall so that people are able to look out. They used a small plastic doll to establish eye level and to create the height of the front door. The children also learned that our school is five units wide and that the church next door is only one unit wide. Lorraine has planted very deep roots. These six-year-olds are going to be very ready to study more complicated concepts related to scale, ratio, and proportion when they are older. Above all, they've begun to lead very wide-awake lives. They are lucky to have studied with a teacher who teaches in ways that allows learning to occur when there is no teacher around. They will not walk down a city street in just the same way. They have an architect's eye and an architect's language now. They are prepared to observe and question.

We are always open to the fevers that sweep through our students' lives. Over the years I have seen classrooms become totally immersed in snails, whales, the stock exchange, chess, the Beatles, bridges, chicks, dinosaurs, and outer space. There are plenty of occasions for individual students as well as small groups of students to explore an incredible array of very personal areas of inquiry. The topics and settings differ, but all teachers demonstrate a passion for living alongside inquiring minds, a rich array of strategies for gathering and organizing information, an attitude toward revising and rethinking the learner's questions, techniques for using reading, writing, and the arts to make sense of data, as well as a multitude of ways to teach others what has been learned.

I recently interviewed an inexperienced teacher for an early-childhood special education position. Halfway through the interview I asked her what a day might be like in her classroom. "How the day goes," she began, "would depend on the theme the class was studying." "How would you choose the theme?" I asked. "Oh," she responded, "there are so many to choose from, the possibilities are limitless." I asked her to give me an example of a theme she thought might be appropriate for five-year-old language-delayed children. "Maybe we would study parks," she answered. I then asked her to describe a day in her class if "parks" was the theme. "I'd choose a few books about parks to read aloud and then I'd plan some art projects that are connected to the books." I stopped this young teacher-to-be and offered her some suggestions. I reminded her that she wasn't teaching parks, she was teaching children. I guided our conversation with the following questions:

- What do you think young children should know about parks?
- How would you find out what your students already know about parks?
- Are there big important understandings you would hope very young children would come to appreciate as they study parks?
- Are there books and activities you would choose deliberately because they might help children appreciate key concepts?
- How would you find out what the children wonder about parks?
- How would you help them find the answers to their own questions?
- How would you invite students to select their own theme for whole-class study?

I also asked this prospective teacher if she could imagine teaching without any theme. Themes are not a constant in our school; rather, they punctuate the school year and add a colorful feel to classroom life. Schools can be rigorous, content-rich places without thematic teaching. After all, I reminded my guest, you can't read and write about nothing, and we read and write for big blocks of time every day. You can always eavesdrop on interesting conversations, even if everyone is *not* immersed in an organized study.

This interview turned into a brief seminar, but I couldn't resist. Teaching is not coming up with a clever or cute topic, then squeezing your brain to come up with a zillion theme-related activities. Teaching requires a deeper, reflective stance. Selecting, designing, and teaching curriculum involves realizing possibilities, establishing priorities, negotiating with members of a community, rethinking schedules, resources, and goals, forging new grounds, and continuous revision of plans and activities.

The Importance of Adequate Time

I always suggest that prospective parents read Vera John Steiner's *Notebooks of the Minds*. I want them to understand the value the researcher has placed on allowing young people to be obsessed with things. I want parents to understand why we value sticking with content studies for a long time. I tell prospective parents about my son's long-term interest in bubbles, from blowing them as a toddler to his high school science research project on the symmetry of soap film and soap bubbles. Schools become different places when people aren't rushing through curriculum, anxious to click off topics "covered." Instead, we value long-term commitment to fewer topics.

A parent who recently toured our school sent me the following follow-up letter.

Dear Shelley,

I loved your school when I visited last winter—the whole place felt like a library. I loved the kids' poems and stories up on the walls. I loved the way the teachers spoke to the children—how they spotted the questions and led the kids to the answers. It's a great place.

I especially liked your defense of creative obsession for lack of a better phrase. At that point my three-year-old had memorized Snow White—*the book and the audio versions. She had been Snow White for Halloween and continued to wear the costume every day since. We spent the months of February and March making papier mâché puppets of Snow White, the Wicked Queen, and the Prince. She acted out the story several times a day, insisted that it be read to her—she had four different versions—before her nap and before bedtime, and had collected miniature versions of the characters, sticker books, coloring books, plates, toothbrushes, posters—her room was a shrine to Snow White.*

And then a week ago she said to me. "Mommy, in all these princess books there's a beautiful princess, a wicked ugly witch or queen who doesn't want to get married, and a prince. All of them. They're all the same." I was amazed, she got it—the template, the paradigm, the formula, whatever you want to call it—she got it. Because, I'm convinced, she was allowed to wallow in her interest. I clipped this article after hearing you speak and it's been sitting in a pile of stuff on my desk ever since. I think it's saying the same thing—deep thinking wins the day.

Zoe's still in preschool—and we're way the hell over here on the West Side, but I hope somehow we can work it out so that she can come to your school. It's an oasis.

Have a good summer,

Elizabeth Page

The article Elizabeth is referring to appeared in *The New York Times* in a description of the IBM computer Deep Blue, which was used as the opponent in a chess match with the world chess champion Gary Kasparov. Experts praise chess computers that have deeper information over those with shallower information, even though the latter may have greater across-the-board information. Deep Blue plays chess well because of its ability to calculate more deeply.

Once again that Ladino proverb rings true, "It's not how many commandments you fulfill, but the spirit in which you fulfill them." Likewise, it's not how many thematic units and courses of study we boast having studied during a school year. Rather it's the spirit, depth, joy, and commitment that we bring to those carefully chosen studies that leave a lasting impression on our students and ourselves.

Reading, 'Riting, and 'Rithmetic

Visitors, weaving in and out of classrooms in our school, see many similarities in the amount of time devoted to the teaching of reading, writing, and mathematics as well as similarities in teaching techniques within these workshop areas. It's no surprise that teachers and children feel so much at home when they take part in one another's workshops. Successful practices are contagious in school buildings in which people admire one another and are eager to collaborate and innovate on one another's ideas.

Although this text and its companion volumes, *Lifetime Guarantees* and *Writing Through Childhood*, focus primarily on the teaching and learning of the language arts during the elementary grades, we also take pride in our mathematics instruction. Our district has been rethinking mathematics instruction for several years, and our teachers are privileged to work, study, and research alongside several top mathematics educators. The district provides support for all teachers including summer institutes, professional reading materials, teaching materials and resources, staff developers, and worthwhile workshop series. At each workshop demonstration, I'm awed by what I don't know. Our teachers have been invited to think through the big ideas in mathematics. They have learned how to help students talk clearly as they reason quantitatively. Many years ago, when I was a classroom teacher offering students a daily dose of prescribed mathematics, I don't ever recall having an interesting mathematical tale to share with my family around the dinner table. Today, I simply marvel at what our children are able to do and their ability to talk about what they are doing in mathematics. I know things are going well in mathematics when teachers have stories to tell about their student's thinking.

Our students seem so at home renaming numbers, seeing patterns in hundreds charts, and performing great amounts of mental math. With deep-rooted number sense and little attention to algorithms, our students understand how knowing that $6 \times 7 = 42$ helps you know what 60×70 is, what 12×7 is, what 3×7 is, and so on. Unfortunately to date, I have remained more of a spectator than participant in math workshops, but I'm present enough to realize just how limited I am. I have had very little personal experience in performing mental mathematics, cooperatively solving mathematical problems, and appreciating other people's strategies for solving problems. I have had no experience in creating math menus, teaching replacement units, or providing manipulatives. The teaching of mathematics keeps me particularly humble. I realize just how little I know and how much there is to learn.

The Principal's Role in Curriculum

Lucy West, our district's wonderful coordinator of mathematics instruction, recently distributed a list of ways principals can support teachers' efforts to change their mathematics instruction. She suggested, for example, that principals attend district workshops, buy necessary materials, encourage workshop attendance, schedule big blocks of time, communicate with staff developers, arrange time for teachers to talk, read related curriculum materials, inform parents, remove pressure of instant success, and try teaching a few lessons. In addition to all the tasks listed above, there are several other curriculum-related challenges that I am particularly happy to accept. They include the following:

Maintaining the Organizing Vision

As previously noted, a visitor once referred to our school as teacher heaven. It didn't take long to realize that teacher heaven is a very exhausting place. All of us put in very long hours and we often bring our professional lives into all that we do outside of school. We worry continually about children who aren't making significant academic progress and those who are exhibiting inappropriate social behaviors. We worry about students whose families are in crisis and students who have serious health problems. And of course, just like all reflective practitioners, we always question our own teaching practices. Are we doing enough? Is there a better way? Are we as good as people expect us to be? Teacher heaven is indeed very exhausting, and tired educators can get into trouble. I worry most that when we're tired we will make mediocre choices. It's hard to be discriminating when you're feeling overwhelmed. When too much is on your plate, you can even lose your appetite for perfectly prepared gourmet foods.

Thank goodness we're not all exhausted at the same time. I do think it is the principal's responsibility to bring people back on task when our goals become blurred and the curriculum loses its freshness. It's a role I share, of course, with my colleagues. Everyone on staff needs to feel responsible for putting us back on track when we've gone astray.

If our music teacher were thinking about designing a new course of study, it wouldn't be surprising for me to suggest it include a Broadway musical or the work of jazz musicians from Harlem. After all, we want children to feel fortunate to be living in New York. When we are thinking of trying a whole-school course of study as a change of pace, it wouldn't be surprising for me to suggest we study our one city block. What incredible curriculum there is to be developed if we look at our block through the eyes of a historian, artist, mathematician, and scientist. What a way for children and adults to appreciate their community. When children share their finished written work with me, they have come to expect my usual response. After complimenting them, I usually ask, "What are you going to do with it now? Where in the real world does it deserve to be read?" My responses are fairly predictable, because I stand firm in the notion that children need to see the richness of their world and learn to use their literacies to improve the quality of their world.

Creating Structures to Push Thinking

Whenever enthusiastic teachers get together, new thinking occurs. Ideas are born when teachers eat lunch together, sit next to each other on a long field trip bus ride, or notice what one another are working on as they wait for their turn to use the photocopy machine. There are also structured ways to push people's thinking.

Weekly Staff Meetings   Since the very first week our school has been in existence, Wednesday afternoons, from 3:30 until 5:00 P.M., we have been holding regular staff meetings. The format has undergone lots of changes as our staff has grown in numbers. Today, two of the four meetings each month are devoted to some aspect of curriculum and/or instruction. Once a month we meet in smaller grade-level clusters, and once a month we use this time to meet in reader-response groups to talk about a good juicy novel we have chosen to read. By the time you read this, we will no doubt be experimenting with yet another way to use our time together. (More details on staff meetings in Chapter 7, "Turning Schools into Centers for Professional Study.") I often take the role of discussion leader, although through the years we have come up with alternate plans of sharing this responsibility. Over the years we have used several prompts, structures, and activities to focus our conversations. They have included the following:

- During the week, ask teachers to fill out questionnaires on specific topics and share the results at faculty meetings. (See Content Area Survey and Status of the Staff Worksheet in Appendixes 19 and 20.)
- View videos of colleagues working in different disciplines. The "Star" of the video has an opportunity to target discussion.
- Hold staff meetings in one another's classrooms, beginning with a tour of the room narrated by the host teacher.
- Read aloud picture books that invite talk about curriculum. For example, reading *Archibald Frisby* by Michael Chesworth encourages teachers to discuss what

they would do if they had a science-obsessed student like Archibald in their class as well as how to inspire more lovers of science. Reading *Snow Day* by Moira Fain promotes talk about teacher-student relationships and the role of art and writing. Reading *Phoebe and the Spelling Bee* by Barney Saltzberg brings up talk about how to study spelling words. Reading Sally Grindley's *"Why Is the Sky Blue?"* reminds us that our students can be very fine teachers.

- Share excerpts from adult novels that illustrate children's need for content-rich curriculum. For example, Michael, the main character in Pete Hamill's *Snow in August*, demonstrates a child's total immersion in a self-chosen area of inquiry. Will, Sully's grandson in Richard Russo's *Nobody's Fool,* demonstrates a child's daydreaming moments of inquiry, and Digger in David Malouf's *The Great World* has a third-grade obsession for maps and atlases. Memoirs can also inspire rich talk about the kinds of inquiring lives we would love our students to lead. Memoirs by Margaret Mead, Annie Dillard, and Edward O. Wilson are filled with inspirational passages.

- Read multiple copies of carefully selected professional articles or books in preparation for talk on an agreed-upon topic. Follow up with appointments to visit in one another's classrooms. (See more on making professional reading add up in Chapter 7, "Turning School into Centers for Professional Study.")

- Display content area artifacts across the grades. For example, collect and display letters sent home to inform families about new areas of study, or samples of homework attached to research projects, or forms of logs kept by students during content studies.

- Create a "Have you seen ———?" forum. Meetings begin with staff members recommending that people stop in to see some worthy new project or ritual in a colleague's classroom. Have you seen how Sharon Taberski devotes some of morning meeting time to content studies? Have you seen the way Judy's students keep a weekly class journal? Have you seen the way Regina and her classmates resolve personal problems at the end of the week by giving out stars of forgiveness on Friday afternoons? Have you seen the way Joan's students take turns coming up with closings for each day? Have you seen Karen's collaborative class scrapbooks on famous sites around New York? Have you seen Tammy's kindergartners take part in their daily "News Minutes"? Have you seen Eve's birthday ritual, in which parents tell the story of the child's birth? Have you seen the handmade greeting cards Kathy and her students have made for families living in shelters? Have you seen how David and his students turned their geography studies into a mural for their back wall? Have you seen how Amy has turned her read-aloud time into a read-along time? Have you seen the oneliners Pat hangs on the soon-to-be-filled bulletin boards in her classroom, like "Pining for Poems," "Aching for Art," and "Waiting for Words"?

- Do quick freewriting or brainstorming activities. Begin, for example, by giving instructions such as "Draw two columns. What are you sure of and not sure of about the teaching of nonfiction reading?" or "List your top ten concerns about the new math initiative," or "Write a short reflective piece about how your content studies have improved the quality of life in your classroom. If they haven't, why not?" Teachers can be asked to share in small groups and then bring big ideas to the whole group.

Grade-Level Meetings   Once a month teachers have an opportunity to meet with teachers working with students the same age as their own. Their talk can then be much more targeted to specific age and grade concerns. I am happy to roam the building stopping occasionally to join in on a particularly intriguing conversation. (Some grade levels leave the building and I have to roam from coffee shop to coffee shop to join them.) It is the principal's responsibility to be part of the think tanks that form throughout school buildings. Some days, I must admit, I am too tired after school hours to think an original thought. Often I'm a better listener and note taker at these meetings; I need a wide-awake weekend morning to think through my colleagues' concerns. I suppose this is also true for many of my colleagues. It therefore becomes essential that issues are not "covered" in one-shot meetings. As is true for our students, it's always preferable that teachers study a topic over time. I find some of my best thinking takes place away from school, when I am more relaxed and my mind is less cluttered. A case in point follows.

At one grade-level meeting, the third-grade teachers were rethinking the way their students research and present the stories of their family's heritage and immigration to the United States. (See Joanne's letter, page 190). Students usually begin their research by collaboratively creating a list of kinds of information they could share with their classmates about their family's country of origin. They are given class time as well as resources and strategies for gathering the information they need. Students also work closely at home with family members to enrich and extend their learnings. They are assigned a date for presenting their cultural background and the story of their family's immigration. On the red-letter day, family members, loaded down with cameras, authentic ethnic snacks, and appropriate background music, usually accompany their children to class. Classmates serve as audience to one another's presentations and have the opportunity to touch coins from various countries, taste homemade treats, see family trees, as well as listen to the sound of a few words in the language of the country being presented. Children always look forward to these presentations, and come to appreciate how lucky they are to be learning alongside friends from such diverse backgrounds. The presentations are always well received, but the teachers sensed there might be ways to make the learnings and the presentations more powerful, for both the presenter and the members of the audience.

My thinking about our third graders' research projects began on the following

Sunday morning when my husband walked in with some old three-tiered bric-a-brac shelves that he found at a neighborhood garage sale. I was busy writing at my desk when he walked into my office with this unexpected treasure. It was wonderful to have a real excuse to leave my work for a while to find a place to hang the shelves and to decide on how to fill them. It didn't take too long to do both. I found the perfect nook and decided that the three shelves of three different heights would make a perfect home for the assorted pitchers that were now in cupboards and cabinets in the kitchen and dining room. I had never realized that I owned so many pitchers. By putting them together, side by side, I came to appreciate the varied shapes, textures, colors, and sizes of these dozen pitchers. I began comparing handle shapes, rim designs, and spout sizes. I noticed many things that I had never seen, when the pitchers lived in separate rooms, behind so many closed doors.

I then began thinking about all those children, listening to one another's presentations. I wondered if we could create structures that would enable the students to see all the information presented side by side, as well as design ways for them to interact with the information so that they too might see things they never saw before. I wrote the following note to my colleagues and then met with them to talk through these sketchy ideas. It seems important to point out that I never worry if my ideas are off-target or even inappropriate. They are merely meant to encourage further conversation and exploration of new thoughts. I never expect them to serve as mandates and I never worry that they will be stretched, twisted, collapsed, reshaped, or totally ignored. In fact, I always expect unexpected things to take place when I meet with thoughtful teachers. (Several years ago I visited with Renay, one of our third-grade teachers, when she was teaching in Ecuador. As we drove through the streets of Quito, I noticed that some drivers didn't stop at the stop signs. "They're just a suggestion!" Renay joked. So too, my teaching ideas are just a suggestion.)

> *Dear Renay, Amy, and Joanne,*
>
> *I've been thinking about your third graders and their immigration investigations. I went ahead and jotted down a few thoughts, even though I realize that to do a really good job I'd first need to find out what are the big understandings about immigration you're trying to get across to the children as well as what have been the kids' main concerns and questions. Despite the fact that I'm working from a bit of ignorance, (I'm sure that I've done that before), I went ahead and categorized my thoughts around the different stages of the student's work.*
>
> ### Research Techniques
>
> *Children throughout the school from all the grades, who come from the countries being studied, can be tapped as resource people. (These children can also be invited to the whole-group presentations, serving as special guest members of the audience.)*
>
> *Children can learn to use city resources. For example, we can show them how to read the yellow pages phone directory to search for embassies, cultural organizations, and even ethnic restaurants. We can teach them to make appropriate phone calls, send faxes, and/or write letters of request. (I've learned this from our friend in Denver, Steph Harvey, who is*

working on a book about nonfiction writing. She talks at length about teaching children to use readily available reference material.)

Why not encourage and support collaborative research across the three third-grade classrooms? Students from the same home countries can share resources and even present together. (Should we let scheduling headaches prevent us from carrying this out?)

Countries being studied need to become public knowledge in our school. Perhaps the students can post the countries in a central location. No doubt, visitors and family members will have additional information, stories, memories, artifacts, and ideas to share. Third graders can be invited to any related interviews taking place in other classrooms. (First graders in Paula's class, for example, are always interviewing family members from different cultural backgrounds.)

We can encourage students to videotape older folks in their families to gather their immigration stories. Presentations can include a viewing of these oral histories. (I have some interesting notes from Sheldon Oberman on gathering family stories. Let me know if you're interested.)

We can invite parents in on the search for newspaper clippings from all the countries represented. It would be interesting to discover if the events happening in their countries today are connected to their families' reasons for immigrating.

We can encourage students to write to cultural institutions in the city to find out if any collections are connected to their work at hand. We can be looking into the Internet as well.

Audience Participation

Audience members can keep a special immigration journal, taking notes on one another's presentations. All presentations can be viewed with students' immigration questions as the lens. This would require deeper thinking than just learning about countries. We will need to remind students that they are keeping a notebook about immigration, not merely a scrapbook. They are making notes as well as taking notes.

We can encourage students to read over their notes periodically looking for surprises, threads, patterns, discrepancies, etc., much the way they have learned to use their writer's notebook.

They can also staple in any handouts from their friends' presentations. Looking at the same words in ten different languages, for example, will demonstrate how researchers study data.

We can ask students to do occasional reflective responses in order to tease out important issues. I can imagine our third graders writing in response to the following questions (or any that fit closer with your specific goals) in mind.

> What do you think is the hardest thing about arriving in a new country?
>
> Have you ever visited a different country? What made it feel different?
>
> What do you think the first people listed on our family trees would think about life in New York today?
>
> What do you think is the difference between studying a second language in school and moving to a new country in which you must learn another language?
>
> Have you ever felt different than the people around you? Explain.
>
> What kind of work could you do if you didn't speak a language that most people could understand?
>
> How can we make newly arrived students feel really welcome?

We can also ask students to keep a list of their own growing questions and concerns about immigration, and then classmates could respond to one another's inquiry issues. We can edit and publish student responses in our school newsletter.

At the end of each presentation, we can ask audience members to write a complimentary note highlighting memorable moments. Then we can fold up and ceremoniously pass these little slips of paper on to the presenter, who can take the comments home to be enjoyed as bedtime reading. (This would be similar to the adult writing workshops we've attended.)

In pairs, students can keep dialogue journals with one another, writing back and forth after each presentation. Conversations on paper will push audience members to clarify their thinking and get them to interact with the information presented. We can encourage students to look for elements of presentations that will inform their own work in progress.

Whole-Class Gatherings

We can label children's home countries on one class map, together with date of family immigration, to enable students to see patterns of immigration.

We can create graphs and charts to bring information together and develop big concepts. For example, children can graph all the reasons families first came to America, the number of family members that made the original move, the number of families that have roots in more than one home country, the number of first-generation Americans in the class, the kinds of work newly arrived immigrants were able to get, etc.

Children can respond to the literature read aloud in their immigration journals to deepen their studies. We might consider creating a bibliography of available immigration picture books, poems, and nonfiction texts. In other words, we should all know what one another have. For example, have you all read Megan McDonald's My House Has Stars, *Emery Bernhard's* Happy New Year, *Eve Bunting's* How Many Days to America?, *Riki Levinson's* Watch the Stars Come Out, *Sonia Levitan's* A Piece of Home, *Amy Hest's* When Jessie Came Across the Sea, *Bonnie Pryor's* The Dream Jar, *Jeanette Winter's* Klara's New World, *Marilyn Sach's* Call Me Ruth, *Mary Watson's* The Butterfly Seeds, *and Betsey Hearne's* Seven Brave Women?

We can also invite social action about immigration issues today. We can ask children to reflect on how their studies have influenced their thinking about current life in the United States. We can encourage students to get their voices going and get their pieces published for real. For example, students could write letters to the editor about the issue of using English only or providing health care for all immigrants. (Should we create an ongoing immigration news board in a central location?)

Weave Immigration Studies into the School Day

- *Students can study our school language board. Third graders could be responsible for keeping this board up to date as their related community service.*
- *Students can connect their research to our yearly schoolwide international dinner, preparing meaningful background reading material.*
- *We can add richness to the students' research by collaborating with school subject specialists. For example, music and art teachers can add depth and breadth to students' discoveries by simultaneously studying distinctive art and music forms in students' home countries.*
- *Each child can search for additional picture books that take place in their home country, eventually building a third-grade library of related literature.*

- *Each child can do several pieces of short writing connected to their study. They can write up a short interview, a family story, a recipe, a family tree, and a timeline. If a genre is being studied, that format can also be used. Students can shape their information into poetry, picture books, or photo essay. Students' writing can then become part of permanent, third-grade reference libraries.*

I hope some of these thoughts are worthwhile. As you can tell I've begun to think about ways for the children to use those presentations as a means of thinking new thoughts, much the way they revisit the entries in their writer's notebook. I am wondering if our eight-year-olds can notice patterns as well as differences in their immigration stories. I wonder if the students could ask big questions and construct abstract ideas about geography, language, culture, and history if they placed the presentations side by side. And just as they do with the entries in their writer's notebook, I wonder if the students in the audience could do their own important writing in response to one another's presentations.

Can we get together at the next grade-level meeting to continue this conversation?

With respect,
Shelley

P.S. Perhaps each grade-three teacher can research her own family's immigration story and present it to the class. This invitation can be extended to other staff members.

I am able to think new thoughts when I'm alone at home, but my thoughts never become well-developed, fine-tuned, or practical until I meet with the teachers who are deeply engaged in the topic. Principals need to make sure that teachers have ample time to talk, and they need to find ways to become part of those conversations.

Joint Teaching Sessions   Several years ago our PTA raised funds to renovate our school auditorium. As previously noted, the bolted-down chairs were removed, along with the linoleum squares. The oak floorboards were covered with several coats of clear polyurethane and shiny black folding chairs were stored in rolling carts in the corners of our new "ballroom." This huge space on our fourth floor holds several hundred people. We use this space for dance and music rehearsals and performances, messy, spread-out-on-the-floor art projects, adaptive physical education instruction for students with special needs, large group family meetings, and indoor recess during inclement weather. I've long wondered why we don't take advantage of this expansive room for joint teaching sessions.

It's a natural space for hosting a combined reading or writing workshop. Several years ago Judy, Joanne, and I arranged to meet in the ballroom with Joanne's entire third-grade class and Judy's sixth-grade crew. We wanted to study conferring techniques together. We announced to the students, who came prepared with drafts, writing folders, and their writer's notebooks, that we were not to be thought of as three separate writing instructors to be helping three students simultaneously. Instead, we intended to work together, with one student at a time, in order that we study our own conferring techniques. It was important to let students in on our goals, otherwise it would be too easy for the students to pull us off in separate directions, preventing us from ever listening in on one another's conferences. The students eagerly spread out in this large room, anxious to read their writing with new partners who up until now only occasionally shared playground space and cafeteria tables. Judy and Joanne took turns, inviting a student to share. We each took turns hosting the conference, as our colleagues listened in, took notes, and jumped in when they couldn't resist. After each conference we had time to process our work, and talk about our strengths and weaknesses as conference partners. It was a rare professional opportunity, and of course it needn't be so rare. Teachers and administrators can and should carve out regularly scheduled opportunities to work together. All it takes is a big space, a shared interest, and the commitment to make it happen. (Of course there are other ways for teachers to visit in one another's classrooms. See Chapter 2, "Rethinking the Role of Principal," and Chapter 7, "Turning Schools into Centers for Professional Study.")

Informal Study Groups   There are topics that for short periods of time seem particularly crucial for small numbers of teachers. For example, new teachers, teachers who have changed grades, or teachers with a particular research question in mind may want to study a topic that does not have schoolwide appeal. It makes sense to form an intimate informal study group. Over the years we have had breakfast meetings, lunchtime conversations, and after-school chats. Usually these groups form around a specific line of inquiry. Other times a broad subject is announced, and a come-what-may attitude employed. Just recently I announced that I would reserve Monday afternoons, from three-thirty to five o'clock, for informal talk about the teaching of writing. The meeting place was announced, our poetry reading room, and teachers were encouraged to drop in any week with questions, concerns, ideas, and of course student writing.

Summer Planning Meetings   We're fortunate that, each year, our district provides us with a small amount of funding in order to invite staff members to work together for several days during the summer months. It's a glorious opportunity to prepare for a new school year. Relaxed teachers can prepare very fertile ground for some new and ambitious school-year challenges. Over the years we have used these summer hours to think through the use of portfolios, imagine the possibilities of a whole-school study of our one city block, and most recently to try to capture in writing what our grade-level expectations for each subject are. This challenge brought up big questions concerning assessment as well as the national standards movement. (See related information on standards and assessment beginning on page 225).

Fulfilling District Obligations

Each year our superintendent, Elaine Fink, requires that heads of school write down their school's goals and objectives. She used to tease me that she could always spot mine in the pile. They were the only handwritten ones. I've come to take them a lot more seriously, especially as Elaine has made the district forms more and more open-ended. I rarely get them in on time, however. It just takes so much talking early in the year to really establish where we are headed. Elaine asks principals to explain in narrative form their hopes for the year in terms of literacy, mathematics, interdisciplinary work, parent involvement, English as a second language, professional development, and any other area we are particularly interested in. She often reminds us that our use of budget allocation should demonstrate our commitment to the initiatives we describe (a living example of putting your money where your mouth is). I've always liked that reminder, because it has implications for how we live our life at school as well. In other words, if we determine that real-world writing, for example, is a writing curriculum priority, then the money we spend on materials should support our intention, as should the daily agenda on our wipe-off boards, the materials we choose for read-aloud time, and the amount of time we discuss this issue at grade-level meetings and whole-school faculty get-togethers.

Even though I often procrastinate about getting my goals and objectives together each autumn, I know the task is a valuable one. Any time you write what you are thinking, the experience gives you time to pause and reflect on your interests, needs, obsessions, passions, and priorities. Each time I write, I'm stunned by what I say; what I know and what I don't know. The following is a brief excerpt from one year's response to being asked about our interdisciplinary initiative.

> During our summer planning time we read Jerry Harste's research on inquiry-based curriculum. We then began calling on district experts, e.g. Tanya for science, Anna for social studies, and sharing their input. We then explored the possibility of trying, for the very first time, a school-wide inquiry study. We chose our "one city block" as the broad umbrella of our inquiry. We will begin by imagining what would be important about such a study, asking ourselves what significant learnings might be attached to such long-term work, across the grades. We would then catapult children into living with an extra wide-awakeness by taking several walks around the block, reading related materials, talking to family members and people in the community. We would then ask children to imagine themselves as people with particular ways of viewing the world. Perhaps the children would pretend to be photographers, architects, scientists, environmentalists, physicians, mathematicians, politicians, artists, or musicians. We would then ask the children to imagine walking around the block with each of these different groups of people. "What would they probably notice? What would they probably say? What might confuse them? What might make them happy? What might make them furious?" Once the students understand the different ways these people view the world, we will begin to imagine the questions each might ask. Once the questions are listed and sorted, children, teachers, and parents will begin trying to answer their questions, paying attention to the new questions that pop up along the way. These inquiry projects will no doubt lead to lots of interviewing, firsthand observations, reading of historical documents, sketching, photography, and so on. The children's finished work will no doubt result in lots of public speaking, art demonstrations, and written products. The children will also benefit from many opportunities to work collaboratively, share resources, and teach others what they are learning. The most significant benefit will be that children will view their neighborhood with new eyes, appreciating its strengths and working to eliminate its weaknesses.

It is our hope that conducting a schoolwide interdisciplinary inquiry project will push our thinking about smaller scale, classroomwide studies that take place all year round. Currently there are classes studying Native Americans, the rain forest, the solar system, whales, trees, and skeletons. What we learn to do as a community will have lessons for what we do within the four walls of our classrooms. We will continue to read professionally about inquiry teaching and learning and to try out new ideas in the company of colleagues.

Writing Grants to Support Curriculum

I'm not a very successful grant writer, but I keep on keeping on. I try not to write proposals for unreasonable events, crowd-pleasers that would sound great in a school brochure, but would require head-spinning interruptions, scheduling nightmares, or just too much time away from the regular work at hand. In addition, I only write grants for projects that fit easily into the regular life and curriculum priorities of the school. The following is an excerpt from a grant proposal to bring the performing arts to our students.

> At the Manhattan New School, one of our most heartfelt curriculum beliefs centers on helping children see the richness of their lives. We know that children need not be rich to appreciate the richness of their environments. Our job as educators is to provide hopefulness for our students. In our New York City public elementary school, we want children to realize how fortunate they are to live in such a culturally diverse city. We want our youngsters to take full advantage of parks, libraries, and museums. We want our children to lead wide-awake lives. Many carry writer's notebooks. Some carry sketchbooks. When our students walk down the street, we want them to be awed by architectural detail, to be fascinated by the rich mosaic of faces, and to marvel at cleverly designed store windows. We want them to take pride in the sounds of surprising languages spoken, and the availability of foods from all corners of the globe. We want them to understand our visitors' envy that our school is in walking distance of the Museum Mile. These desires necessarily influence our curriculum decisions, having an impact on the literature we choose, the field trips we make, and the inquiry projects we support.
>
> Many of our city studies require little or few financial resources. We take neighborhood walks; our parents prepare traditional foods from their home countries; and we tap the free resources of Central Park rangers, museum curators, and local public librarians. Then too, we host occasional bake sales to raise funds to rent buses and pay admission fees to special events. We have realized, however, that we have been neglecting one major attribute of New York City—the performing arts. This year Jacques d' Amboise's National Dance Institute has been working with our fourth graders, and their incredible ability to turn nine- and ten-year-olds into quality chorus line performers has awakened our interests in the best New York has to offer. We want our students, throughout the grades, to keep on dancing. So too, we want all our students to understand the contributions made by the jazz musicians in Harlem, the folksingers in Greenwich Village cafés, and the actors, artists, and musicians who bring life to the Broadway stage. In other words, we are particularly interested in developing curriculum that will help students understand the significant contributions diverse New Yorkers have made to the performing arts in this country.

Working with Parents on Issues of Curriculum

Principals can also enrich curriculum studies by working with parents directly and by supporting teachers' efforts to share curriculum with parents. Several effective ways of informing parents about curriculum were described in Chapter 5, "Reaching Out to Families." They include:

- Holding curriculum nights early in the year to explain new grade-level expectations.

- Asking parents to serve as secretaries, preparing summary notes at curriculum night. These notes can then be distributed to parents who were unable to attend.

- Devoting PTA meetings to one particular curriculum area and holding the meeting in a teacher's classroom. The classroom teacher can serve as host, offering a walking tour of how the curriculum area is handled in the classroom. Teachers can also take part in panel discussions of curriculum areas.

- Having teachers and/or administrators invite parents to do as the children do. In other words, parents are asked to take part in evening reading, writing, and math workshops.

- Inviting students to present workshops on curriculum to parents, followed by presentations of their work.

- Devoting school newsletter columns to aspects of curriculum.

- Creating courses of study around specific areas of curriculum. Small groups of parents with specific requests for information meet with a teacher or the principal to explore one aspect of curriculum.

Additional ways to communicate with parents that are particularly effective in exploring issues of curriculum include:

- Sending jargon-free curriculum articles home.

- Inviting district experts as guest speakers to explore curriculum with parents.

- Showing slides of children at work across the curriculum, followed by a question-and-answer session.

- Hosting parent tours specifically highlighting one particular curriculum area. For example, parents can be invited to visit kindergarten through fifth-grade rooms to see how mathematics is being taught. Later they can reconvene to talk about what they noticed, how the teaching differs from their own school memories, what similarities they saw across grade levels, and to ask any questions they might have.

- Asking students to write curriculum columns for school publications. Students can serve as reporters on the curriculum beat. For example, the social studies reporter can periodically survey the building and share schoolwide topics and methods of study.

Sometimes parents initiate dialogue on curriculum. Renay, a second/third multigrade teacher shared with me a beautiful note she received from the father of one of her students, Lathisha (see Figure 6.1). This gracious and concerned parent, Mr. Walker, had a powerful idea—teachers and parents writing books together. What better way would there be for parents to really understand what goes on in classrooms?

Gathering Curriculum Resources

Principals, who regularly wander the building peeking into out-of-the-way storerooms and file cabinets, can become incredible sources of information. Principals who visit every classroom every day are in a way taking informal inventories of all that is available. They know who the experts are. They know where the goodies are. I know which classroom has a great collection of atlases. I know who has a complete set of *Hardy Boys* books. I know who keeps red licorice for snacks in her wooden cupboard. I know who is an expert at drawing animals. I know who plays the piano and who knows how to sing Irish folksongs. Principals who pay attention can take on that switchboard-operator role, hooking up students and teachers with people and places they can learn and teach, nourish and be nourished by. Of course, this extends beyond the boundaries of our one school. Principals need to know what is happening in other area schools. Sometimes, just the right connection is just a phone call or e-mail away.

In addition, I periodically ask teachers to jot down the topics their children are studying. From my classroom visits I always know the whole-class areas of interest, but

DEAR RENAY:

LATHISHA CONTINUES TO HAVE PROBLEMS IN MATH. I AM UNABLE TO APPLY MYSELF TO ASSIST HER AS I WOULD LIKE TO BUT I WOULD LIKE TO EMBARK ON THIS IDEA WITH YOUR COLLABERATION. I WILL DESIGN EXERCISES TO GIVE HER PRACTICE IN HER AREA OF DIFFICULTY. TO BE OF MAXIMUM VALUE I MUST KNOW WHETHER WHAT I HAVE DONE MEETS WITH YOUR APPROVAL. ACCORDINGLY I WOULD APPRECIATE YOUR COMMENTS AS WE GO ALONG. I KNOW THIS IS REQUESTING A SPECIAL FAVOR WHICH MAKES DEMANDS ON YOUR TIME. PERHAPS TOGETHER WE COULD WRITE A NEW BOOK ON TEACHING TECHNIQUES FOR TEACHERS AND PARENTS. (SMILE). YOU ARE A VERY GOOD TEACHER.

BEST REGARDS

SINCERELY,
WINSTON A. WALKER
PARENT OF LATHISHA.

Figure 6.1

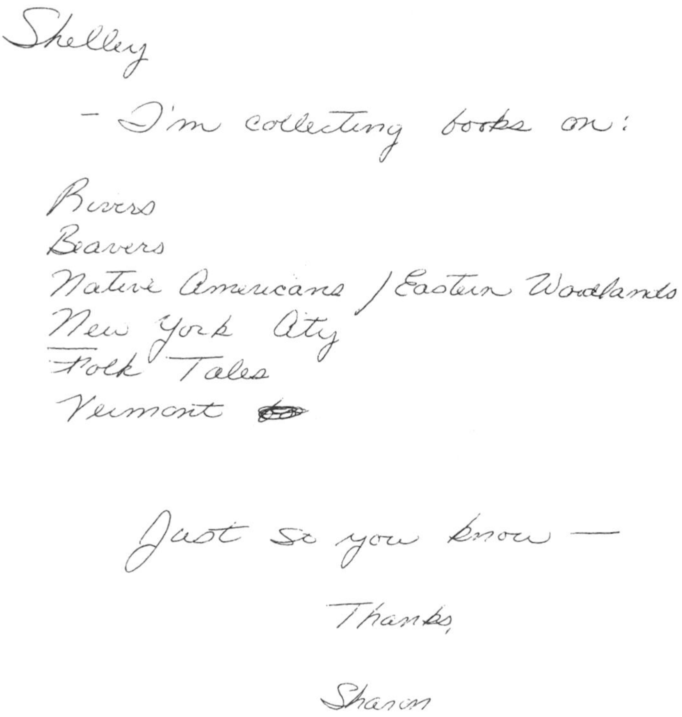

Shelley

– I'm collecting books on:

Rivers
Beavers
Native Americans / Eastern Woodlands
New York City
Folk Tales
Vermont

Just so you know –

Thanks,

Sharon

Figure 6.2

I don't always know individual or small-group studies. I find it helpful to have these topics posted on my office bulletin board as a constant reminder. (The listing should also hang in a more public place, so that everyone in the school community always knows what the current hot topics are.) Included here is Sharon Taberski's response to such a request (see Figure 6.2). When I know the hot topics, I can always be on the lookout for just the perfect article, news clipping, picture book, photo, or phone number of a potential expert. Just as some people prepare stocking stuffers to hang on the mantle on Christmas morning, I take particular delight in stuffing goodies into teachers' mailboxes in the early morning.

Concerns About Assessment and Standards

The phrase *show and tell* brings to mind one of the most familiar kindergarten rituals. It is perhaps surprising, then, that I sat in awe the first time I witnessed Isabel's five-year-olds engage in the daily ritual they call "show, tell, and teach." First the children arrange themselves into a large circle in the carpeted meeting area. Next a child brings out two or three hollow blocks from the dramatic play area and places them in the center of the circle. Then come the brightly colored silk scarves. Yes, silk scarves. They too are borrowed from the dramatic play area and are carefully selected and draped over the hollow blocks, thereby creating a glorious pedestal for the five-year-old about to carefully arrange the goodies he or she has carried to school in a shopping bag. The child lifts each item and carefully places it to guarantee a lovely arrangement as well as easy visibility for the classmates gathered. Show, tell, and teach is ready to begin.

The tools and rituals in Isabel's classroom become sacred to all members of her community. Whenever I visit her room, I am keenly aware of the elegance of design, the clarity of purpose, and the serene sense of order that have been woven into all her classroom procedures. Educators would do well to bring these qualities to all the rituals, structures, and practices that fill our school calendars and daily agendas, including those school practices related to assessment.

Our work with assessment, however, began with none of these qualities. We were not elegant, clear, or serene. We realized that in order to eventually say to parents, visitors, and district office personnel, "This is how we assess our students," we would have to spend many long hours exploring and experimenting with many undefined, tentative ideas.

As our school grew in population each year, I was particularly interested in assessment procedures that would be consistent throughout the grades, or at least one that would be consistent for the early-childhood grades and one that could be implemented for the upper grades.

Designing Meaningful Assessment Tools

In-depth and long-term conversations about assessment took a turn with the publication of Joanne Hindley Salch's wonderful book *In the Company of Children.* During the school year prior to its publication, Joanne and her third-grade teammates had written a list of hopes for third graders, to be given out to parents during evening conferences. The list included expectations for reading, writing, mathematics, social interactions, and work habits. As a school, we had initially used checklists coupled with parent conferences to share student progress with family members. The checklists included descriptors for all subjects as well as such qualitative terms as *always, sometimes, occasionally, rarely.* We were not fully satisfied with these, but were reluctant to move toward narrative reports due to the time involved in carefully completing them for classes that were often filled with thirty students. Joanne and her teammates' carefully-crafted list of hopes moved us away from quick checklists. Teachers across the grades were inspired to create some form of written scaffolding that would help children keep tabs on their own learning and at the same time would provide a means of presenting information to parents.

"Our Hopes"   The third-grade list of hopes became a working document for teachers throughout the building. It is now referred to as the "Our Hopes" assessment. When the fourth-grade teachers created their own, they added a system for students and teachers to reflect upon these goals. Now in addition to a list of yearlong expectations in each subject area, Joan, Kevin, and Sungho designed a way for students to record whether or not they had reached these goals as well as a way for teachers to agree or disagree with student self-assessments. (See sample below.) Their innovation was adopted for schoolwide use in third through fifth grades. Joan, Kevin, and Sungho wrote the following fourth-grade cover letter:

> *To the student:*
>
> *Please read the fourth-grade hopes and expectations carefully for each of the different subjects. These are the things we have been talking about and working hard on this year.*
>
> *Place a check next to the areas you feel you are successful in (you remember to think about them and do them all the time). Write the letter "G" to indicate areas that are goals for you to focus on in the future (things you sometimes do but are trying to remember to do all the time).*
>
> *Be very thoughtful and honest about your responses.*
>
> *To the family:*
>
> *When there is no comment by the teacher, it means the teacher and child are in agreement. Differences of opinion between the teacher and child will show up in the teacher column.*

The fourth-grade team then wrote a list of hopes and expectations for all areas of the curriculum (reading, writing, mathematics, social studies, spelling, handwriting, etc.), as well as a section for work habits, attitudes, and even homework. The specialists in our school added similar sections for each of their specialties (music, art, physical education, science, and Spanish). A brief excerpt from the social studies section illustrates the format and types of hopes that were highlighted.

Teacher	Child	
_____	_____	I take notes as I listen to class presentations, news reports, discussions, as well as when I'm reading.
_____	_____	When taking notes I restate the information I want to remember in my own words.
_____	_____	I participate in class studies by bringing in related news clippings, magazine articles, notes from news broadcasts, internet findings, etc.
_____	_____	I take part in social studies class discussions and conversations.

Some of the fourth-grade math expectations included:

_____	_____	I use mathematical language when writing and talking about math.
_____	_____	I look at problems to first make reasonable estimates of the quantity or amount of an answer.
_____	_____	I add two-digit numbers mentally.
_____	_____	I add three-digit numbers mentally.

(I have made the deliberate decision to not reprint complete sets of these grade-level hopes. There are tremendous advantages to each school community and small clusters of teachers within those communities composing and negotiating their own expectations. The conversations surrounding these documents were perhaps more important than the documents themselves.)

As can be seen from this brief sampling, these documents are not a list of isolated facts that every student must memorize, but rather a way for all members of the school community to become aware of yearlong possibilities. These documents provided a way for teachers to see the power of their teaching and for students to assess their own hard work. Joanne also suggests that the assessment system created in our school was effective and efficient because it, "matched the way we taught, didn't take away from teaching time, thoroughly involved students, and was relied upon throughout the school year."

It should be noted that the "Our Hopes" assessments remain flexible documents. Although we worked hard to create consistency of format throughout the grades (in terms of design, language, font, as well as making sure that there were no gaps as we moved from one grade level expectation to another), the contents of the checklists would be ever changing for several reasons. Our teaching is always being informed by our own professional development work, including professional reading, classroom research, staff conversations and intervisitations, workshops and summer institutes, the arrival of new colleagues, consultants, as well as district and state initiatives. The word processor makes it easy for teachers, working with their students, to revise the document whenever necessary. They can, for example, add unique areas of study, include additional expectations, as well as prepare a shortened version for early-in-the-year distribution. The self-assessment columns can be deleted when parents first see the document at the October curriculum meeting, and then added in November when the document is sent home for the first time. It became evident that these lists of clear, consistent, well-thought-out hopes for each grade level would not only add cohesiveness to our growing school but would serve to educate and inform parents in a straight forward manner.

It should also be noted that, even back in the days of simple checklists, our students throughout the grades had always been asked to do additional narrative self-evaluations. In other words, children had always been asked, and continue to be asked, to write about themselves as learners. At set times throughout the year, children are asked to reflect on their growth across the disciplines. Such teacher-designed prompts might include, "As a writer, what goals are you setting for yourself?" or "How have you changed as a reader?" or "What are you discovering about yourself as a scientist, mathematician, and historian?"

Student Portfolios   Along with implementing the new lists of hopes, the entire faculty studied the ways that other educators were defining, designing, and utilizing student portfolios. Our research and extensive professional reading helped us to see that we could not adopt the way that any other school had chosen to use portfolios. We knew that we had to design a way of working that fit with our community. We continued to study the use of portfolios and eventually accepted the challenge of creating a system for weaving the use of work samples into our daily lives as well as into our family conferences.

The use of student portfolios was eventually established school wide and today they are filled throughout the school year. Students periodically file work samples in all subject areas. In June, students are invited to take home all of their work except for a few carefully selected items. These include breakthrough pieces in all subject areas. In addition, there are certain school wide tasks that students are asked to perform annually. These tasks are done on the scheduled half-days that the central board provides for staff development. It is our hope that the products resulting from these tasks will be saved from year to year. During any one school year we usually have eight of these half-days. As explained earlier, rather than try to make such days feel like typical whole days, we decided to use them to engage in schoolwide events. We therefore have our "Dancing in the Streets" celebration during the June half-day and our Winter Solstice celebration during the December half-day. We invite the entire student population to take part in predetermined portfolio challenges on the remaining half-days. These include:

- Prepare a self-portrait.
- Create a pattern.
- List all the people who work in our school, including their names and jobs.

It's very revealing to observe how children grow over time on all these tasks. Their changing abilities, sense of self, and awareness of others, remind us to appreciate just how much they are learning and how much their sense of community is increasing. Imagine at graduation receiving six self-portraits you have drawn, six patterns you have designed, or six written lists detailing your awareness of the adults in your school community. It's as if our students are opening individual time capsules when they review these materials. Children simply can't believe what they have accomplished and how far they've come.

Additional schoolwide portfolio tasks might include:

- offering suggestions to improve the school
- drawing or writing about what they want to be when they grow up
- presenting the alphabet in a beautiful way
- recording the name of their borough, city, state, and country
- listing the names of all the states they know
- writing the words to a song or poem they know by heart
- drawing a floor plan of their classroom
- making a map of the school
- making a list of favorites (authors, colors, television shows, movies, desserts, breakfast foods, poets, toys, musical instruments, and places in the world).

(See reproducible list in Appendix 21.)

Involving Family Members in Student Assessment

We make it a practice to involve family members in the assessment process, according to the following timeline:

October: Family members receive list of hopes at curriculum night. (This is turned into a checklist of expectations for use in November, March, and June.)

November: The teacher/student checklist is sent home with a parent-response page. Teachers meet with family members at half-hour conferences, looking at work samples. (Formal portfolios are usually not presented this early in the year.) Teachers often invite students to be present at these conferences. (A generic school letter of concerns is available to distribute to families of students who are experiencing difficulties. At this early part of the school year, these are usually problems related to attendance, punctuality, work habits, and social relationships.

March: Family members attend spring conferences with teacher and student. Student is always present at this conference and in fact leads the conference. Child walks family members through his or her portfolio and explains his or her self-assessment on the "Our Hopes" checklist. Student also completes an assortment of narrative self-assessment surveys and questionnaires.

June: Teacher sends home a completed "Our Hopes" checklist for the year, indicating that child is now ready for the next school year. Student creates a supplemental list of goals for upcoming year. Student places additional work in portfolio and selected pieces are added to cumulative file kept in staff room archives. Work samples that are not selected for inclusion are taken home.

Early-Childhood Documents

Our kindergarten, first-grade, and second-grade teachers spent many hours creating parallel checklists for our youngest students. Teachers carefully checked for developmental appropriateness, as well as consistency in content, language, and design. A major difference in the early-childhood checklists is that the young children are not asked to decide, as the older students are, if the behaviors listed are goals or accomplishments. Instead, early-childhood teachers chose to use qualifying descriptors. They currently read, "area of strength," "making progress," "not yet consistent," and area of concern."

Kindergarten teachers call their document "Habits of Work, Habits of Mind," and list their expectations for the developing reader, writer, and mathematician as well as thoughts on student's growing sense of responsibility. The latter includes such abilities as being able to consider suggestions from classmates, ask for help when needed, and deal with difficult situations appropriately. First- and second-grade teachers have prepared very similar checklists.

A few of the expectations for a first-grade writer include:

Is beginning to write for a variety of purposes and audiences

Matches text and illustration

> Considers suggestions from others
>
> Is beginning to use conventions appropriately
>
> Takes risks as a speller

A few of the strategies and behaviors listed in the second-grade reading document include the following:

> Uses contextual cues to create and maintain meaning
>
> Uses visual cues (sound/letter correspondences) to figure out unknown words
>
> Self-corrects to maintain meaning
>
> Uses known words and spelling patterns to figure out unknown words
>
> Uses prior knowledge to understand text and figure out words

In addition, teachers have devised ways for very young children to take part in self-assessments. They periodically interview kindergarten children and take notes about their individual hopes, interests, struggles, and accomplishments. So too, first graders are asked to write simple reflective pieces about themselves as readers, writers, and mathematicians, or to respond to self-assessment descriptors by choosing a smiling face or a frowning one. In the curriculum area of writing, for example, these descriptors might include such items as, "I can think of topics," "I try to spell hard words," "I can read my writing," and "I leave spaces between words." Young children also keep portfolios to share with their families.

Standardized Testing

Our school is a regular New York City public school, and students are required to take all standardized tests. For years, my colleagues and I have not been able to attend the annual convention of the International Reading Association because most standardized tests in reading and mathematics were administered in the first week in May and we couldn't be out of town during these high-anxiety times. Beginning just recently, our testing calendar has been stretched out over the months of January through June, with more tests added for even more grade levels. The good news is that we can now attend the IRA conference. The bad news is that our battery of tests is now intended even for second graders.

My daughter, an attorney, reminds me that *battery* refers to an assault by beating or wounding. Is it any less painful for children to sit through these exams now that they don't all take place in a short amount of time? (See page 69, "The Plague of Standardized Testing.") Even though the majority of our students do quite well on these exams, we work hard to ensure that parents keep these scores in perspective. Our parents realize that they learn so much more about who their children are as readers, writers, mathematicians, scientists, and so on by poring over portfolios, reading homegrown checklists, listening to their children's reflective writing, talking to teachers, and visiting classrooms.

The Standards Movement

I read with interest an obituary column written about ninety-five-year-old Frank Cyr, who was known as the father of the yellow school bus. He was a professor of rural education at Teachers College, Columbia University, and was famous for establishing national standards for school buses. Working with a committee of automotive engineers, he produced a list of forty-four national standards for various parts of the school bus. To this day our country's school buses are yellow with black lettering because these colors offer maximum visibility at dawn and dusk. Creating a list of safety standards on vehicles must have taken a great deal of time and energy, but the task could not have been nearly as complicated and controversial as creating national standards for children's education. Living, breathing human beings are not built to specifications in an automotive shop.

Informing Parents About Standards

Our district is heavily involved in the standards movement, and it became my responsibility to introduce that involvement to our community. The lists of hopes created by our own teachers became a valuable tool in explaining the complex notion of formal standards to our family members. In fact, I referred to these lists as well as to student portfolios when I sent my first standards letter to our parent body. It read,

> *Dear families,*
>
> *Perhaps you have been reading in the newspaper about New York City's involvement in the movement toward developing national educational standards. I am writing this letter to begin the conversation within our own school. Many district educators have been deeply involved in standards research and development, particularly the New Standards work coming out of the University of Pittsburgh and the National Center on Education and the Economy. I have participated myself in a few national standards–related committees dealing with the teaching of the language arts (reading, writing, listening, and speaking). Of course, there are standards for all subject areas, including mathematics, science, and social studies.*
>
> *Briefly stated, there are two main types of standards, content and performance. Content standards refer to "what children should know and be able to do." For the most part, these were developed by major professional organizations in this country including the National Council of Teachers of English and the National Council of Teachers of Mathematics. Performance standards refer to how well children perform in each content area. In other words, performance standards ask, "How good is good enough?" You might think of the grade-level lists of yearlong hopes that our teachers have shared with you as our content standards and the material in your children's portfolios as evidence of their performance.*

I continued my letter by presenting some of the controversies attached to the standards movement.

There are some educators who worry that national standards will not be matched with standards of delivery. In other words, children living in rich districts will continue to receive more services than children living in poor districts do and yet both will be held to the same standards of performance. Some worry that students who do not meet national standards will be quickly labeled and tracked within their school systems. Yet others are concerned that nationwide standards will lead to cookie-cutter teaching without room for creativity and flexibility. There are others who worry that pushing for standards now implies that we didn't have standards prior to now.

We, of course, know that this is not true here in our district, in our school. We have always believed in effort, hard work, rigorous classrooms, and high-quality work.

I then tried to allay any local concerns.

Despite some of these broad concerns over the standards movement, we need to trust that here in our district the standards will not be misused. In fact, we need to believe that any conversation about standards, at the district or the school level, will result in even more thoughtful practice regarding curriculum, instruction, and assessment.

Rest assured that here at the Manhattan New School, we have always talked about rigorous challenges and cutting-edge assessment systems. The district's commitment to the New Standards Project will, however, influence some of the work at our school. I trust that since our standards have always been high, our students will have no problem meeting the standards. In reading, for example, one of the fourth-grade standards reads, "The student reads at least twenty-five books or the equivalent each year." We are hopeful that our students will meet this standard, knowing how many wonderful books surround our students, as well as the amount of uninterrupted time the students are given to read each day. Hopefully similar blocks of time are devoted to reading in the evenings, weekends, and holidays when the children are in your care. . . .

The New Standards researchers have recently published their assessment system for fourth graders and this, too, will impact on our students. This system is made up of the performance standards, an on-demand test, and a portfolio of student work. Our fourth graders will in fact be taking the New Standards reference examination in mathematics this spring. We are expecting our students to do well, as our mathematics teaching requires students to deeply understand concepts and participate in frequent problem solving. In other words, the New Standards testing is a close match to our teaching. . . .

In the next few months, you will be hearing a great deal more about the standards movement. You can be assured that as a staff we will continue to approach all new research, initiatives and mandates with serious and reflective eyes and minds. We always have your children's best interest at heart.

I felt very comfortable in introducing the standards movement to families and in assuring them that we have always had high standards. I like to recall the time when one fifth grader in Judy's class showed me his writing and asked, "Is it Judy material?" Clearly our students know that our expectations for them are high.

What I did not explore with parents at that time was a major concern that remains with me today. Although our district pays a great deal of attention to professional development, I worry that there are districts that spend so much time thinking and talking about standards that there is not enough time left to talk about exquisite teaching. We can list page upon page of standards and create rubrics to accompany them, but without the best practices taking place in classrooms, the work will be in vain. There is a comedian on television who jokes about putting together a difficult, five-thousand-piece jigsaw puzzle: It was all sky! Too much talk about standards, and not enough of the kind of professional development that makes change at the classroom level is like putting together a jigsaw puzzle of the sky. It takes an impossible amount of time and it doesn't add up to much.

Continuing Conversations About Assessment

Our homegrown lists of grade-level hopes and expectations helped us to comfortably explain what we expected would happen as children moved from year to year at the Manhattan New School. In addition, holding these thoughts in our hands pushed us to take a critical look at any gaps, discrepancies, or developmental concerns that may exist. We sensed that this formal document would also force us to think through any philosophical differences that might exist among staff members. I imagine that on any elementary staff, differences of opinion exist about homework, the place of standard spelling, the introduction of formal reading, the role of phonics instruction, and so on. Writing out these lists of expectations helped us to see that we were not immune to such differences and that it is near impossible to see eye to eye on all issues even when a staff appears to share clearly stated and common beliefs about teaching and learning.

The lists of grade-level hopes also became a fulcrum for conversations about growth over time. A case in point took place when I became conscious of a beginning-of-the-year happening. Teachers would occasionally approach me and very graciously and confidentially say such things as, "How many years has Douglas been in this school?" or "Is handwriting taught in all the grades?" or "I'm surprised Cynthia can't read a simple 'I Can Read' book." Their telling questions made me wonder if it weren't time to deal with some of these issues at our weekly staff get-together. I began by asking my colleagues to do something that doesn't come naturally. I asked them to think about what their students could *not* do when they entered their classes in September. In other words, I was asking my colleagues to list any weaknesses, gaps, or inadequacies that they considered surprising. I even gave them a "sentence-starter" to free up their thoughts. Each teacher jotted down responses to, "I'm surprised when children enter my class in September and don't know how to . . . " Below is a sampling of the teachers' responses.

- Teachers of five-year-olds were surprised when children didn't know their last names or that they had one. They were also surprised when children didn't know that some symbols are letters and some are numbers.
- Teachers of six-year-olds were surprised when children couldn't recognize their names, hold a book in an appropriate way, or join in on a repetitive pattern.

- Teachers of seven-year-olds were surprised when children couldn't read independently for fifteen minutes, mixed up lower case and upper case letters, left no spaces between their words, or didn't have strategies for unknown words.

- Teachers of eight-year-olds were surprised when children didn't use a margin and couldn't choose appropriate books or read independently for twenty minutes. They were also surprised when children were not familiar with a sense of paragraphs in a text (they didn't understand the comment, "Let's look at the third paragraph"). Teachers also expected third graders to be familiar with alphabetical order.

- Teachers of nine-year-olds were surprised by students who didn't value keeping a writer's notebook and those who didn't reread their own writing. Teachers were also surprised that some students didn't know the difference between a city, state, country, and continent.

- Teachers of ten-year-olds were surprised when students couldn't spell commonly used words, said they had nothing to write about, or were uncomfortable using a dictionary.

Teachers shared their concerns without placing blame. The activity got us talking about age-appropriate expectations and pushed us to look back at our lists of hopes, rereading them for any needed revisions or shifts in emphases. The activity also got us wondering why children were not learning things that *were* being presented year in and year out. Curriculum talk led to talk about instruction. As it should. The activity also created a rather informal list of "red flags." We have always been reluctant to label children, but the list of concerns served to inspire an honest heart-to-heart talk about children that seem to have very special needs. School settings need to be safe places to engage in these kinds of difficult conversations. (See related information on page 250, "Airing Differences Respectfully.")

Appreciating How Much We've Grown

None of us feels that we've arrived in the assessment arena. There are issues still gnawing at us, and they probably will for a long time to come. Every once in a while though, something happens that makes us pause and appreciate how much we've accomplished thus far. A letter from a former student who moved back to her home country at the end of second grade made us remember how things used to be when we were in elementary school, and reminded us how much more humane and sane our assessment of students is in comparison (see Figure 6.3).

Of course, all of us at school were glad to hear from Joan and, of course, we were as proud of her as we have always been. But we didn't need medals, competitions, or grade point averages to know that she was an accomplished student. And we believe

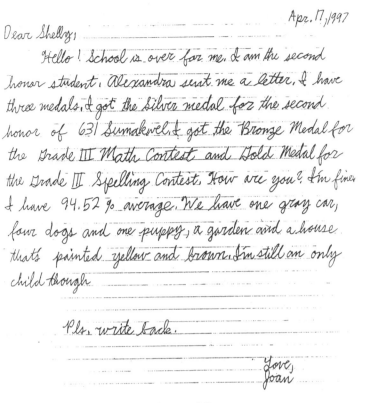

Apr. 17, 1997

Dear Shelly,

Hello! School is over for me. I am the second honor student. Alexandra sent me a letter. I have three medals. I got the Silver medal for the second honor of 631 Sumakwel. I got the Bronze Medal for the Grade III Math Contest and Gold Medal for the Grade III Spelling Contest. How are you? I'm fine. I have 94.52 % average. We have one gray car, four dogs and one puppy, a garden and a house that's painted yellow and brown. I'm still an only child though

Pls. write back.

Love,
Joan

Figure 6.3

that her wonderful parents were as proud of their daughter when we showed them the beautiful work in her portfolio, when we had long conferences with them about what we saw in Joan as a learner, and when they listened to her read aloud the poems that she had written. Maybe even more proud, because our assessment took into account their daughter's full potential and capacities—not her performance in a single "context," but her participation in a full, rich, and wide-awake life.

RELATED READINGS IN COMPANION VOLUMES

Lifetime Guarantees (Heinemann, forthcoming), will be abbreviated as LG.
Writing Through Childhood (Heinemann, forthcoming), will be abbreviated as WC.

Offering lifetime guarantees	**WC**: Ch. 8.
	LG: Ch. 8.
Using literature to improve the quality of school life	**LG**: Ch. 3.
Creating thematic studies	**LG**: Ch. 4.

Designing structures to push thinking	**WC**: Ch. 11.
	LG: Ch. 7.
Sharing picture books that invite talk	**LG**: Ch. 1, Ch. 6.
Sharing adult novels with inquiry connections	**LG**: Ch. 4.
Organizing an immigration study	**LG**: Ch. 4.
Creating multi-grade writing workshops	**WC**: Ch. 7.
Deciding on literacy goals and objectives	**LG**: Ch. 6, Ch. 7.
Thinking through portfolios	**WC**: Ch. 11.
Making decisions about assessment	**WC**: Ch. 8.
	LG: Ch. 8.
Sharing early childhood documents	**WC**: Ch. 6.

TURNING SCHOOLS INTO CENTERS FOR PROFESSIONAL STUDY

Priorities

- Schools must speak the language of professional development.
- Professional development concerns must be uppermost in our minds when we make decisions about spending money, hiring staff, and using time in a school.
- Educators must demand high-quality staff development.
- Staff developers, like teachers, must be nurtured.
- Educators must take care of their own literacy.
- We must welcome opportunities to learn from visiting educators.
- Educators must have professional development priorities.

Practice

- On developing school structures that support teachers' learning, including interclass visits, reading of professional material, and time for reflection.
- On developing criteria to evaluate staff development, including the respectful airing of differences
- On the art of staff development, including being unconditionally pro-teacher, fighting fads, and aiming for elegant arrangements
- On making time for teacher study
- On establishing adult book clubs in school settings
- On meeting the needs of first-year teachers
- On supporting student teachers
- On turning schools into successful sites for visiting educators, including do's and don'ts for visitors, the value of offering courses over time, and suggestions for hosting conference days

When we originally sent a proposal to our school board explaining our hopes for working in their district, I wondered if we should have described our intention as one of creating a Center for Research and Staff Development that happens to have an elementary school attached. That's just how serious I was and continue to be that schools need to be considered as places for teachers to lead scholarly lives. I can't imagine providing quality education for students if schools don't take the teaching of teachers seriously. Rexford Brown has remarked that "anyone who hopes to excite and challenge young people without exciting and challenging their teachers hopes in vain." When teachers delight in their own professional discoveries, their students reap the rewards. How many times have educators asked, "Would you go to a doctor who doesn't keep up with the latest findings and techniques?"

What I hadn't realized when we began this school in Community School District 2 is that the district staff's vision for schools, all schools, is to focus on improved instruction for children through passionate professional development for teachers. We were indeed a perfect match. We had chosen the right neighborhood to set up shop. Several years ago Richard Elmore, of the Harvard University Graduate School of Education, prepared a paper for the National Commission on Teaching and America's Future, in which he describes our district's unique approach to professional development. In it he succinctly describes the life of a District 2 principal. He notes, "Professional development is what administrative leadership *does* when they are doing their jobs." He goes on to say, "It is impossible to disentangle professional development from general management in District 2 because the two are, for all practical purposes, synonymous. . . . In District 2 staff development *is* management, and vice versa." This conclusion perhaps explains, to readers who might have been wondering, how it is that I spend so much time working on issues of curriculum and instruction and related staff development concerns. The explanation is now clear. It *is* what I was hired to do. I am privileged to work in a district that does not ask principals to get good at paperwork. This is a district that asks principals to get good at teaching. And that makes all the difference in the world.

The Language of Professional Development

My district colleagues appreciate the sentiment in the following poem that I wrote one late June afternoon.

What Really Matters
The summer wind made a delivery today
right through the open schoolhouse
window.
It brought the paprika smell
of Wiener schnitzel
from the Hungarian restaurant
next door.

It brought a bouncing, rubber ball—
small, and oh so royal blue.
(Whatever happened to those pink Spauldings,
the color of bubble gum?)

It brought those feathery white, star-like fluffs—
some sort of airborne plant.
I've always meant to look up
their scientific name but
I've never gotten around to it.

The wind made a delivery today,
direct to the principal's office.
Of course, the regular mailman brought
memos, surveys, and standardized tests;
directives, announcements and more.

I much prefer
the smell of Wiener schnitzel
the bounce of a rubber ball
and those star-like fluffs.
I must look up their names.

Of course, I'd prefer painting a mural, responding to a poem, or reading aloud a picture book to hanging out in my office, no matter what good things sail through the open window. As I said previously, I know our superintendent would be concerned if it were too easy to reach me by telephone. I'm not expected to be in my office. I'm expected to be in classrooms. When a kindergartner in Pam's class calls out to me as I walk by, "Hi, Pam's teacher," I know I'm honoring my job description.

So here I stand, a principal in a school district that speaks the language of professional development. It is the only language spoken in the corridors of the district office, at budget meetings, and at monthly principals' conferences. This is a district that:

- publishes monthly professional development calendars that are five pages long
- periodically distributes professional development surveys
- has hosted a professional book fair for teachers and administrators
- hires over sixty staff developers each year to work in classrooms
- enables classroom teachers to maintain their classrooms and simultaneously teach teachers
- devotes principal conference time to issues of best practice
- offers regular teacher-as-researcher courses
- distributes professional articles and books to principals on a regular basis

- orchestrates structures for principals to become mentors for one another
- spends 5 to 6 percent of its annual budget on professional development
- offers the kind of quality summer institutes that make teachers change their vacation plans

Professional Development as a Guide to Decision Making

Professional development concerns are at the heart of all the decisions we make about spending money, hiring staff, and use of time. And this genuine and total commitment to professional development for teachers and administrators makes it a joy to come to work, and enables our school to become a fertile ground for nurturing teachers who delight in the mysteries of teaching and learning.

One afternoon my colleague Judy Davis remarked, "Some days I feel like the odometer on an old car that has reached one hundred thousand miles and registers at zero again." Judy is a brilliant, successful teacher, and yet some days she feels like she knows nothing and has to begin learning how to teach all over again. It's this periodic sense of starting over, of rethinking all that she does, that makes Judy such a master teacher. After the Yankees won the World Series in 1996, I read an advertisement over someone's shoulder as I waited for an airplane flight. I couldn't tell what the ad was for, but it capitalized on baseball fever. It read, "The challenge in life is stepping up to the plate and re-inventing yourself." The challenge in teaching, as well, is to step up to the plate everyday and re-invent yourself. None of us has all the answers. Professional development is our lifeline.

I must admit, however, that when I finally arrived at the penultimate chapter of this book, one set aside for issues of professional development, I wondered if I really needed to say any more about teacher's learning. After all, every chapter in this book, in one way or another, has offered thoughts on professional growth. For example,

In Chapter 1, I listed "taking adult learning seriously" as one of the secrets of our success.

In Chapter 2, I suggested ways for principals to accept the role of instructional leader.

In Chapter 3, I outlined ways to enable teachers to lead scholarly lives.

In Chapter 4, I suggested the need for teachers to create their own curriculum of caring.

In Chapter 5, I suggested ways for teachers to educate parents.

In Chapter 6, I listed school-wide structures to push thinking about curriculum and assessment.

This chapter, then, presents no staff meeting activities, conversation starters, or rituals. Instead, this short chapter is intended to promote big thoughts about professional growth.

I begin with professional growth *within* a school community and then move to the value of inviting outsiders in. In other words, I refer once again to my mother and her brown derby cake. Family comes first. We must make sure that we are satisfied with the professional growth of our own staff members before we orchestrate visits and courses for teachers and administrators outside our school community. It's a lesson I must continually teach myself.

Then too, when we are ready to allow visiting educators in, we must give them the behind-the-scenes tour. They can't just view the polished Broadway act. Visitors must be invited to see the rough drafts of our teaching and become aware of the issues we are struggling with. I've been told that if people ever visited a sausage factory and saw how sausages were made, they would never eat sausages again. This kind of thinking does not apply to education. If people understood all that goes into running an effective classroom, they would be in absolute awe of the teaching profession. Several years ago, in order for the parent community to fully understand how much work really goes into leading a successful classroom, I sent the following letter home:

> Dear families,
>
> When I served as the co-director of the Teachers College Writing Project, I used to be a frequent visitor to schools. Often I'd escort educators from all over the city, all over the country, to wonderful literature-based, child-centered classrooms. I'd make sure our visitors saw effective writing conferences, powerful reader-response groups, productive share meetings, and authentic classroom celebrations.
>
> Now, I no longer visit many schools. Instead, our building has become one of those schools that educators visit, and I've realized that I no longer worry about what visitors see. Instead, I worry about what they don't see. Let me explain.
>
> One day, I found myself admiring a beautiful mural some of our students had painted. I realized that as a visitor to other schools, I might very well have noticed that fine work of art. I probably would have complimented the teacher and the children. Now, however, I have an incredibly richer and deeper appreciation of their work. Now I'm aware of all that goes into creating just that one lovely painting. I had forgotten about all the behind-the-scenes work.
>
> I had forgotten about the hard work that goes into deciding on content, gathering the supplies, organizing the project, learning about paint, brush stroke, use of space, design, color, shape, and even cleanup procedures. I had forgotten about finding the right physical space to do the work, okaying the procedures with the custodian, and even figuring out how and where to hang the masterpiece. There's a lot more behind the mural than meets the eye.
>
> So too, there's a lot more to literature-based, child-centered classrooms than meets the eye. That's why I'm now more concerned with what visitors don't see than with what they do.
>
> The teachers in our school make it look so easy. Visitors see all the beautiful artifacts. They see pocket-charts filled with perfectly printed poems, baskets of frog books sitting next to the frog tank, and graphs of pumpkin sizes, presidential elections, and favorite

kinds of apples. They see math literature alongside math manipulatives, Native-American poetry and prose alongside classroom tepees, and children's original poems, posters, picture books, and petitions everywhere.

And visitors see all the beautiful interactions—between the children, between the children and their teachers, as well as between the children and the student teachers, high school interns, neighborhood volunteers, and of course, parents. I worry that it all looks so easy. "What a joyful place," visitors say.

Yes, the Manhattan New School is a joyful place. I'm delighted that visitors want to capture all these "Kodak moments." But I wish they could see all the behind-the-scenes work that supports our teachers' efforts and makes the classroom work they do possible.

I wish visitors were here to see the teachers pulling together each Wednesday for long after-school meetings. We talk about the tone in the school, the need for new rituals, and mostly about curriculum areas we'd like to explore. We've been rethinking the use of the writer's notebook, the place of formal spelling instruction, and the role of newspapers in our own lives and those of our students.

I wish visitors could attend our adult book groups. Teachers, student teachers and high school interns gather to talk about a book we've all read. We've laughed and cried over Kaye Gibbon's Ellen Foster, *Russell Banks's* The Sweet Hereafter, *and Robertson Davies'* Murther and Walking Spirits.

I wish visitors were here in the very early morning hours or late into the evening to marvel at the way teachers help one another, prepare for their own teaching, or simply swap stories about their teaching and learning.

I wish visitors could pop into room 203 on Monday evenings to see parents working on their own writing. I wish they could see parents slipping articles into my mailbox, helping me brush up on my Spanish, or attend district workshops.

In short, I wish visitors were not just snapping cameras at scenes of children taking their learning seriously, but those of adults doing the same.

Several years ago, Rumer Godden, in Horn Book Magazine wrote, "If books were Persian carpets and one wanted to assess their value, one would not only look at the outer side, the pattern and colorings; one would turn them over and examine the stitch, because it is the stitch that makes a carpet wear, gives it its life and bloom."

I've likewise thought that if schools were Persian carpets, visitors should not only look at their outer sides—the classroom decorations and curriculum designs. They must also turn them over and see their inner sides. I believe that it is the energy attached to adult learning (including that of parents and administrators) which makes a school wear, "gives it its life and bloom."

I look forward in the months and years ahead to have even more space and time to take adult learning seriously at the Manhattan New School. And I look forward to each and every one of you becoming part of our learning community.

With respect,

Shelley

Whenever possible, then, visitors must see our tentativeness, our struggles, our playing of hunches. They must witness the scholarly lives we lead. When visitors arrive, we can't be on "company behavior." It's okay for visitors to see children in conflict, an upset parent, or a frustrated teacher who arrives late because of a traffic jam. I'm convinced that visitors get more out of their visit because our school is a real school.

Visitors appreciate that we are not an elite setting. We face all the problems any teachers in a large city school face and yet we are a thriving educational community. What more could any visitor ask for?

School Structures That Support Teachers' Learning

It's too easy *not* to take care of ourselves as learners. The days are so jam-packed with taking care of our students' learning that it's easy to forget that out students will benefit by our continued study. In order to keep adult learning on the front burner, I have found it helpful to take a few imaginary stances.

> **Imagine** your school as that Center for Research and Staff Development with an exemplary schoolhouse at its core. How would your school life differ?
>
> **Imagine** the principal as the teacher with the faculty as members of the class. What syllabus would you put together for this year-long course? What decisions would you make about curriculum, reading materials, teaching techniques, projects, assessment, and so on, so that everyone is learning all the time? How would you involve your students in these decisions?
>
> **Imagine** that money was not an obstacle. The sky is the limit for substitute coverage, reference material, conference attendance. What would you do? Now, how can you make some of this happen without a lot of extra funding? (More times than not, it's not money that keeps teachers from stepping away from their classrooms, it's time. The teachers I know best are unwilling to leave their classes for extended periods of time because they can't bear to give up precious time with their children. Having a cadre of expert and familiar substitute teachers goes a long way in encouraging teachers to spend time in someone else's classroom or at a district workshop or professional convention.)

When we are able to develop a school culture that gives top priority to professional growth, it's not difficult to devise a long list of school structures to support teachers' learning. These would include:

Formal Demonstration Lessons
These are carried out by colleagues for one another, with follow-up talk time built in.

Informal Interclass Visits
Teachers benefit from an open-door policy that enables them to drop in on colleagues without any planned agenda. It always helps to have another set of informed eyes viewing our practice.

Meaningful Staff Meetings
Our superintendent suggests that our staff meetings be of such high quality that they could be aired on cable TV. We aim for prime-time quality, considering each session to-

gether as a time to solve problems and explore issues that really matter. (See Appendix 22, Quotes to Ponder at Staff Get-Togethers and Appendix 23, Response Sheet to What Really Matters.)

Meaningful Grade-Level Meetings
Teachers must be given sufficient time to talk to colleagues with similar concerns.

Encouragement to Write for Publication
Teachers who regularly reflect on their own practice are always asking, "Why am I doing what I am doing?" They necessarily learn a great deal and realize they have a story to tell.

Reading of Professional Material
Teachers get together to read professional texts and articles, and then arrange to try out these ideas in the company of colleagues. It's too easy for nothing to happen if we don't roll up our sleeves and experiment, innovate, and invent best practice.

Professional "Book Reports"
Teachers volunteer to read the latest additions to our professional library and prepare one-page handouts of key discoveries. (I often hold new books up at staff meetings and announce content, thereby soliciting volunteers to do a first read.)

Professional Videotape Library
Teachers are given access to in-house videotapes as well as published material, including Shelley Harwayne's *A Visit to the Manhattan New School* (Heinemann), Paula Rogovin's *The Classroom Interview in Action*, (Heinemann), Sharon Taberski's four-part series, *A Close-Up Look at Teaching Reading* (Heinemann), and Joanne Hindley Salch's four-part series, *Inside Reading and Writing Workshops* (Stenhouse).

Mentor Arrangements
New teachers apprentice themselves to another experienced and accomplished teacher.

Courses of Study
Teachers form networks, creating both formal and informal courses.

Conference Attendance
Teachers who attend professional conferences prepare notes for those who did not attend and willingly share their learnings.

Inviting Experts In
Staff makes use of in-house experts but calls upon outside consultants and/or district experts when needed.

Breakfast and Dinner Dates

Teachers informally arrange to meet for individual conferences with colleagues outside of school.

Visits to Other Schools

Teachers are given opportunities to visit schools in different parts of the city or country and share their learnings when they return.

Reading of Nonprofessional Material

Reading great novels together, or nonfiction or poetry, promotes professional growth. Teachers need simply ask, "How can we give our students what we have given ourselves?" (This structure is paramount to the life of our school and warrants additional attention. See "Taking Care of Our Literacy" on page 258).

Reflection Time

Teachers must have sufficient opportunities to focus their thoughts and reassess their practice. Of course, most teachers who understand the absolute necessity of having time to think back on all they are doing discover their own ways of creating this white space. They write in journals every night, use their long drives home to take a reflective stance, or count on certain colleagues for frequent and leisurely conversations. Teachers also need opportunities at work to pause and consider all they are doing. Staten Island, the borough where I spend long weekends and summer holidays, is about to become home to a Chinese scholar's garden. *The New York Times* explained this haven as follows. "Based on the Taoist ideas of how to promote meditation and reflection and on 2,000 years of Chinese design tradition, the one-acre garden will become the kind of sanctuary that renowned scholars specializing in literature, mathematics and Confucian philosophy might receive from the emperor if they were court favorites, or that prosperous families might build using their own money." All teachers need to be seen as court favorites, in need of a tranquil space that enables them to look back and look ahead. Of course, school budgets don't allow for the creation of a scholar's garden, but we can make sure our staff rooms are beautiful, calm, and free from constant interruptions, and that teachers are given as much time as possible to take "scholarly breaks."

Having High Standards for Staff Development

Evaluation Criteria

It's not difficult to make long lists of structures like the one above, but what is crucial is that all components of staff development meet high standards. Ideally, they

- have realistic time frames (Teachers should not be expected to make changes in their teaching overnight.)

- are attached to reasonable goals (Teachers should not be expected to focus on too many new curriculum areas at the same time.)

- are scheduled in a predictable fashion (For example, teachers should not be surprised when they arrive at work to discover a consultant in their room.)

- are connected to one's unique community (Teachers should not be asked to adopt someone else's curriculum or teaching methodologies whole-hog.)

- value differences among teachers, never privileging one style above others (Staff developers should actually be promoting variety, and avoiding cookie-cutter results.)

- capitalize on teachers' existing strengths and areas of expertise (Teachers should never be thought of as empty vessels waiting to be filled.)

- provide cutting-edge information (Precious time can not be devoted to already-well-digested material.)

- are presented in empowering and engaging ways (Teachers, the professional group particularly conscious of effective teaching techniques, should never be given mediocre presentations. Workshop leaders must have solid content as well as effective methods of sharing their information.)

- are connected to teachers' felt-needs. (There are so many pressing issues on teachers' minds that it would be disrespectful to orchestrate workshops or visitations on topics of little concern to those teachers gathered.)

- are empowering to teachers (Teachers should leave staff development sessions feeling optimistic about their chosen profession and the contributions they are making.)

- never promote an elite "in" crowd (No group of teachers should be elevated as a result of any professional development. No one teacher should be put on a pedestal.)

- allow for varying points of departure (Not all personnel are ready to take on new challenges at the same time.)

- are respectful of teachers' busy lives (Staff developers need to remain conscious of how unique a teacher's professional life is. They must never forget that teachers often have limited time to eat, make phone calls, or even go to the restroom. They often have limited access to photocopy machines. Then too, staff developers need to keep in mind that teachers are responsible for many curriculum areas as well as many social dynamics. The topic being closely studied is not the only subject on their daily agenda. Teachers also can't neglect issues related to management, standardized testing, parents, and the social tone in their own classroom. Teachers who are heavily engaged in staff development need additional "white space" in their busy lives. See "Making Time for Teacher Study" on page 257.)

- are long-term enough to allow for significant learning (No slap-dash staff development is ever offered.)
- always involve the administrators (Principals should not take a backseat or make a swift exit after introducing a guest speaker.)
- include behind-the-scenes moments (Staff developers need to share the resources and techniques that enable them to know what they know and do what they do.)

Airing Differences Respectfully

In addition to the criteria listed previously, a final essential point remains. We anticipate that during staff development teachers will have differences of opinion. What is crucial is that all members of the scholarly community learn to air differences without placing blame, without insulting or attacking one another. Sometimes it becomes rather difficult to reach consensus at a staff meeting. Fine teachers are often passionate and opinionated. Those qualities serve as strengths as well as weaknesses if teachers are unable to listen respectfully to one another. My husband and I recently bought the apartment next door to our small Manhattan apartment. My husband set out to break through the walls to connect one apartment to the other. He took up a big heavy sledgehammer and started whacking away at the wall. Nothing happened. The wall vibrated a bit, but not even a dent was made in it. He was about to give up when, as a last resort, took out a plain, garden-variety hammer from his toolbox. He made a little nick, and then another, and then another. Pretty soon he could crawl through the opening and a short while later he could walk through the opening in the wall. A hammer did what a sledgehammer couldn't. So too, when we attempt to make change in school policies and teaching practices, we need to leave our sledgehammers at home. Change is slow and people are fragile. Gentle, respectful conversations will get the job done. Harsh, insulting words will not. (See Appendix 24, Learning to Say Difficult Things in Acceptable Ways).

The Art of Staff Development

Those in a position to plan or present staff development need to consider several factors that surround the actual work.

Effective staff development is a tough process, whether it is a principal, teacher mentor, visiting professor, or consultant working alongside a school staff. Workshop presentations, classroom visits, courses of study, demonstration lessons, reader-response groups, and even heart-to-heart talks between professionals are always connected to broader, schoolwide considerations.

The following thoughts on staff development are intended to promote professional growth that is nonthreatening, well received, effective, and long lasting. Each suggestion has implications for the administrator who arranges for or offers staff development as well as for personnel who conduct staff development at the school level. The suggestions may also help teachers who are offering or receiving staff development to assess the strengths and weaknesses of the professional study in their schools.

Be Inclusive

Staff development is more likely to be successful in schools that come close to Frank Smith's description of "learning emporia." Staff development should not be perceived as something we do unto the weaker teacher or reserve for inexperienced staff members. All staff members, including principals, consultants, and teacher mentors, should be able to announce, "This is my year to study ————." There needs to be a genuine feeling that no one has arrived. Everyone needs to be swept up by the deeply engrained value placed on adult learning. (Adult learning doesn't necessarily need to be directly related to curriculum. Teachers have added energy to our school lives because they studied piano, watercolor painting, and photography outside of school. They always find a way for these kinds of studies to benefit the school community.) It's the shift to a learning mode that helps teachers fine-tune their teaching practice and results in memorable and inspirational staff room conversations.

Take Adequate Time

When I say "No Talking in the Halls," I do not use this dictate in the sense of the old school rule demanding silence. Rather, I am suggesting that those perceived to have expertise in any particular area are actually doing a disservice to teachers when they answer serious and far-reaching questions in quick and automatic ways as they pass one another in the hallway. Instead of rattling off answers in passing, staff developers need to carve out time to talk through teacher's concerns in ways that promote professional dialogue. The staff developer can't be seen as the person with all the ready-made answers. Long-lasting change is more likely to be made when teachers are involved in teasing out all the possible solutions to any one problem.

Be Pro-teacher

Staff developers (be they teachers on staff, outside consultants, administrators, or district personnel) must be unconditionally pro-teacher. They can't be what the children call tattletales. If they truly respect teachers, they will not compare one classroom to another or engage in idle gossip about staff members. Teachers take big risks when they invite others to work in their classrooms, rethink their belief systems, try new techniques, and allow others to observe them teach. They deserve to be in caring hands. If staff developers are asked by administrators to comment on their work with teachers, staff developers need to enthusiastically present teachers' successes and *graciously* comment on teachers' struggles.

Marvel at Children

The most effective staff developers I know are those who are in awe of children—their wide-eyed wonder is contagious. These staff developers remind teachers what a privilege it is to be around children. They read aloud student work with reverence in their voices. They pay careful attention to what children say and are eager to share students' surprising insights and observations. The presence of enthusiastic staff developers often reminds classroom teachers how lucky they are to spend time with young people.

Fight Fads and Passing Fancies

People given the honor of helping teachers must be grounded in something that they believe in. They can't switch gears every time a new mandate arrives. In fact, we need to count on staff developers to be outspoken in their skepticism of passing fancies and whimsical approaches. There are too many teachers with file cabinets filled with short-lived pilot programs and useless curriculum guidebooks.

Stay Grounded

Years ago I heard a staff development researcher argue that staff development is like baseball. She was referring to batting averages and reminding the audience that team-mates with a .300 batting average were considered wonderful players. This statistic means that they are able to hit the ball three out of ten times. I suppose her comments were intended to encourage staff developers who are frustrated that they are not able to reach all teachers. I'm not sure that I'd be satisfied with a three-out-of-ten success rate, but I have learned to never engage in magical thinking. Just because I offer a workshop, even one with long-term supports attached, doesn't mean that all members of the audience are able to improve their literacy instruction. Staff development never works quickly. There are no magic potions.

Employ Artful Communication

It is essential that people who take on mentor roles are capable of giving well-deserved compliments. Staff developers must be able to acknowledge any instructional changes teachers have made as well as pay homage to those areas of classroom life of which the teachers are most proud. At the same time, mentors must learn how to say hard things in ways that can be heard. There is a real art to knowing how and when to offer con-structive criticism. Mentors must first establish the kind of trusting relationship that al-lows one to speak frankly. And then those honest comments must be framed in kind and gentle words.

Respect the Host

Staff developers who offer demonstration work in another teacher's classroom should not expect to have things their own way. They must take into account the routines and rituals that have already been put in place by the classroom teacher. They must honor the classroom teacher's methods for such day-to-day necessities as bringing a group to meeting, making transitions, distributing supplies, and so on. Staff developers should expect to feel a little uncomfortable and dependent on their hosts. It is like cooking in someone else's kitchen.

Stand in the Doorway

Earlier in this book, I suggested that teachers and administrators need two lenses in their cameras. They need both a wide-angle lens to see the big picture of school life as well as a zoom lens to study specifics. The same applies to classroom-based staff development work. Staff developers and teachers intent on making change and improving instructional techniques need to stand in the doorway to view the classroom as a whole as well as pull in close to fine-tune their teaching techniques. Standing in the doorway, not being directly involved in the teaching for a few moments, also provides insights into the effectiveness of the classroom management (Do children continue working in acceptable ways?) as well as the independence of the children, (Can children carry on without the constant support of the teacher?). Ineffective management and children who constantly interrupt the teacher are of course interrelated and often prevent teachers from turning their classrooms into successful reading/writing workshops.

Allow for Time Together and Time Apart

Time spent with staff developers is precious. I should feel the blood rush to my face when Sondra Nye, our brilliant math staff developer, arrives and teachers are not prepared for her visit. I should be embarrassed and so should my colleagues. Staff developers must be informed in advance when a field trip, standardized test, or special school schedule will prevent the collegial work from taking place. Then too, the time a staff developer spends with a teacher should be considered sacred. Interruptions must be eliminated. On the other hand, staff developers need to work in ways that guarantee that learning will take place when they are not present. In other words, staff developers need to think through long-term assignments (e.g., giving teachers research tasks), informal supports when they are unable to be present (e.g., creating teacher networks so that colleagues are able to support one another), structures that promote reflection (e.g., asking teachers to videotape their work or keep journals on their teaching), and informal safety nets (e.g., providing teachers with the staff developer's home phone number if urgent questions arise).

Think Big Thoughts

Educators responsible for providing in-services need to begin with those imaginary stances described earlier. They need to think big, asking for *all* the resources necessary to provide the finest staff development possible. They need to imagine having an abundant professional development library, all the extra coverage teachers needed, and unlimited time to talk to teachers. From many years' experience as a staff developer, I have learned that if I ask for a great deal, I will probably get some of what I need, at least enough to get off to a good start. Once the professional development work is going well, it is easier to argue for more support.

Provide Good Teaching

What we ask teachers to give children is no different from what we should expect staff developers to provide for teachers. If we expect classrooms to be filled with scenes of modeling, coaching, individual attention, small-group instruction, collaborative problem solving, and so on, then we should expect professional development work to contain similar elements. Good teaching is good teaching.

Evoke a Literary Mood

In the teaching of writing we suggest that form support content. The same holds true in the teaching of teachers. Staff developers who want to help teachers use literature well, speak in clear and effective ways, value writing as a tool for thinking, and so on, would do well to utilize these very same techniques with their colleagues. Some of the most effective staff development workshops I have offered included choosing effective metaphors to make my meaning clear, sharing evocative poetry, and asking teachers to write in response to an article or videotape. We can't ask students to do things that we ourselves don't do, and the same holds true for folks leading staff development.

Aim for Elegant Arrangements

Unfortunately, the word *elegant* for teachers can simply mean a quiet room with no interruptions. The teaching profession has never been honored with any first-class touches. But that quiet room can become *truely* elegant when it contains a tray of cookies, a basket of fresh fruit, and a pot of good coffee with real milk. It can be made elegant with the addition of carefully duplicated articles, well-thought-out calendars, and invitations to attend relevant conferences.

Discriminate

Traditional in-services often involve a series of workshops for *all* members of the staff or some form of "turnkey" training in which a key person attends professional development sessions and returns to share the information with the *entire* staff. From my past life as a staff developer and the principal-as-staff-developer role I now enjoy, I have learned that you can't give equal attention to everyone. Staff developers can give a substantial amount of time to a few and then move on to others, periodically returning to an earlier study group. They can keep cycling back, empowering teachers to continue learning on their own and especially alongside their colleagues.

Be Willing to Roll Up Your Sleeves

We all appreciate houseguests who pitch in with household chores. Staff developers eager to help teachers improve their instruction should begin by "being one of the guys." Hindy List, an accomplished staff developer, never hesitates to help a teacher rearrange furniture, unpack books, or label students' writing folders. She knows that teachers need to be able to focus on the topic at hand and that they can't do so if their classroom basics are not in order. In addition, teachers are more likely to trust a staff developer (including the principal) if the staff developer's actions indicate that he/she remembers what it is like to be a full-time classroom teacher.

Hang Yankee Banners

It's obvious to my friends that I am an avid baseball fan. I read baseball literature. I follow the games and the players. I root for my favorite home team, the Yankees. My professional life is also marked by this personal interest. As previously noted, I keep a collection of baseball literature in my office and hang Yankee banners and team posters on my wall. Being a baseball fan is part of who I am. It allows me to be me. Staff developers need to be able to bring who they are into their professional lives. They need to be allowed and encouraged to bring their own talents and passions into the work they do. I am not interested in working with staff developers who bring canned scripts along. Staff developers who do, give the wrong message to teachers. Our lives involve more than our classrooms. People who serve as mentors for teachers need to demonstrate a willingness to be fully themselves in front of students.

Understand the Politics

Staff developers need to stay informed about the pressures teachers face (e.g., new state or district mandates, testing procedures, teacher requirements), the history of staff development in the school, and all the sources of influence in the school. These might include community organizations, the school board, local newspapers and politicians, the teachers' union, and so on. Staff developers who take these factors into account when they plan and carry out their professional development work are more likely to meet the unique needs of any particular school.

Don't Window-Shop

Staff developers can not be seen as visitors who merely drop by, hang out, and share a cup of coffee. Together with the classroom teachers, they need to have established very clear goals for their time together. The staff developer's job is not to improve classrooms generically but to help teachers with such specific issues as assessing students' reading needs, improving literacy record-keeping, introducing short genres in the writing workshop, or matching the reading of poetry to the writing of poetry. Staff developers do not have the luxury of casually strolling the avenue, stopping to window-shop along the way. They have important work to do, usually in insufficient blocks of time.

Be Neither Mavens nor Missionaries

Staff developers who come on too strong often meet with resistance. No teacher benefits from being steamrolled by gung-ho educators who carry themselves as if they have all the answers carved in granite. Teaching is necessarily filled with tentative feelings and ambiguities. Trying to take these away from teachers also serves to take the art out of teaching and results in lowered morale. Let's make schools maven (Yiddish for boastful experts), and missionary-free zones.

Have Realistic Goals

Earlier, I suggested that all components of staff development should have reasonable goals and time frames attached to them. There I was suggesting that we should not expect individual teachers to change in too many ways in too short a period of time. Having realistic goals can also apply to entire schools and entire districts. Years ago, when I was first considering working for the central board of education as a staff developer, a friend who always wore her silver hair cropped close to her scalp offered me some professional advice. Pointing to her hairstyle, she explained, "I keep my hair cut short because if I let it grow long, it becomes thin and straggly. Be careful, you can spread yourself too thin as well." My friend worried that I would take on too much and that in the end my work would not add up to much. Staff developers should guard against taking on too many teachers in too many settings. They risk losing their effectiveness.

Share Your Mentors

Educators need to share the roots of their thinking. Staff developers need to let the teachers they are working with know the experts they themselves learn from, the books they read, and the conferences they attend. Teachers should never think that exquisite teaching is simply a gift. Passing on information inspires teachers to continue studying on their own and helps them realize how extensive the field is. It also serves as a professionally gracious protocol. The teachers I know best understand how much I have learned from such important educators as Nancie Atwell, Donald Graves, Jerry Harste, Georgia Heard, Tom Newkirk, Linda Rief, Regie Routman, Kathy Short, and many other experts in the field.

Be Reflective

Staff developers need to feel okay about making mistakes in front of the teachers in their charge. In fact, they need to take full advantage of such occasional mishaps as lessons that go nowhere, weak advice given in a writing conference, or moments of classroom confusion. If staff developers have the courage to process these moments, teachers will learn the value of being reflective. It always pays to look back on our teaching and ask, "What went well that I can build on?" and "What went poorly that I can revise or eliminate?" Staff developers should not only be reflective during the school day, but also when they go home at night. Regularly looking back on their work with teachers will enable each staff developer to create his/her own set of guiding principles for professional development. Staff developers are then more likely to become, along with their content-area expertise, experts in the process of change.

Nurturing Staff Developers

Educators who work as full-time staff developers need professional company, just as teachers in a school do. They need to meet together regularly in order to stay on the cutting edge of content and become masterful at the process of change. They need to read relevant professional literature, offer one another advice, and carve out their own areas of inquiry. They need to live with two antennae out, one for their content field and the other for issues related to staff development. When staff developers attend conferences, in addition to taking notes on content, they should be asking such questions as, "How do presenters begin? Handle questions? Use audio-visual equipment? Structure their presentations?" They should be paying heightened attention as well to any opportunities to watch others give demonstration lessons, lead discussion groups, or deliver keynote addresses. (See related ideas in Lucy McCormick Calkins and Shelley Harwayne, *The Writing Workshop: A World of Difference: a Guide to Staff Development.*)

Making Time for Teacher Study

If staff development is to be effective, no matter the topic or format it takes, it will be enriched if teachers are freed up during school hours to work with one another, visit classrooms together, or even work with small groups of children in one another's presence. To that end, I once sent the following note to teachers:

> *Dear friends,*
>
> *Here are some of the ideas that we discussed during the last staff meeting which might free teachers to work with each other. Please look them over and try to find one that you'd like to try.*
>
> > *Shelley covers two classes together in the ballroom (preferably for reading or writing).*
> > *Parent volunteers host center time in early-childhood classrooms.*
> > *Student teachers provide limited coverage, with licensed teacher in proximity.*
> > *Teachers cover two classes at once for worthwhile events (e.g., singing together).*
> > *Teachers co-teach two writing workshops together in the ballroom.*
> > *Kindergarteners visit first-grade writing workshops.*
> > *An entire upper grade class is assigned community service simultaneously to free up a teacher.*
> > *Back-to-back preps enable two teachers to use this time to study the same issue in one another's room.*
>
> *Let me know if you've thought of other structures. Hopefully, we will also have some substitute funds for professional development to make collaboration much easier.*
> *Thanks,*
>
> > > > *Love,*
> > > > *Shelley*

In addition, teachers are often willing to devote out-of-school time to collegial study. As described previously in this book, our staff meets every Wednesday afternoon for an hour and a half. This may sound like a lot of time, but of course it is never enough. In small groups, teachers also meet before school and after school to share common concerns. They meet on their lunch hours and during their preparation periods as well. Several teachers on staff have even had sleepovers in order to work on projects together.

Taking Care of Our Literacy

Several months ago, my daughter was waiting at Grand Central Station for a train to Washington, D.C. The train was delayed and she sat reading. A man nearby kept trying to engage her in a conversation. She kept ignoring him, but he kept on talking to her. Finally, she looked up at him and said, "I'm sorry. I can't *not* read." Instead of ending with that, the man looked at her in disbelief and asked, "You can't read?" "No," she said, "I can't *not* read!" That sentiment needs to be true for educators. We can't *not* read.

Adult Book Clubs

At school, one of the most important things we do together is to share a good juicy novel every month or so. As noted earlier, one adult restroom in our school serves as a sort of literary archive. On each square tile on the restroom wall, you'll find the title and author of a book we've read together. (A compete bibliography appears in Appendix 25.)

Each June, our district offers us a bit of money designated for summer planning. This enables interested teachers to earn extra money by working together to prepare for the upcoming school year. We have always used a bit of that time to create a reading list for the new school year. Teachers pool their suggestions, make visits to the local bookstore, consult amazon.com, etc. When the entire staff returns to school in the fall, they are eager to see the year's options.

Since our school has grown to almost thirty staff members and student teachers are welcome to join these reading groups, we now have reading groups forming around three different books at the same time. This keeps each response group down to a manageable and more intimate number and keeps the expenses down as well. Teachers do not have to buy copies of all the books but can swap titles with a colleague who has already read the book. (We also try to keep the costs down by including many books that are available in paperback.) At one point last year, teachers chose to read Doris Lessing's *Love, Again* or Charles Frazier's *Cold Mountain* or Rebecca Wells's *The Divine Secrets of the Ya-Ya Sisterhood.* If books are particularly well-received, they reappear as a choice in the next round and then teachers can borrow copies from one another.

Our response groups are very informal. We are tired at the end of the day and are not interested in performing. (This past year we switched our book group to early morning from eight o'clock to nine o'clock and share breakfast treats as well. Children arrive at 8:40, but teachers arrange for guest readers on those days (parents, student teachers, volunteers) to greet the class and read aloud to them for the first twenty minutes.) There are no leaders, no prompts, no response logs required. We just sit around and have a good honest talk about a book. We laugh, sigh, question, and commiserate. We critique, read aloud, snack, and tell stories in response. We get to know each other as readers and as human beings. We make a commitment to reading and we grow as readers. Most of all, we have a really good time. I have long thought that the reason bookstores so often sell calendars is to enable readers to mark dates with their friends to get together and talk about books.

Our teachers' reading groups do not feel like a college course, nor should they. Some people are too busy to read for each round. (Teachers do have lives apart from literacy.) Some people do not finish their books in time. (No demerits are given.) Some people protest the choices. (Staff members have very different tastes in reading.) Some people want to read fewer books a year, some want more frequent get-togethers. (We have had splinter groups who tuck in an extra book and meet outside of school in between the school reads.) Our reading groups are completely voluntary and teachers should never feel otherwise. Our job is to make the choices so wonderful and the meetings so joyful that everyone will say, "I can't *not* read."

The following brief essay appeared as a lead to our review column in *The New Advocate*. I wrote about my own commitment to adult reading groups:

Twenty-five years ago, when I was pregnant with my daughter, my mother used to serve me huge portions of her delicious home-cooked meals, because she said I was "eating for two." Some days when I run up exorbitant bills at my local bookstore, I free myself from guilt by using the same logic. After all, my daughter thankfully shares my taste in reading and I willingly pass my adult novels on to her. That expensive stack of books qualifies in my mind as "reading for two."

Most of my bookstore purchases are required reading for the many book clubs I belong to. In our staff book club at school, we get together once a month to share a good novel. We post our choices on a public bulletin board, to make sure our students and visitors know we get together to read as an activity of choice. The bulletin board also serves as a reminder for all of us of the upcoming titles and the dates of the get-togethers. We are not reluctant to boast about our commitment to reading. We recently got together to talk about Frank McCourt's *Angela's Ashes*. Our staff room filled with talk of poverty, hunger, parenting, alcoholism, child labor, and other big issues that really matter.

I also belong to a principal's book club. The members are heads of other schools in our district as well as a few district office staff members who know our schools well. We hold these meetings every six weeks at each other's apartments. These book talks feel very different from the ones at school because, in addition to talking about the book, we do a lot of social talk. After we spend time swapping school stories and talking about the food that accompanies each gathering, we finally get around to talking about the book. We recently read Louis De Berniere's *Corelli's Mandolin* as we dined on tortellini and chicken francese.

There are two other book clubs I belong to at school. One is a newly started parent reading group [described in Chapter 5, "Reaching Out to Families."] When the group was getting started, the parents asked me to pick the first title. I suggested Wallace Stegner's *Crossing to Safety*, a book I fell in love with several years ago. Parents have been stopping me in the hallways at school to talk about how much they're enjoying the book and how surprised they are to never have read anything by this author. I wouldn't be surprised if this club doesn't inspire some serious author studies, with members determined to read several books by the same author.

Judy Davis, a fifth-grade teacher at our school, invited me to join a special reading group. Periodically Judy invites students and their parents to read a novel together and then to spend an evening at school, eating pizza and sharing their responses to books.

We've spent hours talking about such books as Gary Paulsen's *The Monument,* Susan Creech's *Walk Two Moons,* and Jane Breskin Zalben's *Unfinished Dreams.* Currently, we are preparing to talk about Carolyn Coman's *What Jamie Saw.* These meetings are very special for several reasons. Parents come to understand our way of teaching reading, appreciating how we marvel at different interpretations, not privileging any one person's take on a book. Each book invites family members to talk about important issues that might not have come up had they not read the book together. The book talks also enable parents and children to see each other in a totally new light, as equal members of a scholarly gathering. I especially delight in this group because it demonstrates that bedtime stories need not end once children are reading on their own. Reading can continue as a shared family entertainment in its most elegant form.

I suppose I really do belong to yet another, much smaller book club, the one I share with my daughter. Whether we are sharing responses via an expensive long distance phone call or over dinner when she is home on break from law school, the best of book club happenings takes place. We read beautifully written books, layered with meaning, and we listen to one another's responses, laughing and crying together, reading aloud our favorite parts, making connections to other books, and puzzling over the parts we're not sure of. Reading for two is as much fun as eating for two. [For further information on adult reading groups, see *Lasting Impressions,* Chapter 10, "Book Talk That Makes a Difference."]

As previously noted, there are some New York City educators who believe that we will transform our public schools if we ask our children to wear uniforms. When all children are dressed alike, this reasoning goes, they will have more self-esteem, sense of belonging, and school spirit. I have different thoughts about transforming schools. My tools include the use of humane language, the gracious invitation for people to tell their stories, and the sharing of fine literature. And the sharing of fine literature applies to the adults as much as to the children. We transform schools when adults take care of their own reading lives. I would argue that you can't have a truly successful school if the adults in that school don't read. Not only do we change relationships among staff members, but teachers have a rich well to draw from when they teach reading to their students. A few years back the first Barbie teacher doll appeared in toy stores. The doll had apples and rulers printed all over her flimsy dress. I'd have much preferred a stack of books under her arms and a library card sticking out of her pocket.

Unexpected Professional Growth

In addition to the staff development structures previously described, there are unexpected and surprising means toward achieving professional growth. When the social tone is supportive in a school and teachers and their administrators honestly trust, admire, and appreciate one another, teachers can learn in the company of their colleagues. For example, when a small group of teachers work in a summer school setting, the change of pace and focus of attention can establish new relationships and pave the way for continued camaraderie during the regular school year. Similarly, teachers who take graduate courses or attend summer institutes together can form new professional as well as personal relationships. These too can result in continued shared inquiry studies. Teachers also learn a great deal about their own teaching when they agree to serve as a cooperating teacher for student teachers. Our teachers also grow professionally when they allow their classrooms to become a site for a graduate student's doctoral research. In addition, worthwhile information sent home to families can serve to inform teachers. Likewise, when school bulletin boards demonstrate important concepts, they instruct teachers who are new to the field or new to the subject matter as well as the parents and students for whom they were designed.

Meeting the Needs of First-Year Teachers

Over the years, we have hired several first-year teachers to join our staff, although the majority of new staff members have been very experienced teachers. Often the first-year teachers have been student teachers that the community had simply fallen in love with and taken under their wing. At other times, a prospective teacher arrives with résumé and portfolio in hand and is so impressive, we can't resist taking a chance. The first-year teacher does of course need professional development. Just twelve weeks earlier the student teacher may have been in the caring hands of a university supervisor and a cooperating teacher who placed safety nets under all the student teacher attempted and gave spoken feedback for their every move. They may have met in weekly support groups with other novice teachers, kept detailed journals on their work, and had opportunities to ask all their beginning questions. Once they are hired as full-fledged teachers, these university-orchestrated supports are no longer in place. It becomes the school's responsibility to provide particularly wise and caring professional development for newcomers to the field.

Above all, with a brand-new teacher, the key to wise staff development is simplicity. That very first year, new teachers have to find their voice and feel comfortable in the setting they create with their students. They don't need to be bombarded with tons of curriculum guides and advice from too many senior staff members. They don't need to be encouraged to share their struggles in front of all their well-meaning colleagues at staff meetings. Instead, they need to apprentice themselves to one caring colleague, one who has a compatible way of classroom life. The last thing a new teacher needs is five different teachers suggesting ways to bring a class to attention or smooth moments of transition. Most first-year teachers need to focus on creating elegant management systems and then work on fine-tuning their subject-matter teaching. In order to accomplish this second goal, I have found it beneficial to provide the new teacher with additional preparation periods early in the school year in order to have them observe in a master teacher's classroom. Those visits should be targeted, however, toward specific curriculum areas. New teachers' heads will spin if they try to learn everything at once.

We have also been planning to put together a three-ring binder filled with information for teachers new to our staff in order to familiarize them with the givens of our schoolhouse life. This would be similar to the letter that appears in Chapter 1 reminding new staff members that we avoid store-bought decorations, most contests, religious holiday celebrations, sexist language, random decorations, loud voices in the hallways, whining, and so on. (Compiling such a list of things to avoid would make for an interesting staff meeting.) This binder would also contain helpful union, salary, and benefits information, as well as school calendars, telephone directories, and neighborhood information. I'd also like to have a special section for teachers who are not just new to our school or to our city but new to the profession. I'd probably begin this section the way the late Dr. Spock began his classic for parents, *Baby and Child Care*. His opening line read, "You know more than you think you know." I would add such important first-year advice as, "Don't forget to enjoy the children," "Bring your own interests into the classroom," and "Ask for help." Every school should prepare such a book for their new teachers.

Above all, principals should proceed with caution around first-year teachers. They must be sympathetic to the fact that these teachers may be feeling overwhelmed by their new undertaking, and that they may be in need of a good cry when they go home at night.

Inviting Student Teachers into the Professional Community

Schools fortunate enough to have student teachers need to think through ways to ensure that their hours spent in the school do not merely represent an obligation to fulfill a course requirement. I send the following letter each semester to the new student teachers that have been assigned to our school. (We accept student teachers from six different universities. We really have become a teaching schoolhouse.)

Dear ———,

Welcome to the Manhattan New School. We feel privileged to have so many students working alongside us. We trust that once you get to know our world, you will also feel fortunate and privileged to have been assigned here.

Do take advantage of all we have to offer. Just as we want every minute to count for our elementary students, so too we expect all the adults in the school to lead rigorous, scholarly lives. To that end, don't hesitate to:

- ask honest questions of your cooperating teacher
- read our professional literature
- attend our Wednesday staff meetings
- join our monthly book groups
- share your own research, articles, clippings
- immerse yourself in children's literature
- get to know many staff members

We also believe that students don't simply belong to a class, but to a school. Likewise, we hope that you will take part in school-wide activities. We don't mean merely helping out in the lunchroom, which is of course a necessary and serious responsibility, but you are also welcome to attend such gatherings as:

- *weekend and evening celebrations, fundraisers, and performances*
- *after-school programs*
- *PTA meetings and parent-teacher conferences*
- *courses held at the school*
- *half-day professional development workshops*
- *school day special events including field trips, book fairs, and festivals*

In addition, let us know if you have any special areas of expertise you'd like to share (e.g., a second language, music, journalism, dance, etc.).

Know that most of us are here early in the morning and stay late into the evening. You're welcome to join us as we plan, prepare, and evaluate our work. You're also welcome to pitch in as we turn this old school building into an aesthetically enriched setting. (A school can't look as beautiful as ours does without lots of extra time, energy, talents, and enthusiasm.)

All of us wish you well. We can recall our own student teaching experiences and we know your time here will become an important part of your professional and personal memory bank. No doubt, you will long remember the names and faces of the children and adults who are about to touch you deeply.

To a joyous semester.

With much respect for your chosen career.

Sincerely,

Shelley

P.S. Don't hesitate to stop in and chat with me. I'm usually around my office before and after school hours.

(See Appendix 26 for a reproducible form of letter.)

Signs of a Professionally Alive Community

Each year, before opening our doors to visitors from outside the school, I need to be sure that professional development is alive and well for all members of the staff, including myself. Several years ago, Jane Wagner wrote a great play that starred Lily Tomlin on Broadway. It was called *The Search for Signs of Intelligent Life in the Universe*. The following are a few signs of intelligent professional life in the universe of our school. When these ways of living grow commonplace, I'm confident that we are ready to serve as powerful learning mentors for other educators.

- The daily logbook (see form in Appendix 1) announces daily opportunities to grow professionally. (News of who is doing what in which classroom at what time.)

- Teachers regularly check out the professional library to see what new titles have been recently added. (Waiting lists for hot books appear.)
- Teachers proudly talk about what they don't know in addition to what they know well.
- Student teachers tell us that they are having trouble sleeping because their heads are so filled with children and ideas for teaching and learning.
- Professional articles mysteriously appear in one another's mailboxes.
- Teachers are spotted visiting one another's rooms on their "free" periods.
- People expect written notes as well as oral reports when colleagues attend conferences, and they are not disappointed.
- Staff meetings are productive, dynamic, and engaging forums, and we're wishing we had videotaped our last few meetings.
- People's staff room conversations indicate that they know what is being studied around the building.
- Teachers ask student teachers to videotape classroom moments.
- Our work with any consultants is organized, valued, and rigorous. We make every minute count.

Visiting Educators

Many visitors come to our school. It is a rare day when our daily log book doesn't announce that someone on staff will be hosting a visitor in his/her own classroom and/or walking through the building with a friend, relative, professor, former colleague, and so on. (We have been privileged to show our school to many respected and renowned experts including Donald Graves, Jerry Harste, Tom Newkirk, Regie Routman, Bobby Fisher, Karen Ernst, Irene Fountas, Nancie Atwell, Susan Stires, Georgia Heard, Ralph Fletcher, and Mary Ellen Giacobbe. Peter Johnston has researched in Joan Backer's fourth-grade room. Maureen Barbieri periodically drops in on Judy Davis' fifth-grade class.) During the autumn and winter months, we also host weekly tours for prospective parents. No special provisions are made for any of these rather "informal" visits.

We also get lots of formal requests to visit from educators throughout our city, our country, and in fact from teachers in distant lands. People hear about our school because so many of our staff members have published their writing, produced videos, and/or serve as consultants and keynote speakers. We take every request for a visit as a compliment. We know that we have lots to learn, but we are quite proud of what we have accomplished so far.

Corresponding, scheduling, planning, and orchestrating these visitor requests, however, could become a full-time job—one that no one, of course, has time to add on to his/her already busy life. Our budget constraints also keep us from responding to visitors in a timely fashion. Often we do not have sufficient funds for postage, and long-distance calls and faxes are a complicated business in a public school. And then there is our commitment to keep interruptions to a minimum. If we host visitors on a daily basis, we are no longer practicing what we preach about the need for big blocks of time to accomplish our ambitious teaching and learning goals.

We do set aside days in the spring semester to give interested educators at least a glance at what we are all about, and thankfully we do have structures in place to allow district colleagues to study with us for extended periods. (See descriptions of these events in the following).

Springtime Visits   Usually in late May or early June, when the testing season is over and before the heat and humidity set in, we attempt to accommodate all the visitors' requests we receive in any school year. We send out a letter announcing dates for visitors, and teachers avoid arranging field trips on those red-letter days (see Appendixes 27, 28, and 29, for correspondence with visitors). We don't plan any special demonstrations for visitor days or hang up any fresh bulletin board displays. Visitors see the real school, not a polished "model-home" version. The only accommodation we make to the guests is an attempt to cover all the teachers visited, for a short period of time at the end of the morning, so that they get a chance to talk to the visitors. Visitors hear a brief overview of the school, including a discussion of the issues we are grappling with. Remember that we want visitors to realize that none of us have all the answers. They are then invited on a brisk walk through the entire five-story building, after which they are assigned to linger in one classroom that is closely related to their grade-level interest. They then have an opportunity to chat with the classroom teacher visited. Our visitor's day is actually a visitor's half-day. (No one seems to mind, as there are great restaurants, shops, and museums nearby. Besides, most of their learning probably takes place as colleagues talk about their visit during lunch or on their travels home.)

Schools that host visitors might also consider the following gracious touches. (We consider them, but don't always pull them off.)

- Name tags with space to include the visitor's hometown
- Coffee and cookies (bagels, of course, in New York City)
- Easy access to restrooms
- A printed list of neighborhood restaurants (Students can be asked to prepare this.)
- A packet of articles about the school or samples of school newsletters
- Any professional articles written by staff members
- Welcome notes written by students (Students can be asked to give background information to visitors. Their comments can be quite eye-opening.)

In addition, the school would be wise to include on its invitations to visitors such specifics as travel directions, information about parking and the exact hours of the visit. Visitors to the Manhattan New school are encouraged to make the visit in the company of a few colleagues, including administrators and parents. (Students are also occasionally invited to visit. See "Courses over Time," following.) Visitors might also be told in advance that the host teachers would appreciate copies of teachers' reflections about their visit. (These write-ups increase learning opportunities for the host staff and remind visitors of the value of taking notes.) Finally, visitors frequently ask what they can bring to the school. To that end, our PTA has composed a letter that invites donations of such necessities as paper, postage, markers, and so on. We can't charge admission but we can accept donations. We really are a public school.

Suggestions for Making the Most of School Visits   The following suggestions have been gleaned from years of visiting schools and from hosting visitors in our own school. Let them serve as a sort of etiquette handbook for teachers who are fortunate enough to spend time in other teachers' classrooms. (Joanne Hindley Salch often makes suggestions like these to our visitors before they enter classrooms.)

Dos

- Open doors gently, move chairs quietly, and use soft voices. In other words, be as inconspicuous as possible.
- Bring a clipboard or journal in order to take notes, draw sketches, or jot questions.
- Take cues from host teachers as to whether you should participate or observe. (Teachers have differing styles when hosting visitors.)
- Take advantage of opportunities to talk to the children whenever possible (not during whole-class gatherings, but when children are working individually or in small groups).
- Try to get a sense of the big picture, of how the classroom runs as a whole.
- Zoom in on smaller teaching moments.
- Bend down, sit on the rug, pull in close, and really listen.
- Note interactions between staff members.
- Target your visit to meet your needs. You can, for example, pay extra attention to such issues as management, the quality of classroom talk, record-keeping, etc.
- Send your observations and reflections to the host school. You'll crystallize your learnings and be contributing enormously to the host school.

Don'ts

- Don't spend your time copying bulletin board displays or titles of books. You'll miss valuable teaching moments.
- Don't take samples of student or teacher work without permission.

- Don't take photographs, videotapes, or slides without permission.
- Don't ask the office staff to duplicate work without hosts' permission.
- Don't ask questions of teachers that pull them away from their teaching during your visit. Jot them down for processing time.
- Don't wander around the school on your own if you're part of an escorted tour.

Courses over Time   We know that "one-shot" visits can never accomplish what could be accomplished if we had structures in place that enable visitors to establish teaching and learning residencies for extended periods of time. When a couple of our teachers returned from their visit to the Center for Teaching and Learning in Edgcombe, Maine, they were awed by the structures created by Nancie Atwell and her colleagues to facilitate visiting interns' learning. Their thoughtful planning and weeklong internships guarantee that visitors will be able to effectively think through their own school reform. (Unfortunately, our status as a public school prevents us from making the financial arrangements necessary to create such in-depth study opportunities.)

I recently received a gracious letter from the assistant superintendent of the American School Foundation in Mexico City. Janet proposed an exchange program between our teachers. She would arrange for a teacher to work in our school focusing on Spanish language studies, while one of our teachers would work in her site providing staff development in the teaching of writing and literature-based learning. Janet was most flexible in her offer, suggesting arrangements that extended from a short two-week exchange all the way to a semester-long one. (Of course, our position as a public school once again makes such arrangements difficult. City regulations require all teachers to be licensed by our central board of education and prevent unlicensed teachers from teaching in our schools. Established policy also makes it difficult for city teachers to take paid exchange leaves. We have yet to figure out ways around these obstacles. But we never say "never.")

Karen Ernst proposed yet another long-term plan for mutually beneficial staff development. She suggested visiting with groups of her colleagues and simultaneously sharing with our teachers her expertise in valuing art in our literacy work. In addition, Karen offered to provide regular feedback through excerpts from visitors' journals. Karen's proximity to our school (her site is just a train ride away in Connecticut), and her willingness to provide invaluable feedback made her offer a difficult one to refuse. (The first time Karen came to our school, she sent pages from her sketch journal in response to her visit. Teachers were so bowled over by her insights and her talent that they would have agreed to any long-term relationship.)

We would love to create additional staff development structures that allow us to make professional contributions to the field. At present, several teachers on staff have been asked by our district office to open their classrooms to visiting teachers from other district schools. Our host teacher meets with administrators, staff developers, and teachers from these other schools to determine the staffs' areas of interest and to set aside specific dates for these Courses Over Time to take place. Teachers usually choose a day of the week and then set aside four consecutive weeks to visit. The schools hire substitute teachers for their cluster of visiting teachers and the district provides us with funds to hire a substitute as well. Our substitute teacher makes it possible for the teacher whose work is being studied to step away from her classroom whenever necessary to provide background information, assign research tasks, distribute handouts, answer questions, monitor visiting teachers working with small clusters of our children, and so on. Each of these courses targets a different area of study. Visitors have spent time with our teachers in order to study such topics as moving from notebook writing to finished products, organizing for effective reader-response groups, record keeping in the early-childhood reading workshop, and so on. The district also provides honorariums for our teachers who lead after-school workshops connected to their in-class courses.

The advantages of these courses stretched out over time are many:

- Visiting teachers don't feel like they are away from their own students for too long a stretch at a time. (Host teachers as well do not feel a loss of undivided attention toward their students when visits are spread out over time.)
- Visiting teachers get to know one group of children and can watch progress or conduct brief case studies.
- During the week apart, teachers can try out new ideas in their own classrooms.
- Teachers can bring related work samples and questions to the next week's gathering.
- Visiting teachers can arrange to bring students to classroom visits, adding another dimension to staff development.

Other effective tools and strategies connected to these courses can include:

- Worksheets to focus visitor's attention. For example, Joanne has given worksheets to visitors that ask them to spot examples of such valued essentials in her classroom as "predictablity, choice, and interaction."
- Interactive moments designed so that the host teacher is not the center of attention for the entire day, and visiting educators are able to take on research tasks and try out new techniques. For example, Joanne and Judy have created assignments for visitors to their reading workshops that require teachers to interview a students about his or her reading, listen to the student read aloud, and cull from those experiences ideas for mini-lessons to be taught to the entire class.
- A walking tour of the entire building so that visitors can appreciate the social, professional, and academic culture of the school.
- Inclusion of the visiting teacher's administrator in all activities as well as opportunities for the administrator to speak to the principal of the host school.

- Opportunities to share such nuts-and-bolts materials as ordering information, titles of books, and even names of substitute teachers.

- Longer lunch hours for participating teachers on course days to further conversations and professionalism.

- Time for visiting colleagues to share their own areas of expertise and arrange for possible reciprocal visits to their schools. (Learning is never one-sided.)

Conference Days   Over the years we have also hosted conference days at our school devoted to specific topics. For example, our district's monthly principals' meetings are frequently held in schools throughout our district, and one year we were invited to highlight the study of nonfiction in our school. On such special occasions, in addition to offering keynote addresses and workshops on related topics, we arranged for visitors to observe aspects of reading, writing, and researching nonfiction throughout the grades and across topics and disciplines. On another occasion, the focus of our conference was "Creating the Social and Physical Environment." To target visitor's responses we handed out the worksheet that appears in Appendix 30).

The key to allowing schools to become venues for all-day conferences begins with an agreement on the part of the entire staff that the event is a worthwhile professional contribution. It then becomes essential to think through the availability of such items as:

- time for planning and preparing for the day
- a comfortable space for large-group gathering
- necessary audiovisual equipment
- substitute teachers to cover classes of those teachers presenting workshops and to allow all teachers to be able to get responses from visitors and answer their questions
- duplicating machines to produce pertinent hand-outs
- funds to add such gracious touches as refreshments, name tags, flowers, table-cloths, etc.
- helpers for setting up and clearing up (These could include teachers, student teachers, volunteers, parents, custodial workers, etc.)

It is also important to invite to the conference those parents or community members particularly concerned with issues of curriculum and instruction. In addition, it is worth thinking through how students can take an active role in the various aspects of a conference day. Can students lead small workshops, talk to clusters of visitors, narrate tours, explain finished work, and so on?

No matter the structure of the work with visiting educators, and no matter the attention to detail most visits require, the presence of outsiders can serve an important role in the lives of teachers. Teaching is a profession that can be marked by feelings of isolation. Teachers rarely have time to talk to teachers from other schools. And in some settings, teachers have little time to talk even to their own colleagues. Opening a school to visitors is one way of guaranteeing "news from the outside," fresh eyes to comment on the work being done, and opportunities to swap ideas and begin long-term professional relationships. Schools visited must not be limited to those whose students have high scores on reading tests or math. We know that schools should be judged on many more criteria. There is much to be learned from any group of hardworking educators. Despite my passion for the study of literacy, I recognize that not every sight visit should be devoted to the teaching of reading and writing. I have learned a great deal visiting schools whose educators have particular expertise in the teaching of second-language learners, social studies, science, and mathematics.

The Importance of Having Staff Development Priorities

One time on a flight back to New York, I found myself browsing through one of those glossy airline magazines. So many of the articles appealed to me that I had this uncontrollable urge to keep several of the pages. I flipped to the front of the magazine, searching for the magic words, "complimentary copy." But this magazine was not a giveaway. I knew that the publication would not be for sale in my local newsstand and I sat there coveting several of the articles. That's when I began separating the pages from their binding, ever so quietly, gently, and surreptitiously. (I was trying desperately not to alert the passengers on either side of me, or worse yet, the flight attendants in the aisle.)

Yes, I succumbed to destroying a magazine and taking papers that really were not mine for the taking because, I must admit, I was suffering from "educator-overload." When I am in this state of mind, I see the potential educational value in everything that surrounds me. I connect everything I see to my students, colleagues, and school.

I wanted the article on the artist Manel Anoro because his beautiful paintings were titled in both Spanish and English. "Why can't we do that?" I thought. We could label things in the school in two languages. We could write the daily agenda in two languages. We could hang hallway signs in two languages.

I wanted the cartoon for our staff restroom bulletin board. It showed a tropical drink, complete with a pretty paper umbrella sticking out, next to a man's neck tie. The sketches were labeled "mai tai" and "your tie." We're always playing with language at our school. I knew my colleagues would appreciate this play on words.

I wanted the article entitled "Respecting Your Child," to share with members of the PTA. The author describes the importance of learning to say no to children.

I wanted the article that explained the symbolism of the Chinese dragon. I knew teachers would love to share this information with their students when they celebrate the Chinese New Year.

I wanted the interview with the director of the Smithsonian's National Museum of the American Indian just opening in New York City. No doubt, we'd be making class visits to this new attraction.

I even wanted an advertisement for a new pocket printer. It was filled with a lush list of descriptors and made me wonder if ads might be useful in working with our English as a second language students. I could imagine students studying these inexpensive materials and simultaneously learning English and concepts about American culture.

Perhaps, on occasion, you too have suffered from educator's overload. You can't stop making connections. You can't shut down. You can't stop thinking about your professional life. Your heads spins. Good ideas zoom across your brain like shooting stars in an arcade game.

It's this state of mind that often prevents educators from passing up opportunities to take courses, attend workshops, work with a consultant, and visit other schools. Everything is irresistible. We are compelled to put our names on all those sign-up sheets. There is, of course, a downside to too much professional thinking. We can grow tired, mentally exhausted, and obsessed with learning all there is to learn, trying out all there is to try out.

Several years ago when one of our students, Madeline, was in kindergarten, I visited her class during writing workshop. The five-year-old had stapled a wad of pages together, and across the first page she had written in her best invented spelling, "The Book of Important Stuff" (see Figure 7.1).

When I was granted permission to turn the page and read her book, I was disappointed to find all the remaining pages blank. I asked Madeline why she hadn't filled the pages and she quickly responded, "Nothing important has happened yet. I'm waiting."

Educators need their own books of important stuff. We can't learn everything. We can't take every course, read every book, attend every conference. We must have priorities. We must be able to say, this is my year to learn _____, and we fill in that blank with

Figure 7.1

one topic, one issue, one area of inquiry. (I write this knowing that many teachers are under pressure to rethink too many curriculum areas at the same time. We need to continually make the argument, "Let me feel confident about this one area before I begin to make change in another.") Just as *The New York Times* places the most significant news stories above the fold, educators need to ask, "What's above the fold?" "What's most significant?" "What really matters for me at this point in time?" Setting limits and devoting big blocks of time to one area of study is the only way we can study issues deeply and lead scholarly lives.

RELATED READINGS IN COMPANION VOLUMES

Lifetime Guarantees (Heinemann, forthcoming), will be abbreviated as LG.
Writing Through Childhood (Heinemann, forthcoming), will be abbreviated as WC.

Creating school structures that support teachers' learning	**WC**: Ch. 11. **LG**: Ch. 7.
Airing differences respectfully	**WC**: Ch. 11. **LG**: Ch. 7.
Taking care of our literacy	**WC**: Ch. 11. **LG**: Ch. 7.
Arranging adult reading clubs	**WC**: Ch. 11. **LG**: Ch. 7.
Having staff development priorities	**WC**: Ch. 11. **LG**: Ch. 7.

CHAPTER 8

SING ABOUT IT!

Several years ago, my custodian received a copy of a letter that an angry neighbor had sent to the central board of education complaining about our school. It seems that a burglar alarm went off early one Sunday morning, much to the annoyance of this outspoken resident. I can understand what a nuisance a screeching alarm can be on a weekend morning, but I will never understand the cynicism and sarcasm attached to this particular letter. Midway through his harangue our neighbor concluded, "Just what in hell is anyone going to steal in there, obsolete text books, cafeteria food, chalk, asbestos?"

I'd like to take my neighbor by the hand and give him the royal tour. He'll see floor upon floor of beautiful classrooms filled with hardworking and effective teachers alongside engaged and successful learners. He'll find no obsolete textbooks, in fact, he won't find any textbooks at all, just thousands upon thousands of beautiful books in addition to Internet access to even more resources. He'll find pretty decent cafeteria food, as well as hundreds of children who look forward to and appreciate having a hot meal at midday. He'll find no chalk, but brightly colored markers sitting on the ledge of shiny wipe-off boards. And I'd show him how those markers are used to craft wonderful poems, solve challenging mathematical problems, and create great works of art. He'll find absolutely no asbestos, as all of it was removed years ago. We have the paperwork to prove our clean bill of health.

Why do people find it so easy to attack public schools and public school educators? One day, early in a school year, I pulled up in front of our school and saw a handwritten sign hanging on the front door, apparently written by one of our kindergarten teachers and edited by an anonymous passerby. The sign was written neatly and carefully in thick black marker (see Figure 8.1). The passerby used a carat to insert an *e* into the word *kindergartner*, making it appear as "kindergartener," and wrote in the margin, "Learn to Spell!" I immediately tore down the sign, furious that someone would add such a comment. I forgot about the sign as the school day began, never even asking who had put it up. The next day, and the day following that, I witnessed repeat performances. A teacher, as yet unidentified, hung new signs, and the unknown editor each time changed the spelling and told the teacher to learn to spell. Finally, I began asking around, "Did you hang a sign about the new location for kindergarten arrival and dismissal?" I should have recognized Pam's handwriting. "Yes," she said, "I've hung several and each day the sign disappears!" I explained to Pam that I had been removing the signs and my reason for doing so. It didn't take Pam very long too hang a new sign, in fact she hung two. Alongside her kindergarten arrival and dismissal announcement, she posted a sign about spelling. Pam enlarged the dictionary definition and added her own comment (see Figure 8.2). We never heard from our anonymous critic again.

Our custodian recently hung a display case on the outside of our school building. In addition to a sign congratulating the Yankees on their 1998 World Series championship and one celebrating Jacques d'Amboise upon his receipt of the National Medal of Arts, one other display was very important to me. I hung the following

Kindergart^e_ners ^Learn to Spell^

Should be dropped

off and picked up

in the cafeteria

beginning September 16th.

Figure 8.1

kin·der·gart·ner (kĭn′dər-gärt′nər) *n.* Also **kin·dergarten·er** (-gärt′n-ər). A child who attends kindergarten.

An interesting fact: "Kindergartner" can be spelled two ways!

Figure 8.2

words, written by John Dewey one hundred years ago: "What the best and the wisest parents want for their children . . . the community must want for all its children. Any other ideal for our schools is narrow and unlovely; acted upon, it destroys our democracy." Words like these make it even more disheartening when our neighbors think it's okay to mock us.

Challenging Negative Images

I suppose, however, that it's not surprising that so many people think it's okay to analyze, criticize, ridicule, and condemn public schools and public school educators. After all, the media and pop culture do it all the time. David Letterman has entertained his late-night viewers with a top-ten list devoted to "Signs Your Elementary School Principal Is Nuts." I mentioned earlier a gift I received once, a framed poster highlighting the frazzled administrator surrounded by stacks and stacks of papers (never books, just papers) alongside bottles of headache remedies, antacid, and even a container labeled "Bucket for Pulled Hair."

Even when reporters have positive things to say, they often choose to begin with the negative to grab the reader's attention. We were visited by a group of wonderful educators from Seattle. The kind reporter who clearly appreciated our school began his article, entitled "Making Teachers Better," with the following description:

> The Manhattan New School rises six stories above East 82nd Street on New York's Upper East Side. With no playground, students spend their recess dodging among parked cars in the street, barricaded at both ends to keep moving vehicles out. The ground floor lunchroom of the nearly 100-year-old building is a grim institutional space with green walls and a labyrinth of pipes and ducts for a ceiling. But upstairs, in classrooms vividly decorated with student artwork and writing, the former P.S. 190 is a far cry from a stereotypical grubby, struggling urban school.

The reporter goes on to quote one Seattle educator who found our school to be "an exemplar of fine teaching." I wish he had begun with that lead. I think it's catchy enough.

The powers that be would even have us believe that even children hate school. A recent photograph on the cover of *The New York Times* during a holiday break showed dozens of children waiting in the icy rain to get into a local museum. The caption read, "It's Still More Fun than School." There may have been huge dinosaur replicas in that museum, but our students would still not say that standing in the cold for an hour was more fun than attending school. I hope no educators hung that depressing schoolbased "Life in Hell," cartoon strip by Matt Groening in their staff rooms. It was the one showing a student endlessly complaining about being in an overcrowded classroom, taught by an exhausted teacher, reading boring books, being given unchallenging assignments, and sensing that everyone in the school hates one another. After listening to her son's tirade, the mother comments that things are looking up in the schools. This is not a funny cartoon, not funny at all. Educators should certainly not glorify this kind of pop culture criticism. It is as bad as the teacher who on the first day of school hangs the sign, "Only 179 to go!" Not funny, not funny at all. (See related information in Chapter 2, "Rethinking the Role of Principal.")

Even folks who don't intend to rake schools over the coals often unknowingly give a negative message. I clipped an ad for a new school program produced by an electronics company. It suggested how groundbreaking and innovative school assignments could be if only our schools had high-tech equipment. According to the advertisement, children would no longer be rushing out the door at day's end but instead would sit spellbound, totally engaged in the new assignments. These new tasks, the ad suggests, would involve interviewing, editing videotapes, and even producing documentaries.

Just what do Madison Avenue advertisement folks think is happening in our schools? This description doesn't sound very groundbreaking to me. It sounds like the kind of wonderful scenes you might find in any hands-on, child-centered, inquiry-based, process classroom. One wonders what the public thinks is happening behind our red brick walls. Perhaps our exterior walls should be made of plate glass so that passersby could at least get a visual sense of what was happening in the schoolhouse on their block. Some day I'm going to hang a sign, in that outdoor display case, that simply says, "Congratulations New York City Public Schools!" I wonder if any neighbors would stop by to find out what warranted such a banner.

If they did, I'd show those curious neighbors around. They'd see that our students do spend big blocks of time exploring topics, interviewing experts, and creating polished, finished products. That's primarily what they do at school, all day long. They read about these topics, write about them, make field trips, do firsthand observations, and so on. They think and talk about them, wearing different hats and looking through different lenses. They are asked to analyze issues from the differing perspectives of the artist, mathematician, historian, and scientist. And alongside research in the library (we would never eliminate this scholarly act as the ad suggests), and despite our meager funds, our students have already learned to interview experts, handle camcorders, roleplay parts, and edit their work. And alongside writing research papers, our students choose to write columns for the school newsletter, skits to be performed by friends, letters to editors of real newspapers, speeches to be given to their classmates, as well as songs, poems, and picture books. That electric company has great public relations, advertisement campaigns, and great press. Public schools don't and that's a pity.

I have to admit that sometimes even people in the education field think it's okay to present educators in demeaning ways. Joanne once bought me a present sold at the exhibit hall of a literacy conference, not because she thought I'd love it, but because she knew I'd *hate* it. She knew that I would somehow go public and protest this object, a wall hanging labeled "Top Ten Reasons to Become a School Principal." Included on this list were such sarcastic comments as, "Daily visits from the 'BEST' students in the building." "Close personal relationships you form with 'concerned' parents,"

"Spend lots *more* time each day at your beloved school," and "Might have to work for a living otherwise." Lots of educators must be buying materials like this, otherwise they wouldn't continue being published. They're not funny. They're destructive, and they feed the public's belief that schools are wastelands filled with people who have it easy. (We've all heard the arguments that our day ends at three o'clock and we have summers off and lots of holidays as well!) I've been tempted to create my own wall-hanging proclaiming the real merits of being an elementary school principal. Mine would include such items as

- You get to know hundreds of children instead of only thirty.
- You get to be the first to open cartons of new books.
- Every year, dozens of kindergartners call you Mommy by mistake.
- You get cupcakes every day, lots of love letters, and your birthday feels really special.
- You get to throw out inconsequential mail and avoid wasting teachers' time.
- You get invited to lots of celebrations.
- You can read aloud your favorite book, over and over again, to lots of different classes.
- You can carve out time to paint, sing, snack, and build with blocks.
- You feel appreciated by hundreds of parents who entrust their children to you.
- You get to marvel at exquisite teaching and learning. (You have opportunities to *kvell*, as we say in New York.)

Now, as I near the end of this book, I must admit that I'm pleased to have written it. Above all, I think my story lays counterclaim to those critics who are so quick to condemn educators who are passionate about such important movements as whole language teaching, literature-based instruction, inquiry-based studies, and the process approach to reading and writing. I'm proud to let outsiders know that wonderful things are happening inside the public schools in which these approaches to teaching and learning have been thoughtfully considered, carefully implemented, and continuously reflected upon.

Raising Our Voices

When my children were younger, they attended Stuyvesant High School in Manhattan, an incredible public school filled with accomplished students and teachers. Each year the students would write original, clever musicals, and these "Sings" as they were called would be performed as a competition between the grades. The performers were always memorable, but so were the audiences. Whenever members of the audience detected a forthcoming song, they would call out, "Sing about it!" much to the delight and laughter of the packed auditorium. I have always loved the line "Sing about it!" because the invitation was always said with such gusto. Today when I think about the way the public and the media attack our public schools, I want to say to my colleagues all over this country, "Sing about it!"

I have been singing the praises of the Manhattan New School community throughout this book, and I'd like to encourage public school educators throughout the country to do likewise about their own school settings. Teachers, administrators, school board members, staff developers, librarians, student teachers, and all the other *informed* members of educational communities need to write books, send letters to the editor, open their schoolhouse doors to visitors, post Web sites, make calls to the local news stations, and speak out at town hall meetings.

One day at lunch, I heard Joanne say that she was tired of hearing about fat grams. "Enough!" she said. So too, I am tired of hearing negative stories about public schools. We all need to say, "Enough!" The public needs to understand the work we do. They also need to know that we do care about such "hot" topics as spelling, handwriting, grammar, punctuation, and yes, even phonics, but we know how to teach those things wisely and well without the use of deadly workbooks, boring textbooks, isolated skill and drill sheets, and watered-down and often inane basal reader stories. In a letter to my colleagues, I once urged them to write for publication. I wrote,

> I highly recommend to those of you who haven't attempted to write a book that you do so. It isn't that misery loves company, I actually do love writing. It isn't that I'm jealous of those of you who get to sleep late, have brunch with friends, read the books on your nightstand, or go off to Vermont to ski for a long weekend. (I actually wouldn't mind the first three, but I'd rather sign a contract to write six more books, each in a different language and genre, than do out-of-door stuff. My sports injuries amount to bumping my leg on the corner of a table while playing Scrabble.) And it certainly isn't that I think the royalties from professional books will help make payment on your loans, mortgages, tuition or bookstore bills. (Unless Woody Allen writes the screenplay, Quentin Tarantino directs it, and Kevin Bacon, Denzel Washington, and Michelle Pfeiffer star in it, the money probably won't be worth writing home about.) The reason I highly recommend you all begin to write about your professional lives, is that putting your thoughts and reflections on paper will really help you to stop and appreciate the work you are doing.

Several years ago, when there was talk of privatizing custodial services in the New York public schools, our custodian John sent me a note in which he said, "What bothers me about this situation is that people that have no idea about what's going on in the schools seem to be making decisions they know nothing about!! You have a flat on your car, you change the flat, you don't throw away the car." So too, people who know very little about what goes on in schools seem to be making wholesale judgments about public education. Just as you don't throw out a car if you have a flat tire, you don't bash all public schools because there is work to be done.

Now more than ever we need a deliberate and concerted effort to change the public's perception of what goes on inside the public schools of America. Now more than ever we need informed educators to speak out about ways they are improving their schools. They need to let the world know that public schools are alive and well. (I've gone so far as to have convinced our local pharmacist that when our parents come in to buy those special shampoos that get rid of head lice to be sure and tell them that there has been a run on these shampoos from private school parents as well. Head lice don't only crawl around in the hair strands of children attending public schools!) Mind you, I am no Pollyanna. I don't wear rose-colored glasses. I know there are problems in many public schools. But we don't solve those problems by sensationalizing them, by frightening parents about life in public schools, or by poking fun at public school educators. We don't get people working to preserve the future of public schools if they don't believe there is anything worth saving.

I was once asked to address the New York City School Volunteers at their end-of-the-year get together. In addition to thanking the volunteers for the hours they spend inside New York public schools, I asked a favor of the men and women assembled. I began,

> I'm delighted to have volunteers in our school, not only for the services you provide, but also for the stories I hope you tell your wives and husbands, sons and daughters, grandchildren, neighbors, friends, and colleagues. It's wonderful to have people from outside the profession spend regular hours in our schools and see firsthand what life is like inside a New York City public school. I know you are all witness to lots of tender moments and scenes of compassion, humor, and humanity, but I hope you are also sharing scenes of scholarship and hard work, rigor and high standards. Teaching children to read is not an act of magic. My colleagues and I have been studying literacy for many, many years and we are still puzzling over difficult issues. Making learning to read easier for a struggling child is complicated business. There are no quick-fix formulas. I hope you are telling stories about that hard work when you talk about volunteering in the public schools. We think of you all as our ambassadors, our very own public relations firm.

I want lots of people to know about the good things happening in our schools. I know that my cantankerous neighbors aren't likely to pick up this book, but with any luck an educator may put it into the hands of a friendly politician or two, or perhaps a journalist or media mogul. These influential people need to know that it's time to stop picking on us. We are doing our job. In fact, given the limited funds and the obstacles in our way, we are doing a heck of a job. They should not only stop picking on us, they should start helping us. If they stopped to think about their own educational family trees, I know most of our critics would have a public school to thank. A public school probably made it possible for their great-grandmother to learn English, their grandfather to learn a trade, their mother or father, son or daughter to get accepted into a fine university.

Instead of mocking us, our critics should be writing donation checks to honor the contributions these schools have made to the success of their families. (*The New*

York Times, in an article entitled, "Kofi Annan's Astonishing Facts," summarized the United Nations Human Development Report. It announced that "Americans spend $8 billion a year on cosmetics—$2 billion more than the estimated annual total needed to provide basic education for everyone in the world." Something is terribly wrong with this picture.)

Instead of mocking us, our critics should be joining forces with all the organizations dedicated to the preservation of public schools in America. They should be spending big blocks of time in schools across this nation, telling the real stories, not spreading the all too sorrowful stories based on short visits to a few schools in crisis.

The New York Times has a clever marketing campaign called "Support Education While You're on Vacation." Instead of canceling your newspaper subscription while you're out of town, you can arrange to have your newspaper delivered to a school. At first I thought this was a very admirable campaign. But then I realized that most folks take their vacation when schools are not in session. I want people to support education when they are *not* on vacation. I want that support fifty weeks out of the year rather than only two. That's why it is essential that educators sing the praises of their schoolhouses.

Saying Thank You

My invitation to "Sing about it," extends to parents as well. Parents understand clearly when their schools are doing a great job. The public needs to hear those voices in the national conversation about where public education is headed. The other day, I spotted a woman with a shopping bag emblazoned with the words, "The job of a citizen is to keep her mouth open." I couldn't agree more.

The wonderful writer Susan Cheever is a parent in our school. We're always grateful when she writes about us in her "Mothering" column for *Newsday*. Susan has written several complimentary articles about our school, with such telling titles as "A Public School with a Vision: Happiness," "The Limitations of Dick and Jane," and "A Perfect Perch: The School Yard." In another column, "A Reason to Love New York," Susan, in describing her decision to choose public over private school for her son, notes, "At public school, I knew my son would have career teachers, men and women who had cared enough about teaching to become certified and to continue their own education." In yet another column entitled, "Returning to School," Susan pays us the highest of compliments. She writes,

> My 7-year-old son goes to a public school in our Manhattan neighborhood, a wonderful school knit together by committed teachers and enthusiastic parents, and blessed with a principal who cares about books and teachers almost as much as she cares about children. My son loves school. He says he loves it because he likes to play with his friends, but he learned to read this year and this is his proudest accomplishment. In eight months he has

progressed from being stumped by the simplest words to being able to read himself a complicated story that interests him and makes him laugh. (His current favorite is Jon Scieska's "The True Story of the Three Little Pigs," by A. Wolf). He loves the teacher who taught him to read; he loves being able to look at words and see what they mean. Reading me a story at bedtime has become his favorite ritual of the day.

Most parents are not accomplished professional writers, of course, but they need not be. Over the years, I have received so many powerful letters from parents, first draft, handwritten notes that are worthy of publication. Perhaps parents need to begin their own pro-public school publication. This "Celebration Press," would let the public know that they are proud of their children and their children's teachers and their schools. I might begin such a publication with Laurel Eisenbruch's letter to the staff upon her son Adar's graduation (see Figure 8.3). Thankfully, her younger son Noah is still a student in our school.

Imagine your local politician reading an entire anthology of parent "love letters." How could they argue that we aren't meeting standards? Who better to judge our schools than the parents whose children attend them? Then too, our students can offer testimony themselves. Over the last several years, particularly at graduation, I receive written tributes from graduating seniors. One of these, from a student named Laura, included the following sentiment: "I can hardly find one extremely bad thing to keep me from loving this school like a parent. I have one hope currently: When I get older and have kids, I'll live in this city and be able to send them here to get the same type of experience and lesson in life." A collection of student tributes like this one would make quite a gift for our mayor.

In addition to wanting the world to know that our public schools are thriving, there are several other reasons I am now grateful for having seen this book to completion. I am hopeful that *Going Public* serves as a compliment to the profession as well as a very personal staff development tool I can offer my own colleagues. Perhaps, the teachers I know best will read it and say, "So that's what she's been thinking all these years." Principals should probably be required to put the story of their school on paper. The task makes you clarify what really matters in your professional life, helps you assess your needs and take pride in your colleagues and your accomplishments. Then too, I hope this book encourages a few aspiring teachers to actually become teachers, and inspires a few experienced teachers to dream the impossible dream and start a school of their own.

And finally, this book serves as a very personal way of saying thank you to the New York City public schools. Many city schools appear on my own educational family tree. When I look out at the sea of faces that fill our playground each morning, I can easily imagine my mother arriving from Poland and my father arriving from Cuba. I desperately want our school to do for students from Yugoslavia, the Dominican Republic, China, and some forty other countries, what the public schools of New York City did for my parents, for me, and for my own children.

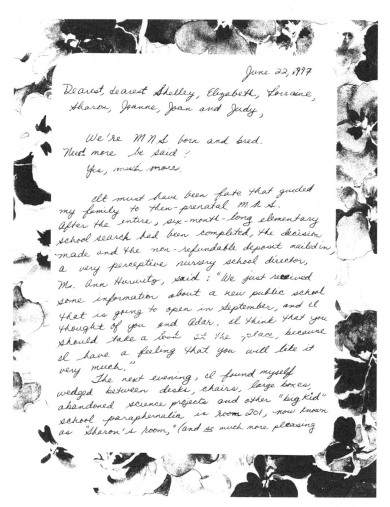

June 22, 1997

Dearest, dearest Shelley, Elizabeth, Lorraine, Sharon, Joanne, Joan and Judy,

  We're M N S born and bred. Need more be said? Yes, much more.

    It must have been fate that guided my family to then-prenatal M.N.S. After the entire, six-month-long elementary school search had been completed, the decision made and the non-refundable deposit nailed in, a very perceptive nursery school director, Ms. Ann Hurwitz, said: "We just received some information about a new public school that is going to open in September, and I thought of you and Adar. I think that you should take a look at the place, because I have a feeling that you will like it very much."
    The next evening, I found myself wedged between desks, chairs, large boxes, abandoned science projects and other "big kid" school paraphernalia in room 201, now known as "Sharon's room," (and so much more pleasing

Figure 8.3 (Continues)

to the eye and the mind!) I listened to Shirley and Joanne as they explained their views and experience of children and how they learn, and the vision that they had for this school-to-be. The only distraction for me was my inner voice saying excitedly, "This is it. This is it!"

So, this letter, although written to all of you, is in part my "thank you" to Ann Hurwitz!

It is also, however, the best way that I know of imparting to all of you (including those MNS staff members not mentioned by name) two things: a) my great appreciation for the six years of your immeasurable devotion, caring and work, from which Adar has benefitted so much, and b) the gut-level, most basic meaning that MNS has always had to us.

As I search for the words to describe what MNS signifies to us, beyond its being the site of my childrens' formal primary education, I'm forced to use words that cannot sufficiently relay my feelings. The best that I can do, nevertheless, is to tell you that M N S is our community, our haven, our family and our home. Aptly, these are the same words that Adar has used when telling me his feelings about MNS.

Although this is a sad time for Adar and me, I am so thankful for our having belonged to your community, and for every contribution that each of you has made to the formation of (let's forget about modesty!) a very fine person. How beautiful it is to have a child who does not know the concept of not wanting to go to school. How can I thank you for a gift as important as that??

As a school with special emphasis on reading and writing, I suppose (hope?!) that you and I have been compatible: I write notes (yes, very frequently) and you willingly read them! I her by bestow upon each of you the Most Patient Reader of Concerned Parents' Notes Award. I am appreciative! (Most of you may have "Round Two" still ahead; I'll try to be very kind!)

Please know that you can consider Adar a ready, willing and able volunteer when you have any need for assistance. At this point, he can't bear to imagine losing contact.

This is (almost) the last note from me for a few months. Relax and enjoy your well-deserved vacations!

With love,
Laurel

Figure 8.3, *Continued*

APPENDICES

CHAPTER 7

Daily Log
Registro Diario

DATE _____
La Fecha

Staff Members Absent/Substitute:
Ausencias de los Maestros/substitutos:

Reminders/Announcements:
Acuerdense de . . . /anuncios:

Staff Development Opportunities:
Oportunidades de desarrollo para nuestros maestros:

Schedule Changes:
Cambios al programa:

Use of Ballroom:
Uso del salon de baile:

Visitors:
Visitas:

Trips:
Excursiones:

APPENDIX 2

Interviewing Questionnaire

This worksheet may be used by administrators, teachers, parents, and any other committee members who are in a position to interview potential candidates for teaching positions in your school. Sample questions are included as well as space for taking notes on the candidates responses.

Name of candidate _____

- If colleagues were visiting your classroom, how would you facilitate their learning?

- How would you plan for an inquiry-based social studies course of study?

- Who are your mentors and what have you learned from them?

- How would you launch a writing workshop?

- How would you organize a classroom library?

- How do you assess your own professional growth and the growth of your students?

- What are you currently reading for your own pleasure and for your professional growth, and what are you reading to your students?

Interested in Making Your School More Beautiful?
Have a Conversation About . . .

Choosing decorative "stuff" that contains people's stories

Framing surprising things

Using collections to add drama

Adding unifying threads

Eliminating eyesores

Aligning design with purpose

Creating literary artworks

Highlighting architectural features

Choosing surprising colors

APPENDIX 4

Does Your School Need a Housekeeping Conversation?

List Your Pet Peeves Here

(Examples:)

Chairs remain upside down on tabletops after start of day

Common areas are being used as attics

List Possible Solutions Here

Assign monitor to check that all chairs are uprighted.

Ask custodian about basement storage possibilities

Personnel concerns regarding housekeeping

Additional tools or materials needed to support housekeeping

Additional school structures, rituals, or activities that would promote housekeeping

Additional ways to involve students in housekeeping responsibilities

Students' Sense of Teacher's Priorities

Name of Student _____

Name of Teacher _____

How important do you think these things are to your teacher?

1=Very important
2=Sort of Important
3=Not that Important

(There are blank spaces for teachers to add additional items)

_____A beautiful room

_____Neatness

_____Finishing what you start

_____Being a fast reader

_____Being organized

_____Respecting what other people have to say

_____Reading in the company of other people

_____Your grade on a test or quiz

_____Having favorite authors

_____Sharing your thinking with classmates

_____

_____

_____

Choose at least 3 things from the list to write comments about on the back of this sheet.

This worksheet is based on the work of Joanne Hindley Salch and Shelley Harwayne at the Manhattan New School.

APPENDIX 6

How Well Do You Know Your Colleagues?

Your name _____   Name of your colleague _____

Rank your colleague according to the following descriptors using the numbers described below:

Number 1=Very important
Number 2=Sort of important
Number 3=Not that important

_____Art and music woven into everyday life

_____Making every minute count

_____Finishing what he/she starts

_____Working closely with parents

_____Having a beautiful classroom

_____Reading aloud across the genres

_____Editing and publishing student work

_____Visiting in colleagues' classrooms

_____Speaking compassionately to students and parents

_____Being gracious to visitors

_____Listening respectfully to colleagues

_____Taking care of his/her own reading and writing

_____Being respectful of school property and common areas

_____Helping students appreciate their community

_____Newspaper reading and other lifelong literate acts

_____Having students perform community service

Share your rankings with your colleagues. How well do you know one another?

Create another list of descriptors custom-designed for your community.

What Do Teachers Need?

Please comment on each factor and then add your own personal necessities.

Compliments

Tranquility

Respect for Differences

Professional Colleagues

Scholarly Lives

Higher Salaries

Supportive and Informed Principals

Big Blocks of Uninterrupted Time

Which needs can we provide for one another? How do we accomplish those? Which require political action? How do we accomplish those?

APPENDIX 8

Additional Formal Teacher Observations.

1.

Dear Kevin,

What fun to observe your teaching on a holiday—the hundredth-day-of-school celebration. I've only seen this acknowledged by kindergarten children and their teachers. The third graders' faces and the goodies they brought in reminded me that the event is probably worth some schoolwide attention.

When I arrived the children were gathered in the meeting area to share how they solved their math homework problems. As usual, the tone in your room is quiet and nurturing. The children always appear attentive and interested in their learning. The incredibly beautiful artwork—the African mural and the stained glass window—also speak of the pride the children have in themselves and their work.

Brian began by reading aloud the math problem. Mattie then explained her process of solving the problem. You then asked the class, "What did you use to solve the problem?" Jennifer responded, "I used things. I put them on plates. I counted . . . " "Hold on," you interrupted, asking the rest of the class, "Did you hear what Jennifer did?" "Jennifer," you continued, "how did you know to do that?" Jennifer answered, "Cause the problem said so." You then probed Jennifer's understanding of the problem.

Other children shared their strategies. Holly drew pictures.

William added, "Since I already knew that $9 \times 3 = 27$, I just subtracted. I used my prior knowledge." Your response to all the children made them proud of their strategies. It's also clear that you have spent a great deal of time thinking about the language of mathematics. You also frequently took on the mentor role, stating, "That sometimes happens to me . . . "

It was lovely to hear you connect the writing process to that of solving math problems. "It's the same thing we talk about in writing at the end of a piece. What do we have to do to make sure it's A-O.K.? Yes, look it over, reread it. Reread it like it's the first time you ever read it."

Your students are eager to share their thinking processes and they are very attentive to one another. I noticed how conscious you are of any moment of non attention. "Nadia, did you hear what was said?" "Jesse and Stefan, stop that." "Esther, did the problem catch you?" You even reminded children that when they went off to work on their research groups to be aware of children who are inattentive. "If someone in the group is in a wandering mood," you suggested, "lasso them in!" It's clear you do not let any students fall through the cracks.

I was particularly moved when Esther explained she was having difficulty with the math problem and Bianca added, "Yeah, Esther told me on the car ride to school this morning that she needs to work on that." How wonderful that you students willingly talk about math in their free time.

At the end of the math homework check, you reminded students how to check on their group research reports if they were finished. Students then went off to work on their projects, with topics ranging from Georgia O'Keefe to various African inquiries.

Thanks again for a lovely visit. It's clear that you are a wonderful addition to the Manhattan New School family. I hope your colleagues will visit during math time and you will find ways to visit them during any curriculum area you would like to study. Do let me know how I can help arrange such intervisitations, as well as your participation in any scholarly study groups.

Sincerely,

Shelley

2.

Dear Regina,

Whenever I spend time in your classroom, I walk out wishing I had even more time to learn alongside you. It is an absolute joy to watch you in your first year as a classroom teacher in our school. I'm delighted that you have brought your great strengths as a teacher of science to your ever-curious-about-the-world second graders. It is also evident that you are now a graduate student at Bank Street. Your room is full of literature, projects, and busy hands.

There is so much to marvel at. Everywhere I look there were centers of interest, as intriguing for adults as for children. I was fascinated by the Women Make History wall, the recycling information, and the menagerie of hamsters, crickets, and iguanas.

Of course, none of these centers would be put to good use if you hadn't worked so hard on building community. The children care about you, each other, their animals, their school and world community. They've learned a great deal from your kindness and compassion. The room feels and sounds like a room where Regina and company live.

When I entered on Tuesday morning, Zara had just announced a "Poetry Break" by holding up a large sign. The children paid great attention to their classmate as she recited an original poem, "Little Mouse." Meeting time began, and Rehan led the share meeting. You guaranteed a successful one when you reminded the audience how to respond with respect and reminded the young writer to read his piece in his loudest voice. Rehan read a narrative about having a playdate with Salman. I was struck by how well you know your children's lives outside of school. You responded to Rehan, "That's your second playdate with Salman, isn't it?" After the children responded kindly to Rehan, you asked him, "Is this your best? What would you rate it?" It is clear that self-evaluation, the most important kind, is woven into all you do.

Share meeting in your room is not just for writing; it is for reading. Next, Rehan read from a question-answer book. He asked, "What is Lightning,?" which led to some lively discussion and much learning. The children's responses included, "thunder," "electricity," and "God's gift."

I was particularly struck with the sense of ritual in your classroom. From the poetry-break, to the share meeting routines, the children feel secure because they understand how the room runs and they know what to expect. I also loved the class chart on, "Look at all the places we've visited in our reading." Byron responded that day letting the class know that his story took place in Japan, California, and the Pacific Ocean.

Your teaching is engaging, so full of surprises. I enjoyed learning that Friday would be, "No Electricity Day." I was intrigued by your old suitcase time capsule that sits atop a cupboard. I loved watching the children's faces when you dismissed them by announcing, "If you have 2+2 letters in your first name, line-up, 2+5, 10+2, etc." Every minute counts in your classroom.

My only regret, Regina, is that your important commitment to Bank Street makes it impossible for you to participate in most Wednesday afternoon staff meetings. I look forward to the time when you will be able to be an active member of our own adult learning community. For now, I intend to visit more often and encourage our colleagues to join me.

We still have a breakfast date to keep. With respect for the had work you do.

Sincerely,

Shelley

APPENDIX 9

Rethinking School's Social Tone

Please comment on each item, thinking through your school's strengths and weaknesses.

A curriculum that supports a caring social tone

A careful use of language

Literature valued as a humanizing tool

Gracious invitations for all to participate and share their gifts

Moments of hearty laughter

Schoolwide, multigrade gatherings

Frequent celebrations

Are there additional factors that contribute to your school's supportive social tone?

Are there factors that get in the way of a supportive social tone?

How can you begin to remove these obstacles?

PROMOTING MULTIGRADE MOMENTS

Do your students have opportunities to . . . ?

- Serve as guest speakers in one another's classrooms.
- Share books and other materials from one another's classrooms.
- Serve as interview resources for one another.
- Join one another's reader-response groups.
- Take part in one another's math workshops.
- Read to children in different classes.
- Share their writing with new audiences.
- Teach one another how to keep writer's notebooks.
- Make teaching appointments to share areas of expertise.
- Serve as tutors for one another.
- Read the same school anthologies and perform poetry together.
- Sing together in the school chorus.
- Perform together in the school orchestra.
- Serve as translators for one another.
- Go on field trips together.
- Visit siblings' writing workshops.
- Serve on the student council together.
- Join clubs across grade levels, playing chess, talking baseball, etc.
- Travel on the school buses together.
- Attend after-school programs together.
- Play in the yards together.
- Attend English as a second language and resource room classes together.
- Offer computer guidance to friends of many ages.
- Perform community service alongside older and younger children.
- Participate in joint workshops with other whole classes.
- Spend time in classrooms engaged in similar content studies.

Add Additional Opportunities Unique to Your School

What You'd Like Them to Understand About

What you'd like them to understand about	Publishing	Notebooks	Assessment	Drawing	Recordkeeping
Students					
Parents					
Administrators					
Colleagues					

What you'd like them to understand about	Genres	Grammar	Good Writing	Handwriting	Literature
Students					
Parents					
Administrators					
Colleagues					

What you'd like them to understand about	Topic Choice	Spelling	Conferring	Punctuation	Sharing
Students					
Parents					
Administrators					
Colleagues					

Manhattan New School Newsletter:
Summer & Autumn Wishlist

DIRECTOR'S VOICE

Dear families,

It's hard to believe that in just a few weeks we will be wishing one another a happy summer. The children are beginning to talk about day camps and sleepaways, family vacations and visits to grandma.

My summer plans sound almost too hectic to be true. They include Australia, England, Sweden, and a few stops in the U.S.A.

For this last column of the year, I've jotted down my summer wish list for our students, followed by a playful autumn one. When we return in the fall, we will have the additional space needed to make our school dreams come true. The autumn list hints at some of the possibilities.

SUMMER WISH LIST
FOR MNS CHILDREN

1. Your local librarian calls you by your first name and can't help but remember the kind of books you love.

2. You run out of pages in your writer's notebook and have to search for just the right new one.

3. You visit lots of zoos, parks, museums, and beaches and you ask lots of hard questions.

4. Your markers begin to run out, your crayon points become blunt, and you start to empty that drawer filled with scrap paper.

5. You find one new author to admire and you read all the books you can find.

6. You find a few minutes to send postcards or letters to classmates, teachers, or to me.

7. You stare at the stars, the clouds, the waves, and the flowers and you ask lots of tough questions.

8. You listen to lots of good music and you sing and dance along joyfully.

9. You memorize a few favorite poems so you can recite them to us in the fall.

10. You find a good friend to spend long hours playing checkers, chess, or scrabble; playing house or playing school; setting up lemonade stands, putting on backyard or front-stoop shows, telling stories, inventing games, giggling at jokes.

11. You pay close attention to fireflies, ladybugs and caterpillars and yes, you ask lots of real important questions.

12. You pack a good book and some paper and pencil into your camp trunks, vacation suitcases, beach bags, and picnic baskets.

13. You watch a few baseball games, root for the Yankees, and get ready to watch them play in the World Series.

14. You return to school happy and healthy and filled with the joys of childhood.

AUTUMN WISH LIST
FOR MNS CHILDREN

1. You'll paint murals everywhere, even on our front door.

2. You'll work on long-term projects in our little block room.

3. You'll develop photographs in our very own dark room.

4. You'll paint, sketch, collage, sculpt, and make prints, in our art studio.

5. You'll experiment in our own science lab.

6. You'll climb, run and make-believe in our new playgrounds.

7. You'll perform on the stage of our full-time auditorium.

8. You'll read in cozy reading rooms throughout the building.

9. You'll have a regular meeting room for clubs- cooking, print-making, pottery, computer, arts & crafts, etc.

10. You'll plant flowers in windowboxes and backyard gardens.

11. You'll work on computers throughout the building.

12. And yes, you'll arrive by 8:40 and be picked up by 3:00.

With Love,
Shelley

Handwriting Letter to Families

Manhattan New School
311 E. 82nd Street
New York, NY 10028

Dear Families,

Neat and legible handwriting is important for many reasons. It helps the writer to read what he or she has written. It helps the reader get the message the writer is sending.

Legible handwriting is honored in our school. We spend time talking with children about correct letter formation. We talk about the quickest way to form letters and words. We watch as children grasp a pencil and comment on their grip. Holding a pencil in the standard way helps many children to form their letters easily.

The best way to teach handwriting is on an individual basis. In this way the writer can get immediate feedback on his or her work and if necessary, corrections can be made. In school, handwriting is worked on individually and in small groups. In order to support this work handwriting sheets will be sent home weekly. This homework is required for all first graders. However, some of the kindergarten students may find it taxing. It is not my intention for homework to become "homewar." If your kindergarten child balks at this work, please don't press it. Send me a note and I'll help out in whatever way I can.

As you help your child complete the sheets, encourage him or her to use the complete space. Uppercase or big letters should touch the top and bottom lines. Many lowercase or small letters start at the middle line. In school we will use the words vertical and horizontal to describe how the pencil moves. We will also use the words clockwise and counterclockwise to describe the round letters.

Working together, we can help the children concentrate on this aspect of our curriculum.

Thank you for your help,

Sincerely,

Pam

APPENDIX 14

Joanne Hindley Salch's Letter to Families
About Children's Work Habits

Dear Families,

It's that time of year again in third grade. I can almost set my clock by its occurrence. I call it the "good enough" disease that seems to attack most 8 and 9 year olds in February. Disappearing are the days of "I need to try and do my best" and appearing are the days of "As long as I've put something down on paper it's 'good enough'.

The symptoms include:

- *a sudden backslide in neatness and organization of schoolwork*
- *an incredibly strong desire to be the "first one" done regardless of the quality of work*
- *an increased occurrence of "I can't find it" and "I forgot to do it"*

Sound at all familiar? The good news is that with some guidance and support from both you and I, the cure rate is generally 100% and takes place rather quickly.

In school, I am returning to a slower paced pack up in the afternoon, including going over the homework sheet together. We also had (and will continue to have) some lengthy conversations about the above issues.

For your part, I'm asking you to please do two things:

One is to resume (if you've stopped), looking over your child's homework sheet of assignments each and every evening after he/she has completed the work. Simple questions such as those listed below are great for opening up conversation about homework, and are also a way of checking to make sure that everything has been completed:

- *Did you finish reading and fill out your log? May I see what you've recorded?*
- *Is the entry in your writers notebook at least one full page long? or How much did you get done on your writing project this evening? Please let me see what you're working on...*
- *Did you solve your math problems carefully? Which one did you find to be the most challenging? Please show me what you did.*
- *Did you collect new words for the spelling pattern? Or, Are we supposed to study any spelling words together this evening?*
- *Do you have any homework due tomorrow for your specialist teacher (i.e. Spanish or science)?*

Please don't hesitate to ask your child to redo any assignment that you feel doesn't show they have applied their best effort.

My second "at home" request is that your child packs his/her knapsack in the evening after their work is completed and not to wait and do it in the morning. This may sound like a minor thing, but I've found that it does help many children who tend to be "scattered" or inconsistent in getting everything together.

As always, I thank you for all your help. If you've found any (or all!) of the above issues to really be of concern to you regarding your child, please be sure to bring it up at our parent-teacher conference which will take place in a couple of weeks.
And let's be optimistic - you may even have noticed an improvement by then!

Thanks again,

Joanne

Pam Mayer's Classroom Newsletter

News From Pam:

Mayaguez Children's Library
We've already sent 2 boxes filled with books to Puerto Rico. I mailed a letter explaining our plan to Esther Castro, the librarian. I'll keep you informed if she writes back. We found out that there is a library rate that is significantly lower than a regular mailing rate. (The library rate is even better than the book rate.) Thanks to all of you who so generously signed up to mail a box of books. There is a sign-up sheet outside the classroom.

Do you have books at home that you'd like to donate to the Mayagüez Children's Library? If so, bring them to school and I'll pack them up.

K-206 Yearbook
Kathy Powell, our computer staff developer, plans to help us with an end-of-the year yearbook. It's not too early to start putting it together! We need volunteers to be on the yearbook committee. We need help with:
- Desktop publishing (layout & design)
- Digital camera pictures
- Scanning pictures
- Typing
- Making color copies (when yearbook is finished)
- Book binding (when yearbook is finished)

If you're not familiar with the technology involved, Kathy will teach you! Kathy and I meet most Tuesdays from 1:05-1:50. Please let me know if you're available to join us on Tuesday, 3/17 to begin work. Thanks!

K-206 Auction Items
We plan to make several items to be bid on at the auction on March 20th. Several families will come in and help during centertime so that we'll have some creations to be auctioned off. Joni and Tracey bought an unfinished chair and step stool that the children will paint. We also plan to paint a pasta dish from *Our Name Is Mud*. Please have your child wear casual painting clothes tomorrow. If you'd like to help, let Joni, Tracey or me know so that we can organize the activities. There was a letter that went home yesterday about the raffle to win a playdate with a teacher. Mine will be custom made. If your name is pulled, your child and I will decide on just the right date.

Dell Computer
Do you have experience with Windows 95? Our Dell computer is now hooked up and ready to go! Please let me know if you'd like to come in to work with a small group of children on our new Dell. It's new to me, so I'd like to learn too! Does anyone have an old sheet to donate as a computer cover?

Sincerely,

Pam

Pam Mayer

A Few Poems from Poetry Folder for Parents

Richard Margolis's "All My Hats," in *Secrets of a Small Brother* (Macmillan, 1984).

Barbara Howe's "Early Supper," in Helen Hill and Agnes Perkins's *New Coasts & Strange Harbors: Discovering Poems* (Hill, Perkins, Crowell, 1974).

Ann Turner's "Here It Is," in *Street Talk* (Houghton Mifflin, 1986).

Gary Soto's "Teaching Numbers," in *A Fire In My Hands* (Scholastic, 1989).

Barbara Esbensen's "The Visit," in *Who Shrank My Grandmother's House?: Poems of Discovery* (HarperCollins, 1992).

Daisy Zamora's "Canto de Esperanza" in *IXOK AMAR GO: Central American Women's Poetry for Peace* (Granite Press, 1987).

David Chin's "Sleeping Father," in Liz Rosenberg's *The Invisible Ladder* (Henry Holt, 1996).

Myra Cohn Livingston's "Growing: For Louis" in Lee Bennett Hopkins and Misha Arenstein's *Potato Chips and a Slice of the Moon* (Scholastic, 1976).

John Ciardi's "All I Did Was Ask My Sister A Question," in Isabel Joshlin Glaser's *Dreams of Glory: Poems Starring Girls* (Atheneum, 1995).

Paul B. Janeczko"s "How to Hug Your Three-Year-Old Daughter," in Paul B. Janeczko and Naomi Shihab Nye's *I feel a Little Jumpy Around You: A Book of Her Poems & His Poems Collected in Pairs* (Simon & Schuster, 1996).

Gwendolyn Brooks's "A Welcome Song for Laini Nzinga" in Susanna Steele and Morag Styles's *Mother Gave A Shout* (Volcano Press, 1991).

Constance Levy's "Color the Tiger," in *When Whales Exhale and Other Poems* (Margaret K. McElderry Books, 1996).

William Trowbridge's "Taking My Son to Kindergarten," in Naomi Nye's *What Have You Lost?* (Greenwillow, 1999).

Roger Jones's "First Grade," in Naomi Nye's *What Have You Lost?* (Greenwillow, 1999).

Carl Sandburg's "Arithmetic," in Stephen Dunning, Edward Luedeer, and Hugh Smith's *Reflections on a Gift of Watermelon Pickle . . . And Other Modern Verse* (Scott, Foresman and Company, 1966).

Arlene Mandell's "Little Girl Grown," reprinted in Shelley Harwayne's *Lasting Impressions: Weaving Literature into the Writing Workshop*, Heinemann, 1992).

PTA Donation Letter

Dear Friends,

As visitors leave, after having spent a jam-packed morning at the Manhattan New School, they often ask Shelley, teachers, or a member of the P.T.A. what they can offer as a way of saying thank you to the children and teachers of our school. Guests, I suppose, enjoy surprising their hosts with a treat.

As you know, ours is a public school, so we can not charge any fees for coursework, observation, or study here. Instead, we can only accept donations. We have, therefore, compiled the following list of frequently needed items, if you would like to make contributions to our community.

Know, that fortunately we are well endowed with books, so these do not appear on our list.

***   ***   ***   ***   ***   ***   ***   ***   ***   ***   ***   ***

Polaroid film   postage stamps
plants   Xerox paper
slide film   coffee
blank notebooks   paper cups
markers   paper napkins
blank notecards

Thanks,

Members of the P.T.A.

APPENDIX 18

Be a Buddy to a New MNS Family!!

As the Manhattan New School continues to grow, we believe we can still maintain that strong sense of community that attracted so many of us to our school. To make this possible, we thought it would be a lovely idea for our "old" families to volunteer to be buddies to our incoming students and their families, particularly those who enter the school after kindergarten. As a buddy, you might meet your assigned family at school events, introduce them around, answer their many questions about their new school environment, and simply be a friend! Who knows what great friendships might develop!!

If you'd like to volunteer for this "act of kindness," please fill out the form below and return it in an envelope marked "PTA" to your child's classroom teacher. If you have any questions or suggestions, please call me at _____.

Thanks,

_____

Name_____ Child's Name_____

Child's Class and Teacher _____

Your telephone number _____

Content Area Survey

1. What big topics do you expect to study this year? What are you currently studying?

2. How are your students involved in choice of topics to be studied?

3. How much time peer week can you imagine devoting to such studies?

4. Will you integrate your content studies into your regularly scheduled meeting times, reading and writing workshops, reading-aloud times, or work on content studies apart from these daily rituals?

5. What kinds of instructional materials do you need to support these content studies?

6. Are you working alongside any colleagues? Are you planning to invite our specialists in on the studies? (In other words, is there a place for art, music physical education, science, or Spanish to enrich these studies?)

7. Do you need help in tapping family and wider community resources?

8. What kind of literature would support your work?

9. Will your students also have time to take part in individual and personal inquiry projects? Will the same instructional supports be present?

10. How might your students share their discoveries with the whole school community?

APPENDIX 20

Status of the Staff
Colleague letter

Dear Colleagues,
Please take a few minutes to jot down brief descriptions of your approaches to the follow-ing classroom practices. We will do a quick "status of the staff" when we share these re-sponses at our next staff meeting. I think the range of responses will help us to learn from one another's unique ways of doing things and inspire people to drop in on one another's classrooms more frequently. I've tried to include issues that we rarely talk about. Let me know if you'd like to include others.

Thanks in advance.
Shelley

Morning Meeting
(Include your procedures, rituals, or routines as well as any ways of working that you think your colleagues probably aren't aware of or ideas you are thinking of implement-ing. You might also refer to your manner of announcing the day's agenda).

Homework
(Include selection procedures, methods of distributing, systems for checking, range of subjects, any resources used, and/or attach samples).

Methods for Getting Whole Group's Attention

Methods for Making Transitions Smoother

Handwriting Instruction
(including resources used, frequency of instruction, materials, etc.)

Use of Portfolios
(Include any individual classroom uses as well as use of schoolwide portfolio)

Methods for Handling Disciplinary Issues
(In other words, when children engage in inappropriate acts, what are the main ways you handle these situations?)

Yearly Schoolwide Portfolio Tasks

Below are a few challenges that can be offered throughout the grades and repeated each year. Imagine graduating from elementary school with six attempts at the following:

- Prepare a self-portrait.
- Create a pattern.
- List all the people who work in our school, their names and jobs.
- Draw or write about what you want to be when you grow up.
- Present the alphabet in a beautiful way.
- Record the name of your city, state, and country.
- List the names of all the states you know.
- Write the words to a song or poem you know by heart.
- Draw a floor plan of your classroom.
- Make a map of the school.
- Make a list of favorites-(authors, colors, television shows, movies, desserts, breakfast foods, poets, toys, musical instruments, and places in the world).
- Offer suggestions to improve your school.

Other possible tasks include:

APPENDIX 22

Quotes to Ponder at Staff Get-Togethers

1. "All the classroom methods we appreciate—process reading and writing, inquiry-based studies, reader-response opportunities, real-world problem solving—all these add up to raising activists."

2. "I disagree with those textbooks on administration that suggest that the teacher's main area of concern is the classroom and the principal's is the school at large. No, we both need two lenses in our cameras, the wide angle and the zoom. Schools become better places when all of us can step back and see the big picture and pull in close to do the nitty-gritty work."

3. A quote from a church wall in Sussex, England—"A vision without a struggle is only a dream. Works and deeds without a vision are mere labor. A vision and action together bring hope to the world." These are words for educators to live by.

4. "When you know people's stories, they become a well to draw from."

5. "Principals, heads of schools, can't be the kind of "grandparents" who are only there for the birthday cupcakes and the holiday celebrations. They also need to be the kind of grandparents who are willing to stay up all night with the feverish child."

6. "In New York, when you buy a dozen bagels, you get one free. I think the same principle should apply to our schools. For every twelve teachers, you get one free."

7. "Isabel Beaton likes to think of our school as a garden in which each teacher is given an individual plot of land. Teachers are not handed an overall design and then assigned little jobs in order to achieve a predetermined effect. Instead, she believes, all the teachers are invited to create very individual gardens. What adds wholeness to our setting is that all of us are gazing in the same direction. We have shared beliefs, much as all committed gardeners put their trust in the soil, the sunshine, and abundant rain showers."

8. "I once heard a radio commercial for Mercedes-Benz. The announcer was listing oxymorons, including student teacher. He couldn't have been more wrong. Aren't we all students and teachers at the same time? And if we are not, shouldn't we aim for this noble goal?"

9. "If children are to believe that they belong not only to a class but to a school and a community, we have to live our lives accordingly."

10. "I learned a long time ago that it doesn't matter what curriculum decisions we make, what instructional strategies we try, or what assessment tools we select, if students and teachers don't care about each other. So too, it doesn't matter how brilliant our mini-lessons are or how clever our conferences are

if children make fun of each other's handwriting, dialect, or choice of topic. These things don't matter at all if the really important stuff isn't in place."

11. "When our school first opened, I suggested that teachers imagine that every-thing that they say to their students is somehow broadcast throughout the entire building on a public-address system. 'We shouldn't say anything, in any tone, that would embarrass us if our colleagues overheard,' I added . . .We transform schools when we carefully watch how we talk <u>to</u> and <u>about</u> students, parents, and our colleagues.

12. "Curriculum decisions need to be made by the people whose lives are touched by those decisions."

13. "When my colleagues ask me if I think a certain topic is worthy of a big block of time for individual, small group, whole-class or schoolwide study, I sug-gest they ask themselves two broad questions. First, 'Will this study help students see the richness of their world?' Secondly, 'Will this study provide students with opportunities to use their literacies and talents to improve the quality of their world?'"

14. "We can list page upon page of standards and create rubrics to accompany them, but without the best practices taking place in classrooms, the work will be in vain."

15. "I am privileged to work in a district that does not ask principals to get good at paperwork but expects principals to get good at teaching. And that makes all the difference in the world."

APPENDIX 23

Reader Response Sheet: What Really Matters at the Manhattan New School

1. Having a beautiful setting

2. Watching our language

3. Trusting one another

4. Seeing the walls tumble down between school and community

5. Viewing second language as a strength, not a weakness

6. Helping children see the richness of their lives

7. Helping children use their literacies to improve the quality of their lives

8. Valuing big blocks of time

9. Placing literature at the heart of all we do

10. Knowing one another's names and stories

11. Believing in the importance of trading places

12. Keeping a supportive social tone on the front burner

13. Offering real tasks/providing real-world pay-off

14. Loving school

15. Honoring rigorous scholarly teaching and learning

Readers can suggest evidence of the above priorities from the text as well as from their own professional experiences

Learning to Say Difficult Things in Acceptable Ways

The following schoolhouse scenarios would all result in members of a school community having to have difficult conversations. All are based on priorities presented throughout this book and can be used as conversation starters or role-plays at staff meetings, network gatherings or courses in administration, reform or teacher mentoring. To really help members of a school community walk a mile in one another's shoes, it would be beneficial if people chose roles that they ordinarily don't find themselves in. In other words, principals might role-plaly teachers and teachers might role-play administrators.

1. You notice that an empty water cooler jug that the third graders have been using to collect a million pennies in is being treated disrespectfully. People have tossed broken pencils and soiled tissues into the narrow opening. You call a schoolwide meeting to address the students.

2. A few students reveal that their families have bought commercially prepared skill and drill phonics kits. You are about to speak to family members at a curriculum meeting.

3. Your principal has just hung a new hall display. Unfortunately, you notice glaring spelling errors in the writing.

4. Some children in your new class seem overly interested in reading poorly written, formulaic books, the kind you might see on sale in a supermarket check-out line. They explain that they were allowed to bring these in for independent reading all last year. You want to discuss better literature choices with your students as well as chat with their last year's teacher.

5. Some teachers forget to be good listeners at staff meetings and engage in sideline conversations. You are determined to speak to them privately.

6. A student tells you that a volunteer has screamed "Shut up!" to a noisy crowd in the cafeteria. You want to be sure this never happens again.

7. When you visit your colleague's classroom you sense that many of the students are choosing books that are too difficult for them. You'd like to help.

8. The teacher next door is beginning to store unsightly items in the hallway near your classroom door. You'd like to eliminate this eyesore.

9. You have been encouraging your students to use their "indoor voices," and not to talk across the classroom, but rather walk over to the person they are addressing. Your principal does just the opposite, speaking in a booming voice and calling across the classroom.

APPENDIX 25

Bibliography of Book Club Choices

Books I've been reading in various book clubs over the last eight years:

Felicia's Journey, William Trevor

Nobody's Fool, Richard Russo

Ellen Foster, Kaye Gibbons

All the Pretty Horses, Cormac McCarthy

Like Water for Chocolate, Laura Esquivel

Time and Again, Jack Finney

From Time to Time, Jack Finney

Fried Green Tomatoes at the Whistle Stop Café, Fannie Flagg

The Book of Ruth, Jane Hamilton

Murther and Walking Spirits, Robertson Davies

The Great World, David Malouf

Body and Soul, Frank Conroy

A Thousand Acres, Jane Smiley

Mao II, Don Delillo

Crossing to Safety, Wallace Stegner

Angle of Repose, Wallace Stegner

Pigs in Heaven, Barbara Kingsolver

Miss Smilla's Sense of Snow, Peter Hoeg

Tales of the City, Armistad Maupin

Stones from the River, Ursula Heggi

Picturing Will, Ann Beattie

Angela's Ashes, Frank McCourt

Snow in August, Pete Hamill

Corelli's Mandolin, Louis De Bernieres

Love, Again, Doris Lessing

Divine Secrets of the Ya-Ya Sisterhood, Rebecca Wells

Little Altars Everywhere, Rebecca Wells

The English Patient, Michael Ondaatje

The Shipping News, E. Annie Proulx

The Sweet Hereafter, Russell Banks

Rule of the Bone, Russell Banks

Hotel DuLac, Anita Brookner

Dead Man Walking, Sister, Helen Prejean

Seeing Calvin Coolidge in a Dream, John Derbyshire

An Italian Education, Tim Parks

Mrs. Ted Bliss, Stanley Elkin

Sabbath's Theater, Philip Roth

In the Time of the Butterflies, Julia Alvarez

A Patchwork Planet, Anne Tyler

Ladder of Years, Anne Tyler

The Stone Diaries, Carol Shields

Happenstance, Carol Shields

Small Ceremonies, Carol Shields

Swann, Carol Shields

Snow Falling on Cedars, David Guterson

The Romance Reader, Pearl Abraham

The Wedding, Dorothy West

Cold Mountain, Charles Frazier

The Color of Water, James McBride

The Debt to Pleasure, John Lanchester

Naked, David Sedaris

Black and Blue, Anna Quindlen

Memoirs of a Geisha, Arthur Golden

The Giant's House, Elizabeth McCracken

A Gracious Plenty, Sheri Reynolds

The Rapture of Canaan, Sheri Reynolds

The God of Small Things, Arundhati Roy

Midnight in the Garden of Good and Evil, John Berendt

Fugitive Pieces, Anne Michaels

Into Thin Air, Jon Krakauer

Margaret Atwood, Alias Grace

Reading in the Dark, Seamus Deane

Lady with a Laptop, D. M. Thomas

The White Hotel, D. M. Thomas

Walking on Walnuts, Nancy Ring

A Widow for One Year, John Irving

Paradise, Toni Morrison

Blue Glass, Sandra Tyler

The Bone People, Keri Hulme
The Sixteen Pleasures, Robert Hellenga
The Riders, Tim Winton
Oscar and Lucinda, Peter Carey
Martin Dressler, Steven Millhauser
Echo House, Ward Just
Here on Earth, Alice Hoffman
So Long, See You Tomorrow, William
    Maxwell
A Year in Provence, Peter Mayle
Cave Dwellers, Dorothy Allison
Cloud Chamber, Michael Dorris

Dreams of My Russian Summers, Andrei
    Makine
Charming Billly, Alice McDermott
Fall on Your Knees, Ann-Marie
    MacDonald
Four Letters of Love, Niall Williams
Evening, Susan Minot
The Poisonwood Bible, Barbara Kingsolver
Iron and Silk, John Saltzman
The Nuisance Lady, Paige Stein
American Pastoral, Philip Roth
Caucasia, Danzy Senna

APPENDIX 26

Letter to Student Teachers

Dear _____ ,

Welcome to _____. We feel privileged to have so many students working alongside us. We trust that once you get to know our world, you will also feel fortunate and privileged to have been assigned here.

Do take advantage of all we have to offer. Just as we want every minute to count for our elementary students, so too we expect all the adults in the school to lead rigorous, scholarly lives. To that end, don't hesitate to:

- ask honest questions of your cooperating teacher
- read our professional literature
- attend our staff meetings
- share your own research, articles, clippings
- immerse yourself in children's' literature
- get to know many staff members

We also believe that students don't simply belong to a class, but to a school. Likewise, we hope that you will take part in schoolwide activities. We don't mean merely helping out in the lunchroom, which is of course a necessary and serious responsibility, but you are also welcome to attend such gatherings as:

- weekend and evening celebrations, fundraisers and performances
- after-school programs
- PTA meetings and parent-teacher conferences
- courses held at the school
- professional development workshops
- school day special events including field trips, book fairs, dancing in the streets

In addition, let us know if you have any special areas of expertise you'd like to share (e.g. a second language, music, journalism, dance, etc.).

Know that most of us are here early in the morning and stay late into the evening. You're also welcome to pitch in as we turn this school into an aesthetically enriched setting. (A school can't look beautiful without lots of extra time, energy, talents and enthusiasm.)

All of us wish you well. We can recall our own student teaching experiences and we know your time here will become an important part of your professional and personal memory bank. No doubt, you will long remember the names and faces of the children and adults who are about to touch you deeply.

To a joyous semester.

With much respect for your chosen career.

Sincerely,

_____

Response Letter to Visitor Requests

Shelley Harwayne
PRINCIPAL

PS 290 ✓ The Manhattan New School
311 East 82 Street, New York, NY 10028

T: 212 734-7127
F: 212 772-8879

February 1, ___

Dear friends,

Our spring-cleaning rituals include taking care of the many visitor requests that accumulate during the summer, autumn and winter seasons.

We spend the first half of the school year making sure we know our children and their families well. In addition, we spend abundant time making new colleagues feel at home and making sure that we are taking care of our own professional development needs. It isn't until this point in the school year that we feel ready to invite visiting educators to spend time at our school.

To that end, we are inviting you to visit on the morning of _____ If you are able to come on that date, won't you fill out and return the attached form. (We are very sorry but we can not honor individual requests for specific dates. As school people you can appreciate our need to keep these special events down to a minimum. If you are unable to visit on the assigned date, don't hesitate to write to us again for a possible visit during the next school year). Travel directions, parking suggestions as well as background material recommendations are enclosed. When you visit, we will suggest wonderful local restaurants that will allow you and your colleagues to linger over lunch and have ample time to chat about your morning visit.

Thank you for being patient and for your interest in our work. We look forward to showing you the Manhattan New School and learning from your responses to our school.

Sincerely,

Shelley Harwayne

Shelley Harwayne
and all the staff members of
the Manhattan New School

Visitor Return Form

Name of School_____

Date of Visit_____

Address of School_____

Names of Colleagues Visiting (Please limit your visit to three people as educators from several sites will attend on the same date).

Name	Title	Grade Level Interests
1.		
2.		
3.		

Telephone Number of School_____

E-Mail Address of School_____

Fax Number of School_____

Name of Contact Person for Visit _____

Home Phone Number of School Contact_____

Please explain below how you heard about our school and what you hope to gain from your visit.

Return this form to Shelley Harwayne
Visitor Confirmation
Manhattan New School
311 East 82nd Street
New York, New York 10028   **Or Fax to 212-772-8879**

Background Materials About Our School

Materials You Might Consider Taking a Look at Before Your Visit

Books

In the Company of Children, Joanne Hindley (Stenhouse, 1996).

Classroom Interviews: A World of Learning, Paula Rogovin (Heinemann, 1998).

Standing on Solid Ground: Strategies for Teaching Reading in the Primary Grades, Sharon Taberski (Heinemann, forthcoming).

Lasting Impressions: Weaving Literature into the Writing Workshop, Shelley Harwayne (Heinemann, 1992).

Going Public: Priorities and Practice at the Manhattan New School, Shelley Harwayne (Heinemann, 1999).

Lifetime Guarantees: Literacy Lessons from the Manhattan New School, Shelley Harwayne (Heinemann, forthcoming).

Whole Language: The Debate, Carl Smith, Shelley Harwayne editor, Erudite Commentary: "Whole Language: Now More than Ever," (ERIC Clearinghouse on Reading, English and Communication, 1994).

Writing Through Childhood: Lessons from Young Writers at the Manhattan New School, Shelley Harwayne (Heinemann, forthcoming).

Articles

Teaching Pre K-8, May 1994, Cover story, "In New York City there are Schools that Work," and "Publisher's Memo," "Dreaming the Impossible Dream . . ."

New York Teacher, (UFT), Volume XL, Number 10, January 13, 1999, "Teachers have the Write Stuff," Joe LoVerde.

New York Teacher, Volume XXXIX, Number 19, May 25, 1998 "Qualities of Leadership," David B. Sherman.

Our Town, Volume 27 #44, October 7, 1998, "Class Conscious: Pushing Dem Education Platform, Rep. Maloney Tours P.S. 290," Christopher Moore.

New York magazine, (Feb. 27, 1995), "Parental Guidance Suggested in Public Schools," Martha Fay.

Voices from the Middle, Message from the Editors, Volume 3 Number 3, September 1996, Maureen Barbieri and Linda Rief.

*Talking Points,*Volume 6 #3 (Winter, 1995), "The Manhattan New School: You've Got to Have a Dream," Shelley Harwayne.

Scholastic News, Cover story "Voices of America," Volume 58, Number 14, January 12, 1996.

Colorado Reading Council Journal, (Spring, 1995), "Somewhere Over the Rainbow: A Visit to the Manhattan New School," Laura Benson.

Newsday, Susan Cheever's "Mothering," column "A Public School with a Vision: Happiness," (Nov. 22, 2997), "The Limitations of Dick and Jane," (Dec. 14, 1996), "A perfect Perch: The School Yard," (March 14, 1998), "Choosing a Battle and an Attitude," (Feb. 21, 1998), "Returning to School, With Kids," (Nov. 7, 1997), "Books as a Bridge," (May 15, 1998), "Public Schools Make the Grade," (May 8, 1999).

The New Advocate, our school column, "Connecting Readers & Writers with Books, Weaving Literature into the School Community." (Volumes 9, 10, and 11, Numbers 1-4, 1996-1998).

The Seattle Times, "Making Teachers Better, Dick Lilly, May 25, 1998.

The New York Times, "When War Visits the Classroom," Nichole M. Christian, June 12, 1998.

Videos

A Close-up Look at Teaching Reading (four-part series), Sharon Taberski (Heinemann 1996).

Inside Reading and Writing Workshops (four-part series), Joanne Hindley (Stenhouse 1998).

Classroom Interviews in Action, Paula Rogovin (Heinemann 1998).

A Visit to the Manhattan New School, Shelley Harwayne (Heinemann, forthcoming).

Things We're Working on Worksheets

Shelley Harwayne
PRINCIPAL

PS 290 The Manhattan New School
311 East 82 Street, New York, NY 10028

T: 212 734-7127
F: 212 772-8879

Manhattan New School Visit - March 25, 1999

Looking at School Environment

What evidence is there of the following school priorities?

- **Respectful language when talking to or about students, colleagues, parents**

- **Creation of beautiful settings**

- **Supportive social tone**

- **Serious academic tone**

- **The spirit of a "teaching" schoolhouse**

- **Respect for diverse teaching styles within same philosophical base**

- **Involvement of parents and community members**

PS 290 The Manhattan New School

<u>Looking at any one Classroom-</u>
What evidence is there of the following priorities?

➢ Rigorous and simultaneously joyful classrooms

➢ Realistic and appropriate goals for children

➢ Well-informed teachers who aren't afraid to teach

➢ Abundant opportunities for children and adults to talk, listen and respond to one another

➢ Children who understand how their classrooms operate as well as what is expected of them

➢ Big blocks of uninterrupted time

➢ Teachers with effective management techniques

➢ Rich classroom libraries

➢ Safety-nets for struggling children

➢ Full participation of the second language learner

➢ Children who understand what reading and writing are for

➢ Opportunities for self-evaluation

Things We're Working On...

• ROOM arrangements to allow for social interaction

• Class libraries and their accessibility to children...

• Art woven into curriculum...

Stationery designed by Liliana and Caitlin

- <u>Bulletin boards that invite interaction</u>...

- <u>Children working independently</u>...

- <u>A supportive social tone</u>...

- <u>Use of time (structures of the school day)</u>...

REFERENCES

Harwayne, Shelley, 1992. *Lasting Impressions: Weaving Literature into the Writing Workshop.* Portsmouth, NH: Heinemann.

Hindley, Joanne. 1996. *In the Company of Children.* York, ME: Stenhouse.

———. 1998. *Inside Reading and Writing Workshops* (videotape). York, ME: Stenhouse.

McCormick Calkins, Lucy, and Shelley Harwayne. 1987. *The Writing Workshop: A World of Difference: A Guide for Staff Development.* Portsmouth, NH: Heinemann.

Rogovin, Paula. 1998. *Classroom Interviews: A World of Learning.* Portsmouth, NH: Heinemann.

———. *The Classroom Interview in Action* (videotape.)

Taberski, Sharon. *Standing on Solid Ground: Strategies for Teaching Reading in the Primary Grades.* Portsmouth, NH: Heinemann. Forthcoming.

———. 1996. *A Close-Up Look at Teaching Reading* (videotape). Portsmouth, NH: Heinemann.

Smith, Carl B. 1994. *Whole Language: The Debate.* Bloomington, IN: EDINFO Press and ERIC Clearinghouse on Reading, English and Communication.

Lifetime Guarantees: Literacy Lessons from the Manhattan New School. Portsmouth, NH: Heinemann. Forthcoming.

Writing Through Childhood: Lessons from Young Writers at the Manhattan New School. Portsmouth, NH: Heinemann. Forthcoming.

INDEX

MORE Praise for *Going Public*

When elementary teachers dream of Paradise, they dream of the Manhattan New School and principals like Shelley Harwayne.

In this hugely important book, Shelley demonstrates how to reach the highest educational standards in a public school (or any school) in spite of less than perfect buildings and less than adequate resources. In amusing and clear prose, Shelley shares a school-management style that conveys power and status upon individual, highly talented teachers in such a way that the very best education is able to occur. She explains how to deal with the big issues and the small without being bogged by bureaucracy, and how to run a school that is brilliant for teachers, superb for children, and deeply comforting for parents.

With wide readership, this book could change the education of a nation, let alone the lives of the happy multicultural children who attend the Manhattan New School.

—Mem Fox
Author of *Radical Reflections* and *Possum Magic*

Revealed in this magnificent book are the priorities and practices of one pioneering school and principal—and a world of possibilities for all public schools. Read it and discover what deeply intelligent, rigorous education can be, should be, and must be for all children.

—Anthony Alvarado, Chancellor of Instruction, San Diego City Schools

The future is now at the Manhattan New School. Everyone is a teacher/learner—from children and teachers to specialists, parents, the lunchroom helpers, street-crossing guard, and custodian. Written in sparkling prose, *Going Public* invites you to visit every classroom in this neighborhood public school and know that what is happening now at the Manhattan New School is possible for teachers and children everywhere. Shelley Harwayne is the consummate teacher educator who happens to be the principal. I've visited this unique school six times. Each time I visit I long to share the school's remarkable story with others. At last the book is here and is must reading for every administrator, teacher, parent, and all who care about public education.

—Donald H. Graves
Author of *A Fresh Look at Writing*

Harwayne celebrates the possibilities for living and loving life in a public school by demonstrating how she creates a caring community, common vision, and rich curriculum for and with teachers, students, and their families.

—Regie Routman, Language Arts Resource Teacher, Shaker Heights, Ohio City Schools
Author of *Conversations: Strategies for Teaching, Learning, and Evaluating*

As an instructional leader, Shelley Harwayne is distinguished in her belief that a school building should and can be as welcoming and nurturing as a home filled with dedicated and caring adults who support children's learning. Readers will discover in *Going Public* both a celebration of and a model for exemplary public education.

—**Karen Feuer**, Parent and President, Community School Board Two

An extremely important book for anyone who cares about education. . . . All will gain from Shelley's brilliant descriptions of the birth, growth, and inner workings of the Manhattan New School.

Shelley Harwayne is an extraordinary woman of high intelligence and positive energy. The book shines with her love, humor, and imagination, and that most uncommon virtue, 'common sense'! To read this book is to want to go to school again, Shelley's school, with her there and her family of teachers!

—**Jacques d'Amboise**, Founder, National Dance Institute